A Year in the Life of a Third Space Urban Teacher Residency

Bold Visions in Educational Research
Volume 49

Scope:
Bold Visions in Educational Research is international in scope and includes books from two areas: *teaching and learning to teach* and *research methods in education*. Each area contains multi-authored handbooks of approximately 200,000 words and monographs (authored and edited collections) of approximately 130,000 words. All books are scholarly, written to engage specified readers and catalyze changes in policies and practices. Defining characteristics of books in the series are their explicit uses of theory and associated methodologies to address important problems. We invite books from across a theoretical and methodological spectrum from scholars employing quantitative, statistical, experimental, ethnographic, semiotic, hermeneutic, historical, ethnomethodological, phenomenological, case studies, action, cultural studies, content analysis, rhetorical, deconstructive, critical, literary, aesthetic and other research methods.

Books on *teaching and learning to teach* focus on any of the curriculum areas (e.g., literacy, science, mathematics, social science), in and out of school settings, and points along the age continuum (pre K to adult). The purpose of books on *research methods in education* is **not** to present generalized and abstract procedures but to show how research is undertaken, highlighting the particulars that pertain to a study. Each book brings to the foreground those details that must be considered at every step on the way to doing a good study. The goal is **not** to show how generalizable methods are but to present rich descriptions to show how research is enacted. The books focus on methodology, within a context of substantive results so that methods, theory, and the processes leading to empirical analyses and outcomes are juxtaposed. In this way method is not reified, but is explored within well-described contexts and the emergent research outcomes. Three illustrative examples of books are those that allow proponents of particular perspectives to interact and debate, comprehensive handbooks where leading scholars explore particular genres of inquiry in detail, and introductory texts to particular educational research methods/issues of interest to novice researchers.

A Year in the Life of a Third Space Urban Teacher Residency

Using Inquiry to Reinvent Teacher Education

Monica Taylor
Montclair State University, USA

and

Emily J. Klein
Montclair State University, USA

With contributions from
**Linda Abrams, Priyank Bhatt, Matthew Brewster, Ada Beth Cutler,
Michael De Antonio Jr., Alexander Diaz, Marisol Diaz, Carolyn Granato,
Antonio Iglesias, Walter Kaczka, Kim Scott Kallai, Dave Koethe,
Marc Kolb, Douglas Larkin, Roger Leon, Rosiane Lesperance-Goss,
Maria Cristina Morales, Erin Mooney, Anna Karina Monteiro,
Fernando Naiditch, Anthony Orsini, Gail Perry-Ryder, Suzanne Poole,
Jennifer Robinson, William Romney, Mario Santos, Kathryn Strom,
Janae Taylor, & Susan Taylor**

SENSE PUBLISHERS
ROTTERDAM/BOSTON/TAIPEI

A C.I.P. record for this book is available from the Library of Congress.

ISBN: 978-94-6300-251-6 (paperback)
ISBN: 978-94-6300-252-3 (hardback)
ISBN: 978-94-6300-253-0 (e-book)

Published by: Sense Publishers,
P.O. Box 21858,
3001 AW Rotterdam,
The Netherlands
https://www.sensepublishers.com/

All chapters in this book have undergone peer review.

Printed on acid-free paper

for Tom
-EJK

for Mark, Michael, & Griffin
-MT

TABLE OF CONTENTS

ACKNOWLEDGEMENTS

We are well aware that one advantage of being scholars is that we get a chance to narrate the work to which we are deeply committed, that of providing the most caring, skilled, and socially just teachers for Newark's children. Collaboratively narrating the story of our third space urban teacher residency has been a labor of love. Our book offers a rich kaleidoscopic view on teacher preparation because of the insightful and honest contributions of our Newark Public School partners and our Montclair State University colleagues, particularly Cindy Onore, our initial collaborator, mentor, colleague, and friend and Jennifer Robinson and Ada Beth Cutler for inviting us to do this work in the first place. Additionally, we would like to thank Mario Santos for opening up his school to the partnership and believing in its impact for his students. We would also like to acknowledge Tania Seibert, our graduate assistant, who provided tremendous editorial and formatting support. Finally, we appreciate the guidance of Michel Lokhorst from Sense Publishers who enthusiastically encouraged the publication of the book.

MONICA TAYLOR AND EMILY J. KLEIN

1. A YEAR IN THE LIFE OF A THIRD SPACE
URBAN TEACHER RESIDENCY

A PROLOGUE

In March 2014, T. Bone Burnett organized a collective of musicians who had never before worked together to develop an album based on the newly uncovered 1967 handwritten lyrics of Bob Dylan. Elvis Costello, Marcus Mumford, Taylor Goldsmith, Jim James, and Rhiannon Giddens were invited to work on the album, *Lost on the River: The New Basement Tapes,* because, as Burnett (2014) explained, "Not only do they have the talent and the same open and collaborative spirit needed for this to be good, they are all music archaeologists. They all know how to dig without breaking the thing they are digging" (para. 4). Each artist received 16 lyrics prior to their two-week recording session at Capitol Records in Hollywood. Some came with a couple of melodies, others came with more, but once together they received an additional eight lyrics. As Burnett (2014) emphasized, those additional lyrics, "which no one had time to think about, led to some of the freest recordings" (para. 4). The interesting aspect of this creative project was the collaboration among the musicians. Each created his or her own music for many of the lyrics so that the end result was multiple versions of the same song, allowing what Lewis (2014) described as "a perspective on the ways different artists respond to Dylan's lyrics. Each artist [took] the lead on the tracking of his or her song, and all provide[d] suggestions and whatever instrumental and vocal support the others require, with Burnett overseeing final production" (para. 9).

We were struck when we read this by the kinship we felt between the creation of the secondary cohort of the Newark Montclair Urban Teacher Residency (NMUTR) and the creation of *The New Basement Tapes.* They have both been constructed in what we, and others, refer to as a third space—a place located between other entities and continually under construction. In the case of *The New Basement Tapes*—the third space allowed for a new kind of musical creation as it brought together artists outside their traditional individual studio realms; in the case of the NMUTR, the residency was conceptualized as a third space and it brought together educators from the district, school, and university to think differently about teacher education. This negotiated third space has attempted to combine the features of the formerly separate domains through multi-vocal dialogue with one another, and has become an entirely new and unique territory. We borrow the concept of third space from the fields of cultural studies, post-colonial theory, geography, and most recently critical

1

literacy (Bhabha, 1994; Gutierrez, 2008; Moje et al., 2004; Moles, 2008; Routledge, 1996; Soja, 1996). Much like Oldenburg (1999) who describes the "third place" as a social setting that is neither home nor the workplace/school where members of a community can be involved in civic engagement, we hoped that our residency would be neither governed by the university (first space) nor led by the schools (second space). We envisioned that the residency would exist in a unique and new third space that was perpetually negotiated. It strives to be an epistemological space, "a site of praxis, a place where the theory and the method meet ... where theory and method blur together, where theory is method and method is theory" (Moles, 2008). Routledge (2006) notes that too often in the academy, we produce "theory that is distanced from ... direct, lived experience" (p. 401). We considered a third space to be a process that would allow for the potential to "live theory in the immediate" (Routledge, 1996, p. 401) and "deconstruct the barrier between the academy and the lives of the people it professes to represent" (Routledge, 1996, p. 400). Rather than privileging the university over the school or vice versa, the residency as a third space always under construction could act as a hybrid program which embraced the essential elements of each space while also having room to build new features, practices, and tools. Like in *The New Basement Tapes,* in the NMUTR, faculty, mentors, community organizers, residents, and students have collaborated to prepare urban preservice teachers and incite change in schools, but we are located in a space that is neither the purely theoretical realm of the university, nor what is considered to be the traditionally practice realm of the classroom. Our interactions have not been limited by rigid hierarchical parameters which often situates the university in a position of power, determining what knowledge is valued and how it is operationalized; rather we have attempted to nurture a fluidity that allows for new and multiple inventions and interpretations. We are educational archeologists, digging at the roots of teacher preparation and school/university partnership without destroying them. Just as Dylan's 1967 original lyrics served as the inspiration for the project, our third space work derives from a long-term partnership between Montclair State University (MSU) and Newark Public Schools (NPS) involving preservice and inservice teacher education. For both *The New Basement Tapes* and the NMUTR, the third space has become "a place of invention and transformational encounters, a dynamic in-between space that is imbued with the traces, relays, ambivalences, ambiguities and contradictions, with the feelings and practices of both sites, to fashion something different, unexpected (Bhabha, 1994)" (Routledge, 2006, p. 406). It allows us to construct multiple versions of how to prepare urban teachers and foster teacher leadership and change in schools, rather than projecting that there is one singular linear process to become an urban teacher. Inviting a continuum of approaches, ways of knowing, and interpretations, which are continually being reinvented, challenges the rigid dichotomized perspective of "good" teaching and "bad" teaching often espoused in academia and schools. Just as this musician collective created multiple song versions of the same Dylan lyrics, so too could one mentor/resident relationship, for example, look completely different than another. These different renditions, in our third space production, all may exist within the same program.

Similar to *The New Basement Tapes,* this NMUTR third space work has not been easy or simple. Bhabha (2004) likens a third space to "a stairwell" in terms of its "hither and thither" and "the temporal movement and passage that it allows, prevent[ing] identities at either end of it from settling into primordial polarities" (p. 5). Ours has been a continual construction, a utopian prospect that we have not fully achieved. Many versions of how to do this work have emerged as we negotiate across multiple entities and honor the voices and perspectives of all of the participants. We have understood that to attempt to do this third space work well there has needed to exist, what Burnett (2014) called "a deep well of generosity" (para. 6) from all of the participants. We are thankful for the trust and generosity of all of our partners who have contributed to the secondary cohort of the NMUTR. We know that this work could never have been accomplished without them.

This book, like *Lost on the River: The New Basement Tapes,* weaves together voices of faculty, residents, mentors, administrators, community organizers, and students who have lived together in an urban teacher residency program in Newark as they reinvent math and science teaching through the lens of inquiry. Each chapter includes narratives from multiple perspectives – the faculty, mentors, residents, and administrators – as well as tools we have used within the program to support and build change, providing readers with both real cases of how an urban teacher residency can impact school systems, and concrete tools and examples to help the reader understand and replicate aspects of the process. We have intentionally chosen to include this multivocality as it attempts to put into practice the tenets of a third space, where multiple narrations of this negotiated space are constructed and many understandings of a single concept may exist. More concretely, the authors of each chapter navigated the writing process in their own unique ways. Some authors co-wrote their chapter, while others allowed one author to take the lead incorporating the prompted narratives of their partner authors throughout the text. In other chapters in which the lead author indicated that they collaborated "with" others, the representational voices of their partners were drawn from interviews, field notes, and resident artifacts. Again in the spirit of a third space always under construction, each chapter has a unique interpretation of multivocality.

Capturing both the successes but also the tensions and challenges, we offer a kaleidoscopic view of the rich, complex, and multi-layered ways in which multiple participants work together to make enduring educational change in urban schools. As Goldsmith, one of the musicians, reflected:

> But what I really learned from this project—and not just from Dylan's words, but from everyone involved, who I'm sure took inspiration from him, too—was that everything is better when you don't treat things too preciously. Instead, you get in there and do what you do, and work hard, and hope for the best. (Slate, 2014, para. 7)

Our third space NMUTR has been a fragile utopian enterprise that requires continual tedious tending, one that has relied on a shared commitment of all involved and a deep sense of hope that working collaboratively has the potential, even if not perfect potential, to make a difference.

INTRODUCTION

We, Monica and Emily, have been colleagues at MSU in the Secondary and Special Education Department for the past nine years. Our official collaboration began when we worked with a team of departmental faculty to create and teach a Masters program in Teacher Leadership. But as we look back at that now, we realize that in many ways our collaboration then was superficial compared to what it would become during our work in the NMUTR. Working within a third space construction has helped us to invent a collaboration that blurs lines between scholar, teacher, administrator, leader, friend, and team member, as well as build on our strengths in all of those areas.

In November, 2009, we, as well as Cindy Onore, were approached by Ada Beth Cutler, our Dean at the time, to conceptualize, design, and teach in the urban teacher residency program to prepare math and science teachers for Newark's middle and secondary schools. MSU and NPS were one of 28 partnerships that had just received a five year Teacher Quality Partnership Grant from the Office of Innovation and Improvement in the U.S. Department of Education to create an urban teacher residency program. As we sat in the initial meetings with our MSU colleagues and NPS partners, Ada Beth enticed us when she emphasized that this was an opportunity to reflect on our past research and teaching experiences, think outside of the box, and put our dreams into practice. She urged us to "radically imagine" (Greene, 2000) what this residency program could become.

We were daunted by the task of developing this program in six months, writing and processing the new curriculum, finding schools and teachers with whom to work, recruiting and admitting students, and getting it all off the ground by June 2010. That said, we were comforted by the fact that we knew we shared similar orientations to teaching and learning and deep commitments to urban teacher preparation and partnerships with schools. None of us, not Monica, Emily, or Cindy, was willing to take this project on individually, but as a team we knew that it could be accomplished. Monica agreed to be the lead faculty and Emily and Cindy agreed to work alongside her.

And so we began…

In this chapter, we provide a foundation for navigating the second cohort's year in the life of a third space urban teacher residency through the upcoming chapters. True to the qualities of this third space we attempt to create, we narrate this chapter in three voices: each of our own individual voices as well as a collective voice. It begins with a dialogic description of our own backgrounds and theoretical histories to this work. Bringing our voices together in order to simulate a third space, we then explain the principles of the secondary cohort of the NMUTR in the context of the urban teacher residency movement in the United States. A brief exploration of the ways in which we conceptualized the program using inquiry in the third space follows. Finally we outline the details of our program and we share our vision for this book as well as the rationale and format of each chapter.

WHO ARE WE AND HOW DID WE BECOME URBAN TEACHER EDUCATORS?

Monica

To begin with, I think it is really important for us to share a little bit about how we became urban teacher educators and what our beliefs are about urban teaching. Sharing this sets the stage for our collaboration and background to the NMUTR. It illustrates some of the rationale behind our goals and objectives for the third space inquiry framework, which guided the work of the residency. So Emily, tell us a bit about how you became an urban educator.

Emily

I grew up in Queens attending PS 101 there and middle and high school in Manhattan at Hunter College High School, fondly known as the brick prison. For years I trained to be a ballet dancer and it never occurred to me that I could love anything as much as I loved dance. I would later attend college at Barnard in New York as well and go through their teacher education program, but I attended the program mostly because it had been ground into me that I should have a career when I graduated. However, the day I walked into my student teaching classroom, I knew I had found the profession I was meant to be in; it was love at first lesson plan. In many ways, teaching was like dance – it was all encompassing, intellectual, and creative, and even physically exhausting. When I was working with teenagers I thought of nothing else. After graduation I spent two months driving cross country and as I was traveling back and forth in a beat up Buick, I knew that I wanted to teach in an urban, rather than suburban, classroom, and that I was interested in how schools could get better.

After I got my MA in education I started looking for teaching jobs, and I remember walking the streets of Manhattan in August with my resume in hand going from school to school smiling at rather grim school secretaries. One day I found a job at Norman Thomas HS, but by the time I made it to the district office I was bumped by someone senior to me. Finally I got a position teaching 9th grade English at Martin Luther King Jr. High School in Manhattan. Despite all my fancy degrees I had no idea what I was doing. That first September I would ride the subway home and cry the whole time. I had a boisterous 9th period class that I could never get to all sit down in their chairs at one time. One day teaching them with a fever of 102 I burst into the classroom and lectured them, "You guys don't know! This is your future. I care about you and I want your lives to be better!" After my outburst they were all silent for a moment and I thought, "Wow I really got to them. I reached them." After a beat, one student noted to the others, "Dude do you see how blue her eyes get when she cries?" and they all burst back into chatter. And yet still, by the end of the year I was hooked. I loved the job, the school, and the kids. But I knew there had to be a better way to teach teachers so that first year wasn't the disaster for them that it was for me.

Monica

I grew up very close to my maternal grandmother, Nanny, who was a kindergarten teacher in the Bronx for 25 years. Although she would have never called herself a social justice advocate, she had a deep commitment to her students and an openness to their cultures and identities. She understood, perhaps because she was the daughter of immigrants, the school classroom needed to be a place where students and their families were valued and appreciated. She loved her students unconditionally and she found great delight in their observations and insights. She never raised her voice and she was always warm and loving.

As a young child raised by a single divorced working mother, I often ended up with Nanny in her classroom when I had days off from my own private elementary school. Watching her engage and interact with her urban kindergarten students was the foundation of my teaching career. Not much older than her students, I was given small teacher like tasks like reading to a small group, putting out the peg boards, or reviewing number work one on one with a child. I loved everything about teaching! The principal at the time adored me and said that I should come and talk to her when I was ready to be a teacher because she would hire me in a heartbeat. Of course, at 8, this seemed like an impossible promise.

But of course, when I graduated from Penn, I decided that I wanted to be a teacher even though I only had a couple of education courses under my belt. Why teaching was not my goal throughout college I will never totally understand. Throughout my schooling, I always opted to work with younger children, either as an assistant in a classroom or as a tutor after school. Even in college, I worked with urban children in a local elementary school in West Philadelphia. So at graduation, I asked Nanny to give me advice about finding a teaching job in New York City. Retired, she reached out to her former principal who was also retired, and asked for some advice. She was reminded that Mr. Mazza, who had replaced her principal, was now an assistant superintendent in District 3 in Manhattan and well the rest is history. He met with me and I was hired within two weeks to teach Spanish and French at Lincoln Academy, an alternative progressive middle school.

Emily

The turning point in becoming a teacher came at the end of year one when I got involved in a professional development program called the American Social History

6

Project (ASHP). Paired with a history teacher, we spent a few days in the summer and a series of weekends during the school year, receiving professional development on how to create and implement interdisciplinary curriculum in the classroom. There were four teams of teachers at King led by an experienced team who mentored us as we stumbled our way trying to figure out how to navigate team teaching, interdisciplinary English and Social Studies curriculum, and shared assessments. The opportunities for community and collaboration were invaluable, but mostly I learned from watching my co-teacher interact with kids in ways that taught me how I might build relationships more effectively. I stopped trying to control students through threats of failing grades and punishments. I started asking them to engage in projects and work that mattered to their lives and asking questions about who they were. I watched my colleagues, I collected ideas from them, and I opened up my classroom. I began to learn how to teach.

Monica

My years at Lincoln Academy made me realize how naïve I had been about urban life and how much of the city I really did not know at all. My middle school was made up of African American, Caribbean American, and Latino students who opened their worlds to me. They invited me to visit their families, neighborhoods, and communities. They helped me to see the complexities of their lives and cultures and the importance of understanding and valuing their identities for our teaching/learning community.

It was in my second year of teaching that I met Cindy Onore who changed my teaching career forever. Having become a teacher through alternate route, I was required to take several courses to maintain my certification. Determined to be independent in this next stage of my life, I decided to take courses at City College. An incredibly different university culture from Penn, I was overwhelmed and intimidated as I tried to navigate the hallways there. Seeking some educational foundations courses, I stumbled into Cindy's office and that detour changed my life. Cindy took a look at my transcript, heard that I was teaching languages at Lincoln Academy, and said emphatically as only Cindy can, "I know what you should do. You should take my course in Language and Literacy." And so I did and it was the perfect beginning to my educational career. We read Freire, Dewey, and Vygotsky, theorists to whom I return over and over again. Cindy's course provided the space for me to develop as an urban educator. All of her students were struggling as urban teachers and she facilitated deep honest reflection about our teaching, how to address our students' needs, how to make up for the lack of resources in our schools, and how to teach in empowering ways. She modeled a true democratic pedagogy that focused on negotiating the curriculum and promoting authentic inquiry. She was the real deal and helped me explore theories that supported many of my teaching instincts in the classroom.

Emily

After a number of years at King and at ASHP, where I eventually became a professional development teacher leader in the organization, I became curious about the role of professional development and learning in the lives of teachers. I truly felt that without this organization I would not have survived those early years of teaching. As I became more interested in figuring out how to support and help other teachers in the organization, I began to think about the work of teacher education, and I sought out doctoral programs that would let me pursue these questions. I ended up at New York University and spent the next five years looking at innovative teacher education designs that support teacher learning. My dissertation work and a book published in 2009, looked at the Big Picture Learning schools, a fascinating and innovative school design. My research examined how educational organizations support teachers in doing innovative and student centered teaching, both in terms of curriculum, but also in terms of coaching, leadership, and training.

Monica

Once I completed my Masters in Language and Literacy, it was pretty clear that I wanted to become Cindy Onore and hence I pursued a doctorate at the University of Arizona in Language, Reading, and Culture. Studying with people like Dana Fox, Ken and Yetta Goodman, and Luis Moll extended the theoretical foundation that I had begun to build with Cindy into the areas of whole language and teaching for social justice. For my dissertation I worked with Mexican American adolescent women around how they constructed their identities through multiple sign systems. Feeling marginalized in school, these women invited me to conduct ethnographic research in every aspect of their lives including their families, peers, work settings, and communities. Building reciprocal relationships with them helped me to understand the value and importance of their "funds of knowledge" (Moll, Amanti, Neff, & Gonzalez, 1992) and the limited perception of what knowledge was accepted in schools.

Emily

When I started at MSU, I knew I wanted to continue to work with teachers, both inservice and preservice teachers, but I was not sure how to do that. Although research had been deeply interesting to me and I was thrilled to be applying all that I had learned to preservice education, I also knew that I wanted opportunities to work with teachers along the continuum of their careers. While there were opportunities to teach in the MA program, I missed the experience of working in and with whole schools. A few years into my work there, Cindy Onore invited me to teach some of my classes on site in Newark and I began to build relationships there, hopeful there would be more opportunities to work with inservice teachers.

Monica

Leaving Tucson and beginning my career as a teacher educator first at Wagner College in Staten Island and later at MSU, I wanted my courses to be field based. Being mentored by Cindy in the early days of my teaching career and then working alongside Ken and Yetta Goodman who always valued the professional knowledge base of teachers, I was worried that the ivory tower implicitly constructed a hierarchy of expertise with university faculty being favored over teachers.

At MSU, I was hired to start a professional development school partnership with Grover Cleveland Middle School in West Caldwell, New Jersey. My first opportunity to work with a privileged school, I was unclear how to address social justice issues in this setting. Working collaboratively with Gennifer Otinsky in her sixth grade class, we brought together sixth graders and preservice teachers to explore issues of injustice and racism through inquiry in the language arts and social studies curriculum. This was particularly important for the preservice teachers as many of them had never examined these issues and were uncomfortable with the idea of doing so with middle school students.

Emily

I would have been extremely hesitant to take on the NMUTR without Monica and Cindy. While I had worked with both pre and inservice teachers, I still knew I lacked some of the necessary knowledge and skills to take on a project like this on my own. Yet it also brought me back to the work I wanted most to do in the place I wanted most to do it. I felt that between us we would be able to draw on each other to create this program, but still it felt overwhelming and unknown.

Monica

And yet when we were asked to potentially design and lead the secondary cohort of the NMUTR we jumped at the chance. Drawing from our experiences of doing partnership work, we wanted to foster a much more explicit partnership with schools where our mentors were valued as teacher educators. Continually concerned with the disconnect that seems to pervade teacher education between theory and practice, we hoped to create a space where residents would be able to focus on the ways in which theory and practice intersect. We knew that this was going to be a messy and non-linear experience but we were willing to take the plunge.

THE URBAN TEACHER RESIDENCY

We also have our social imagination: the capacity to invent visions of what should be and what might be in our deficient society, on the streets where we live, in our schools. (Greene, 2000, p. 5)

9

As will be discussed in much more detail in Chapter Two, our NMUTR was constructed in the context of a long-term, strong, and rich partnership between MSU and NPS. These already established partnerships helped us to identify schools in which the program could reside. Interestingly, in the cohort two year, we worked primarily in two schools: East Side High School and Arts High School. Although East Side High School was a relatively new site for us, we had only been there for the first year of the residency, we felt welcomed and supported by Mario Santos, the principal, as well as the faculty. In fact, Mario generously, and strategically, allowed the mentors a load reduction as a way to show his support and acknowledgement of how time intensive working with a resident would be. Because our numbers doubled, we expanded to Arts High School for the second cohort. This was a natural decision as Emily had been working at Arts for several years prior to the residency and had a productive relationship with some of the mentors, like Kim, an experienced master math teacher. We purposely selected schools that were representative of Newark's diverse population (See Appendix 1 for demographic details of each school) but also were high functioning and had strong administrators who were committed to high student achievement and innovative teaching. Both East Side High School and Arts High School seemed to meet those criteria. As is discussed in Chapter Two, this was not originally the intention of the superintendents who requested that residents be placed in higher needs schools. Aligned with the research on urban preservice teacher education, we knew that during that residency year, it was essential that residents were apprenticed in high functioning schools (Ronfeldt, 2012) with mentors who were successful and had effective math and science teaching practices even if some of those were traditional.

The Urban Teacher Residency model was developed in 2007 as a means of addressing urban teacher shortage and quality (Berry, Montgomery, & Snyder, 2008). Created in the image of medical residencies, residents serve a one-year clinical apprenticeship under the tutelage of an experienced co-teacher in a district school (Solomon, 2009). Coursework and training are tailored toward preparing residents for the specific district in which they are teaching. Although there is only preliminary research on this work, there is already an indication that retention rates for residency graduates are higher than for graduates of other traditional and alternate route programs (Papay, West, Fullerton, & Kane, 2012; Urban Teacher Residency United, 2014).

As we sat down to brainstorm what we hoped for this residency, we first looked to the original UTRs in Denver, Boston, and Chicago to get a sense of their structures. Interestingly their programs tended to be led by community organizations that were affiliated with a teacher education program at a university but not led in collaboration with one. We wondered what our role would be in the NMUTR as teacher educators and how we could work collaboratively with our partners in NPS.

INQUIRY IN THE THIRD SPACE

And then the line was quiet but not dead. I almost felt like he was there in my room with me, but in a way it was better, like I was not in my room and he was not in his, but instead we were together in some invisible and tenuous third space that could only be visited on the phone. (Green, 2012, p. 73)

While we embraced some of the features of other UTRs, we saw the NMUTR as having the potential to become a third space in teacher education (Zeichner, 2010). In fact, although we were already familiar with the third space theory, it was Zeichner's article, that came out just as we began to design our residency vision for the program, which pushed us to dialogue across the three separate entities of MSU, NPS, and Newark community organizations and construct the NMUTR, a potentially new democratic negotiated third space that had its own characteristics and features. We hoped to disrupt the traditional power relationships and participate in a space where the roles of the university, school, teacher candidate, and community were reimagined. We wanted the NMUTR to invite faculty, mentors, community members, residents, and students to share and construct knowledge and cross customary role boundaries. For example we knew that mentors did not set curriculum in university courses and we knew that faculty did not teach in high school classrooms. We wondered if maybe those types of boundaries could be crossed in this program (and in fact both would be). We realized that for this to work we would need to allow the third space to be dynamic, ambiguous, ever-shifting, and always under construction. That required continuous generative conversations among all participants to determine roles and responsibilities, common goals/objectives, instructional strategies, assignments, and assessment tools. We hoped that asking participants to share their knowledge, experiences, and expertise would lead to the co-construction of a blueprint for the program. We were not exactly sure what our final product would be but we understood that there was no other process.

As we mentioned earlier, we each had extensive experience with inquiry and negotiating the curriculum (Boomer, Onore, Lester, & Cook, 1992; Freire, 2000; Onore, Goeke, Taylor, & Klein, 2009), and realized the NMUTR generative process would take on a similar form. In a sense, we asked all of our partners to be inquirers in a third space and shift their identities from being passive receivers of knowledge to active knowledge constructors, problem posers, and problem solvers (Freire, 2000). We knew this would involve listening, dialogue, and action. It would be complicated and it was – in many of the chapters within we detail the ways it could be complicated, the ways we would get stuck, and some of the ways we got "unstuck." We also wanted to extend this negotiation to the residents themselves and so we hoped to invite them to help us co-construct the curriculum. Engaging as co-teachers and co-learners, the faculty, mentors, and community representatives had opportunities to model inquiry for the residents and residents in response were able to be inquirers for themselves. Some non-negotiable assignments were designed to provide residents with ownership of their learning. These included: developing UBD units that would be taught in their classes, conducting action research to examine teaching practices, and designing Inquiry Cycle Experiences (ICE) to explore social justice issues with their students. However much of the NMUTR curriculum was emergent and negotiated with the residents (Boomer, Onore, Lester, & Cook, 1992). Our mentor meetings, observations, instructional rounds, and class discussions provided us with a window into the needs and questions of the residents. These would often grow out of experiences in the NPS classrooms with mentors and students. Our insights would help us to construct formal curriculum or at other times we would add additional workshops to address the residents' concerns. For example, during cohort two, the residents were anxious about socially just classroom management. In response, Katie, one of our doctoral students, designed a multi-part workshop on the topic.

Creating this third space residency also involved negotiating key equally valuable roles for mentors and faculty (Klein, Taylor, Onore, Strom, & Abrams, 2013), yet we had few blueprints to help guide us in constructing this new dynamic. Our program was unlike traditional teacher education programs where the cooperating teacher is only responsible for the clinical experience and often invites the student teacher into her classroom for part of one semester during which time she gradually hands over her class preparation and teaching. In the NMUTR, the mentors acted as primary teacher educators and invited residents to work alongside them for an entire school year. They were involved in the co-construction of preservice teacher education curriculum, co-teaching and co-planning with their resident, and learning alongside the resident through joint participation in workshops, collaborative action research, and instructional rounds.

Shifting roles took time. It was not a simple process of just naming the mentors as teacher educators (Bullough Jr., 2005), although we were very deliberate about giving them that title as well, knowing that language is powerful. They were looking for a set of concrete roles, defined and discrete tasks, and top/down professional development. We began by rethinking what the mentor/resident relationship would be in the classroom. We thought that co-teaching models (Friend & Cook, 1996) might feel more appropriate for a third space. We hoped that the residents would take the lead *for* rather than *take over* the classes gradually during the course of the school year and recognized that we needed to put structures in place to enable this. Initially, mentor-resident relationships resembled the more familiar student/teacher model but as we, and they, continued to transform the relationship between mentor and mentee, we all moved to more of an apprenticeship model. Working alongside the mentor, rather than in tandem, provided access to her moment-by-moment thinking and decision-making.

Striving for a third space also required a different type of relationship between faculty and mentors. We needed to build trusting and authentic relationships that allowed for honest and open communication, something that can be challenging when we are inhabiting each other's work spaces and often struggling and taking big risks – with new practices, new teacher/student relationships, new identities, and new curriculum. This meant positioning ourselves in ways that were, at times, unfamiliar and uncomfortable with constant attention to language and actions and whose voices are privileged. We realized that we had to find a means to open a true third space for the mentors and the faculty, where we could share our experiences and think about our practices as teacher educators. Reflecting on the first year, as we moved into the second year of the residency, we developed a more formal meeting structure for the mentors and the faculty. It was in those meetings where we began to position ourselves as active knowledge-creators and full subjects in our own learning as we provided support and critique of one another. We were transparently examining our practices together and being vulnerable to critique and change. This was the start of a shift in power and authority over how to nurture new teachers (Taylor, Klein, & Abrams, 2014). This dynamic is discussed in more detail in Chapters five and seven, which address some of the pedagogical strategies led by the mentors, like action research and video protocols.

THE NMUTR SECONDARY COHORT PROGRAM

We now turn briefly to the details of the program, in order to provide the appropriate backdrop for the book. Our NMUTR secondary cohort focused on preparing math and science teachers for NPS over a period of twelve months. During this time, residents received a $26,000 stipend as well as free tuition for a Masters of Teaching from MSU. In exchange, they were required to commit to three years of teaching in NPS with NMUTR induction support. During their residency, they were guided through the certification process and received mentoring and support for hiring.

We began our program in June with an intensive week-long course at MSU which we co-taught with Fernando Naiditch. We asked residents to reflect on their own learning experiences, analyze learning theories, unpack issues of identity and social justice, and develop their own goals for the summer. In the second week, they participated in a professional development workshop on inquiry based learning facilitated by the staff at the Newark Museum. These first two weeks provided residents with some useful teaching strategies for their six-week internships at the Newark Museum, La Casa De Don Pedro, and the Newark All Stars. Beginning to see themselves as "public professionals" (Onore & Gildin, 2010), residents taught science and math inquiry lessons at the summer camps at both the Newark Museum and La Casa De Don Pedro, helped to organize the Newark All Stars Talent Show, and acted as "relationship managers" with the Newark All Stars interns.

In August, residents began to meet with their mentors to curriculum map and develop lesson plans for the upcoming school year. Residents helped mentors set up their classrooms and reported to their schools for beginning of the year professional development workshops. On the first day of school, mentors and residents greeted their students as co-teachers. Residents would spend the next ten months completely immersed in their NPS school communities. Once a week, they would meet with faculty for three hours as a formal "university" class. These were held onsite at East Side High School, Arts High School, or American History High School.

As we moved into the regular school year, the mentors were involved in all aspects of the program including curriculum development, observations, and evaluation. Together we created new processes for writing and reviewing lesson plans, conducting informal and formal observations, and ultimately evaluating the residents. We developed a lesson plan format that would scaffold the kinds of thinking that the mentors and faculty valued for instruction. Periodically, towards the later part of the first semester, we collaboratively analyzed lesson plans in depth, looking for how they supported students' inquiry. We used a modified version of the tuning protocol (McDonald, Mohr, Dichter, & McDonald, 2003) when we would ask residents to present the lesson plan, mirror what we heard in the presentation, share warm and cool feedback, and then have the residents respond. In general, the tuning protocol enabled mentors, residents, and faculty to engage equally as authorities of teaching in the third space.

We also had to adjust how we approached resident observations. We emphasized scripting the lesson, or writing down everything that was said by the resident and the students during the lesson. This helped mentors and faculty have discussions about concrete moments in the lesson rather than making statements that were judgmental or based on assumptions. We used a modified version of "Reformed Teaching Observation Protocol" (RTOP) (Piburn, Sawada, Falconer, Turley, Benford, & Bloom, 2000) – a tool developed at Arizona State University in support of constructivist math and science inquiry teaching and supported by the standards in those fields. This tool was also used collaboratively during instructional rounds (City, Elmore, Fiarman, & Teitel, 2009), a valuable and productive addition to cohort two that facilitated important conversations that were generated from the deconstruction of a shared teaching observation. These moments seemed to provoke the most "aha" moments for residents as they had a chance to observe action, collaboratively reflect, and act again by tweaking their teaching practices. In the fall, we began the instructional rounds by observing mentors and then gradually moved to observe residents. We divided the cohort in half and each individually led four instructional rounds.

In the spring, we continued to observe each resident through both instructional rounds as well as individual observations. We purposely made sure that residents were observed by a variety of faculty so that they have different lenses on their practices. Additionally, the residents participated in a series of workshops, which addressed the learning needs and modified instruction of English Language Learners and of Students with Disabilities. Our spring curriculum also involved two significant projects aside from rounds and teaching, both of which are detailed in the book. Residents engaged in designing and implementing an action research project as well as a social justice inquiry project. The year ended with presentations of artifacts from the year that reflected their growth and learning. Finally, we spent the last months preparing the residents for the job market through writing resumes and educational philosophy statements, conducting mock interviews, and generally debriefing about the job application process.

A YEAR IN THE LIFE: THE ORGANIZATION OF THE BOOK

The book is organized around a year in the NMUTR and shares the various key moments during the learning trajectory of the residents.

Chapter two, written by Jennifer, Ada Beth, Julianne, Mathew, Marisol, Carolyn, Roger, and Sue, traces the history of the partnership between MSU and NPS that led to the development of the NMUTR.

Chapter three, composed by Emily, Monica, Walt, Marc, and Dave, details the admissions process that was co-created between the university and the district to choose residents for the program.

In Chapter four, Monica, Alex, Janae, Katie, and Gail discuss how the residents developed their social justice stance as urban educators. They explain the Inquiry Cycle Experience (ICE) project and share the graphic organizer created for that assignment.

Chapter five, written by Emily, Suzanne, Antonio, and Erin, describes the mentor led action research project residents engaged in during the spring semester. Mentors guided residents, drawing from their own experiences of conducting action research alongside faculty. At the end of the chapter they include the graphic organizer that supported this research.

Chapter six, by Fernando and Alex, narrates the ways in which theory and practice can be interwoven to address the needs of and modify instruction for English Language Learners (ELL). They provide both the assignment of the portrait of an ELL as well as some concrete examples of work produced by residents.

In Chapter seven, Emily, Kim, William, and Linda depict how the faculty, mentors, and a doctoral assistant created a video protocol to help them make transparent the often unspoken decisions and actions teachers make throughout a lesson. It includes a sample video protocol.

Chapter eight is narrated by Doug, Karina, and Suzanne. It examines the development of science pedagogical content knowledge in building science educators. They share the assessment module as a tool used to rigorously strengthen practice.

In chapter nine, Monica, Emily, Alex, Pri, and Suzanne describe how the summer internships in Newark community organizations like the All Stars Talent Show Network and La Casa de Don Pedro influenced the residents in their first years of teaching.

Chapter ten, written by Katie and Rosie, focuses on the secondary induction program for resident graduates in their first year of teaching. The Artifact Package Project, a teacher inquiry project, is also discussed in detail.

In Chapter eleven, Monica, Karina, Cristina, Michael, and Mario tell the story of how our residents and mentors have developed as socially just teacher leaders through the support of NMUTR faculty and administrations. Blending multiple personal narratives, it provides a longitudinal perspective of the work of the NMUTR.

Finally the book concludes with updates about our residents in their schools and our thoughts about the implications of our third space work not only for Newark, but for preservice teacher education programs in the United States.

REFERENCES

Berry, B., Montgomery, D., & Snyder, J. (2008). *Urban teacher residency models at institutes of higher education: Implications for teacher preparation.* New York, NY: Center for Teaching Quality.

Bhabha, H. K. (1994). *The location of culture.* London, UK: Routledge.

Boomer, G., Onore, C., Lester, N., & Cook, J. (1992). *Negotiating the curriculum: Educating for the 21st century.* New York, NY: Routledge.

Bullough, Jr., R. V. (2005). Being and becoming a mentor: School-based teacher educators and teacher educatoridentity. *Teaching and Teacher Education, 21*(2), 143–155.

Burnett, T. B. (2014). T. Bone Burnett: How I set lyrics for Bob Dylan's new basement tapes to music. *The Guardian.* Retrieved from http://www.theguardian.com/music/shortcuts/2014/jul/20/lyrics-bob-dylan-new-basement-tapes-t-bone-burnett

City, E. A., Elmore, R. F., Fiarman, S. E., & Teitel, L. (2009). *Instructional rounds in education: A network approach to improving teaching and learning.* Cambridge, MA: Harvard Education Press.

Freire, P. (2000). *Pedagogy of the oppressed.* New York, NY: Continuum.

Friend, M., & Cook, L. (1996). *Interactions: Collaboration skills for school professionals.* New York, NY: Allyn & Bacon.

Green, J. (2012). *The fault in our stars.* New York, NY: Speak.

Greene, M. (2000). *Releasing the imagination: Essays on education, the arts, and social change.* San Francisco, CA: Jossey-Bass.

Gutierrez, K. D. (2008). Developing a sociocritical literacy in the third space. *Reading Research Quarterly, 43*(2), 148–164.

Klein, E. J., Taylor, M., Onore, C., Strom, K., & Abrams, L. W. (2013). Finding a third space in teacher education: Creating the MSU/NPS urban teacher residency. *Teaching Education, 24*(1), 27–57.

Lewis, R. (2014). Lost Bob Dylan lyrics make for 'new basement tapes' project. *Los Angeles Times.* Retrieved November 11, 2014.

McDonald, J., Mohr, N., Dichter, A., & McDonald, E. (2003). *The power of protocols: An educator's guide to better practice* (2nd ed.). New York, NY: Teachers College Press.

Moje, E., Ciechanowski, K. M., Kramer, K., Ellis, L., Carrillo, R., & Collazo, T. (2004). Working toward third space in content area literacy: An examination of everyday funds of knowledge and discourse. *Reading Research Quarterly, 39*(1), 38–70.

Moles, K. (2008). A walk in thirdspace: Place, methods, and walking. *Sociological Research Online 13*(4), 3. Retrieved February 9, 2012, from http://www.socresonline.org.uk/13/4/2.html

Moll, L., Amanti, C., Neff, D., & Gonzalez, N. (1992). Funds of knowledge for teaching: Using a qualitative approach to connect home and classrooms. *Theory into Practice, 31*(2), 132–141.

Oldenburg, R. (1999). *The great good place: Cafés, coffee shops, community centers, beauty parlors, general stores, bars, hangouts, and how they get you through the day* (1st ed.). New York, NY: Paragon House.

Onore, C., & Gildin, B. (2010). Preparing urban teachers as public professionals through a university-community partnership. *Teacher Education Quarterly, 37*(3), 27–44.

Onore, C., Goeke, J., Taylor, M., Klein, E. J. (2009). Teacher leadership: Amplifying teachers' voices. *Academic Exchange Quarterly, 13*(2), 78–83.

Papay, J. P., West, M. R., Fullerton, J. B., & Kane, T. J. (2012). Does an urban teacher residency increase student achievement? Early evidence from Boston. *Educational Evaluation and Policy Analysis, 34*(4), 413–434.

Pilburn, M., Sawada, D., Falconer, K., Turley, J., Benford, R., & Bloom, I. (2000). *Reformed teaching observation protocol (RTOP).* Tempe, AZ: Arizona Collaborative for Excellence in the Preparation of Teachers.

Ronfeldt, M. (2012). Where should student teachers learn to teach? Effects of field placement school characteristics on teacher retention and effectiveness. *Educational Evaluation and Policy Analysis, 34*(1), 3–26.

Routledge, P. (1996). The third space as critical engagement. *Antipode, 28*(4), 399–419.

Slate, J. (2014). What Bob Dylan's basement tapes teach us. *Esquire.*

Soja, E. W. (1996). *Thirdspace: Journeys to Los Angeles and other real-and-imagined places.* Malden, MA: Blackwell Publishing.

Solomon, J. (2009). The Boston teacher residency: District-based teacher education. *Journal of Teacher Education, 60*(5), 478–488.

Taylor, M., Klein, E. J., & Abrams, L. (2014). Tensions of re-imagining our roles as teacher educators in a third space: Revisiting a co/autoethnography through a faculty lens. *Studying Teacher Education, 10*(1), 3–19.

Urban Teacher Residency United Report. (2014). Retrieved from http://www.utrunited.org/EE_assets/docs/14102-UTRU_Building_Effective_Residencies-Full-ingle_Pgs.pdf

Zeichner, K. (2010). Rethinking the connections between campus courses and field experiences in college- and university-based teacher education. *Journal of Teacher Education, 61*(2), 89–99.

Monica Taylor
Department of Secondary and Special Education
Montclair State University
Montclair, New Jersey

Emily J. Klein
Department of Secondary and Special Education
Montclair State University
Montclair, New Jersey

APPENDIX

ARTS HIGH SCHOOL 2012–2013

Free/Reduced Lunch Programs: 82.2% of student population
Limited English Proficiency: 0.1% of student population
Special Education Programs: 6.3% of student population

Linguistic Diversity	
2012–2013	Percentage
English	75.5%
Spanish	18.0%
Portuguese	5.3%
Haitian Creole	0.6%
Igbo	0.3%
Creoles and Pidgins	0.2%
Other	0.2%

Enrollment of Students by Ethnic/Racial Subgroup	
Black	52.7%
Hispanic	38.8%
White	7.9%
Asian	0.3%
American Indian	0.3%

College Readiness Test Participation		
2012–2013 Percent of Students	School Average	State Average
Participating in SAT	85.9%	75.3%
Participating in ACT	100%	20.6%
Participating in PSAT	0%	52.5%

Composite SAT Score			
2012–2013	School Average	Peer Average	State Average
Composite SAT Score	1,241	1,205	1,512
Critical Reading	398	396	495
Mathematics	426	413	521
Writing	417	396	496

AP/IB Courses Offered		
AP/IB Course Name	Students Enrolled	Students Tested
AP Physics B	50	17
AP Chemistry	20	2
AP Art—History of Art	15	7
AP English Literature and Composition	13	7
AP U.S. History	13	10

Postsecondary Enrollment Rates by Racial Subgroup		
Racial Subgroup	2 Year Institution	4 Year Institution
Black	32.1%	67.9%
Hispanic	38.5%	61.5%
Economically Disadvantaged	40.7%	59.3%

EAST SIDE HIGH SCHOOL 2012–2013

Free/Reduced Lunch Programs: 85.9% of student population
Limited English Proficiency: 17.9% of student population
Special Education Programs: 14.3% of student population

Linguistic Diversity	
2012–2013	Percentage
Spanish	39.2%
English	39.2%
Portuguese	19.4%
Bengali	0.6%
Gujarati	0.3%
Arabic	0.2%
Other	1.2%

Enrollment of Students by Ethnic/Racial Subgroup	
Hispanic	53.8%
White	30.5%
Black	14.6%
Asian	0.7%
American Indian	0.3%
Pacific Islander	0.1%

AP/IB Courses Offered		
AP/IB Course Name	Students Enrolled	Students Tested
AP Calculus AB	23	23
AP Spanish Language	19	19
AP English Language and Composition	18	18
AP Statistics	13	14
AP Spanish Literature	11	9
AP U.S. History	11	11
AP English Literature and Composition	10	10
AP U.S. Government and Politics	8	8
AP Biology	8	8
AP Physics B	5	5

College Readiness Test Participation		
2012–2013 Percent of Students	School Average	State Average
Participating in SAT	50.2%	75.3%
Participating in ACT	81.3%	20.6%
Participating in PSAT	17.5%	52.5%

Composite SAT Score			
2012–2013	School Average	Peer Average	State Average
Composite SAT Score	1,239	1,205	1,512
Critical Reading	399	398	495
Mathematics	437	413	521
Writing	403	398	496

Postsecondary Enrollment Rates by Racial Subgroup		
Racial Subgroup	2 Year Institution	4 Year Institution
White	56.1%	43.9%
Black	63.6%	36.4%
Hispanic	73.2%	25.6%
Students with Disability	78.6%	14.3%
Economically Disadvantaged Students	66.7%	32.6%

MEET THE AUTHORS FROM CHAPTER TWO

Jennifer Robinson, I began my work in urban education as a teacher and supervisor in the Chicago Public Schools and in Evanston, Illinois. When I started as faculty at MSU over 20 years ago, I worked with many teachers including, Susan Taylor, at the Harold Wilson Professional Development School (PDS) in Newark. There, we collaboratively developed a structured experience for prospective teacher education candidates who were taking the Initial Field course to help them critically examine their beliefs and conceptions of urban schools. As an instructor in Project THISTLE, I taught a curriculum development course to NPS teachers and challenged them to realize their role as stewards of the schools who provide their students with access to best learning experiences possible. When I taught the course, Education in the Inner City, I was able to introduce MSU graduate students to urban schools through two intensive field experiences that took us into University High School where I first met Walt Kaczca and other dedicated NPS educators. Over the years, I have had the privilege of leading several grant-funded projects to recruit and retain new and experienced educators in partnership with the Paterson, Newark, Jersey City, and East Orange Public Schools.

When I became the Director of the Center of Pedagogy (CoP) in 2005, Ada Beth charged me to further our college mission and be the catalyst for excellent, equitable education in Newark. She encouraged me to use the Partnership for Instructional Excellence and Quality (PIE-Q) as our primary vehicle to deepen our partnership work with the Newark Public Schools. When we were awarded the grant in 2009, I wanted to amass all that we had learned over the years about urban teacher preparation and school/university partnership in the development of the residency. Moreover it was important that the NMUTR become an avenue whereby other like-minded faculty from across the university would engage in preparing socially conscious teachers for our partner schools.

Ada Beth Cutler, I came to MSU as a faculty member in 1994, when the university was in partnership with NPS and the Newark Teachers Union (NTU) at the Harold Wilson Professional Development School (PDS). With expertise in teacher professional development and a commitment to working in urban schools forged in the beginning of my career in New York City, I quickly became involved in the partnership at Harold Wilson. That is where I first worked closely with Jennifer Robinson, also a faculty member at MSU at the time, and where I met Sue Taylor and many other educators who later took on leadership roles in NPS. I led workshops for the professional development staff members at Harold Wilson, taught teachers who were on assignment there, and first came to know the landscape of teaching and learning in NPS. As a teacher educator at MSU, I knew that NPS was an important setting for our teacher education students to immerse themselves in striving urban schools and learn good practice from many fine educators in the district.

Part of my job in my early years as a faculty member at MSU was to direct our school-university partnership, now called the MSU Network for Educational Renewal (MSUNER), of which NPS was a member district. In that capacity, I worked with NPS leadership in the central office in Newark and had a hand in policy and politics affecting the partnership. My work in and commitment to Newark and its public schools also developed through the Education Law Center, where I volunteered my expertise by serving on various Abbott committees and task forces at the state level.

In 2000, I became dean of the College of Education and Human Services at MSU and my hands-on work with teachers and schools in Newark lessened, but my ability to affect and deepen the overall partnership with NPS increased in this new role. I was able to commit university resources, especially faculty time, to the partnership and I actively supported and developed grant proposals to advance the partnership. Our partnership with NPS has had its ups and downs, but I always knew it was key to our efforts to simultaneous renew and improve urban schools *and* teacher education. In many ways, the NMUTR was the culmination of those efforts.

Julianne Bello, I had been teaching seventh grade and then humanities at First Avenue School (FAS) for five years when my principal, Tony Orsini, invited me to join him at a PIE-Q meeting. I can remember feeling overwhelmed, sitting at the table with fellow teachers and administrators from neighboring schools, MSU faculty, and NPS leadership, and hearing them discuss "the work" of PIE-Q. As my understanding of the partnership grew, it was empowering for me as a teacher leader to help Tony establish our school as a site for university students to thoughtfully consider urban teaching. My role was to coordinate the on-site component of the Public Purposes of Schooling course through collaborating with Monica Taylor and Vanessa Domine to host an orientation session as an introduction to our school, coordinating the teachers they would shadow, and providing opportunities for the ten hours of community service they would complete. A product of these orientations was the development of the FAS teacher handbook, which would become a valuable tool in the induction process of our new hires. For new hires coming from MSU, I was an additional layer of support in their beginning years of instructional practice.

I was invited by MSU to become an adjunct professor in 2006, and my work with both district and university leaders inspired me to complete my degree in Administration and Supervision in 2007. Following Tony's retirement, I continued to act as liaison until January 2010, when I left Newark to become a middle school vice-principal, first with Dover and then with the West Orange Public Schools. In September 2014, I became an elementary principal with the Roselle Park school district. Professional development and innovation in teacher preparation continue to be areas of interest for me.

Matthew Brewster, I currently serve as special assistant for high school operations in NPS. I have worked in various capacities in NPS for the past 22 years. I taught at South Seventeenth Street School, supervised school management teams in School Leadership Team V, and then was the vice principal and principal at Vailsburg Middle School. My central office work began when I was appointed director of professional staff development in the fall of 2006. It was in that capacity that I became involved with PIE-Q and MSUNER.

The NPS office of professional staff development was, at the time, the link between the district and the university. As the director of that office I was responsible for representing the district on various committees and stewarding initiatives and programs that came about as a result of the partnership. I contributed to the development of the proposal for the NMUTR and lead my staff as we participated in interviews associated with the selection process for the first few cohorts of residents and mentors.

Marisol Diaz, engaging in partnership work is not for the faint of heart. I am the principal of Benjamin Franklin Elementary School in NPS. My leadership journey formally began in 2004 when I was invited as a "teacher leader" to co-develop PIE-Q. That work was at once deeply rewarding, formative, and grueling. It was rewarding because it enhanced my beliefs in the critical importance of developing highly competent teachers; formative because it made sense of my academic development both during my undergraduate at MSU, graduate work at Seton Hall University, and my decision to become an urban school administrator; and grueling because to achieve excellence in teacher preparation an administrator must embrace the complexity and deep personal and professional challenge of the work. Collaboration done well has the power to provide the resources critical to the support required to create an excellent school, one that responds purposefully to the needs of each of its students.

PIE-Q laid the foundation for the work of the NMUTR, in which I naturally and gratefully remain involved, this time as a principal. The NMUTR brought our partnership work to a deeper level. Through this collaboration I have had opportunity to work with MSU faculty to craft the experiences and content for residents. Lessons learned through these experiences helped push my thinking and practice in how to support teachers throughout the teaching continuum. It has been a privilege to be among the pioneers of better education through the work of developing and nurturing passionate, caring, and competent teachers.

Carolyn Granato, I currently work as the principal of McKinley Elementary School, located in the Central Ward of Newark. It is a PK- 8th grade elementary school serving approximately 1025 students of which 1/3 are of special needs. I have served in this position since August 1999. In 2001, I became involved in partnership work with MSU. My colleague and mentor Susan Taylor suggested that my school become one of the original sites for PIE-Q.

In spring 2009 the PIE-Q Leadership Council discussed the pending opportunity to take our partner work to another level. We decided to respond to the Teacher Quality Partnership (TQP) grant RFP from the Department of Education by submitting an application to start a residency style teacher preparation program. We were thrilled and honored when we were selected to be one of the first TQP grant recipients in October 2009. Even more wonderful was the fact that McKinley Elementary School was selected to be one of the first school sites for the new NMUTR.

My involvement in the partnership between MSU and the NPS has had a profound impact on my professional growth and development as an educator and person. I currently have approximately 15 teachers employed as a direct result of this grant serving the most fragile children at McKinley and other NPS. The NMUTR is such a well thought-out and thorough approach to the recruitment, preparation, and retention of strong, effective urban educators. Teachers are prepared beyond theory and can apply practice because of this incredible grant.

Roger León, I am a proud product of NPS and remain a resident of the renaissance city. As a graduate of Rutgers University–Cook College with a Bachelor of Arts in Biology, I felt the need to teach in Newark schools that I attended—Hawkins Street School and Science High School—and I aimed to and indeed helped to improve them. I taught in the Algebra Pilot, which afforded 8th graders a demanding Algebra curriculum throughout the city while providing future mathematics teachers with intensive professional development. As a result of my Master of Arts in Education Administration from MSU, I was afforded various professional opportunities early in my career, including becoming principal of Dr. William H. Horton School and the prestigious University High School of the Humanities for several years.

One of the things I remember about the numerous PIE-Q meetings we held at University High School when I was principal there was the incredibly profound reciprocal relationship that existed between the school district, the university, and the teacher education program. We had professors who moved the instructional program for us by providing professional development that demonstrated the practice of theory. Our English and Social Studies Departments used the Socratic Method because of the MSU professors who led us in that method of teaching. So, the teacher education candidates were seeing master teachers and the master teachers were seeing professors who profoundly understood the craft of elevating instruction. Having the opportunity to actually work in a high performing urban school allowed MSU students to see how it was very possible to educate children, regardless of their life circumstances, at really, really high levels.

NPS students remain my greatest pride and joy because of their abilities to accept all of the challenges that are presented to them with the understanding that their success is the only acceptable outcome. Since I firmly believe that every child is a genius, every adult is required to provide unique opportunities to demonstrate this fact. Currently as the Assistant Superintendent in NPS with an unwavering commitment to the improvement of student achievement, my knowledge and understanding of issues and concerns related to public education and administration, superior human relations skills, and supervision of the development, organization, and delivery of curriculum and instructional programs and services are amongst my highest priorities.

Anthony Orsini, I was employed by NPS as a classroom teacher directly after receiving my degree from Kean University. My employment at NPS covered 42 years, the last twelve as principal of the First Avenue Elementary School (FAS). Shortly after our school received Fordham University's National School Change Award (the first school in New Jersey to be so honored), I was asked to participate in MSU's PIE-Q program. As a participant in the program, selected members of our staff and I would meet monthly with Jennifer, other CoP members, faculty, and teams from the other PIE-Q schools. During these sessions we discussed various issues related to improving the quality of instruction in our schools, specifically, how we could improve teacher retention. The ideas generated in these sessions led to the creation of the FAS New Teacher Handbook and we scheduled monthly meetings with all student teachers and non-tenured staff. During these meetings we would discuss any issues the teachers would request as well as provide presentations from various members of the school's support staff. FAS also hosted between 20 and 30 MSU students from the Public Purposes of Schooling course each semester. Students would commit to 10 hours of service to the school. They contributed to a variety of school programs and also served as tutors to selected FAS students.

After retiring in 2009, my association with MSU continues to this day. I work as an Adjunct Professor and Education Mentor. I thoroughly enjoy sharing my experiences and providing assistance to current students in the teacher education program.

Susan M. Taylor, I currently work as the Director of the NMUTR. I have served in this position since August 2010 when I retired from NPS after 39 years of service as a teacher and principal. In addition to receiving my Master's degree in Educational Leadership from MSU I have been involved in partner relationships with MSU as a teacher and principal. During my final 14 years in NPS I was the principal of Benjamin Franklin Elementary School. Our school was one of the original sites selected by NPS and MSU leadership to be part of the PIE-Q.

In the spring of 2009 the PIE-Q Operations Committee discussed the pending opportunity to take our partner work to another level. We decided to respond to the Teacher Quality Partnership (TQP) grant RFP from the Department of Education by submitting an application to start a residency style teacher preparation program. The PIE-Q partners were thrilled and honored to be selected as one of the first TQP grant recipients in October 2009. Additionally, I was pleased when Benjamin Franklin School was selected to be one of the first school sites for the newly formed NMUTR.

My involvement since the early 1990s in the partnership between MSU and NPS has had a profound impact on my professional growth and development as an educator and person. In my current role as Director of the NMUTR I am able to utilize much of my experience as an urban educator and administrator in alignment with the knowledge I have gained regarding the growth and development of effective teachers. The NMUTR is such a well thought-out and thorough approach to the recruitment, preparation, and retention of strong, effective urban educators.

JENNIFER ROBINSON WITH ADA BETH CUTLER,
JULIANNE BELLO, MATTHEW BREWSTER, MARISOL DIAZ,
CAROLYN GRANATO, ROGER LEON, ANTHONY ORSINI
AND SUSAN TAYLOR

2. PARTNERSHIP

Origins of an Urban Teacher Residency

An urban teacher residency would contain all our dreams of what an authentic partnership between a district and teacher education program should embody: a finely-tuned shared governance structure supported by regular meetings, retreats, and professional development. It should include MSU faculty members in residence in schools for on-site teacher education and professional development; MSU students conducting inquiry projects with NPS students; NPS students attending summer pre-college programs at MSU to prepare and motivate them for college; intensive job-imbedded professional development for NPS teachers; NPS staff as instructors and teachers who are dedicated to the successful implementation of on-site teacher preparation; a cutting edge induction support program for new teachers, including MSU grads who were prepared on-site in the district to assist; and a rigorous, outside evaluation of all partnership aspects and activities. (PIE-Q Leadership Council Retreat, April 2009)

A PRELUDE TO THE BEGINNING

The arduous task of planning, writing, and submitting major grant proposals is all too familiar to many in academia and in large school districts. Normally, the most regrettable circumstance is submitting a topnotch proposal that does not get funded. In reality, we experienced a worse-case scenario.

Early in 2003, the US Department of Education released a Request for Proposals (RFP) for the Teacher Quality Enhancement (TQE) Grant program. The grants of up to $5,000,000 were designed to fund partnerships between large urban school districts, their teachers' union, and nearby universities that were dedicated to improving teacher education, teaching, and learning in urban schools. This grant brought the possibility of establishing a strong foundation for deep partnership between Montclair State University (MSU) and Newark Public Schools (NPS). Rather than submitting a proposal to fund a "project" with a specific life span, we wanted to propose a way to build a healthy, sustained relationship that would meld our mutual goals of making instructional excellence the norm in all Newark classrooms.

The grant was not to be the first venture between MSU and NPS. We already had a history of over 40 years of collaboration. In the 1970s, MSU's Project THISTLE (Thinking Skills in Teaching and Learning) helped NPS teachers strengthen children's creative and critical thinking skills (Oxman & Michelli, 1984). In the 80s NPS joined MSU's Clinical Schools Network to help prepare new teachers and support experienced ones. In 1991, MSU, NPS and the Newark Teachers Union (NTU) signed a bold agreement to establish New Jersey's first professional development school to link teacher professional development and teacher preparation through a range of activities and collaborative projects that resulted in positively affecting teacher attitudes and teacher candidates' views about teaching and learning in urban schools (Walker et al., 1995). All of this activity was further validated when MSU joined the National Network for Educational Renewal (NNER), a membership network of school districts and universities dedicated to the ongoing renewal of schools and the institutions that prepare teachers (Goodlad, 1994; Heckman & Mantle-Bromley, 2004). After forty years of successful collaboration on individual projects, we saw the TQE grant as an opportunity to build a lasting partnership with a sophisticated infrastructure.

While the College of Education and Human Services (CEHS) at MSU was anxious to forge a sustained partnership with NPS, one persisting challenge was the scattershot nature of our prior endeavors, in particular working with different schools and principals on each project and never building school or district capacity. Our work lacked collaborative practices and policies between NPS and MSU that were necessary to affect systemic and substantive change for the P-12 students we aimed to reach. The TQE grant seemed tailor-made for us to do something dramatically different to rectify these gaps in our prior work together.

As the CEHS dean and director of the Center of Pedagogy (CoP),[1] we knew how competitive federal grants were and pursued this with serious intention and all the resources we could muster for success. That meant garnering support from MSU's president and provost and the NPS superintendent, including their commitments to provide a good portion of the required match.

We met with the NPS superintendent and deputy superintendent at the time, to discuss establishing an interdependent system for urban teacher recruitment, preparation, retention, and professional development for the continuous renewal of the schools and teacher education. With a history of high quality teacher preparation, MSU wanted an operational base to better prepare its students to be excellent urban educators. Experience had taught us that spreading a thin veneer of resources across this large school district was not the right approach. We wanted to work in schools led by dynamic principals who wanted to partner with MSU and welcome cohorts of student teachers into classrooms to learn about teaching. Initially, the superintendents liked the idea of concentrating efforts in a cluster of schools, but they had concerns about the schools we recommended.

A BRIEF LOOK BACK IN TIME

As the oldest and largest school district in the state, NPS had a history of struggling to serve the needs of its low-income, culturally, and linguistically diverse student population. In 1995, NPS had become a state-operated school district when it was determined that the district was fiscally and educationally mismanaged, and not able to meet State standards (CTAC, 2000). Under the superintendent's leadership, the district had invested heavily in professional development. However teacher recruitment and retention were the district's critical needs when we were discussing the TQE grant. Anecdotal data and exit surveys of teachers who had left the district indicated that support for novice teachers was lacking and it was clear from students' academic performance that highly skilled teachers were needed.

The superintendents wanted to know why we wanted to work in the better schools, and why we weren't proposing to work in the neediest and "hard-to-staff" schools. They pointed out that it's easy to prepare good teachers in good schools. They wanted the grant to help the weakest teachers, administrators, and students. Though unsaid, we believed focusing the grant on those schools would also off-load their burden of having to face many of the ingrained systemic problems that ailed the district.

We gently explained that, to attract the best teachers, you need great schools where they could learn from seasoned teachers and work (Hargreaves & Fullan, 2013). We also wanted to dispel negative impressions of urban schools that teacher education candidates often carry with them from their largely segregated schooling experiences (Burdell, 2006; Domine & Bello, 2010; Feistritzer, 2011). The majority of today's teacher education candidates continue to be white, middle-class, and monolingual (Cochran-Smith, 2004; Cochran-Smith & Villegas, in press; Onore, 2006). As a teacher education program dedicated to promoting democratic principles and social justice, we faced back then and continue to face the moral dilemma of preparing teachers for culturally diverse classrooms. In fact, most MSU teacher education candidates have never been nor do they want to teach in Newark initially.

The so-called good schools we requested as partners still needed lots of work, we asserted. We argued that, even though these schools were not chaotic and many children tested at the proficient level, the students were not receiving the highest quality education. We also wanted to expose NPS teachers and leaders to innovative instructional practices, not to mention wanting NPS staff to educate our students about how to advocate for their students' communities (Klein, Taylor, Onore, Strom, & Abrams, 2013). The superintendents relented, but they also insisted we work with a new middle school.

We hired an expensive, highly regarded writer who could ensure quality, adhere to the grant proposal requirements, and work across our different operating cultures. As dean, Ada Beth used precious CEHS discretionary funds to pay for that. Fortunately we were able to accomplish all of these tasks despite challenges and moments of doubt. After months of meetings and negotiations with NPS, we crafted a final proposal called the Partnership for Instructional Excellence

31

for Quality Education (PIE-Q) (See Appendix). This new concept of school/ university collaboration was very different from what we had before. It was integrated in quality, linking together elements of earlier efforts, with vision, and far-reaching purpose. What many of us had experienced in our own schooling and professional lives, we desperately wanted for the NPS children (and teachers): teacher leadership and decision-making, a sense of community and agency for all students, and democratic school leadership. These schools would be the primary settings in which MSU teacher education candidates would develop their teaching skills. Perhaps graduates would elect to teach in NPS. We wanted PIE-Q to be a representation of what the NNER calls the "simultaneous renewal of the schools and teacher education" (Goodlad, 1994).

Unlike reform, renewal assumes that partners will question assumptions and continue to make changes where improvements can be made and gaps in quality education exist. Simultaneous renewal is an effort to create between two cultures, the mechanisms and processes of a new, mutually beneficial culture that has within itself the seeds of continuous renewal (Goodlad & McMannon, 2004). Renewal requires a type of connectedness that is time-consuming and labor intensive. Much like a marriage, renewal is real work, requiring persistence and loyalty, at times in the face of insurmountable odds. At the time, we were not familiar with the concept of the third space, but there are clear connections. The tentativeness of teacher education in a third space suggests the negotiated nature of partnership roles and relationships. Clearly, the utopian dimension of the third space is in concert with what we hoped would be a new vision of partnership (Klein, Taylor, Onore, Strom, & Abrams, 2013). This chapter will provide more examples of how the NPS/MSU partnership established in 2005 became the launching pad for preservice teacher education in the third space.

Once the proposal was written, and submitted, we waited for word from the U.S. Department of Education. This was one of the early electronic submissions of federal grant proposals with a deadline for when the submission portal would shut down. The sad and painful truth is that our proposal never left our office because the grants administrator underestimated the time needed and had not completed the uploading process when the portal shut down. Nothing was submitted, absolutely nothing.

It is difficult even now, over ten years later, to revisit that awful event. How could this have happened? How were we going to explain this to the president and provost at MSU, the NPS superintendent, and all the principals, teachers, faculty members, university leaders, and union officials who had worked on and committed to this proposal to our vision of what PIE-Q could be? What about all our hopes, dreams, and plans? As dean, Ada Beth took ultimate responsibility for the disaster and dealt with the fallout, anger, frustration, and deep disappointment shared by all of the partners in the proposal. She reflects, "I will never forget my meeting with the MSU president when I told her what happened." Without exaggeration, we had to go through a period of mourning.

Sometimes though, out of the ashes of a disaster, something good and important and fruitful is born. That's exactly what happened here. As we began to recover from the shock and disappointment of our failure, some of us thought PIE-Q was too good an idea to abandon. Besides, we had already begun forging respectful professional relationships. Just as we began to move forward without funding, the New Jersey Department of Education (NJDOE) launched an application for P-12 Higher Education /Public School Partnership grants of up to $100,000. We returned to the earlier texts, assembled, and quickly submitted a successful proposal. In January 2005, MSU, NPS, and the NTU officially launched PIE-Q. In the remainder of this chapter, we will elaborate on the critical partnership themes that led from the formation of PIE-Q to the NMUTR in 2009.

PRESSING TOWARDS PARTNERSHIP

Initially, PIE-Q consisted of a 4-school feeder-pattern cluster:

- *University High School of the Humanities:* A 7–12 college-preparatory magnet school in the South Ward, with an enhanced humanities curriculum that prepared over 500 students each year;

- *Benjamin Franklin Elementary School:* A K-4 school in the North Ward in which 86% of its 545 children were from homes where Spanish is the first language;

- *McKinley Elementary School:* A P-6 school in the North Ward which served 800 students, many of whom had special needs, through an inquiry-based discovery approach to learning; and

- *Gladys Hillman-Jones Model Middle School:* A 6–8 middle school which served 331 students from McKinley and Franklin schools and used a literacy-rich approach to learning, an extensive ESL program, and an advisor-advisee program. This school no longer exists.

Three themes characterized these schools. First, they all had exisiting positive working relationships among MSU faculty, school faculty, and administrators. Franklin's principal, Sue Taylor, was a long-standing colleague, having worked with MSU faculty at the PDS before it was closed in 1996 following State takeover. Franklin hosted the Art Backpacks program, led by MSU Fine Arts professor, Dorothy Heard, and her students, in which 4th graders engaged in art-making and family literacy activities. Another MSU faculty member, Nancy Lauter, taught her student teaching seminar at McKinley, having developed a relationship with the principal, Carolyn Granato, to work in inclusive classrooms for students with disabilities. The principal of the high school, Roger Leon, supported a Future Educators Academy, considered MSU professor Cindy Onore a member of his faculty, and welcomed cohorts of student teachers each year. His vision was to hire and induct MSU teacher education graduates, thereby cultivating a community of high quality teachers whom he had a hand in preparing at his school.

A second theme, teacher development and teacher leadership, was also evident in these schools. Principals were already challenging and stretching their middle career teachers, a teacher development stage most often overlooked by school leaders (Hargreaves & Fullan, 2013). These principals encouraged their teachers to take responsibility for school projects and lead professional development for groups of teachers. With Sue's encouragement, several teachers at Franklin were enrolled in educational leadership programs.

Third, these schools had strong administrative leadership. We knew that positive, strong, supportive leadership was key to the success of our work with the schools (Foster & Taylor, 2010). Each principal had her own strengths. Known for taking on new challenges as a principal, Carolyn successfully integrated a new pre-school program into her school in one summer, expanding the enrollment by 25% practially overnight. Sue wrote and won a Title VII grant to establish a highly successful dual language program to serve the large population of English Language Learners in her building. According to Roger, "I had a very strong administrative team and I felt that I was modeling for them that which we would want to see a school leader do for their students." Roger was known around the district as a no-nonsense principal; perhaps even a bit eccentric, but effective nevertheless.

TOWARDS BECOMING A COMMUNITY OF PRACTICE

In many respects PIE-Q had PDS[2] characteristics. PIE-Q participants had varying degrees of experience implementing the NCATE Standards for PDS partnerships, but we did not consciously use them to guide our work. While the PDS standards provided benchmarks for the developmental stages of school/university partnerships, they lacked the thick contextual dimension necessary to guide the evolution of team-building and navigate the complexities of crossing institutional boundaries. In fact looking back upon our work together, PIE-Q more resembled a community of practice characterized by collective learning and sustained over time in the pursuit of a shared enterprise, teacher development, with attendant social relations and a common identity. The community members do not necessarily work together every day, but meet because they find value in their interactions, share information, insight, and advice, and help each other solve problems by discussing their situations, aspirations, and needs (Wenger, McDermott, & Snyder, 2002). The community of practice is a framework we use to describe the ways PIE-Q developed the three essential elements of practice in a community: mutual engagement, joint enterprise, and a shared repertoire (Wenger, 1998).

Mutual Engagement

The ability to engage with other members and respond in kind to their actions, and thus the ability to establish relationships in which this mutuality is the basis for an identity of participation. (Wenger, 1998, p. 137)

Monthly after-school meetings that were chaired by Jennifer, CoP director, were held at McKinley School with 10 to 15 participants including principals, teachers, central office administrators, a union representative, MSUNER school/university partnership director, and MSU faculty liaisons to the PIE-Q schools. Early meetings focused on establishing the Leadership Council and developing policies for decision-making, defining short and long-term partnership goals, and discussing strategies to recruit, prepare, support and develop urban teachers. Matthew Brewster, Director of the Office of Professional Staff Development remembers:

> When I first got to central office, someone gave me a whole stack of stuff saying "This is from Montclair State." It wasn't just, "Oh we are doing this project with Montclair State." There was actually substance behind it and it took me the entire summer to read through that stuff and go back and forth with Jennifer to figure out what exactly my office's role was supposed to be. There was more to it than just *saying* that there was a partnership. There was really *a process* that we were trying to establish.

The meetings were cordial and respectful at first. No one broached the topic of "good teaching" or "best practice," despite the fact that multiple and sometimes opposing views were expressed from time to time. Everyone was getting to know each other and feeling comfortable not only across institutions, but between schools in the district where communication and collaboration were neither encouraged nor supported in any significant or formalized way. While the overarching goals of the partnership were to develop good working relationships between university and school faculty, the leadership council, as the group called itself, struggled initially to define the purpose and direction of the meetings. Mutual engagement required that we recognize our competencies, value learning from one another, and acknowledge what we did not know individually (Wenger, 1998). Goal-setting became a negotiated endeavor in PIE-Q meetings. At times, MSU faculty held back in order to leave room for our school-based counterparts to speak into the situation. It is this space-making that enabled everyone at the table to feel they had a stake in the work. Each month schools reported on partnership work, discussed how MSU students were included in the school community, exchanged information about existing activities, and shared how MSU and NPS faculty were collaborating in the work of teacher preparation. According to the First Avenue School (FAS) principal, Tony Orsini, "[A] nice thing about PIE-Q was that you could steal from your other colleagues, see some of the things that they were doing that were working in their buildings with student teachers and first or second year teachers, and implement them in your building."

Through mutual engagement, we also attempted to cultivate a cadre of effective and skilled cooperating teachers in each school. We began by recruiting experienced teachers to become clinical faculty so they would learn MSU's conception of good teaching through three required mini courses: "Teaching for Critical Thinking," "Coaching and Mentoring," and "Culturally Responsive Teaching." Besides mini courses, the MSUNER offered a range of teacher-directed professional development experiences, including funded teacher study groups and action research teams. Despite the fact that NPS was a member district, few teachers and principals took advantage of the free professional development. At one PIE-Q meeting, a participant stated, "The voice of the Network is not loud enough; not being marketed the way it should be. Many district teachers aren't aware of the possibilities and resources available to them." Recruiting clinical faculty in PIE-Q schools was one way the Leadership Council believed it could address this issue.

Accountability to the Enterprise

> The ability to understand the enterprise of a community of practice deeply enough to take some responsibility for it and contribute to its pursuit and to its ongoing negotiation. (Wenger, 1998, p. 137)

Discussions were not enough to hold the group. Later, in addition to the school reports, the group made two important decisions: to establish sub-committees to focus, plan, and oversee PIE-Q work at each school, and to begin addressing deeper issues and challenges facing school partners, such as hiring and retaining new teachers. Short-term objectives were translated into manageable projects, which forced a mix of ideas and collaboration across schools, institutions, and grade levels. Events such as a cooperating teachers' dinner and an Urban Educators' Institute to attract MSU faculty and students to better understand urban schools were projects the sub-committees owned, planned, and implemented. This gave the leadership council a sense of accomplishment and momentum. Having a tangible product was mutually satisfying and helped the group coalesce into an authentic professional community.

The annual Urban Educators Institute, a 4-day experience in spring, was when PIE-Q schools invited MSU faculty, teacher education candidates, and NPS colleagues to observe in classrooms and learn about each school's innovative practices. NPS students conducted the school tours, and teachers and administrators gave talks about the school's points of pride and accomplishments that year. As Marisol Diaz, a vice principal at the time, recalls:

> We had groups of professors whose image of working with NPS was one way and we wanted to highlight the great things that were going on. So having them come and do those rounds and go to different schools was another [way] to show people that this is what's *really* happening. You don't have to be fearful. These are great kids, these are great schools. You could be part of it. I think people walked away saying, "Wow! My perception and perspective are very different now."

Opening the doors of PIE-Q schools to visitors led to a new and normalized practice between the school and the university. PIE-Q's second year coincided with the launch of a new sequence of teacher education courses at MSU, including one course designed to introduce prospective teacher education candidates to the purposes of schools. The curriculum and teaching department decided to embed a field experience within the course that would expose teacher education candidates to urban schools in an authentic way. Instead of reading about urban schools, all pre-admission students were required to conduct extended visits, observations, and community service hours at PIE-Q schools; a truly bold and necessary step on the part of the MSU faculty. We became mutually accountable for the impression MSU students had of NPS; it wasn't just left to the schools to prove they had value. Our responses to this situation—similar and dissimilar—were interconnected because we were engaged together in a joint enterprise (Wenger, 1998).

As director of the CoP, Jennifer regularly received phone calls and emails from fearful and sometimes irate parents who did not want their college-age children going into urban communities for field experiences. One parent wrote a letter insisting that she did not want her daughter "left behind like those Newark kids." MSU had always taken a hard line when it came to placing students in Newark and we made no excuses, but it was like pulling teeth. Rather than force, we wanted to invite our students to see the positive possibilities of making a difference for urban students through the eyes of the talented and innovative teachers and leaders who worked in Newark. Working with CoP staff, the faculty who taught the Public Purposes of Schooling course led their classes (sometimes under protest) into the schools as a sign of their commitment to educating their students about social justice issues. This helped wear down student resistance to learning about teaching and schools in Newark. Tony recalls:

> We used to get about 20 or 30 sophomores who might not have declared majors... we hosted them twice a year [to] give them a taste of what kinds of programs are working in our building. The nicest thing was that they all had to donate ten hours of service to the building so we had some working with teachers, we had some doing individual tutoring with kids, and we had some working field day.

Julianne Bello, a FAS teacher leader, remembers:

> I always worked with our building teachers in terms of hosting, and I think it gave our staff a layer of recognition. To veteran teachers I said, "Yes you're teaching the [P-12] student, but realize that you still have a responsibility, and also something to offer and shed light on for these people who are considering teaching." When we put together the orientations, teachers were willing and eager to be part of that and to interface with the Montclair students ... shepherd the new ones in and [give] that piece of stewardship.

The return on this investment was huge for everyone. Complaints and resistance to going into NPS schools dropped dramatically, primarily because MSU students understood that the PIE-Q experience was a requirement of admission to the teacher education program. There was also a decrease in the number of calls, emails, and protests from students who were placed in NPS for clinical experiences. As reported by faculty after initial school visits, many MSU students were pleasantly surprised to learn how much the students in Newark wanted to learn. NPS students grew accustomed to teaching their college peers about their school. And grade school students' aspirations soared because many of them came to believe they could attend college in the future (Domine & Bello, 2010).

Another lesson we learned along the way was how productive disagreement can be to the enterprise. Practice led us to develop the courage to confront each other to define our commitment to the children and youth of Newark. For example, during one Urban Educators' Institute, MSU faculty voiced their objections to the middle school principal when he characterized his students as budding juvenile delinquents. Other PIE-Q principals did not come to his defense, equally appalled at how he described his students. They also began questioning his methods of instituting school lock-downs and speaking in demeaning ways to youth in his school. Matthew notes:

> I think that speaks to the selectivity of the partnership, and determining what principals were going to be involved. It wasn't just, grab a principal and bring them into the fold. There was a very deliberate attempt to make sure that we were selecting the right people, to make sure that student teachers were going into a situation where they would be supported, where they would really learn. And that the principal would use those resources to benefit their school and not just have people sitting around doing nothing. I think the partnership was really good at identifying principals who would move the work along.

The middle school principal's eventual departure (precipitated by the district), and the subsequent re-organization of the middle school, forced the partnership to suffer its first casualty, but this did not deter progress. By this time, central office administrators expressed their support of the results they were seeing from the partnership in terms of P-12 students' interest in academic achievement and going to college, which was spurred by the presence of MSU students in PIE-Q schools. That is also when FAS and Maple Avenue Elementary School as well as Science High School joined PIE-Q.

Forging into 2007 was pivotal for PIE-Q, because by then the grant money had run out. Jennifer asked the leadership team members at the end-of-year retreat what they wanted to do. The decision was unanimous to continue with each school agreeing to host a monthly meeting. The community showed its willingness to take responsibility and contribute to its continued success when principals dipped into their school budgets to provide refreshments and other resources for accomplishing projects. Jennifer committed CoP budget to host the year-end retreat and continued seeking new funds to support our work. The group also decided to focus on a pressing issue: attracting the most promising MSU students to urban education and getting them hired by the school district annually. Frankly, despite district satisfaction with the partnership, it was nearly impossible to get MSU graduates hired—a problem endemic to urban school districts nationally (Ingersoll, 2003; Levin & Quinn, 2003).

Little did anyone realize that this unifying goal would sharpen the focus of the partnership overall and it would lay the necessary groundwork for the establishment of the Newark Montclair Urban Teacher Residency.

Negotiability of the Repertoire

> The ability to make use of the repertoire of the practice to engage in it. This requires enough participation (personal and vicarious) in the history of a practice to recognize it in the elements of its repertoire. Then it requires the ability—both the capability and the legitimacy—to make history newly meaningful. (Wenger, 1998, p. 137)

With the help of MSU director of Organizational Development and Training, Charlie Matteis, PIE-Q monthly meetings evolved into authentic discussions addressing the teacher development continuum. School teams and MSU faculty established plans to attract and support preservice, novice, and experienced teachers. A new air of accountability developed when teams reported their progress at the annual retreats. Over the next two years, PIE-Q sustained focus on planning and implementing professional development for student teachers, first-year teachers, second and third year teachers, and experienced cooperating teachers, led by teams of university and school district personnel, and a shift in conversations occurred. Instead of pointing at ways the district or union should change, PIE-Q participants began describing their own practices. Sue remembers, "We had a retreat up at the university and did this activity where we all had to list what we do for our first, second, and third year teachers. I remember feeling very convicted because I wasn't doing anything for anybody in any formal way."

Though we gained strength as an organized body, the ultimate goal, hiring well-prepared MSU graduates, remained elusive. The leadership council worked with the NPS Human Resources Department to create a smooth hiring process for MSU candidates. The district agreed to host a Job Fair in January 2007 if all student teachers—not just those from MSU—were allowed to attend. This was a significant breakthrough as far as the leadership council was concerned, so we agreed that any student teachers could participate.

MSU student teachers were professional and prepared to share portfolios of sample instructional units and lessons plans, but disorganization prevailed. Principals were not notified until the last minute and those who attended and showed interest in candidates couldn't offer contracts. The lack of serious intent on the part of the district resulted in candidates taking jobs in other communities. It was clear that, despite claims of teacher shortages, the district had no aggressive or organized plan to hire eligible candidates, even those who had already been vetted by schools during their 14-week student teaching experience.

Finally, at the direction of the leadership council, Jennifer arranged a meeting with district central office administration to present the data and request that the superintendent send a directive to Human Resources to commit to hire a minimum number of MSU teacher candidates who showed skill, ability, and an interest in teaching in Newark. In fall 2007, the superintendent agreed to hire 25 of the best MSU candidates as a show of her intent to establish a teacher preparation pipeline. That promise, along with the fact that the Prudential Foundation had just committed $1.6 million in grant funding to recruit and prepare new math and science teachers for Newark, catapulted these efforts forward. Marisol recalls: "I remember having different conversations at that time. 'So how do we get people hired?' Then we started to expand the people sitting around the table, and that's when some people from HR came, and that helped [us] make the process and the procedure for being able to retain [teachers]."

As a sign of true commitment, Jean Stefani from Human Resources was asked to serve on the leadership council. Her faithful attendance at meetings and insider knowledge regarding hiring procedures and timelines proved invaluable to our work and is still critical. She has been instrumental in sustaining the commitment to hire MSU graduates since 2007. The first year this policy went into effect, the district hired seven MSU graduates. There was a brief celebration following this breakthrough, but a new equally important PIE-Q challenge emerged: addressing the problems related to the degree and depth of district-level induction support for new teachers. It is important to note that this was not a self-serving endeavor on the part of MSU or the leadership council. According to Matthew, hiring MSU graduates was considered a win-win proposition: "From the district perspective, PIE-Q offered an opportunity to have that pipeline of teachers that we knew received a specific level of preparation. They would come in with their substitute card, which was a great advantage in the building. Just knowing that we have that pipeline coming, to see where we could draw from to fill those vacancies, [is significant]." A shared repertoire of stories, actions, historical events, tools, and concepts began to define us as a community of practice.

An unanticipated outcome was that PIE-Q participants began attending national meetings and conferences to deliver presentations and we gained recognition for our partnership success. This was at the height of several national school/university partnership initiatives. Leadership council members were invited to participate in *Strengthening and Sustaining Teachers, Leaders for Teacher-Preparing Schools, Teachers for a New Era Learning Network,* and *NCTAF's Urban Teaching Academy* to share about the progress of the work and to learn new ways to cultivate our work together (AACTE, 2008; AED, 2011; Foster & Taylor, 2010; Goldrick, 2009).

In June 2008, the American Association of Colleges for Teacher Education (AACTE) selected PIE-Q as one of several exemplary school/university partnership models for a panel presentation to congressional representatives in Washington, D.C. Newly-appointed as a NPS assistant superintendent, Roger Leon, spoke on behalf of the partnership; the only one from New Jersey and the only team for which both the school and university partners were present. He remembers:

I was next to Linda Darling-Hammond. She turned to me and said, "I just want to thank you for the work that you are doing." This is a person that I highly respected who paused to remind me of the important work that we have been doing in urban school districts. We were going to challenge the best school districts and if we improved Newark, we improved the State. If we were capable of improving the state of NJ it was going to elevate all the other states and make our country so far superior.

Roger, now an assistant superintendent in the district, has continued to play an advocacy role for PIE-Q and the NMUTR as the face of the partnership in the Central Office of NPS. His steadfast support and his continued favorable comments about the partnership at mutually advantageous times, have served to protect the partnership during turbulent times, much like shock absorbers on a car or truck in a pothole-strewn roadway.

During the new NPS administration that was initiated in 2008, along with a broad-based constituency of community leaders, PIE-Q members helped create a far-reaching strategic plan that included the continuation of the policy to hire high quality MSU graduates. Recognizing that good teachers are the key ingredients for improving student academic performance (Darling-Hammond, 2006), the district developed a strategic plan that identified the recruitment, preparation, support, and retention of well-prepared and highly qualified teachers as central priorities for the district. Strengthening professional development across the teacher development continuum was also a top priority (NPS, 2009). By this time, our participation as an evolving community of practice was seamlessly interwoven in a context of shared histories and we were negotiating meaning individually and collectively through mutual engagement and joint enterprise (Wenger, 1998).

At the May 2009 PIE-Q retreat, when a Teacher Quality Partnership RFP was announced, the leadership council voted unanimously to apply for the grant to establish a teacher residency in Newark. Marisol recounts:

I think we wanted to continue the work we were doing with PIE-Q and the conversations were going a little bit deeper: how do we really prepare the teachers to be excellent educators in an urban context? There would be more alignment between what was happening with teachers who were being taught at the university so that when they came into the public school practicum experience they were well-versed. I do think that's what paved the way for those deeper conversations to happen, that don't necessarily happen anywhere else, to help give birth to the residency. People could have that conversation and not just say, "Everything's great, everything's fine, everything's beautiful." But then be able to say, "Well this is what we're seeing is great and this is some of the stuff we need to adjust." I think it was just a natural shift to say, "We are doing all this work; we want to sustain it. Let's look at how we can create a master plan and fund it to get more teachers into the schools, where we would not only have the university's input but also the school would do the preparation."

The Newark Montclair Urban Teacher Residency (NMUTR) was a logical next step in the evolution of collaborative efforts to prepare highly effective teachers for the district. It took PIE-Q a step further with the financial resources to affect systemic change, beginning with a school-based model for teacher preparation, school-based renewal, and capacity-building of teachers and administrators. When the positive news of the grant arrived in fall 2009, PIE-Q had already proven its stability and readiness to take on a new and larger-than-life project. The partnership had the ability to withstand change, in personnel (NPS district leadership, principals, MSU faculty, staff, and deans) and even state leaders (governor and NJDOE commissioner).

Becoming a community meant that practice offered us something to do together around which we negotiated diverging meanings and perspectives. We engaged, rather than just talked about our connections and they meant more than our regular encounters. We had built deep working relationships and an indispensible bridge between organizations such that the lines of allegiance became blurred (Wenger, 1998).

By the end of five years of intensive partnership, PIE-Q had significant results. First, MSU student negative attitudes towards urban schools began shifting 180 degrees. As Tony relates:

> When I became an adjunct at Montclair, I'd say "We're done with the fall semester. Spring semester we're having seminar at a school." "Where's it going to be?" "Umm First Avenue." "Where is that?" "It's between Sixth and Seventh Streets in Newark." And you could almost see the PANIC! And then to watch the transition after they were there for several weeks. "Hey, it's not so bad!"

Matthew recalls, "Prior to PIE-Q, we did not have a large number of student teachers from MSU. But once that relationship was established they began to place more student teachers, which of course I always thought was a benefit for the school and for the teachers that worked with the student teachers."

One section of Public Purposes raised funds to help improve the playground at Maple Avenue School. And many MSU students now spent more than the required 10 hours of community service. Though pleased with our progress, we recognize that more must be done to ensure that MSU candidates have a reciprocal experience and realize they have as much to gain from their involvement in urban schools as the students they aim to help. Otherwise, we may inadvertently reinforce a "missionary" mentality (Onore, 2006).

University faculty also examined their views about urban students and schools, as a result of engaging in PIE-Q activities. One faculty member who teaches the Public Purposes course shared his experience during a class visit after speaking to a high school student about her aspirations. He was surprised when the student asserted her desire to attend an Ivy League school upon graduation. He later expressed shame, admitting his low expectations for her. He had not anticipated her knowledge, let alone interest, in attending a school his own children might attend.

Second, we established a credible teacher pipeline from MSU to the district, with high-level support from the superintendent. Tony recounts, "There were quite a few who, as a result [of Seminar] would attend the job fairs hoping to get something in Newark because it opened their eyes." By spring 2009, Jean reported that the district had hired 50 new teachers in a range of certification areas from MSU in two years.

Teacher induction, retention, and development became a new priority to school leadership. According to Tony,

> I think that was probably the most important contribution that PIE-Q made because, as a principal, I gave very little thought to the problems with teacher retention. When you're right there in the middle of the whole thing you don't realize how many people come and go rapidly and what you can do to try and get people to stay. Teacher retention was something new to me and it was brought to life as far as the things you can do through the partnership. I think the New Teacher Handbook was one of the most meaningful things [we did at FAS]. We gave it to every student teacher who came in … and also every first year teacher.

And, PIE-Q helped ignite deep discussions about the shared responsibility of teacher preparation. Marisol remembers:

> We started to have conversations about what first year teachers need to know when they come into the classroom. That opened the dialogue for the elementary, middle, and high school people to talk to the professors at MSU about some of the things that we were seeing teachers were coming very prepared with and what things we felt they needed more focus on while they went through their preparation.

As one can see, PIE-Q paved the way for a preservice teacher education program owned by the university and school-based faculty and their students, all situated in the third space. Our new conception of partnership included community-based organizations that contributed to educating the residents about the inherent richness of the neighborhoods surrounding the schools (Klein, Taylor, Onore, Strom, & Abrams, 2013) and further expanding our community of practice. Almost immediately, leadership council members rolled up their sleeves to begin the hard task of establishing the parameters of the NMUTR. Six work groups were formed to drive the beginning engines of the residency.

Monthly PIE-Q Meetings evolved into work group sessions until the launch in February 2010 of the elementary cohort consisting of candidates seeking early childhood, elementary, and special education certification. The secondary cohort, the focus of this book, would begin in June the same year with a mathematics and science cohort.

Having graduated 62 residents in high-need certification areas such as mathematics, science, and special education since 2010, we consider the NMUTR a successful partnership venture. Every graduate resident has been successfully hired as a teacher. Nearly 92% of them teach in NPS; the balance teach in other high need districts or schools. We estimate that, to date, these graduates have positively impacted 4,020 NPS students. The results not only reflect successful teacher recruitment and retention, but also school stability and positive culture.

LESSONS LEARNED

Communities of practice evolve in organic ways that tend to escape formal descriptions and control. Practice defies institutional affiliations and structures, and may bridge institutional boundaries that are critical to getting things accomplished, sometimes in spite of bureaucracies. Boundaries of practice are constantly renegotiated defining much more fluid and textured forms of participation, such as a third space for teacher preparation (Wenger, 1998).

School/university partnerships must be built on giving as well as getting. Too often universities and teacher education programs focus on what is in the best interest of the university or the faculty's research and self-advancement, not on the best interests of the school district, the schools, or the P-12 students. The tension caused by different priorities has plagued partnerships in the past because university faculty are not rewarded for their direct work in schools (Snyder, 2006). Instead, universities have been accused of doing research on, not with schools, which often leads to bad feelings and mistrust. In the case of PIE-Q, however, MSU leveraged much-needed resources through its larger network of school districts and affiliations with other national organizations to benefit the district. Matthew notes:

> One of the things I found out quickly is that everybody wanted a piece of Newark. Every university and organization wanted to give to the kids, study the schools, bring in their program, but it wasn't that they wanted to "partner." They said that they wanted to partner but they really just wanted to use [us]. It was like we were a laboratory. [MSU] was all about, "We can give this to you; this is to benefit you. Yes we need you as well: your students… your schools and all, but it's not just about us. It's a two-way street all the way around… "
> Just having a structure where I could ask for something (was different).

Sue expressed this sentiment differently: "I felt that a lot of times you [MSU] would bring opportunities and I think I generally had a yes attitude about them even though I didn't realize what I was saying yes to. The more that I said yes, the more I increased my savvy about using the university resources. Because I think in the beginning I was pretty blind about them."

Investing in the leadership of well-functioning schools benefited the district as well as the teacher education program. In many urban school improvement projects, district leaders rarely dedicate resources to develop stronger good schools; they do not build upon what works. Funders often drive this, but more often than not, this is to the detriment of higher-functioning schools. PIE-Q provided a healthy community of support for school leaders that resulted in better education for students, an enriched environment for teacher development, and school capacity. Our meetings and partnership work augmented some of the high quality professional development the district had provided for school leaders. Roger reflects:

> Cindy was always giving me research. A lot that I know now is because she was feeding me data. "This is what you're supposed to be doing; what you're supposed to be moving; things that you're supposed to be thinking about." She was pushing me to read a lot ... the research she was giving me was so much appreciated; it was more needed than not. She was making sure that I was on my toes. I lead better because I knew more because of her.

As Sue reflected, "A lot of the times it would be the monthly meeting day and I would have to force myself to go because I would be so overwhelmed and busy running the school. I would say, 'Ohhh, I gotta go to the PIE-Q meeting!' and I would get to the meeting and it would end up being a really rich PD experience and I would be glad I went."

In closing, becoming a community of practice is a complex, dynamic, and iterative process, requiring tremendous dexterity and the ability to tolerate ambiguity. The leadership council constantly revisited and reflected on short-term goals and responded to new opportunities for the benefit of goal achievement. When PIE-Q was awarded a professional development mini-grant from the New Teacher Center, principals saw it as an opportunity to involve more teachers, rather than another burden or distraction. We must also conclude as Wenger (1998) cautions us, not to see communities of practice as inherently beneficial or harmful, but as they truly exist in the world: "forces to be reckoned with for better or for worse. As a locus of engagement in action, interpersonal relations, shared knowledge, and negation of enterprises" (p. 85) for real transformation. We also understand now that the partnership must reflect the ideals of the third space: an utopian entity where all stakeholders advocate for students and their communities, and strive to be experts in their fields, but continue to be inquisitive, imaginative, and generative (Klein, Taylor, Onore, Strom, & Abrams, 2013).

NOTES

[1] The Center of Pedagogy (CoP) is the institutional structure at MSU that coordinates all aspects of teacher education for undergraduate and graduate initial teacher certification programs; a network of nearly 30 school districts; grant-funded projects for recruiting and preparing new teachers; and professional development for faculty on campus and in the schools. As the CoP director it was important to me to establish a teacher residency that became an avenue whereby like-minded faculty from across the university engage in the work of preparing socially conscious teachers for our partner schools.

[2] Promoted in the late 1980s by the Holmes Group and the National Network for Educational Renewal, the PDS is a joint endeavor of P-12 schools and schools of education to create places where entering

teachers combine theory and practice in a setting organized to support their learning; veteran teachers can renew their own professional development and assume new roles as mentors, university adjuncts, and teacher leaders; and school and university educators together engage in research and thinking of practice (Darling-Hammond, 2005).

REFERENCES

Academy for Educational Development. (2011). *Pursuing excellence in teacher preparation: Evidence of institutional change in TNE learning network universities.* Washington (DC), WA: Academy for Educational Development.

American Association of Colleges for Teacher Education. (2008). *Partnerships that work: Turning around low performing schools: Congressional briefing report.* Washington (DC), WA: Author

Burdell, P. (2006). Whiteness in teacher education, In J. L. Kincheloe, k. hayes, K. Rose, & P. M. Anderson (Eds.), *The Praeger handbook of urban education* (Vol. 1, pp. 101–111). Westport, CT: Greenwood Press.

Cochran-Smith, M. (2004). *Walking the road: Race, diversity, and social justice in teacher education.* New York, NY: Teachers College Press.

Cochran-Smith, M., & Villegas, A. M. (in press). Research on teacher preparation: Charting the landscape of a sprawling field. In D. Gitomer & C. Bell (Eds.), *Handbook of research on teaching.* Washington (DC), WA: AERA.

Community Training and Assistance Center. (2000). *Myths and realities: The impact of the state takeover on students and schools in Newark.* Boston, MA: Community Training and Assistance Center.

Darling-Hammond, L. (2006). *Powerful teacher education: Lessons from exemplary programs.* San Francisco, CA: Jossey-Bass.

Domine, V., & Bello, J. (2010). Stewarding urban teacher education in Newark: In search of reflection, responsibility, and renewal. *NNER Journal, 2,* 155–168.

Feistritzer, C. E. (2011). *Profile of teachers in the U.S.* Washington (DC), WA: National Center for Education Information.

Foster, A., & Taylor, S. (2010). Leadership development in high-need schools: A case study. *NNER Journal, 2,* 73–93.

Goldrick, L. (2009, June). *A teacher development continuum: The role of policy in creating a supportive pathway into the profession: New teacher center carnegie policy brief.* Retrieved June 23, 2009, from http://www.newteachercenter.org/pdfs/NTC_Policy_BriefTeacher_Dev_Continuum.pdf

Goodlad, J. (1994). *Educational renewal: Better teachers, better schools.* San Francisco, CA: Jossey-Bass.

Goodlad, J., & McMannon, T. J. (Eds.). (2004). *The teaching career.* New York, NY: Teachers College Press.

Hargreaves, A., & Fullan, M. (2013). The power of professional capital: With an investment in collaboration, teachers become nation builders. *Journal of Staff Development, 34*(3), 36–39.

Heckman, P., & Mantle-Bromley, C. (2004). Toward renewal in school-university partnerships. In J. Goodlad & T. J. McMannon (Eds.), *The teaching career* (pp. 69–95). New York, NY: Teachers College Press.

Ingersoll, R. M. (2003). *Is there really a teacher shortage?* Philadelphia, PA: University of Pennsylvania, Consortium for Policy Research in Education.

Klein, E. J., Taylor, M., Onore, C., Strom, K., & Abrams, L. (2013). Finding a third space in teacher education: Creating an urban teacher residency. *Teaching Education, 24*(1), 27–57.

Levin, J., & Quinn, M. (2003). *Missed opportunities: How we keep high-quality teachers out of urban classrooms.* New York, NY: New Teacher Project.

Newark Public Schools. (2009). *Moving forward together: Preparing students for college, work, and life.* Newark, NJ: Author. Retrieved from http://www.nps.k12.nj.us/StrategicPlan/Strategic%20Plan%20-%20FINAL%20REPORT%20-%204-09.pdf

Onore, C. (2006). Rewriting the curriculum for urban teacher preparation, In J. L. Kincheloe, k. hayes, K. Rose, & P. M. Anderson (Eds.), *The Praeger handbook of urban education* (Vol. 1, pp. 208–216). Westport, CT: Greenwood Press.

Oxman, W., & Michelli, N. (1984). *Project THISTLE: Thinking skills in teaching and learning: A model college-school collaborative program in curriculum and staff development.* Paper presented at the annual meeting of the American Association of Colleges for Teacher Education, San Antonio, TX, February 1–4.

Snyder, J. (2006). Perils and potentials: A tale of two professional development schools. In L. Darling-Hammond (Ed.), *Professional development schools: Schools for a developing profession* (pp. 98–125). New York, NY: Teachers College Press.

Walker, E. M., Hochwald, E., Kopacsi, R., Cai, Y., & Ramswami, S. (1995). *An evaluation of the professional development school in Newark: The impact of training on teacher attitudes, teacher behaviors, and student outcomes.* Newark Board of Education, NJ: Office of Planning, Evaluation and Testing.

Wenger, E. (1998). *Communities of practice: Learning, meaning, and identity.* New York, NY: Cambridge University Press.

Wenger, E., McDermott, R., & Snyder, W. (2002). *Cultivating communities of practice: A guide to managing knowledge.* Boston, MA: Harvard Business School Press.

Jennifer Robinson
Center of Pedagogy
Montclair State University
Montclair, New Jersey

Ada Beth Cutler
Distinguished Professor of Education
Montclair State University
Montclair, New Jersey

Julianne Bello
Ernest J. Finizio-Aldene Elementary School
Roselle Park, New Jersey

Matthew Brewster
Special Assistant for High School Operations
Newark Public School
Newark, New Jersey

Marisol Diaz
Benjamin Franklin Elementary School
Newark, New Jersey

Carolyn Granato
McKinley Elementary School
Newark, New Jersey

47

Roger León
Newark Public Schools
Newark, New Jersey

Anthony Orsini
First Avenue School
Newark, New Jersey

Susan M. Taylor
Newark Montclair Urban Teacher Residency Program
Montclair, New Jersey

APPENDIX

PIE-Q as Communities of Practice

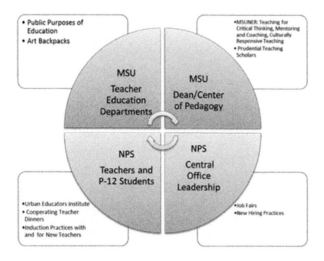

MEET THE AUTHORS FROM CHAPTER THREE

Walter Kaczka, I worked as a high school science teacher and department chairperson for NPS. My career spanned thirty-nine years and three high schools: Central High School, Arts High School, and University High School. My involvement with the NMUTR evolved from my work as a subject and education mentor for the Prudential Teaching Scholars, a precursor of sorts for the NMUTR. After retiring from NPS, I also began working as a student teacher mentor for the CoP at MSU. During the last dozen or so years of my work in Newark, I became involved with MSU at multiple levels to expose students to urban education.

My involvement on the admissions committee grew as a result of my professional relationship and various partnerships with NPS and MSU. In the early 90s Jennifer, as a teacher education professor, brought her students to University High School where I would talk to them about the school and my experiences of teaching in Newark. Later, while assisting Susan Taylor with the Prudential Teaching Scholars, I became familiar with the NMUTR. What intrigued me was the format of the program, similar to medical students doing rotations in various hospital departments. Because I viewed the NMUTR as the best teacher preparatory program for future urban educators, I offered my services and volunteered to be part of the admissions committee for the secondary cohorts two, three and four, and the elementary cohorts three and four.

Marc Kolb, as a middle son of two Jewish immigrants, I find that some stereotypes can be true. I was raised to value and treasure education as long as it was a means to becoming a doctor. Chemistry sets, trips to museums, and books were my parents' chosen method of raising an intelligent child who could weather the years of schooling required to achieve this American dream.

Like any good son, I wanted my parents to be proud and happy, so I took school very seriously. I went to Orthodox religious schools all the way through college. These emphasized studious behavior and consistent inquiry. I started at the Jewish Educational Center in Elizabeth, where an inspiring chess coach, Dr. Hyman Lewis, challenged me to rise above mediocrity and never accept or allow for failure. If I lost a game, he would encourage me to analyze my games until I found my error. Two championships later, I found myself at Kushner Yeshiva High School in Livingston.

The summer between my sophomore and junior years of high school, I made the first absolutely pivotal discovery that would change me. I discovered the New York Renaissance Faire. It may sound silly or fantastical, but to a boy who grew up reading fantasy and stories of dragons, fair maidens, and the incredibly non-mediocre hero this was an amazing thing. I learned that, no matter the background, regardless of social caste, at the Faire, you choose who you are, and no actor or 'playtron', a term for a patron of the Faire who dresses like an actor and creates his own character, is ordinary and average.

After college, at Kushner Yeshiva High School, I was a long-term sub and taught one track of physics. This was my first foray into education. Without proper training, I went by scientific instinct and did well enough, but came the end of the year and a middle school science position opened, my lack of schooling in education proved a hurdle I could not get over in order to secure the position.

Over the summer, I secured a job as a computer repair specialist at Geek Squad in a brand new Best Buy store in Manhattan. I enjoyed this position, but my aspirations were still to teach. When an old high school mentor, Arthur Glaser, suggested I apply for a doctorate in Applied Science and teach at NJIT, I jumped at the opportunity. As a graduate student, I taught three labs. Still without formal training, I went by both theatrical and scientific instinct to educate my undergrads in the best way I knew how. About one year later, the research I was doing in a laboratory on campus to fund my doctorate was cut and I was without money for tuition to continue. Having just gotten engaged to my wife, I needed a job so I went right back to Geek Squad, this time in New Jersey.

My time at Geek Squad was productive, but it was never something I wanted to do as a career. I was a teacher at heart and this manifested through my extracurricular activities within my job. I volunteered to be the PC build instructor at the Geek Squad Summer Academy. I tried to start a computer education and training program at my store. I was always looking for ways to teach. One day, in a very unlikely place, I found something that would change my life. I responded to a Craig's List ad about the NMUTR.

I entered the NMUTR with an absolute and arrogant confidence in my abilities. I had always heard that teaching was simple. How much more could I learn about teaching? After all, I had taught in middle school, high school, and college by then. That first summer in Newark was a very humbling experience. With my preconceived notions of the simplicity of teaching shattered, I began, with careful humility, to learn, from the very beginnings of pedagogy, how to teach and reflect.

Dave Koethe, I first heard about the NMUTR through an online post on Craig's List under the category of education jobs. At the time I was working as a teaching assistant at an alternative school in South Jersey. I had been there for two years and though I was interested in teaching I had become disenchanted with the school and the career prospects that I had there. I knew that I wanted to teach high school science and I already had experience working with students from urban settings at my current job. Before I applied I had taken and passed the Praxis II testing in biology, which was the content I wanted to teach. My tentative plan was to pursue my alternate route certification with a school district in South/ Central New Jersey.

When I first applied to the NMUTR I had little to no knowledge about Newark, the historic struggles of the NPS, or the cultural background of my potential students.

This lack of knowledge led to extensive research on my part before the first day of the interview process. What I learned was that the students and district were probably going to be different from anything I had experienced in my life. The school where I would be interviewing was one of the most racially and ethnically diverse schools in the city of Newark with a huge ESL population of Spanish and Portuguese speaking students. As I would later learn most English speaking students still spoke either Spanish or Portuguese at home.

As a self-proclaimed average white kid from the suburbs my background and upbringing were very different from the students with whom I would be working. What made me want to teach in Newark and the appeal of NMUTR was a common belief system; that every student has the capacity to learn and be successful. The term successful might look very different to different people but that just shows that all people including students are different and unique individuals. Even though my background, culture, and learning style might be very different than my students I can bridge that gap by getting to know them as individuals. I still firmly believe that the personal connections you develop with students are more important than where you are from, what culture you identify with, or your native language.

The NMUTR's emphasis on student centered learning and the ability to build relationships in the classroom appealed to me because it aligned with my view of what good teaching looks like. The people I met through the program like my mentor Karina Monteiro and fellow cohort resident Alex Diaz embody what a good teacher looks like because they focus on building a community of high expectations based on the relationships they have with their students. When I was in high school the teachers who impacted me the most, were the ones who took time to get to know me. I was not the ideal high school student but when I felt a connection with a teacher, I was willing to try new classes like anthropology.

EMILY J. KLEIN, MONICA TAYLOR, DAVE KOETHE,
MARC KOLB AND WALTER KACZKA

3. CONSTRUCTING AND NEGOTIATING
A RESIDENCY ADMISSIONS PROGRAM
IN THE THIRD SPACE

INTRODUCTION

Day Two of Admissions

Our first face-to-face experience with 25 applicants. The atmosphere is electric, filled with nervous energy, anticipation, and enthusiasm. We gather together in one of the classrooms in University Hall, bringing together applicants, faculty, NPS mentors, and HR personnel to determine cohort two. The evaluation process begins from the moment the group congregates, as we connect faces and names to application files. We are looking for signs, indications of whether or not the applicants have what it takes to be a successful urban teacher in Newark. We go around the room, introducing ourselves and sharing our roles in this third space community. We review the jam packed agenda for the day. Our tone is serious and intense. We know that by the end of the day our pool of applicants will already be smaller.

The day starts with a collaborative group task. The evaluators position themselves as researchers to observe behaviors and eavesdrop on conversations. They have data sheets on clipboards, ready to jot down any insights. Marc, one of the residents, describes the task through the eyes of an applicant:

> As a part of the full-day admissions gauntlet, our observers wanted us to perform a team task: building a bridge. I'm sure there was a certain amount of symbolism involved in the bridge-building, but it was the constraints and guidelines that really challenged our faculties. The six of us had to build a bridge out of various paper flotsam that could both support a gallon of water and be tall enough for an object to pass underneath. If that wasn't challenging enough, we had about five minutes of planning where we could not touch the materials, followed by a five minute silent time to assemble the bridge.

> The admission process was competitive. I knew we were being observed and judged and that our performances here would determine the outcome of admissions to the UTR. I knew that failure at this task would reflect badly on each of us. We needed to work together and communicate effectively without words. I realized by then that the task was not about the ideas of the individual,

but the implementation of our collective ideas. As individuals, we each seemed to have a very strong showing, but this task forced us to put our individual will and ego aside in favor of the whole group.

In planning, the first thing we needed to do was understand the parameters. The guidelines were very clear, but they allowed for a certain degree of creative thinking. The jug of water did not need to travel the span of the bridge and we could support the jug using reinforced paper columns while still accomplishing the task. This is what I proposed. Unfortunately, only some of the members of the group agreed with me. Others thought that my design did not fall within the parameters of the activity. I asked them to think of a design that would. After a few moments (time was running short), we collectively, although not unanimously, decided to go with my interpretation of the parameters.

Dissension continued to plague Marc's group experience and he told us it was "frustrating" when he perceived that his teammates were "deliberately not assisting because their interpretations of the rules were different" from his own. Even in the debrief, tension arose as some members of the team felt that their disagreement with Marc's understanding of the rules justified their decision not to engage in the task. Observers questioned him, both about his interpretation and the group's outcomes.

As Marc describes, the admission tasks are carefully designed to tease out what we look for in a potential resident. In particular, this group task quickly raises concerns about individual applicants who appear glowing on paper. We see applicants lose their temper and grab materials out of the hands of other applicants. We view other applicants shut down and become unable to engage with others, take any leadership, or even contribute. Conversely, we see some residents become leaders in ways that involve soliciting the contributions of others, respecting a variety of perspectives, and figuring out how to do so without using oral language. Although we do occasionally accept residents whose behavior in the group activity raised concerns, those concerns *consistently* follow us throughout the program; over the course of the residency we have recognized that this admissions component, as well as a number of others described, proved to be valid means of assessing residents for our program (based on our anecdotal evidence and small sample size).

PURPOSE/CONTEXT

In this chapter we describe how we came to choose the residents for the NMUTR, particularly those in cohort two, and how the process reflected our developing notion of the third space and how we continuously built and rebuilt it. We organize the chapter as we "lived" it during the process – as three days where we all came together to do the work of choosing the cohort. Day One includes the "paperwork" day, where we read biographical data, admissions essays, and other traditional entrance materials. Day Two marks the first time we meet our applicants; they come to campus and engage in a number of different activities: a team building activity used to help us understand their ability to collaborate, an individual interview using the Haberman protocol which helps us to understand their suitability for teaching in an urban district, and an individual technology presentation. Finally, Day Three brings the final "cut" to Newark to meet with students, current residents, mentors, administrators, and the neighborhood. We organize it chronologically to bring the reader into the experience of participating in the process, both as we tried to construct it, and also as we engaged in it. While teacher education professors often are the sole decision makers in admissions decisions, many programs have experimented with engaging teachers, district personnel, and content area professors in the process (Caskey, Peterson, & Temple, 2001; Denner, Salzman, & Newsome, 2001). Similarly, we knew that not only did we need to engage all stakeholders in deciding who would become a resident in our program, but that they all should contribute to building the admissions process as the residents would go on to be Newark teachers. It sounds obvious and yet as we, Emily and Monica, and our initial collaborator Cindy looked around us, there were few examples of substantial collaborations between universities and schools in the area of *admissions*. We saw partnerships in many areas of teacher education, but choosing who should become teachers tended to be owned by the university. Breaking that pattern, and therefore taking another step into a third space dynamic between us all, involved making a significant change in the status quo for how this happened. After some consultation with Jennifer Robinson, director of the MSU CoP and the principal investigator of the grant, we decided that our admissions community should include district HR personnel, assistant principals and principals of our partner schools, mentor teachers, faculty from the math and science departments at MSU, faculty from our department of Secondary and Special Education, staff from the CoP, students from the NPS, and after year one of the residency – past residents. As, Walt, an NPS partner, notes:

> In addition to direct observations of the candidates interacting in the schools there was added input from NPS teachers and supervisors. All stakeholders were empowered to share their thinking about the candidates. All perspectives were welcomed. It was interesting to observe the dynamics of the committee members in evaluating the candidates, each employing his/her unique background. The university professors, the pedagogical specialists, the experienced Newark teachers, supervisors and administrators, and the MSU CoP administrators all brought their strengths to the decision-making process. Of considerable importance was the fact that nothing was done in isolation. Potential residents were never screened or evaluated by just one admissions committee member. The selection of each UTR resident was collaborative and open among all committee members.

All voices had to both help to create the process, but then also engage in the selection. Together in the year before the program began, we worked to develop admissions criteria that reflected our notion of what makes a potential good urban math and science teacher and how we might screen for one. By ensuring that all stakeholders participated in the admissions process, we were able to begin this process of creating and engaging in the third space. We hoped that this would set a precedent for all endeavors in the UTR, although it also came with challenges of any community attempting to institute democratic decision-making.

Figuring out how to raise the quality of teachers in the classroom has plagued teacher educators and policymakers for decades and a number of researchers have reported about this problem (Ballou & Podgursky, 1995; Brantlinger & Smith, 2013; Kosnick, Brown, & Beck, 2005). From increasing teacher pay, to raising admission standards, to upgrading criteria for exit standards, there have been few overall successful attempts to ensure that higher quality teachers make it into, and stay in, the classroom. Increasingly however, programs have begun to look for richer assessment measures for admissions (for one example of such a program see Kennedy, 2000). Our work in admissions builds on this assumption—that in order to have higher quality teachers, particularly urban teachers who will stay in the profession and stay in urban schools, we need richer means of assessing who should enter the profession. We hope that rigorous admissions criteria ensure that our residents become effective urban teachers in 12 months. We recognize the limitations of what we can do in a short period of time and therefore have come up with standards that address socially just dispositions and resilient behaviors.

Purpose of Admissions: Theory of Action

Deeply ingrained in our admissions policy is the notion that this process is part of learning. As Denner, Salzman, and Newsome (2001) write in their program description, they are less concerned with the absolute numbers rejected or admitted through the admission process, but more focused on how "participation in the admission interview process had a socialization impact on the other 181 who were qualified" (p. 174) for their program. Recruitment and admittance "set the selection of prior commitment" (p. 175) and create the earliest stages of community building. For us, admissions gave potential residents opportunities to learn about the NMUTR's vision of inquiry based science and math teaching. It served as the commencement of the program and therefore throughout their residency year, was often a point of reference. Admissions had an impact on the residents emotionally, since the challenge of it bonded them, intellectually, because it communicated the vision of inquiry based science and math instruction about which we cared, and socially, for the meaningful ways in which the residents, mentors, faculty, and staff got to know each other as learners, educators, and people.

There were certain NMUTR program limitations and conditions that strongly influenced the qualities we sought in our residents: the first was the length of the program. Given the one-year duration of the program, we needed to choose residents who were primed to be able to participate fully in a residency that advocated for inquiry based science and math teaching; that promoted socially just schools and classrooms where residents would act as teacher leaders. We sought a racially, ethnically, and linguistically diverse group of teachers who might reflect the diversity of the students they would teach. While we did not necessarily expect them to be knowledgeable about either of those two commitments, we did want them to be open and willing to engage in discussions about them, anticipating that there would be resistance at different points. The second condition was that the residents were dedicated to serving students in Newark. Our targeted student is diverse in terms of race, ethnicity, language, and financial circumstances. We wanted residents who were comfortable with such populations and who were dedicated to being a teacher there for at least four years (and hopefully much longer). As Falkenberg (2010) suggests—the working conditions or the nature of Newark's educational system, including the kinds of jobs available post graduation, the administrators, the other teachers, the curriculum, and the testing were also important to consider as we thought about choosing candidates. We knew we needed to select candidates who could navigate this particularly complex ecological system. We wanted to prepare teachers both to teach within the system but at the same time we were preparing them to "teach against the grain" (Cochran-Smith & Lytle, 2004). We also needed residents who would be willing to take risks as learners and engage with a primarily inquiry-based and emergent NMUTR curriculum. Experience from our first cohort suggested that even when residents were open to this new paradigm, as the realities of teaching in urban schools came to the forefront, we would face some resistance to inquiry (Taylor, Klein, Onore, Strom, & Abrams, 2011). Knowing this, we wanted to ensure that our residents had at least positive, foundational attitudes that would serve to support them when they became unsure in any of the above conditions.

Falkenberg (2010) argues against a "fixed-components approach" to admissions—where teacher candidates enter with a "belief system about teaching and learning that matches to a good part the belief system by graduation" or where they would begin their program with "some kind of flexible belief system that can be influenced within the program" (p. 17). Instead he argues for a more *responsive* approach, a less "linear and mechanistic" notion of how teacher education candidates develop that is "concerned with understanding where admitted students come from, where they need to go from where they currently are, and what help they need in order to get there" (p. 23). He suggests a "team of instructors" who teach "from a *developmental* perspective over time of the whole program" (p. 23). In many ways we balanced both a fixed components approach with a responsive approach. Although the limitations above guided portions of our admissions process, we rarely had an image of a single candidate. Rather, within these limitations we accepted a wide range of candidates and developed working plans for each. By the end of the admissions process we would speak with all the stakeholders about the strengths and challenges of each candidate, and set up individual meetings with residents who had been accepted into the program, taking the opportunity to tell them what we felt each needed to work on in the following year. In each case, these profiles would guide our next steps in terms of summer placements, mentor placements, and other curricular decisions. At each stage of the program, the NMUTR team would reflect, revise, and re-evaluate based on the growth and development of the resident. We discovered that oftentimes, the challenges that we identified for each resident were something that needed to be addressed throughout his or her residency. Like Falkenberg, we believed that in the bi-directional nature of teacher education, that "it is not just the program context that influences an admitted applicant's attributes, but that it is also the admitted applicant's attributes that shape the context" (pp. 24–25).

Criteria

One critique of the teacher education admissions process is that often it is not connected to a conceptual framework, something we were cognizant of as we began crafting our own admissions process. As Kosnick, Brown, and Beck (2005) write, "… deciding which qualities to look for in applicants is inextricably linked to determining the qualities we attempt to foster during the program: if we are unclear about the one we will be sure of the other, and our program will lack direction" (p. 102). In year one we used a combination of criteria we had used in our general teacher education program, criteria that related to urban teaching and Haberman's criteria, discussed further within. During a number of daylong retreats all stakeholders collaboratively developed the following criteria:

Successful NMUTR resident candidates must possess:

- excellent written and verbal communication skills,
- passion and devotion to urban education and Newark,
- respect and appreciation for individual and cultural difference,
- critical thinking skills,
- willingness to accept major responsibility for student learning and growth,
- desire to bring fundamental change to classrooms and schools,
- persistence to identify creative solutions to daily classroom challenges,
- determination to engage students in learning that goes beyond the prescribed curriculum,
- ability to challenge the status quo without insubordination,
- an emerging vision of teaching and learning that translates into dynamic classroom practice,
- self-renewal skills to utilize collegial networks,
- leadership skills,
- flexibility, and
- self-reflectiveness.

We had instincts about which of these might be more important, but no data at that point. By year two, after reflecting on data from the experience of teaching cohort one, we had some ideas about which of these criteria were particularly important for success in OUR program. For example, we knew that Haberman's emphasis on persistence and resilience seemed to prove useful for our residents' success, as well as a tendency towards "open mindedness" as a general fit with the philosophy of inquiry. Therefore, informally, we began to weigh certain criteria over others.

Pre-Dispositions

A key pillar of our admissions process was an attempt to measure the "pre-dispositions" that were necessary for becoming an excellent urban teacher. Dispositions are "the values, commitments, and professional ethics that influence behaviors toward students, families, colleagues, and communities and affect student learning, motivation, and development as well as the educator's own professional growth" (Kent, 2005, p. 345). Although more and more teacher education programs are attempting to measure pre-dispositions necessary for teaching now that NCATE standards require disposition evaluation,[1] there is still a relatively uneven policy implementation nationwide (Ginsberg & Whaley, 2003). In part, this is because it is unclear which dispositions are associated with effective teaching and also because they can be challenging to measure. One recent study (DeLuca, 2012) focused on admitting students who had the "propensity for inclusive teaching" (p. 12), but found a "lack of a common conception of inclusivity" which "led raters to rate applicants' propensity for inclusivity differently and inconsistently" (p. 25). We were also open to incorporating pre-dispositions into our admission criteria in an attempt to build on the thoughtful research that had been conducted in our general teacher education programs at MSU. Over a decade ago, MSU integrated dispositions into both their Portrait of a Teacher as well as their admissions rubrics (see Appendix 1 & 2). We adapted these dispositions to reflect the needs of urban teachers.

CREATING AN ADMISSIONS PROCESS

What does it look like to negotiate a third space through an admissions process? In what ways could we gather enough evidence to choose residents that we were certain would be successful through our program? And how were we able to stay true to our commitment of honoring the voices of all of the stakeholders in our decision-making? Below we narrate our admissions process for the second cohort, illustrating the tenets highlighted above.

In order to assure that we would get to know our candidates in some depth, we decided to organize a three day admissions process; this would allow all of our stakeholders to participate in the selection process. We would be given an opportunity to see the applicants in a variety of different contexts, and we would be able to discern both their strengths and the areas in which they would need work.

Day One

We gathered together at 2 Cedar Street, NPS's central office, in a board room with seating around a large table. We met in Newark in order to make it convenient for our NPS stakeholders. We had representation from NPS HR personnel, school principals, department chairs, MSU faculty both from the College of Education and Human Services and the College of Science and Mathematics, and mentor teachers. We came ready to work hard and make the first cuts of the applicant pool for cohort two. It was a reunion of sorts: we greeted one another warmly, happy to see each other, and eager to commence this important process. We were organized into pairs with a university faculty or staff matched with a NPS staff or teacher. Toyin Adekoje, our administrative director from the CoP, handed each of us our packets of rating sheets and criteria, and then the pair received a pile of candidate folders. There was talk of why the number of applicants was low (we had about fifty applicants)—this seemed to come up every year as we worried about recruitment and reaching our goal of eight residents per cohort—but we only detoured from the process briefly and then began our difficult task. There was a hushed energy as pairs attempted to decipher the folders and look for clues and insights into the candidates.

Much like what we know about the data used for admissions in the general teacher education programs, that day we focused on the written applications of our candidates. This included: GRE scores, Praxis scores in their content areas, letters of recommendation, resumes, transcripts, and essays about their background and why they want to become teachers; we looked at what have traditionally been the main tools for admissions decisions (Casey & Childs, 2007; Denner, Salzman, & Newsome, 2001). Additionally, since Toyin was the only one to interact with resident applicants prior to this process, she included her own notes about the phone and email interactions she had with candidates. She indicated whether candidates were motivated, polite, professional, independent, or in need of a lot of coaxing. Her insights helped us to create a more holistic portrait of the applicant.

Content knowledge and student profile: Praxis scores and transcripts. We used information from transcripts, as well as the state mandated passing scores on the Praxis content tests, as two means of helping us assess applicants' content knowledge. Because of the relatively short duration of the program, we needed to ensure that applicants had completed the state requirements for content level courses and also that we felt secure in their understanding of content—there would be no formal opportunities for content area coursework. There has been a movement within a particular strand of educational reform that sees content knowledge as the means of raising teacher quality and improving the profession (Bratlinger & Smith, 2013; Zeichner, 2003). Accepting residents with strong content knowledge was a high priority to us, but we were interested in subject matter knowledge that was organized in such a way as to help students develop a "cognitive map" (Kosnick, Brown, & Beck, 2005). As Kim, one of our math mentors, notes:

> Having a deep understanding of your content is vital, but I think on many levels even more so with science and math. There are many math/science teachers who are currently employed who lack the deep conceptual understanding of

the subject and in turn fail to relay this deep conceptual knowledge to their students. We know as educators, that a majority of students are failing to interpret math /science on a deeper conceptual level, instead engaging them on more of a procedural level. This stems from the ways in which these students have been taught math and science.

Similarly, Will, a science mentor, emphasized that "to teach INQUIRY well, a teacher must be well rooted in their subject matter." What our mentor teachers are referring to here is a kind of content knowledge for teaching, similar to Shulman's (1986) pedagogical content knowledge.

Later we would find the transcript to be an insufficient measure of content knowledge readiness for the program, as we will discuss further on. Similarly, Praxis scores measured some degree of content knowledge, but not always the kind of content knowledge we valued. Kim noted that, while "[the Praxis] does not measure deep conceptual knowledge of a subject," a Praxis score *could* be "a red flag as to an applicant's lack of content knowledge."

But we "read" transcripts for other things as well; we looked for gaps in attendance, discrepancies between major course GPA and their overall GPA, and the courses they chose to take within their major in order to better understand the depth and breadth of their content area expertise as well as their interdisciplinary knowledge. As Will remarks:

> Classes teachers choose to take and how well they do always interest me. I feel it tells a lot about what they will bring to the table as a teacher—what their perspective is on education. Our kids mimic us in so many ways. A teacher that hates math/is not very skilled at it may generate students that have a fear of it because the teacher steers away from using it. Same goes for any other subject. We shed our biases, so it would be good to know or make inferences into the potential biases of a future teacher through the examination of their coursework and decision making.

We attempted to mine the transcript for information about the candidate, but also for the spaces and questions that we needed to pay attention to when we later met them if they made it through round one.

We knew that this data had some use for us in making predictions about the candidates' success as urban teachers. For example, a number of studies have found a statistically significant correlation between grades and student teacher ratings (D'Agostino & Powers, 2009; Roth, BeVier, Switzer, & Schippmann, 1996), as well as a correlation between GPA and "academic competence" (Freeman, Martin, Brousseau, & West, 1989, p. 39). On the other hand, we understood the limits of some of this data, like test scores, because of the decidedly mixed reviews of the roles of test scores in predicting future teaching success; most research shows almost no correlation between current tests and student teaching ratings (D'Agostino & Powers, 2009; Memory, Coleman, & Watkins, 2003). Overall our review of the admissions literature suggested a weak link between test scores, GPA, and a means of determining qualified candidates, so we tended to "over" invite rather than "under" invite (Quirk et al., 1973). This resonated for Emily in particular, because many of the brilliant teachers she had known, who had done terribly in school themselves, ultimately found themselves in teaching. She was always afraid we would miss a "gem," and thus, unless the red flags were *everywhere,* we made fewer cuts in this round than we might have. Monica also tried to be more open-minded on this first day of admissions, much like you would on a first date with someone or the first encounter with someone new. We always wanted to give the candidates the benefit of the doubt.

Certainly there is evidence that deep content knowledge matters for teaching, but in our program, given the length of time, we were more concerned with that "pedagogical content knowledge" we referred to above. Emerging from our second cohort, Doug Larkin, another faculty member, would develop a new measure to help us gauge our residents' knowledge for teaching (Larkin, Robinson, & Perry-Ryder, 2014). This content knowledge "probe" was adapted from Kennedy, Ball, and McDiarmid's (1993) Teacher Education and Learning to Teach (TELT) study and interview protocol. Taken with transcripts and the Praxis score, we were able to develop a richer sense of our residents' content knowledge and knowledge for teaching.

Detecting pre-dispositions for urban teaching: Pre-Haberman screener. Another limitation of test scores and grades is that they do not help to measure dispositions for teaching, an important component of our application process. Denner, Salzman, and Newsome (2001) suggest that the best way to measure pre-dispositions is "by engaging prospective teachers in multiple activities across both real and simulated contexts that afford opportunities for their appearance" (p. 168) and that the best assessment of them involves "multiple sources of evidence" (p. 168). Zeichner (2003) offers that one of the most effective means to build a diverse teaching force is to broaden our criteria from simply looking at GPAs and test scores to a "range of attributes and skills ... such as the kinds of characteristics valued in the Haberman…" (p. 500). Our first piece of evidence of a candidate's pre-disposition was the Haberman pre-screener.

The Haberman protocol is a selection tool for urban school teaching that purports to distinguish "Star" teachers from "Failures" based on how well they respond to certain questions on particular "mid-range functions." These functions are based on personality research that situates teachers somewhere between ideal personality traits on one end of a continuum with situational demands on the other end (Haberman, 1995). The mid-range behaviors Haberman identified represented the behaviors that strong urban teachers exhibit. The pre-screener includes 50 multiple choice questions online and "gauges how close an applicant's answers match those of Stars" (Pillow-Price, 2003, p. 34).

The use of the Haberman protocol was hotly contested over the years we used it. Haberman (1988) suggests that "competences and demonstrated behaviors must replace predictive testing" (p. 41), and his test attempts to measure some of the competencies and behaviors of effective urban teachers. While we all believed it measured certain qualities very well, we knew it was used in Newark to measure these qualities in candidates who had already been through an education program, rather than preservice teachers. Kim, a mentor teacher, admitted, "I have always had issues with it. I know that I might have failed the Haberman if I had been an applicant fresh out of school with no educational coursework under my belt. There have been applicants who have failed but have turned out to be amazing… " Yet Walt, a long time district teacher and administrator, felt it provided "standardization and uniformity." Both perspectives were important to us.

Essays. Some of the research literature indicates that application essays can reveal a "motivation related to student needs … a congruence with the program and mission of the institution … a vision of need or quality in schools, and … ability to express oneself in a compelling way" (Caskey, Peterson, & Temple, 2001, p. 19). Some programs have used essays and other biodata to mitigate "the more extreme effects of admissions based on academic background alone … success in the teacher education program has not been threatened and may even have been enhanced by the use of personal statements in teacher selection" (Smith & Pratt, 1996, p. 50).

Our essay questions, which came from the admission process of the general teacher education programs, focused on dispositional aspects of the residency and the prompts we used helped to illuminate the applicants' understanding of culturally responsive and democratic teaching, two of our philosophical pillars. Over the years, we were continuously frustrated with the essays and we often swore we would re-write the prompts to include mention of why residents wanted to teach in Newark; we felt that the questions did not get at enough of the issues we wanted. However, they *did* often give us information both about a candidate's background as well as his/her writing ability, something that was essential to our program as it requires a great deal of writing from the residents. Residents write almost daily as a means of reflection, assessing their students' work, and conveying their own understanding of curriculum and instruction; extremely weak writers would struggle in the program.

Recommendations. We also reviewed two recommendations from applicants. Although recommendations overwhelmingly tended to be positive, they were sometimes revealing when they came across as superficial and contrived. Some candidates made the mistake of asking for recommendations from either people who were too close to them and could not be unbiased, or others who did not really know the candidates at all. Some recommendations were thoughtful, moving in their sincerity, something we noted. Overall though, recommendations were rarely something that would make or break an application.

As the review process wound down, the stakeholders would gather to discuss and often justify their decisions of whether or not candidates moved to the next day of admissions. These could be tense conversations as many of the reviewers seemed to have already made a significant conscious commitment to the candidates. Usually if there was indecision about a candidate, we would decide to bring them in for an in person look. Sometimes we flagged candidates whom we felt needed a closer look. Monica, for example, often volunteered to follow a particular candidate who did not exhibit socially just dispositions within their written application. She would have some informal conversations with a candidate to get a better sense of their openness and potential commitment to teaching in Newark.

Day Two

As we described in the chapter opening, Day Two involved a variety of different opportunities for stakeholders to determine whether candidates would be appropriate for the residency.

Writing prompts. Prior to meeting their evaluators, the applicants arrived early and were asked to respond to two questions. The first asked them to identify why they wanted to teach in Newark, supporting their reasoning with examples from personal experiences, texts they had read, and world events. The second invited them to engage in a thought experiment where they would imagine teaching in Newark without any constraints like testing, curriculum, or tenure. We had them describe their teaching practices and their beliefs behind those practices. We pushed them to think about what their students would be learning and doing to learn, how they would assess learning, and how they would address students who were either struggling or excelling.

Their writing gave us many insights into the applicants, including their ability to write, to be thoughtful and reflective, and to articulate their reasoning behind why they wanted to become an urban teacher in Newark. We were often surprised to hear candidates state superficially that they wanted to teach in Newark because they heard that there had been some improvements of late, including the new Prudential Center. It was often clear that they had not really thought about their reasons for teaching in Newark—many applicants had not even considered the unique qualities that Newark has to offer as a community. Other candidates made it apparent that they had socially just dispositions and were eager to work in a vibrant, diverse, and interesting community like Newark. They described the research they had conducted to understand Newark's student population, some of the community resources, as well as the school system structures. Some applicants, like Dave, demonstrated a deep commitment to Newark, inquiring about the possibility of moving to Newark to be closer to work and more accessible for his students. The second part of the writing helped us to see if the candidates could imagine teaching in a less traditional way.

Building a bridge together: The group task. As we narrated in the beginning of this chapter, Day Two commenced with the group task. This was a central component of our admissions process and one that, over time, we increasingly saw as important. There are some research findings indicating strong face validity for admissions of simulated group activities (see Caskey, Peterson, & Temple, 2001). While observing the candidates participate in this task, we asked the following questions: Who is more of a leader and what kind of leader are they? Who is more of an observer and how do they use that to their advantage? An underlying assumption of how we see the teaching profession is that we understand the change process in urban schools to be collaborative rather than individual (Taylor, Klein, & Abrams, 2014). As Achinstein and Ogawa (2006) contend, individuals are rarely able to make large-scale change: "There are limits to individual resistance which leave the individual vulnerable and can even result in reproducing the status quo" (p. 57). We also note the work of Oakes, Franke, Quartz, and Rogers (2002), which describes how young urban teachers often decide to remain in teaching because of the strength of their school communities. Therefore, for admissions, observing how applicants collaborated was particularly important. Dave, one of the admitted residents, noted his frustration in the task when somebody handed him a rather large knife to cut materials, but while we observed him that frustration with others was never noticeable. This bridge-building assignment is only a small taste of the kinds of frustrations residents will face in trying to collectively make change in Newark schools. We looked for other things as well: Who does the talking? Who does the listening? How do resident candidates negotiate differing opinions? Quickly, this became a core activity in helping us decide who was going to be successful in being able to constantly negotiate and construct our third space residency, something that is a continual process, rather than a fixed product. As Karina, another mentor, reflects, "This activity really gives insight into how people act under pressure, but also helps to identify what leaders and team players stand out."

The Haberman interview: A pressure cooker. When we sat down to craft our admissions process, we knew that we would include an interview as we do in all our teacher education programs at MSU. Overall there is mixed research on the role of the interview in admissions, with some indicating a connection between interview ratings and success later in teaching (Casey & Childs, 2007) and others, such as Caskey, Peterson, and Temple (2001) and Schectman (1988) finding it less reliable as criteria for admissions. Instead of a traditional interview, our partners in Newark suggested using the Haberman protocol that at the time was required of all Newark teachers. Again we complied with their request as an attempt to make collaborative decisions about the admission process; this is part of what it looked like to construct a third space. Thus the Haberman became our interview protocol, piggybacking on the Haberman pre-screening that the candidates did as part of their written application.

Some research studies that have looked at the use of the Haberman teacher interview protocol to select teachers indicate that those teachers have higher rates of retention in urban schools than teachers chosen with other means (Frey, 2003). Other studies such as Basking, Ross, and Smith (1996) and Klusmann (2004) indicate the Haberman is limited in its predictive value and therefore should only be used as a single source in determining who should be admitted into a teacher education program.

Key categories of the Haberman interview include: persistence, response to authority, application of generalizations, approach to at risk students, personal versus professional orientation to teaching, burnout, and fallibility (Baskin, Ross, & Smith, 1996). Although there was never full agreement about using the Haberman, we found certain parts of it evolved to become more significant in our assessment of candidates than others. For example, as we mentioned earlier, persistence was a quality that, over time, we noticed was particularly salient in whether or not a teacher was successful both in the program and with students over the years (Taylor, Klein, Strom, & Abrams, 2012). Research about the Haberman protocol confirms the validity of the persistence measure (Pillow-Price, 2003). Other research indicates that teachers who "believed their students did not have to love them in order to learn were perceived as doing a better job of evaluating their own students. One explanation might be that these teachers view children more objectively than other teachers and are more ready to accept and employ a variety of methods to measure their students' performances" (Baskin, Ross, & Smith, 1996, p. 17). Similarly, research on Teach for America (TFA) found that of all the qualities (dispositional and otherwise) they screened for: academic achievement, leadership experiences, perseverance, critical thinking, organizational ability, motivational ability, respect for others, and commitment to the TFA mission, one of the most significant ones in relation to student achievement in mathematics was perseverance (Dobbie, 2011). Other research has measured "commitment to teaching"—by which researchers mean teachers whose work has a "special meaning and importance" (Firestone & Pennell, 1993, p. 491). Additionally some suggests that initial commitment to teaching in urban schools is the single most important factor in commitment at the end of the student teaching semester (Taylor & Frankenberg, 2009).

Sometimes we found ourselves noting qualities from the Haberman in other portions of the interview process. For example, on Day Three, Barb, one of the resident applicants, struggled when her car broke down two hours from Newark on her way to the interview. Undeterred, when she discovered it could not be fixed in time to get to the interview, she called a car service to bring her all the way to Newark, telling nobody except the program assistant who whispered the story to others throughout the day. We all noted it as an indication of her persistence, a quality that would characterize her throughout her work in the program. At other times, we felt keenly aware of the limitations of the exam. None of us could agree about an interview question that asked a teacher to decide about how to manage an issue where a principal shut down a curricular or pedagogical initiative taken by a teacher. Informing students that the principal had, in fact, been the source of the canceled program was an immediate "zero." The prescribed answers to certain questions seemed more intuitive to some of us than others. Most of us found the question of whether or not urban teachers could work with students they did not love (the answer should be "absolutely") seemed far more obvious than other questions. Over time Emily would grow to understand the thinking behind

Haberman's questions and scoring, but never would she find it intuitive. Monica, on the other hand, felt comfortable with the Haberman questions and often joked that she would use them at her next dinner party to determine potential friendships. Only stakeholders who had been through the Haberman training through the Newark HR department were permitted to administer the interview protocol. Usually two stakeholders, representing MSU and NPS, were paired to conduct the interview. Each person would take a turn reading the scripted question and prodding the applicant for answers. Both interviewers were required to fill out the rating sheets and upon completion of the interview they would have a discussion to determine the applicant's fate.

Residents had mixed reactions to the Haberman interview as well. As a timed interview that was supposed to only be conducted for 30 minutes, some came close to tears as they were pushed to respond to the questions under pressure. Dave found that if he stayed consistent in his answers, it was not quite as challenging as others suggested. He saw it as fundamentally a test of his "resolve and creativity." Antonio saw it as far more intense:

> The Haberman was easily my biggest challenge during the interview process. I was incredibly out of practice when it came to interviewing, let alone, a rigorous interview. I had entered the interview with a hesitance about education. I knew it was a field I wanted to enter, but as the questions came, it was obvious that I didn't have a full grasp of what was happening in education. Essentially, I was incredibly misguided, if not, deluded. My college experience, filled with idealized ivory tower perspectives, had me entering the real world with a robotic savior mentality. As the interview progressed, it had an almost immediate transformative effect. My mind began to return to my high school years, a time when I had a more genuine connection with the world. Also, it was a time when I had a truer sense of why education is valuable—not just for the accumulation of knowledge, but the human interactions between students and teachers and among students. So as the questions continued to be asked, I remembered how human high school was to me, but I also began to see how human it was for my teachers. It wasn't a sterile occupation, but a multifaceted one, and, to that, an especially gritty one. Teaching requires you to push, to constantly retool your ideas. And I don't really remember any of the questions that were asked, I only remember the way they were asked. They would keep pushing with the same question again and again. Nothing ever seemed good enough. But, as my thinking was transforming throughout the interview, so were my responses. Not to say my answers were getting "better" as the interview progressed, rather, my answers became less clinical and more human. I was more thoughtful. Obviously, though, I didn't realize any of this as the interview was progressing (nor later that day). The whole day was a surreal experience. It had me question my motives and my logic, but more importantly, it helped wash away a lot of the disconnects accumulated in college.

In addition to the Haberman interview protocol, we would also ask applicants some background questions during these smaller group settings. Applicants would talk about why they wanted to be urban teachers of their particular content area. They would also prepare a two-minute technological presentation that would give us some insight into who they were. Applicants created imovies, powerpoint presentations, and other creative endeavors to satisfy this requirement.

Again at the end of Day Two of admissions, the stakeholders met to discuss which applicants would be invited to return for the last selection day. These conversations continued to be intense as evaluators became more and more clear with their perspectives about candidates. With one more possible face-to-face encounter, we often decided to give applicants about whom we were unsure the benefit of the doubt. We hoped, however, that Day Three would determine our final cohort two of residents.

Day Three

Day Three we moved the admissions process from Montclair to Newark. Having two of the three days of admissions occur in the district and in a Newark public school conveyed an important message to the candidates that this is all about Newark students and schools. It also seemed to represent to the stakeholders that this residency was indeed acting in a third space.

We chose to meet at Eastside High School, the first Newark school with which we partnered for cohort one. We began the day by asking candidates and stakeholders to gather in the library on the second floor. Dr. Mario Santos, the principal, as well as Michael De Antonio, the Math department chair, greeted the group and gave some background about the school. We reviewed the schedule and then proceeded to begin the third day of admissions.

Student interviews/Classroom activity. Reviewing the literature on admissions we found almost no indication that students were used in any systematic way in the decision making process. Although they face the immediate and direct consequences of the choices educators make, their voice is rarely included in the process. We believed that part of living in the third space meant involving students in the admissions process so we designed two parts of the day to include them. First residents sat down to talk to students in a whole class. Originally we discussed the idea of having residents teach something to students, but ultimately decided instead to have them engage them more informally in discussion. With little to no teaching experience, we realized that it would be difficult for residents to prepare a lesson that would follow the curriculum of a particular content area. The interaction with students in a class setting would allow stakeholders to determine if the candidate had some teacher presence, was comfortable facilitating discussion, and could think on his/her feet.

We also brought together small groups of students to interview two residents at a time. As Karina shared, "I believe this is the most valuable part of the application process. The ability to connect with kids is difficult to measure, but can be very intuitive. Observing their interaction with students really permits for a means of identifying how they work with the most valuable stakeholders, the students." After the interview, we debriefed with the students, asking for their reflections and analysis about each of the candidates. In many cases we found they had insightful and interesting thoughts about why one or another candidate might be a good teacher. Often these opinions aligned with our own and sometimes they provided a window that helped us see potential that we had not yet seen. For example, a number of us had some concerns about one of the residents, Pri, and his Indian accent. We worried that he would struggle to communicate with students and that the frustration that would stem from this issue would hinder his ability to build personal and academic relationships with kids. In fact, students told us they found him quite approachable and were able to connect with him. They noted the accent, but did not seem daunted by it at all. In actuality, the students were absolutely correct; Pri became one of our warmest and most thoughtful residents. When we made our final decision that piece of information was quite significant.

Interacting with the students was as powerful for the residents as it was for us. Monica recalls watching a difficult conversation emerge with several high school girls and Dave. Dave too describes this unexpected discussion. He reflects:

> Being interviewed by the students was intense. A student, who I would come to know the following year, asked me a question about what I would do if I knew a student was being abused by her father. I told her that I would have to report it to the police even if she told me in confidence. She was upset that it would break up the family and ruin the relationship between the student and me. This led to a 30 to 40 minute breakdown of what has to happen in that situation. Wow, talk about getting a precursor to the type of challenges we would face as teachers in Newark.

Antonio's experience being interviewed helped him to get in touch with why he wanted to become a teacher and connect with youth:

> What I enjoyed about the student interview at East Side was the return to my own adolescence—a time when everything was both carefree yet overly complicated. The sense of carefree came when they were honest and candid with their opinions and feelings, which is very much how I saw myself interacting with them as well. However, the key difference was how unfiltered they were, but, there was no malice at all in their comments, just a refreshing honesty with the best intentions. And yet, on the other side of the spectrum was an emphasis of how complicated life could be, more so, the minutiae of life. The littlest things in life create the biggest concerns, and a lot of their questions focused on how I would play out a scenario. As their follow-up questions proceeded, it wasn't about the big picture, but one specific part of my answer and they clung to it. Why I decided on a certain action. Or what I meant by a certain phrase.

And the questions kept coming until we seemingly did surprisingly return to the big picture. As a result, throughout the course of the interview, I became less concerned about the questions per se and more interested in their discourse and thought process. And I think that's why I ended up in high school. I miss the way I used to think—a way that was unaffected by outside influences. A creative way of thinking. And somewhat selfishly, I wanted to regain that, but I also selflessly wanted them to keep it.

Part of what makes Antonio's narrative so powerful is that it reveals the ways in which the admissions process was not only about gate keeping and assessment but also about socialization and learning. The residents themselves were beginning to learn about teaching, about adolescence and who their students were and would be, and about how to reflect on their learning experiences.

Similarly there were moments in the classroom where some candidates really had the opportunity to shine. Dave and Alex were sent to engage with students in the biology classroom of Karina. They began by helping Rosie—the resident that year in Karina's classroom—with a classroom activity, but spontaneously began to co-teach a mini-lesson. As Dave put it, "The students were fun and we made fools of ourselves as we continue to do." It was in observing their dynamic together that the faculty and mentors were inspired to pair them together in Karina's classroom for the following year.

Walk around/Fishbowl. We always reminded the residents that the entire day was an interview, and as observers we were constantly collecting data, from how they transitioned from one activity to another to how they spoke to each other during those moments and interacted with us. One year, we noticed it was difficult to get a candidate to leave the classroom activity as he was deeply engaged in working with some students in math. Despite being asked multiple times by faculty, staff, and mentors, it took several prompts to get him to leave. Later when we debriefed that moment, some of us were struck by his engagement with students, while others were concerned that he would not follow instructions. We wondered how that might have played out in the program. For us that single moment became an important piece of data (and later would return to haunt us about that candidate who, in fact, was terrible at following instructions from anyone in authority!).

The final activities of the day were examples of capitalizing on every moment as a source of data and included a walk around the neighborhood and a fishbowl debrief. During lunch, we asked candidates to go out into the school neighborhood in Newark and find lunch (or just walk around if they had brought their lunch). They were asked to get a sense of the neighborhood and to be able to reflect upon it by the time lunch was over.

Later, residents debriefed this experience and the entire day in a fishbowl with mentors and past residents while faculty, staff, and district participants observed and took notes. A fishbowl is a pedagogical tool to facilitate and observe dialogue. The applicants were asked to sit in a circle in the center of the room while the stakeholders gathered around to observe and listen to their conversations. One of the faculty, as facilitator, provided guiding questions for the focused dialogue. As they talked we asked them to reflect on their observations both inside and outside of the school. We paid attention to what they noticed about the neighborhood; many were often "surprised" by how centrally the park was located and by the food they could find— particularly, how delicious the Portuguese pastries were. We sought to understand how they connected this with their insights about the students they had met that day—did the students match or break stereotypes they previously held about urban youth? In what ways? How did this day influence their overall feelings about why they did or did not want to teach in Newark? As Karina noted, "Although very awkward, the fishbowl is valuable because it shows the applicant's personality and how they present and hold themselves." Listening to them think and process their reflections out loud often helped alert us to issues of cultural responsiveness, a vital lens for our program.

Decision Making

The decision making process for residents came at the end of Day Three. During this time, all members of the third space community sat down at the table to discuss each candidate, reviewing his/her performance, strengths, and challenges on each day of admissions, and whether or not anyone had strong objections to them. This was often where our real concerns about candidates came to a head and we had to make decisions. As Falkenberg (2010) urges, we admitted applicants "that are weaker with respect to certain desired attributes while being stronger in others" (p. 28) and it was in the final day that we confronted which characteristics residents possessed with which we could ultimately live. For example, we noticed Marc had a tendency to repeat the same story when asked about why he was drawn to teach in Newark—about playing the chess team in Newark in high school, and about being drawn to the energy of urban youth. We were impressed by his energy, fascinated by the choice of an orthodox Jewish male to commit to teaching in Newark, but concerned that his repetition of the same rehearsed narrative over and over again prevented him from listening carefully to the students and other interviewers. We wondered if, perhaps, he was going to have trouble really hearing and connecting to youth. We noted that in our final evaluation of him, arranging to find a number of methods for supporting him in working on learning to listen to young people and build responsive relationships, something that would go from being a weakness to a strength over the course of the next few years of his work.

In year two, part of the decision making process often involved a mentor stepping forward to agree to work with a resident. As we reviewed each candidate we listed his/her strengths and weaknesses; these would become the basis for the first meetings with Monica Taylor and program director Sue Taylor. Often we felt that if we had a resident who had very specific needs, we wanted to ensure we had a strong mentor who could support those needs. While this was not a pre-requisite for acceptance, a mentor who agreed to take on a particular resident was an important part of the decision making process. For example, in year two, Kim felt strongly that she was a good match for Janae (a topic discussed further in chapter seven). Our youngest resident yet and just out of college, Janae was born and raised in Newark. During admissions we were concerned that she might have trouble separating her own experience as a student who had "made it" from other students with similar backgrounds who might have more struggles. We wanted someone who would both relate to those struggles, but also firmly guide and push her beyond that level of relationship to her past experience. Kim stepped forward immediately to volunteer to work with her. She felt a close connection to her during Day Two of admissions, and believed she would be able to work well with her. In doing so, the admissions group felt more comfortable with our decision to admit Janae.

Overall the final decision making process was difficult. We had a lofty goal, as part of our ongoing creation of the third space, of making the selection experience as democratic as possible through respecting the perspectives of all decision makers. But as we have mentioned repeatedly, the third space is a fragile enterprise that needs constant negotiation, and our residency existed within the constraints of two institutions: MSU and Newark Public Schools. No matter what our intentions, in the end our selection process was never fully democratic, as we were bound by the programmatic regulations that required us to admit eight cohort members. As we built each new cohort, this pressure from the university continued to grow and impacted the ways in which we made decisions about applicants.

There were two significant consequences that resulted from this pressure. The first was that no matter how hard we tried to contain the admission days to one set of three days, we always added an extra admission set to attempt to build a full cohort. In cohort two, this occurred as a one day process in June with two candidates: Pri and Antonio. Pri had applied to the initial admissions process but because of a missed email, he did not receive the details of the interviews days. Antonio was a late applicant but someone with whom we were somewhat familiar because of his on campus job in the English Department. Luckily for us, they were available to come to Eastside for an all day interview in June. On this particularly hot summer day, Emily, Karina, Luba, and Sue observed Pri and Antonio as they demonstrated their flexibility in terms of adapting to a more pressured interview setting as well the oppressive heat. And as we look back now, we realize how important both Antonio and Pri became to the residency. They are currently successfully employed as second year teachers. Pri has worked at Newark Early College High School, a school environment that has had tremendous upheaval in terms of leadership, and yet he has committed himself to being a stable force for his students. Antonio is thriving at East Side High School and has become one of the most important nurturers, not only within his cohort, but also across the entire residency. Although our second makeshift admissions day may sound a bit unorthodox, we believe that it exemplifies some of the assets of working in a third space framework. Our residency has been guided by the principle that there is not a one size fits all model for urban teacher education. With a deep commitment to finding the best possible residents, we understand that rules and constraints sometimes need to be more fluid. If we encounter candidates like Antonio and Pri who already have deep persistence, commitment to teaching urban students, and a rich understanding of their content areas, then we are willing to make concessions about such things as deadlines. This is a positive result from veering away from the parameters of the admission process.

Second, on the other hand, the pressure to fill a cohort also led us to accept some residents in cohort two, and later in cohort three, who had some glaring issues from the onset. And as we mentioned earlier, these red flags followed us throughout the twelve-month residency and into the residents' first years as teachers. There are some important implications to learn from this in terms of admissions to any teacher education program. As we discuss further below, the admissions process is a significant gate-keeper in deciding who is allowed to enter the profession. There is only so much personal change that can happen within a 12 month period and many of the challenges that we faced with the residents involved personality traits and interpersonal skills that required work outside of the usual content of a teacher education course. As we illustrated with our example of Marc earlier in the chapter, we were helping residents with interpersonal skills. Although these may be addressed tangentially in teacher education, they are usually not the focus of a program.

In the end we were left with a diverse and fascinating group of eight: one white man from Southern New Jersey, two Latino men, one fluent in Spanish, one African American female from Newark, an older white woman still young—but already a grandmother—a white orthodox Jewish man, a white woman in her 20's who had lived abroad, and an east Asian man also with foreign language fluency.

IMPLICATIONS

Our discussion of the admission process takes place within a conversation where we can identify the challenges and concerns around admissions but where there is little existing data from research studies. We are cognizant of the growing sense in teacher education that those being admitted to the teaching profession are not becoming the teachers we want. It is apparent that often those admitted into teacher education programs require much more support and hands on experience than can be provided in a program that spans a reasonable time frame. In fact, there are few studies focused on finding rich assessment measures for teacher admission. Some of the best examples of programs with multi-layered admissions processes, such as TFA, share very little about the process they use to decide who they admit; these programs are noticeably not connected to a university and do not necessarily prepare the sort of life-long career urban teachers that our residency hopes to produce (Crawford-Garrett, 2013; Veltri, 2010). Additionally, although TFA claims to recruit teachers who possess critical thinking skills, perseverance, and leadership capabilities (www.teachforamerica.org), much of the research demonstrates that successful TFA teachers are good at "following orders, obeying rules, and trusting curriculum that they find problematic and fallible" (Crawford-Garrett, 2013, p. 29).

For us, the admissions process serves a number of purposes; it is not merely just a tool for gatekeeping and deciding who is allowed into the profession, although that is a primary and important one. We outline our objectives here.

Gatekeeping for Particular Programs

We do not want to underestimate the role that admissions played in gatekeeping. Every teacher education program faces certain restrictions on the amount of time it has with a candidate and what it can provide in terms of intellectual and emotional resources. Given those limitations, stakeholders have to decide who they can reasonably support well and they must move towards some version of the teacher professional they hope to educate. This vision needs to be tied to the actual program and the program needs to create an admissions program that is well connected to that vision. The feedback loop must be ongoing and continuous: Do the people admitted seem able, with support, to fulfill the expectations of the program? Over time, do they develop into the kinds of teachers we hope to see in the profession? Any program has to decide where the holes are—are they caused by the admissions process, the program, or the support or lack thereof provided to the candidates?

We were lucky that the residency was small enough that what we learned from each year's admissions cycle and cohort experience could be fed back directly into the following year through informal conversations. For example, our concern that the Praxis scores did not assess whether candidates had ample content knowledge for teaching resulted in Doug developing a new tool, which was piloted in year three. Similarly, we noted how successful some of our quieter candidates were and felt that we were not always paying enough attention to them in admissions; that perhaps a larger more extroverted personality was taking precedence as a first impression, something we noted for later cohorts when we were able to reflect upon a few cohorts worth of graduates. We found that although it was complicated to fill slots in the program, our experience in the residency only made us committed to a more competitive process.

Most importantly, if we really are morally committed to preparing social justice activist teachers, then gatekeeping becomes more complex as potential teachers may be possibly qualified to teach but questionably able take on these orientations. This is another characteristic of our program that sets us apart from others like TFA. Our program is explicitly grounded in the understanding that structural and systemic inequity in society leads to student underachievement. We are committed to developing career urban teacher leaders who are able to, collectively, act as agents of change to disrupt the status quo of Newark schools. This charge requires us to carefully select residents who either already possess this orientation or are open to developing it.

Additionally, if we wanted to elevate the teaching profession we needed to screen for teachers with significant intellectual potential for teaching, a quality that a single measure simply would not capture. Constructing a variety of situations was one way we were attempting to capture this intellectual potential, as was Doug's developing measure of pedagogical content knowledge. However, at the end of three cohorts we are left knowing that we need continued experimentation and debate about what true intellectual potential looks like. Over the course of our work with the residents, we found that our more successful residents were ones that could think critically and self reflect, and also those that had an ambitious work ethic that drove them to take initiatives and commit a tremendous amount of "thinking" time.

Formative Assessment of Residents

The notion that teaching should be one size fits all has been roundly cut down in the public rhetoric about education for years. Despite a near universal belief that students come to the classroom with various needs and abilities, teacher education most typically provides its graduates with a one size fits all model. Using a third space framework, and viewing it as a living dynamic which takes into account all of the various participants including the residents themselves, our program was designed to provide a more differentiated curriculum, but all differentiation is premised upon high quality assessments.

Even for admitted residents, the admissions process provided us with rich information about candidates' strengths and needs in order to better understand how to support them during the academic year. Before they were even admitted, we were able to know them in a variety of ways that would inform how we met their needs, from summer placements to residency sites, to our individual work with them as faculty. If we begin to think about admissions as formative assessment, then there are implications for the ways in which we design our teacher education curriculum and run our programs; we believe there need to be more individualized and differentiated ways to prepare effective teachers. Similarly to what we know about good teaching, good teacher preparation cannot just teach to the middle; it needs to be re-structured to better prepare individuals, something we discuss further in our final chapter.

Socialization

Additionally, as we describe above, the admissions process can be a part of the socialization of preservice teachers. Whether or not we consider it as such, all aspects of selecting residents sends a message to future teachers about the values of the program; what we ask, what we omit, whether they perceive the process as rigorous, just, or caring of them as whole people. Because of the intense nature of the residency, its cohort structure and relatively small nature with residents clustered in groups at a few schools, it was particularly important that we could build community among the residents from the beginning. Many felt the intensity of the Haberman protocol was something that brought them into the Newark teaching community; it was unique among New Jersey teachers, often stressful (some residents almost broke down in tears during it), and far beyond the easy kinds of questions they had come to expect from an interview for an education program (i.e., "Why do you want to be a teacher? What do you think makes a good teacher?"). Similarly, the team activity worked both as a means of helping us gauge their ability to work with others, but also actually as a way of building community. The final admissions day in Newark immersed them into the current community of residents, mentors, administration, and students. Current residents spoke about the unique and rigorous nature of the program, how they had grown in their understanding of teaching and learning, and usually how powerful the experience had been for them. To reiterate, if we want our teachers to be agents of change, we also need to help them see themselves not as lone agents in the process of learning to teach, but part of a larger community of teachers and change agents. This counters prevailing popular notions of teachers as isolated players in their individual classrooms, working on their own, often in opposition to other teachers and administrators. We want to offer a vision of a teacher education system where teachers see themselves working in collaboration for common shared and constructed goals, something that begins at admissions.

Assessment As Learning

Finally, tightly related to both assessment and socialization, the admission process is one of learning for the candidates as well. Each resident reflected on how parts of the admissions process provided introductory opportunities to learn about Newark youth, the community and its schools, the residency, its mission, and how we conceptualize math and science inquiry, as well as the change process.

A richer, multi layered admissions process that serves many purposes is possible even at a scaled up version. Finding ways, through group interviews and activities, to both engage candidates in learning experiences that convey the nature of the program and help assess strengths and weaknesses in addition to gate keeping, can help significantly deepen the learning for candidates. Because we have such limited time with our preservice teachers, we must revise teacher education as something that begins from the day they begin their applications. If we approach the process with the same urgency that we want our teachers to bring to their own teaching, we also help convey an understanding of assessment as learning.

NOTE

[1] For example please see: DeLuca, 2012; Harrison, Smithy, & Kent, 2005; McAffee & Weiner, 2006; Wasicsko, Wirtz, & Resor, 2009.

REFERENCES

Achinstein, B., & Ogawa, R. (2006). (In)Fidelity: What the resistance of new teachers reveals about professional principles and prescriptive educational policies. *Harvard Educational Review, 76*(1), 30–63.
Ballou, D., & Podgursky, M. (1995). Recruiting smarter teachers. *The Journal of Human Resources, 30*(2), 326–338.

Baskin, M. K., Ross, S. M., & Smith, D. L. (1996). Selecting successful teachers: The predictive validity of the urban teacher selection interview. *The Teacher Educator, 32*, 1–21.

Brantlinger, A., & Smith, B. (2013). Alternative teacher certification and the new professionalism: The pre-service preparation of mathematics teachers in the New York City teaching fellows program. *Teachers College Record, 115*, 1–44.

Casey, C. E., & Childs, R. A. (2007). Teacher education program admission criteria and what beginning teachers need to know to be successful teachers. *Canadian Journal of Educational Administration and Policy, 67*, 1–24.

Caskey, M. M., Peterson, K. D., & Temple, J. B. (2001). Complex admission selection procedures for a graduate preservice teacher education program. *Teacher Education Quarterly, 37*, 7–21.

Cochran-Smith, M., & Lytle, S. (2004). Practitioner inquiry, knowledge, and university culture. In J. Loughran, M. L. Hamilton, V. LaBoskey, & T. Russell (Eds.), *International handbook of research of self-study of teaching and teacher education practices* (pp. 601–650). Dordrecht, The Netherlands: Springer Press.

Crawford-Garrett, K. (2013). *Teach for America and the struggle for urban school reform: Searching for agency in an era of standardization.* New York, NY: Peter Lang Publishing.

D'Agostino, J. V., & Powers, S. J. (2009). Predicting teacher performance with test scores and gradepoint average: A meta-analysis. *American Educational Research Journal, 46*(1), 146–182.

DeLuca, C. (2012). Selecting inclusive teacher candidates: Validity and reliability issues in admission policy and practice. *Teacher Education Quarterly, 39*(4), 7–32.

Denner, P. R., Salzman, S. A., & Newsome, J. D. (2001). Selecting the qualified: A standards-based teacher education admission process. *Journal of Personnel Evaluation in Education, 15*, 165–180.

Dobbie, W. (2011). *Teacher characteristics and student achievement: Evidence from teach for America* (Monograph). Cambridge, MA: Harvard University Press. Retrieved from http://blogs.edweek.org/edweek/teacherbeat/teachercharacteristicsjuly2011.pdf

Falkenberg, T. (2010). Admission to teacher education programs: The problem and two approaches to addressing it. *Canadian Journal of Education Administration Policy, 107*, 1–29.

Firestone, W. A., & Pennell, J. R. (1993). Teacher commitment, working conditions, and differential incentive policies. *Review of Educational Research, 63*(4), 489–525.

Freeman, D., Martin, R., Brousseau, B., & West, B. (1989). Do higher program admission standard alter profiles of entering teacher candidates? *Journal of Teacher Education, 40*(3), 33–41.

Frey, P. (2003). *Ability of the urban teacher selection interview to identify teachers who are likely to be retained in the Buffalo public schools* (Doctoral dissertation, Accession order no. UMI 3130117). South Orange, NJ: Seton Hall University.

Ginsberg, R., & Whaley, D. (2003). Admission and retention policies in teacher preparation programs: Legal and practical issues. *The Teacher Educator, 38*, 169–189.

Haberman, M. (1988). Proposals for recruiting minority Martin Haberman teachers: Promising practices and attractive detours. *Journal of Teacher Education, 39*(4), 38–44.

Haberman, M. (1995). *Star teachers of children in poverty.* West Lafayette, IN: Kappa Delta Pi International Honor Society in Education.

Harrison, J., Smithy, G., McAffee, H., & Weiner, C. (2006). Assessing candidate disposition for admission into teacher education: Can just anyone teach? *Action in Teacher Education, 27*, 72–80.

Kennedy, H. L. (2000). Assessing preservice teachers: Developing and implementing a model. *Contemporary Education, 71*(2), 42–51.

Kennedy, M., Ball, D., & McDiarmid, G. W. (1993). *A study package for examining and tracking changes in teachers' knowledge* (Technical Series 93–1). East Lansing, MI: The National Center for Research on Teacher Education.

Kent, A. (2005). Acknowledging the need facing teacher preparation programs: Responding to make a difference. *Education, 125*(3), 343–348.

Klussmann, D. F. (2004). *The impact of teachers selected by the star teacher interview process on student achievement* (Doctoral dissertation, Accession order no. 3130126). South Orange, NJ: Seton Hall University. Retrieved from ProQuest Dissertations and Theses.

Kosnick, C., Brown, R., & Beck, C. (2005) The preservice admissions process: What qualities do future teachers need and how can they be identified in applicants? *The New Educator, 1*(2) 101–123.

Larkin, D., Robinson, J., & Perry-Ryder, G. (2014). *Evidence for growth in secondary science residents' knowledge for teaching in an urban teacher residency.* Paper presented at the American Educational Research Association, Philadelphia, PA.

Memory, D. M., Coleman, C. L., & Watkins, S. D. (2003). Possible tradeoffs in raising basic skills cutoff scores for teacher licensure: A study with implications for participation of African Americans in teaching. *Journal of Teacher Education, 54*(3), 217–227.

Montclair State University. *Portrait of a teacher.* Retrieved from http://www.montclair.edu/cehs/academics/departments/ecele/about/portrait-teacher/

Oakes, J., Franke, M., Quartz, K. H., & Rogers, J. (2002). Research for high-quality urban teaching: Defining it, developing it, assessing it. *Journal of Teacher Education, 53*(3), 228–234.

Pillow-Price, K. (2003). *An evaluation of the Haberman urban teacher selection interview in rural settings* (Doctoral dissertation, Accession Order No. 3323288). Jonesboro, AR: Arkansas State University. Retrieved from ProQuest Dissertations and Theses.

Quirk, T. J., Witten, B. J., & Weinberg, S. F. (1973). Review of studies of the concurrent and predictive validity of the national teacher examinations. *Review of Education Research, 43*(1), 89–113.

Roth, P. L., BeVier, C. A., Switzer, F. S., & Schippmann, J. S. (1996). Meta-analyzing the relationship between grades and job performance. *Journal of Applied Psychology, 81*(5), 548–556.

Schectman, Z. (1988). Agreement between lay participants and professional assessors: Support of a group assessment procedure for selection purposes. *Journal of Personnel Evaluation in Education, 12*, 5–17.

Smith, H. A., & Pratt, D. (1996). The use of biodata in admissions to teacher education. *Journal of Teacher Education, 47*, 43–52.

Taylor, A., & Frankenberg, E. (2009). Exploring urban commitment of graduates from an urban-focused teacher education program. Equity & *Excellence in Education, 42*(3), 327–346.

Taylor, M., Klein, E. J., Strom, K., & Abrams, L. (2011). Finding a third space in teacher education: Creating an urban teacher residency with Montclair State University and the Newark public schools. In S. Dickstein (Chair.), *Developing and sustaining UTRs: How do we provide effective preparation experiences and build resident efficacy?* Paper presented in symposium at the American Educational Research Association conference, New Orleans, LA.

Taylor, M., Klein, E. J., Strom, K., & Abrams, L. (2012). A year in the third space: The praxis of inquiry. In M. Taylor & K. Strom (Chairs), *Urban teacher residencies, year one: Looking across models and contexts.* Paper presented in symposium at the American Educational Research Association, Vancouver, Canada.

Taylor, M., Klein, E. J., & Abrams, L. (2014). Tensions of re-imagining our roles as teacher educators in a third space: Revisiting a co/autoethnography through a faculty lens. *Studying Teacher Education, 10*(1), 3–19.

Teach For America | Home. (n.d.). Retrieved from http://www.teachforamerica.org/

Veltri, B. T. (2010). *Learning on other people's kids: Becoming a teach for America teacher.* Charlotte, NC: Information Age Publishers.

Wasicsko, M., Wirtz, P., & Resor, C. (2009). Using dispositions in the teacher admission process. *SRATE Journal, 18*(2), 19–26.

Zeichner, K. M. (2003). The adequacies and inadequacies of three current strategies to recruit, prepare, and retain the best teachers for all students. *Teachers College Record, 105*(3), 490–515.

Emily J. Klein
Department of Secondary and Special Education
Montclair State University
Montclair, New Jersey

Monica Taylor
Department of Secondary and Special Education
Montclair State University
Montclair, New Jersey

Walter Kaczka
Retired Science Department Chair
University High School
Newark, New Jersey

David Koethe
East Side High School
Newark, New Jersey

Marc Kolb
Florence Township Memorial High School
Florence, New Jersey

APPENDIX 1

Portrait of A Teacher

The Montclair State University community is committed to the continuing development of teachers who exemplify the dispositions, knowledge, and skills reflected in this portrait. They:

1. Have expert knowledge of the disciplines they will teach and can use various strategies, including media and technology, for creating learning experiences that make the subject matter accessible and meaningful to all students.
2. Understand how children and adolescents learn and develop in a variety of school, family and community contexts, and can provide learning opportunities that support their students' intellectual, social, and personal development.
3. Understand the practice of culturally responsive teaching. They understand that children bring varied talents, strengths, and perspectives to learning; have skills for learning about the diverse students they teach; and use knowledge of students and their lives to design and carry out instruction that builds on students' individual and cultural strengths.
4. Plan instruction based upon knowledge of subject matter, students, families, communities, and curriculum goals and standards; and taking into account issues of class, gender, race, ethnicity, language, sexual orientation, age, and special needs in designing instruction.
5. Understand critical thinking and problem solving, and create learning experiences that promote the development of students' critical thinking and problem solving skills and dispositions.
6. Understand principles of democracy and plan and carry out instruction that promotes democratic values and communication in the classroom.
7. Understand and use multiple forms of assessment to promote the intellectual, social, and physical development of learners and to inform instruction.
8. Create a community in the classroom that is nurturing, caring, safe, and conducive to learning.
9. Are reflective practitioners who continually inquire into the nature of teaching and learning, reflect on their own learning and professional practice, evaluate the effects of their choices and actions on others, and seek out opportunities to grow professionally.
10. Build relationships with school colleagues, families, and agencies in the community to support students' learning and well-being, and work to foster an appreciation of diversity among students and colleagues.
11. Possess the literacy skills associated with an educated person; can speak and write English fluently and communicate clearly.
12. Develop dispositions expected of professional educators. These include belief in the potential of schools to promote social justice; passion for teaching; and

commitment to the ethical and enculturating responsibilities of educators, to ensuring equal learning opportunities for every student, to serving as agents of change and stewards of best practice, and to critical reflection, inquiry, critical thinking, and life-long learning.

APPENDIX 2

Montclair State University Initial Teacher Education Program

ADMISSIONS EVALUATION SCALE (REV. 7-08)

Student _____ Evaluator ___ Student ID# _____

Semester: Fall _____   Spring _____   Year _____

Please circle the appropriate rating for each performance category below *using the accompanying RUBRIC.*

RATING SCALE:

Does not meet expectations		*Meets expectations*		*Exceeds expectations*
1	*2*	*3*	*4*	*5*

1.	Subject matter knowledge.	1 2 3 4 5
2.	Written English thinking and communication skills.	1 2 3 4 5
3.	Oral English thinking and communication skills.	1 2 3 4 5
4.	Understanding that a person's perspective is influenced by his/ her life experiences. Appreciation of multiple ways of knowing.	1 2 3 4 5
5.	Belief that all children can learn and that all children bring talents and strengths to learning.	1 2 3 4 5
6.	Respect and appreciation for individual and cultural differences.	1 2 3 4 5
7.	Reflectiveness. Commitment to critical reflection and critical thinking.	1 2 3 4 5
8.	Understanding of and commitment to principles of democracy.	1 2 3 4 5
9.	Initial commitment to the ethical and enculturating responsibilities of educators and to being agents of change.	1 2 3 4 5
10.	Commitment to teaching.	1 2 3 4 5
11.	Personal qualities.	1 2 3 4 5

Be sure to rate each item.   Total = _____ / 55
Comments (use back if necessary)

MEET THE AUTHORS FROM CHAPTER FOUR

Alexander Diaz, I am a light-skinned Cuban American. I am one of four men from a first generation immigrant family. My parents both went to college and I grew up in a suburban neighborhood as one of the only Latino families in the area. I grew up with all the privileges of being Latino without any of the costs. I first wanted to be a teacher after I entered college. Many of my friends in college were not as lucky as I was. They spoke a lot about the kind of experiences they had and the classes they went to during their time in school. They told me about teachers who would put slides up on the board and the whole class would be spent copying the information, they told me about how people in and outside of school would make demeaning comments to them about their heritage and their color, they told me about the dearth of opportunities in their school to explore what interested them through clubs and extracurricular activities, and they told me about how they would often not have enough to be comfortable.

The more they spoke, the more I realized how privileged I had been, the more I realized what all the people in my family who were first generation and my friends in college had to go through to get where they are. In thinking about everything they had been through, I decided that I wanted to be a part of the solution. I did and still do believe that access to a quality education can make all the difference in someone's life. It can mean the difference between finding a way to live comfortably and having trouble keeping your head above water. So, I started searching out experiences that I could get in college that would allow me to teach so that I could get a taste of what it was like. I ended up teaching a first-year interest group as well as tutoring for a program that was designed to help minority youths in the field of science. My initial impetus to teach came from the desire to give back to my community, but I did not anticipate how much I would enjoy teaching; developing relationships while trying to create challenges that would push my students beyond their own limits. Teaching is something that is both intellectually stimulating and emotionally rewarding. Those experiences made teaching change from being just a cause to something that could be a lifetime career.

With my doubts erased, I began searching for teaching programs. I had come across a few residency programs, one was in Colorado and another was in New York. I applied to each just to be safe. A few weeks into that process, my mother told me about the NMUTR. She had found out about it through an old friend that lived in Clifton. Initially, when looking up the specifics of the program, I was a little nervous because I understood how big of a commitment it was, but I knew it was what I wanted to do. It fit in with everything that I hoped to stand for and, more than that, it was the most challenging and rewarding thing I had ever done. I contacted the director, Susan Taylor, some time during my fall semester of my last year in college. In our meeting, I asked what I needed to make sure that I would be the best candidate for the position. She told me that I needed to take one more up-level course in Biology to qualify to teach as well as take the Praxis. I did everything that needed to be done, I applied, and here I am today.

Janae Taylor, I grew up in the heart of the "danger" in Newark, Brick City, New Jersey. Of course I didn't see it as immediate danger so I continued to play outside while the drugs and violence still ensued. It was life; it was the adrenaline from running whenever there was a shootout in the courtyard; it was survival. Things in Newark are ten times better now than when I grew up. So when people talk about things going wrong in the city, I'm numb to it because "this is nothing."

My solace was school. My parents would remember at parent teacher conferences how shocked they were to hear I was a model student, a model citizen. At school I was a completely different person, I had a switch that I was able to turn on and off because like I said, it was all about survival. I learned early on that to survive you need to adapt to your surroundings. In school they needed you calm and respectful in order to be successful. But outside of school they needed you capable of fight. I had both and it came easily to me.

School was my passion since I was 5 years old. I've always wanted to be a teacher. I had my chalkboard in my room and my some fifty plus stuffed animals that were my students. I made my parents and teachers get me old and new workbooks so that I could give my students, my stuffed animals, work to do and me assignments to grade. It was my peaceful zone. It kept me calm. What was happening outside my room's walls and outside my apartment's walls, was no longer occurring in my mind. I just taught, and learned and it was an amazing feeling.

Even at a young age I faced criticisms and racism for wanting to be something other than a "hoodlum." One experience that was really prevalent in my mind was when a white substitute teacher told me that because I was black, I would never be successful just like everyone else out there in the outside world. At six years old I cried my eyes out. All I wanted to do was to finish the book I was writing during reading time. He didn't like that I was told I could do something different. It took me a long time to be able to write my own narratives again. I proved him wrong. I'm one of the youngest (I started at 21) black female teachers of mathematics in Newark, Brick City, New Jersey with a Masters degree. And I am successful!

Kathryn Strom, I am a former secondary history teacher who taught in Southern California in urban settings. A White woman from a lower-middle class background, I grew up in Alabama acutely aware of racial inequality, which later shaped my agenda as a social justice educator. After teaching middle and high school social studies for a few years, I became a school leader at a high-needs school that suffered from high teacher attrition, which caused instability. I began to view teacher preparation and on-going support as a key way to stem teacher turnover as well as pursue goals of social justice in education. These understandings, and my own isolated experiences as a beginning teacher, spurred an interest in the preparation of urban teachers and eventually, the pursuit of a doctorate at MSU in teacher education and development.

During the first two years of the NMUTR, I worked with the program as part of my doctoral fellowship. In the first year of the program, I mainly helped with program and coursework logistics, led a few workshops on language and social justice, and oversaw data collection for research efforts. During the second year, I took on the role of induction coach, a support for the new cohort of resident graduates that faculty hoped would provide a bridge between their NMUTR experience and their new experiences as teachers of record. Because I had been intensively involved in the resident graduates' residency year, attending every NMUTR class, observing their teaching multiple times, and building personal relationships, uniquely positioned me to be able to tap into their previous coursework to reinforce an inquiry-as-stance teaching perspective with the new residents while they navigated their new settings.

Gail Perry-Ryder, I am a middle-class, heterosexual African American woman who is also a product of public and alternative education. As a doctoral candidate in teacher education and development at MSU, I study how Black women teachers' particular knowledge inform the ways they engage their institutions, and how they do their work with youth entangled between multiple systems. My personal and professional experiences are what inspire me to explore the intersection of teacher biography, teacher practice, and the social systems that influence them both.

Prior to beginning doctoral study, my early career was spent entirely in the New York City metro area working as an arts-education administrator, high school social studies teacher, and college counselor. I went on to become a lecturer in African American Studies at the City University of New York and program coordinator for an alternative-to-incarceration program for youth. In these and other settings, I worked to better understand the ways power and privilege operate to undermine educational opportunity for marginalized youth, and developed what has become a lifelong commitment to promoting social justice in education. I had the pleasure of conducting social justice workshops for cohort three of the NMUTR.

MONICA TAYLOR, ALEXANDER DIAZ, JANAE TAYLOR,
KATHRYN STROM AND GAIL PERRY-RYDER

4. TEACHING FOR SOCIAL JUSTICE
THROUGH FUNDS OF KNOWLEDGE
IN THE THIRD SPACE

You could save yourself,
you could save us all,
Go on living, prove us wrong,
Your leap of faith,
Could be a well – timed smile,
Survival never goes out of style.
(Fall Out Boy, "Save Your Generation")

D seemed determined to show me that he was different from the other kids, from the stereotypical concept of a kid from the "ghetto." He continually emphasized, "I don't listen to gangsta rap, I listen to rock music." Or "I'm not like the other kids, I just do not go around with girls I do not like, I like one girl and that is it." This lessened over time as I got to know him; however, that "stereotype" or concern about "the wrong path" was particularly powerful for both D and his mother. D carefully selected his clothing, music, and behaviors ensuring that they fell outside of the "gangsta" scene.

D is really into rock music, bands like Fall Out Boy, My Chemical Romance, the Republic, and writing his own tunes while learning to play the guitar and piano. This passion seems like a negotiation between his identity at home as the "Good Son" and his need for autonomy and self-expression without being associated with or falling victim to the "wrong path." I was so surprised by his musical taste as this music is not what is commonly associated with urban kids, even though often times this genre often deals with themes of liberation, self- expression, and intense, sometimes anger-driven, behavior. It seems like, from the way D and even his mother talk about it, rock music is associated with "White" culture, making it acceptable. This acceptance allows D to spend all his time listening, contemplating and writing his own rock music without his mother fretting. He tells me, "Sometimes I wake up with a song in my head and I have to write it down." Furthermore, his rock music is also what connects him strongly to his two childhood friends N and C and gives him an outlet where he can express himself.

Drawn from a case study of a Newark youth, Alex's narrative illustrates some of the insights he developed while mentoring a student during his initial summer semester in the program. A central goal of the secondary cohort of the NMUTR in general, and the summer semester specifically, was to provide the residents with opportunities to really get to know Newark youth within their own community rather than to support, confirm, or enhance the typical deficit ways in which we think about urban youth. We wanted to combat the stereotypes that often place "school failure on the heads of students or their families, languages, culture and communities" (Dudley-Marling, 2013, p. 68) and, instead, invited our residents to construct rich, complex, sociocultural portraits of their students and their potential as learners (Banks & Banks, 2010; Ladson-Billings, 1995; Nieto, 2007). We believed that disrupting these stereotypes laid the foundation for developing a social justice stance (Au, Karp, & Bigelow, 2007; Cochran-Smith, 2004). We envisioned this stance as a means to inform a teaching philosophy and practice that would recognize and break traditional structures and patterns of schooling that maintain and expand entrenched inequalities in our society (Cochran-Smith, Shakman, Jong, Barnatt, & McQuillan, 2009). We were clear that merely teaching about related pedagogic traditions, such as culturally responsive/ relevant teaching (Gay, 2000; Ladson-Billings, 1995; Villegas & Lucas, 2002), linguistically responsive teaching (Villegas & Lucas, 2011) critical pedagogy (Freire, 1970; Freire & Macedo, 1987; Giroux, 1988; Hinchey, 2001; Shor, 1992) and democratic teaching (Apple & Beane, 1995; Ayers, 2009; Dewey, 1916) and teaching for social justice (Ayers, Quinn, & Hunt, 1998; Cochran-Smith, 2004) is not sufficient to prepare future teachers to interrupt the status quo in Newark classrooms.

In this chapter, we, Monica, a NMUTR faculty, and Alex and Janae, two cohort two residents, narrate our experiences of working toward actively developing a social justice teaching stance based on the funds of knowledge of our students.[1] Monica invited Alex and Janae to co-write this chapter because of their differing perspectives of social justice teaching. Alex represents a more traditional liberal understanding of social justice teaching whereas Janae draws from her own experiences of growing up in an urban community. In a negotiated third space, where all members are continually in the process of becoming, there is not one model of being a social justice teacher. Rather juxtaposing these perspectives provides a fruitful and rich space for discussion and problematizing. We begin with an in depth description of the summer experience, highlighting curricular aspects, and the initial foundation of a social justice/funds of knowledge orientation. We then describe the Inquiry Cycle Experience (ICE) assignment, which we developed to provide residents with an opportunity to begin to think about and put into action their beliefs about teaching for social justice through inquiry. Finally we share what we learned about preparing residents to teach for social justice and some implications for more general teacher education programs.

LAYING A SOCIAL JUSTICE FOUNDATION: BUILDING AN
UNDERSTANDING OF FUNDS OF KNOWLEDGE

Monica

To begin to develop a social justice lens (we say *begin* because we understand that this is a lifelong dynamic process), our residents from the get-go engaged in a variety of learning endeavors within the third space that encouraged their listening to and caring about the students that they would teach. As Schultz (2003) writes:

> The phrase "listening to teach" implies that the knowledge of who the learner is, and the understandings that both the teacher and learner bring to a situation, constitutes the starting place for teaching... It is an active process that allows us both to maintain and cross boundaries. (p. 13)

We hoped that our residents would develop a habit of mind that helped them to "listen to teach" as a way to develop curriculum and teaching that served as a bridge between their students' needs and interests and the essential questions, skills, knowledge, and understanding of their content areas (Wiggins & McTighe, 2005). Similar to the work of Buck and Sylvester (2005) in Philadelphia, our goal was for the residents to move away from the feelings of "self-consciousness, vulnerability, and suspicion" and instead to embrace "respect, confidence, and humility" (p. 220) when they spent time among Newark youth. And like Buck and Sylvester, we understood that this would involve the residents recognizing and reflecting on their own positions of power and privilege that could cause them to feel uncomfortable in their interactions in the various communities of Newark. But rather than focusing the residents on the "culture of poverty" of their students and the ways in which their own privilege contrasts with that, we believed that their summer interactions with Newark students and their active meaning making of the experiences would help them to identify "evidence that reservoirs of human strength and talent, as ready-made, untapped resources, do exist in urban communities" (Buck & Sylvester, 2005, p. 228).

We hoped that participating in a variety of distinct internships in community-based organizations, as we discuss in detail later in Chapter Nine, would create a window into the many dimensions of the young people in Newark. We purposely constructed these experiences during the initial summer session because we wanted the residents' first interactions with kids to be in settings where there is real, authentic learning that has yet to be infected by standards, curriculum, and testing. Before these internships, however, we did spend several intensive weeks with the residents beginning to lay a historical and conceptual social justice foundation as well. Prior to our first week together, we asked residents to read *Hope in the Unseen* (1999), a text written by Ron Suskind, a reporter from the *Wall Street Journal*, about the very honest story of a young African American man who went through the Washington D.C. public school system and eventually was accepted to Brown University. The narrative illustrates the complex tensions and challenges of low-income students of color who are often extremely successful academically in their urban public school settings but severely underprepared for a rigorous college environment and frequently lack the "cultural capital" (Bourdieu, 1973) that facilitates success in elite institutions.

Janae

Before discussing this text, we spent several sessions together talking about identity in terms of the intersections of race, class, gender, language, sexuality, and ability (Crenshaw, 1991). Some of us were more open to discussing these topics than others, either because of having past experiences examining inequity like Suzanne who had traveled to do social justice work in Africa or because our consciousness had already begun to be raised through real life situations or courses that we had taken in college. Because I was the only one who grew up in Newark, I was skeptical about talking about this with the other residents. I appreciated the ability to hear about their individual experiences because it helped me to realize that many others had also had challenging life experiences. They showed me that I wasn't the only one with a "story." I put story in quotations because I will never see others' lives as a 'story.' I'm not a story. I'm an individual. I'm another life in this hectic world. And one world is not worse or better than anyone else.

Alex

We also spent some time refreshing our memories about adolescence and some of the complexities of this particular age. Addressing one of the summer objectives that is most relevant to this chapter, "understanding urban youth and communities," we were invited to first think about urban adolescents through the lens of our own life experiences, then through perspectives that were raised in the readings and discussions, and finally, through getting to know some Newark students. In my summer goal reflection prior to beginning the internships, I wrote, "Although my family has grown up in Newark and I spent a lot of time there growing up, I am only beginning to understand what it means to be a part of an urban community and the challenges that people face as well as some of the intricacies that make it so beautiful."

Monica

Besides teaching at the Newark Museum and La Casa De Don Pedro (see Chapter Nine), residents were assigned to mentor a Newark All Star youth who was interning in a corporate setting. The Newark All Stars Project, Inc. is a 32 year old, privately funded non-profit that sponsors outside of school development programs for poor, urban youth of color. At Newark All Stars, they believe that development is what is needed to move young people and communities from chronic poverty and all of its effects. They emphasize that through a focus on community, performance, and creativity, in and out of school settings, young people can learn the developmental tools necessary to become interested in acquiring knowledge, rather than relying on a more traditional approach that privileges school experiences as the only ones that matter in growth and development. In an effort to meet the needs of all inner city youth, Newark All Stars is committed to being "radically inclusive" (All Stars Project, p. 3). What this means is that ALL students, kids getting into trouble, talented athletes who are college bound, gang members, academically successful students, and/or so-called "at-risk" youth are invited to become part of the All Star community. These young people are brought together with corporate executives, artists, dancers, and others to create a different sort of community where "new kinds of conversations, new relationships, and new performances occur" (All Stars Project, p. 4). Their message to the youth is: "You don't just live in your socially over-determined, parochial neighborhood. You live in the world. And your participation in the new community can develop you to be a builder of the world, a more cosmopolitan citizen" (All Stars Project, p. 4). Their programs focus on the social, cultural, and creative development of youth through a focus on performance where they can be both "who they are" and "who they are becoming" (p. 4). They see performance as a way for the young people "to actively create new ways of how to be in the world" (p. 4).

Alex

In preparation for our work with the adolescents, we participated in a morning orientation at Newark All Stars, where we learned about the principles of youth development and spent an afternoon meeting and getting to know the Newark teens to whom we were assigned through a variety of ice breaker activities. Although the faculty called our work with the youth mentoring, in many ways this relationship was one where there would be an exchange of insider information, where we would support the youth in learning how to navigate a professional corporate setting and where the youth would introduce us to adolescent life in Newark. When I was first asked to mentor, my first reaction was "I don't feel like I'm old enough to mentor anyone. I don't have enough experiences to do that." But I also remember that "the faculty's response was 'you're not meant to be guiding them, per se, but just having a relationship with them and cultivating that relationship with them.' So for me, it took some stress off." As part of our mentorship role, we were asked to organize at least one social experience with our youth either in Newark or in a place of their choice and then also visit our youth at their assigned internship site.

After six weeks of mentoring, we were asked to write a case study about our mentee and reflect on the implications of our experiences with him or her and on our emerging identity as an urban teacher. Specifically, we were asked to describe our young person physically as well as in terms of personality and interests. Then we were to describe, analyze, and interpret our experiences with the adolescent in the various settings, using the artifacts that we had collected to *show* rather than *tell*. To guide us in writing the case study, some prompts were:

What are the different settings in which she/he interacts? What did you learn about her/his identities? What did you learn about the roles and responsibilities of her/his life? What surprised you? What did you learn about urban communities and/or families? Did your experiences contradict some beliefs or assumptions about urban youth and communities that you have? What implications does this have on you as a teacher?

My case study provided me with a space to reflect on what I had learned about D and the ways in which I would incorporate what I learned in the classroom. In my opening narrative, I wrote:

D and his family consciously combat their fears of taking the "Wrong Path." This comes from their own life experiences of observing friends and neighbors who have fallen victim to bad influences. Since this is such a strong archetypal image, in urban culture and within his life, it tends to pervade D's perception of the world. Sadly, these very ideas, although useful in the case of D and his family, are also part of the prejudice that can lead people to discriminate against others from both within and outside of urban culture. Only through acceptance can we hope to positively affect anyone, without judgments made based on how they express themselves musically or otherwise. If we preclude an entire group of people based on these characteristics, we lose the fight of education long before it has started.

My experiences with D greatly influenced the way I began to think about myself as a teacher. I concluded my case study with the following reflection:

If nothing else, I am more aware of what we will be battling within the school system, a problem I hope to solve by leading through example. Through my experiences with the kids at the museum, hearing about their home lives, dealing with the lack of resources, space, etc., sadly, a lot of these students, even in the classroom, face the challenges of teachers who do not understand them and/or are quick to pass judgment. Through my interactions with D, I have gotten to know some of the realities that urban youth face regarding safety, mobility, and common differences in family structure. Regardless of these differences, I believe that all people, both adults and children, desire respect, autonomy, and acceptance. I learned that a lot of them are looking for connections, something which is particularly important in the urban environment. When the students got to know us they were more than happy to work with us to do something or to help us even. That was particularly valuable and getting to know them as individuals was crucial to that process. They want to talk about things and themselves as long as you are willing to ask. Respect comes to mind. I think it was the most valuable resource we had. The fact they respected us was crucial. The students knew we were there for their benefit. Also, a lot of the students have so much going on outside of school, be it different or changing family compositions, family or home responsibilities, and/or work. There is a lot going on in terms of what a student has to do when they get home as opposed to my own experiences.

Janae

I came to mentoring my Newark All Star youth, M, from a completely different perspective than Alex. I have an insider view since I grew up in Newark, attended NPS schools and Rutgers University Newark, and now continue to live in Newark. I was born and raised on Martin Luther King Boulevard – the hospital where I was born, the house where I lived. I lived in the same building that Corey Booker used to live in, Brick Towers, and I live here now and I work at Arts High School on MLK too. I saw my first murder when I was 6. It happens. I lived in the Brick Towers and they were shooting behind the buildings. I was looking out the window and there was a guy shooting another guy for his sneakers. Next thing I knew he was laying there dead, uncovered and you could see the blood. And the next day I saw the guy who shot him with the new sneakers and no one said anything about it. I have been through it; a lot of people have and I guess I am numb to it.

I feel like a lot of teachers because they are not from Newark say that you need to pity the students here and give them more leniency. I think you should treat them as you would treat any other student from any other area. My parents never gave me any excuses. They would say "Oh your cousin just died, well you still need to finish your paper for school."

In a sense, when I mentored M from the Newark All Stars, I was already trying to think about her not as conforming to a stereotype but rather in a more complicated, intersectional (Crenshaw, 1991) way. In my case study, I wrote:

M is the cynical fighter, fighting for success in her world. She is the role model for her family, she is the resilient daughter constantly emerging from a case of severe tough love, she is the girlfriend keeping her boyfriend in check, she is the introverted student staying away from school activities, she is the student reading for an escape, she is the planner who makes her life better for everyone, she is the intern doing what's told of her with no questions asked, and she is "PJ" an endearing family nickname. She juggles all identities, showing that adolescents have just as many intricacies as adults. This discovery of mine is something not to be neglected and forgotten when dealing with adolescents.

She works hard to succeed in spite of the role models she's previously been exposed to. Just to start, she comes from a long tradition of teenage pregnancy, that she is determined to break, despite that it's hitting her from all directions. Her grandmother was sixteen, her mother was seventeen, and her sister was sixteen when they each had their first child. Now her only two best friends just recently at the age of seventeen told her they were pregnant at the same time and she felt confused as to what her obligations were. When I say M is a fighter; she's not a physical fighter but she fights mentally every day to keep her priorities in check a little bit more than any other average teenager. Her father left when she was younger to start a new family in Oregon, something she says is "whatever." I am told, in a conversation we had as we watched the Liberty basketball game, that she used to talk to him on at least a monthly basis and after her mother refused to let her father take her to Oregon to live, the father and daughter relationship became even more distant. She doesn't believe in long distance relationships.

I knew, drawing from my own life experiences, that although I had faced and experienced many of the stereotypes of urban youth, I would not let them define me. I felt like my relationship with M was more authentic because I could relate to her. I wanted to see her as a whole person and not let some of the challenges that she faced living in Newark define her.

HOW DO THESE EXPERIENCES TRANSLATE INTO SOCIAL JUSTICE TEACHING?

Monica

The summer experiences provided an excellent foundation for our model of social justice teaching. From our perspective, social justice teaching involves a Freirean problem posing pedagogy (Freire, 1970) that incorporates the research and practices of funds of knowledge (Gonzalez, Moll, & Amanti, 2005). Using a lens grounded in these theoretical frameworks combats a "banking" model of teaching that focuses on transmitting information to students. A "banking" model works from the assumption that students are blank, empty slates that need to be filled with information and works toward teaching them the norms and ideologies of the dominant culture (Apple & Beane, 1995; Bourdieu, 1973) through the stated and implicit school curriculum. Additionally students are expected to be quiet, obedient, rule followers who do not question teachers or authorities with school (Foucault, 1980). As Freire (1970) writes, "Translated into practice, this concept is well suited to the oppressors, whose tranquility rests upon how well men fit the world that the oppressors have created, and how little they question it" (p. 63).

In contrast, within a dialogic "problem posing" pedagogy, teachers and students work together as active learners to figure out the world. They both play the role of teacher and learner, blurring the traditional power roles of the classroom and making possible the negotiation of the curriculum between the two. Freire (1970) explains, "The teacher is no longer the one who teaches, but one who is himself taught in dialogue with the students, who in turn while being taught also teach. They become responsible for a process in which all grow" (p. 57). There are no right answers – "questions and not answers are at the core of the curriculum; open-ended questions prod students to critically analyze their social situation and encourage them to ultimately work toward changing it" (Peterson, 2009, p. 306).

Students are considered active constructors of knowledge and teaching "relies on the experiences of students and implies respect and use of the students' culture, language, and dialect" (p. 306). It means "moving beyond thought and words to action," and creating a third space where students feel comfortable and empowered to "interrogate their own realities, see them in different light, and act on their developing convictions to change their own social reality" (p. 306). In adopting inquiry-as-stance (Cochran-Smith & Lytle, 2009) in their teaching, residents can encourage students to investigate and question their world, interrogate their own beliefs, and explore multiple and sometimes contradictory perspectives (Freire, 1970; Freire & Macedo, 1987).

Additionally, building from "the funds of knowledge" research (Gonzalez, Moll, & Amanti, 2005) and embracing the notion of a third space, we encouraged our residents to think about their teaching through a lens of intersection between theory and practice, rather than presenting them as two opposing, separate ideas. We expected them to theorize the practices of their students' lives so that they could begin to understand the complex contexts in which their experiences occur, both in and outside of school. Within these interpretations, we wanted them to focus on, as Gonzalez, Moll, and Amanti (2005) emphasize, contradictions rather than coherence and nuances instead of linear connections (Bourdieu, 1977). Giroux (1992) reminds us that "the ways in which students' experience is produced, organized, and legitimated in schools has become an increasingly important theoretical consideration for understanding how schools function to produce and authorize particular forms of meaning" (p. 180). While the residents gained valuable insight from theorizing their students' experiences, they wondered, *how do we incorporate this knowledge into the classroom? How do the practices of the students' lives dialogue with the practices of school?*

GETTING TO "KNOW" OUR STUDENTS AND THEIR FUNDS OF KNOWLEDGE

From the standpoint of the child, the great waste in the school comes from his inability to utilize the experiences he gets outside the school in any complete and free way within the school itself; while, on the other hand, he is unable to apply daily life to what he is learning in school. That is the isolation of the school—its isolation from life. He the child gets into the schoolroom he has to put out of his mind large part of his ideas, interests and activities that predominate in his home and neighborhood. So the school, being unable to utilize this everyday experience, sets painfully to work, on another tack and by a variety of means, to arouse in the child an interest in school studies. (Dewey, 1902, p. 75)

We understood that our residents needed to construct bridges between their own experiences, their students' lives, and the school curriculum. Using their students' "funds of knowledge" (Gonzalez, Moll, & Amanti, 2005) as the cultural artifact in a Vygotskian sense (1978) helped mediate the residents' comprehension of social life within the students' school lives. Residents recognized that the students of Newark exist in hybrid cultures (Bhabha, 1994) or third spaces, combining where they are from with where they are now, where there is always "difference and identity, inside and outside, inclusion and exclusion, past and present" (Gonzalez, 2005, p. 38). Their third space involves what Moje, Ciechanowski, Kramer, Ellis, Carrillo, and Collazo (2004) describe as a combination of "the 'first space' of people's home, community, and peer networks with the 'second space' of the Discourses they encounter in more formalized institutions such as work, school, or church" (p. 41). It adds a new dimension to the third space of the residency, expanding to include the rich and diverse experience of the residents' urban students. Early childhood teachers value and build on funds of knowledge from family, community, and cultural backgrounds (González, Moll, & Amanti, 2005) through home and neighborhood visits and building relationships with the parents. Chu (2014) describes the process:

> At the heart of this approach is collaboration with teachers who are willing to learn from families about how to engage in culturally sustaining practices. Observing teachers who are aware of social contexts helps early childhood students consider the response to the question: How does life outside of school influence life inside the school (Bronfenbrenner, 1989)? (p. 82)

This approach to working with urban students, where the knowledge and experiences that they bring to school are acknowledged, valued, and used as building blocks for learning, sharply contrasts with the ways for example organizations like Teach For America (TFA) position urban teachers in relation to their students. Popkewitz (1998), in an early study of TFA gathered ethnographic data to comprehend how teachers "construct" urban kids through their discourse. His findings demonstrate that "many of the teachers' pedagogical and curricular decisions are guided by unstated white, middle-class norms which consistently cast the urban/rural student as 'other'" (Crawford-Garrett, 2013, p. 16). Darling-Hammond (1994) furthers this critique by describing TFA as a domestic missionary organization, which expects teachers to rescue poor urban students rather than appreciate their cultural capital. When they face challenges in the classroom with a "deficit" perception of students partnered with unpreparedness as beginning teachers, they have no other option but to blame the students for their own teaching failures. We agree with Veltri (2010) who contends that TFA's paradigm is the antithesis of social justice teaching as it perpetuates the status quo and sends a message to urban youth that the only way to be successful is to leave their cultures and communities behind. As Moll and Gonzalez (1997) write, home communities are considered "places from which children must be saved or rescued, rather than places that, in addition to problems (as in all communities), contain valuable knowledge and experiences" (p. 98).

Alex

What does this look like when you are working with adolescents? How do you gain access to their home cultures when they are in the process of constructing identities that are separate from their families? How do you respect their space in their process of becoming and yet still draw from where they come? Interestingly, combining my summer work with Newark youth and my co-teaching in the classroom, I came to the realization that it was essential for me to really get to know my adolescent students and value what they have learned through their own life experiences. At the end of my residency year I reflected,

> I think the biggest mistake I made, coming from a suburban community, was thinking that at some time that I was in some way more equipped than my students to deal with the real world; that I could 'save' the urban youth in Newark. Throughout this year I have learned that many of my students deal with issues and complications that I, as an adult, would have trouble managing. I learned that a lot of them, in facing these challenges and issues, are braver than me and stronger than I ever hope to be. I was mistaken in thinking that I could 'save' them because they have all the potential and ability to succeed. My role as a teacher means providing them with the right environment to reach their potentials.

One of the central issues which came up early on in the year was that *I did not know my students well enough.* I was so focused on providing the education that they needed and ensuring that not a moment of class time was wasted that I did not allow them to see a different side of me nor did I allow them to show a different side of themselves. I trapped myself by trying to move forward without truly acknowledging the differences among the students and each of their own needs. The more I pushed to continue, the more they pushed back. Students were getting into arguments in the class, when I asked them to stay quiet the volume would intensify, and when I set expectations they were all falling asleep.

Eventually I started keeping kids after school for detention. During that time I would talk with them and try to figure out what was going wrong. In doing so I inevitably started correcting the problem that I created. By getting to know them, they became more comfortable with me and were less likely to be combative. Also, as I got to know them, I learned what was going on with them and I was able to adjust accordingly if I felt that something was amiss. Similar to me, Dave, a resident with whom I co-taught, echoed these beliefs when he said,

> I think teaching for social justice is simply about hearing our students' voices, and respecting them. Our students aren't used to having what they say, what they think in class, be worth a lot. You know we hear a lot of complaining by administration or other teachers like, "oh, you can talk with him," or "you can't talk with her," I think, by acknowledging them and helping them express their

voices and their views and ideas, that's the biggest move in social justice and empowering students to do other things outside the classroom.

Janae

Although I understood the importance of identifying with the Newark students and listening to their perspectives, I was concerned that my resident colleagues and even myself in some ways would have a hard time doing so. When we started talking about social justice and identity I thought to myself that these people don't know what they are talking about. They could never identify with these kids, never understand where they come from, and never see a glimpse of what they go through. Not even I, when I'm the one that came from the core of this environment. I was raised in it, engulfed by it, sheltered by it, yet not in it at all. They wanted me to tell my story but it would never help them because they still will never see because they haven't experienced it, haven't lived it, haven't grown numb from it, hadn't had to claw their way out of it the way that I did. I know of these experiences through my eyes and my eyes only. Each child has his or her own pair of eyes through which they see every situation differently and if I, the black, self-helping child from the hood, could barely see what these students saw through their own eyes, how could the other residents?

When they accepted that they could not identify with Newark students, then they were successful at social justice. So I just sat back and listened to the uncertainty, the lack of knowledge, because the good teachers in my cohort eventually figured it out on their own and are still teaching in Newark today. Now I'm not saying I knew all about social justice and identity in Newark, what I'm saying is that when you go through the battle first hand, there's skepticism with others who never have tried. I still think some will never be able to see it through their eyes and will continuously get frustrated when teaching our youth. I get frustrated sometimes, but then I have to just remind myself that the students have a different "story"/ life and have yet to cope. They may never heal from some things in their life but they can cope. I just have to be patient because it's affecting them now and eventually all the frustration will pay off for them as long as the fight is still alive in their eyes, in their lives.

Monica

Janae's perspective is important because it points to the very real challenges of operationalizing a problem based pedagogy that truly relies on funds of knowledge in a third space. This entails deliberate, honest, and humble reflection, which helps to avoid the all too easy slippery slope of taking on the "teacher as savior" stance that enables a deficit judgmental view of urban students. Embracing some humility helps the residents to understand that they will not have all of the answers and to some extent need to accept the uncertainty and unknowability (Coia & Taylor, 2013) of teaching as part of the process. Janae's deeply insightful comments about her colleagues demonstrate that some of this uncertainty involves realizing how their privilege limits their identification with their students. This third space framework borrows from the work of poststructural feminists like Lather (2006), Saint-Pierre (2000), and Ellsworth (1989) and presents quite differently than both the neoliberal agenda that promotes charter schools and TFA and the social justice teacher education programs that advocate for a particular brand of social justice activism. We do not want our residents' teaching beliefs to become "routinized, static and predictable" (Lather, 2006, p. 1). Instead we hope for them "to try and always be open, to never be fixed in belief or judgment" (Coia & Taylor, 2014, p. 165) and to continually work toward a social justice teaching stance. We hope that they will recognize like Ellsworth (1989) that their social justice goals are never fully actualized and that their positions as teachers always privilege them over students. The key is that their constant reflection raises their honest awareness of their positioning and encourages power negotiation with their students.

INQUIRY IN THE THIRD SPACE: THE ICE PROJECT

Monica

We were all clear about meeting the needs of the students and had begun to embrace a socially just teaching stance, but many questions also arose. How could we operationalize these beliefs? How could we design socially just curriculum in math and science classes? And finally, how would the third space of our NMUTR facilitate a socially just inquiry based curriculum? When the program was initially designed, the inquiry concept that drove us centered around the tenets of critical literacy. For us, inquiry "begins with voice, inviting all learners to name their world. It ends in reflexivity and action, inviting all learners to interrogate the very constructs they are using to make sense of their world" (Harste, 2001, p. 15). Within a dialogic, democratic space, we adopt a critical focus to probe the social and cultural norms that are produced and reproduced in schools. We strive to uncover how some are privileged and have access to wealth and power and others live as objects of discrimination and injustice, asking, "Who makes decisions and who is left out? Who benefits and who suffers? Why is a given practice fair or unfair? What are its origins? What alternatives can we imagine? What is required to create change?" (Bigelow, Harvey, Karp, & Miller, 2001).

One way we attempted to address the above-noted questions and issues was through an inquiry cycle project [ICE]. A typical inquiry cycle might begin with questioning or problem posing, followed by an investigation of the question or problem, creation or synthesis from investigative results, sharing and discussing the synthesis, and reflection on the process (perhaps to be followed by revising the question and beginning the cycle anew) (Bruner, 1965). Others present a variation on this cycle that perhaps might begin with a "wondering and wandering" phase to spark a question or investigative impetus (Short, Harste, & Burke, 1996; Taylor & Otinsky, 2007) or result in action that emerges out of the problem posing, investigation, and dialogue (Freire, 1970). These recursive cycles or spirals of investigation, dialogue, and reflection/action lead to the practice of *education as freedom* as students become increasingly agentic in their learning:

> Students, as they are increasingly posed with problems relating to themselves in the world and with the world, will feel increasingly challenged and obliged to respond to that challenge ... their response to the challenge evokes new challenges, followed by new understandings; and gradually the students come to regard themselves as committed. (p. 57)

With the first cohort of the program, we were largely focused on developing an inquiry based science and math curriculum with a social justice stance. After realizing our residents needed increasing support in becoming social justice educators, for cohort two, in the spring semester, we developed an assignment that would invite them to plan, conduct, and reflect on an authentic social justice mini-inquiry cycle with one of their classes. We first modeled the inquiry process by constructing rotating learning stations that provided the opportunity for residents to engage in "wondering and wandering" (Short, Harste, & Burke, 1996, p. 265) with visual, print, and media sources reflecting school-related social justice issues. After reflecting on the learning station experiences, they were asked to develop and enact an ICE unit within their own disciplines that invited students' interests to drive the curriculum, revolved around authentic open-ended student questions, required various kinds of data to be collected, and concluded with a dissemination of findings (see Appendix). Residents presented their ICE projects, including a rationale, lesson plans, graphic organizers, student work examples, and learning reflections.

Alex

Until we were asked to create curriculum that engaged students with a social justice focus, most of us had not found a way to explicitly theorize our practices within math and science. Those of us who already demonstrated a social justice inclination welcomed the ICE project as a way to connect our moral principles to our teaching and engage students in social action. Using the inquiry cycle modeled when the project was introduced, I invited my students to develop burning questions about the environmental issues that plagued them living in Newark. Their topics ranged from asthma rates, the availability of organic food, the production and processing of garbage, to the amount of electrical energy used. My students designed research projects to examine these issues, which obliged them to collect data in the field and then present their findings. For example, one group problematized the access Newark families have to fresh organic produce. The following year, as a continuation of the social justice inquiry, another resident, Antonio and I in our new role as high school teachers, co-planned, developed, and maintained an urban garden where students could grow fresh fruits and vegetables. To a great extent, our students were invited to apply a social justice lens to biology. From this inquiry project, I learned that when students have projects "that are their own"—that they generate themselves—the quality of their work and the level of their motivation increases greatly. I reflected:

> As much as we like students to question, it is only our questions we want them to ask; it is only our answers that we want them to focus in on. They often do not have space for autonomy and ownership, so it is not surprising that they really came to life during the course of the project.

I also recognized the critical importance of social justice teaching because it provides students with opportunities to "cultivate their own voices on issues that are relevant to them." I continued:

> Pollution and environmental contamination is constantly plaguing urban neighborhoods and that injustice continues to wreak havoc on the health of our students and their families. To make them aware and provide them the resources to study this issue gave me a sense of satisfaction that I did not experience in other assignments. I have never been more proud than when I was able to see my students presenting their work for the ICE project.

Janae

It was really difficult to infuse social justice inquiry in the high school mathematics class. I think this was true for a number of reasons. In my inquiry project, I focused more on using inquiry to talk about how mathematics played out in my students' daily lives. Since I didn't see social justice teaching as fixing society or fighting injustice, I preferred to work on strengthening my students' general critical thinking. Together my students and I explored the question of how math relates to the real world. This gave them the opportunity to both increase their interest in mathematics and identify their real life connections to math too.

Finding a way to use social justice inquiry in mathematics was also difficult for my resident colleague Pri. I do not know if it is a coincidence that he is also a mathematics teacher. He wanted his inquiry project to be authentic to the students but in doing so it did not integrate rigorous mathematics knowledge. He attempted to create an inquiry project that bridged real life, tangible injustices that his students identified in their school lives and the content curriculum. He explained,

> I've always had trouble with social justice and math, relating them together. But I would say the first thing is getting to know students, and the social justice theme comes from, like what are some of the things happening in their lives, that address, what they bring with them, and how is it impacting their learning?

Specifically, one of Pri's honor students wrote an article in the school newspaper about the unfair ways in which the uniform policy was enforced. Her premise was that the school athletes seemed to be permitted to break the policy with more frequency whereas other students were required to strictly adhere to the rules. Once the article was published, the honor students from his class felt like they were being singled out and picked on by security and the school administration. Pri thought that this could generate an interesting research question about which students could gather data and find out whether their hunch was correct. Was there a correlation between one's identity in school and how one was treated in terms of school policy? Unfortunately, Mike, the math department chair, quickly nixed the project as being too political. Pri attempted several other inquiries focusing on school life injustices that students had identified, but they were all discouraged from the administration. This experience heightened his awareness about some of the challenges of conducting authentic social justice inquiry with students.

SOCIAL JUSTICE TEACHING: NURTURING A CRITICAL LITERACY LENS

Alex

> We argue that the active integration of multiple funds of knowledge and Discourse is important to supporting youth in learning how to navigate the texts and literate practices necessary for survival in secondary schools and in the "complex, diverse, and sometimes dangerous world" they will be part of beyond school (Moore, Bean, Birdyshaw, & Rycik, 1999). (Moje, Ciechanowski, Kramer, Ellis, Carrillo, & Collazo, 2004, p. 42)

Echoing the above quote, I think that social justice teaching is about finding ways to build bridges from my students' lives to the curriculum. It is about connecting students to the issues that both surround and affect their lives, whether the students are aware of them or not and helping students cultivate the skills necessary to express themselves, both orally and in written form, in a way that is informed and effective.

My resident colleague, Antonio, says it well when he talks about his role as "empowering students to think critically with science as the lens: looking at the world around them, getting as much information as possible, and then making the decision that best suits their needs. That's the focus, and not being robotic or mechanical or conforming." He continues, "If you are happy because you were able to make a decision based on a reasonable amount of information you should feel fulfilled....but it's problematic if you don't have the ability to do that or have all the information given to you, if it is withheld for some reason or covered up, or you don't have access to it."

Encouraging my students to be critical thinkers also involved developing their literacy skills to "read the word, and the world" (Freire & Macedo, 1987). Like many of my colleagues, I began realizing that the majority of the students lacked the basic skills that they needed to express themselves and to cultivate informed opinions through the deliberate and skillful consumption of information via text or video. Without helping them to develop said skills, the students were just being taught in a way that maximized the amount of memorizing that they had to do without providing them any long term benefits. The issues of reading and writing effectively were left for each successive teacher with the constant quotations of "That is not my job" and "There is not enough time." The problem is that after years of being passed through the system, these problems still exist and the students will leave high school without being prepared for the real world.

I was shocked by my students' inexperience with critical literacy and I was tired of passing the responsibility off to the English teachers like I had heard so many other teachers do. I wanted to be accountable for teaching my students how to critically read science. For me, social justice teaching has become about preparing my students to be able to critically examine the real world regardless of my biology expertise, so that they would be able to make informed decisions in their future.

Janae

I approach social justice teaching slightly differently from Alex. First of all, I think social justice teaching is about seeking to find out what interests my students and believing that they are motivated and willing to learn. That is what I realized. Too often people think that urban students do not want to learn. They seem to believe the stereotypes that they see in the media, but I think it is just the opposite. It is just about finding their motivations. I agree with Delpit (2006) when she writes about students of color, "We live in a society that nurtures and maintains stereotypes ... So as a result of living in this society ... their teachers make big assumptions ... They judge their actions, words, intellects, families, and communities as inadequate at best, as collections of pathologies at worst" (pp. xxiii–xxiv). Because of my own experiences of growing up in Newark and being successful against all odds, my social justice teaching stance begins with the belief that all of my students are motivated and capable of learning.

With this in mind, I want to equip my students for the real world but from my perspective this is less about "fixing society or about fixing injustice" and more about teaching them to "deal/cope." Social justice is about helping others deal with the injustice that has and will inevitably fall upon them, especially when they reach out into the real world and escape from their sheltered and segregated institutions that they call school. It's all about teaching them the tough love situations and that it will not be easy for them. It never will be easy, at least not in their lifetime. There will be amazing times of happiness in their "story" but the story that society wants to make for them will make it difficult. It is about how they fight against that story, by acquiring effective ways to deal with their situations.

So what does this look like in my teaching practice? I think social justice teaching for me is about helping my students to be successful in school by encouraging them to have a strong work ethic and nurturing their abilities to be persistent, resistant, and resilient (Haberman, 1995), all of the traits that have helped me to be successful as a student and a resident and now as an urban teacher. I know that developing their critical literacy and numeracy skills as strategies to navigate the world will prepare them to face problems and scenarios in the real world. This means focusing on the "'skills' within the context of critical and creative thinking" (Delpit, 2006, p. 19).

DEVELOPING A SOCIAL JUSTICE STANCE IN THE THIRD SPACE: LESSONS LEARNED

Writing and reflecting together with some distance from cohort two's residency year about developing a social justice stance has been a powerful experience for all as it has helped us to tease out some of the complexities of this third space work. Below are some of our lessons learned that we feel have implications for general teacher education programs.

1. *Never underestimate the power of learning about the urban youth experience from insiders, urban youth.* As we think about some of the successes of the NMUTR curriculum, we are certain that to truly understand the funds of knowledge of our students we have to spend time with them outside of school settings to discover the multi-dimensions of their identities. By opening a third space between the university, school, and community organizations, we were able to create opportunities for our residents to build authentic relationships with adolescents that provided insights into their lives. As our residents think about social justice teaching, each of them refers to the value of getting to know their students and developing curriculum that serves as a bridge between.

   This was not always an easy endeavor. Some of the cohort two residents, like Marc, struggled to find ways to connect with his All Stars adolescent. He attempted to connect with him using the means that he was comfortable using such as email and texting, which may have worked for some teens but unfortunately did not work at all for his assigned one. We made assumptions that the residents would know how to engage with adolescents intuitively but we soon realized, in preparing the residents for their mentoring roles, that we would need to suggest communication strategies as well as appropriate activities. In fact, in cohort three, we required that they invite their adolescent to do one activity that the resident planned and another that the adolescent planned.

   Connecting our preservice teachers with adolescents is more daunting in a general teacher education program but it can be done. Adolescents can be selected by a mentor teacher and preservice teachers can engage with them in their various classes, at lunch, and in after school programs. This experience adds another dimension to the third space—the voice of the urban student and a window into the strengths and diversity of urban communities.

2. *Becoming a social justice teacher in a third space can take shape in diverse ways.* Too often as teacher educators we only value and accept a particular way of teaching for social justice, explicit, provocative, and deeply action oriented. We judge our preservice teachers through a binary lens of either being a certain kind of social justice teacher or not. As Delpit (2006) reminds us: "Why do the refrains

of progressive educational movements seem lacking in the diverse harmonies, the variegated rhythms, and the shades of tome expected in a truly heterogeneous chorus?" (p. 11). Working in this third space where we strove to listen to all of the members, including the residents, continued to push us to think past our own assumptions and biases and become more open to the individual experiences of our residents. We understand now that our residents enter this social justice work from a variety of different backgrounds and perspectives. We recognize that we have to be careful not to allow "the worldviews of those with privileged positions … to be taken as the only reality" (Delpit, 2006, p. xxv) and to realize that committing to a social justice agenda is a lifelong individual endeavor that will look and feel different for each resident.

3. *Before you can theorize practice for social justice, you need to theorize your own experiences around issues of power and inequity.* As we continued to develop our pedagogy to prepare cohort three residents for social justice, we came to the realization that we had not explicitly given our cohort two residents enough opportunities to problematize their own experiences around power and inequity. In other words, we expected them to develop a particular social justice stance for their students without having multiple scenarios where they thought about what it meant for themselves in their own lives. We addressed some of these identity issues in the summer but then more implicitly throughout the fall. It is not a wonder that the ICE projects for cohort two were varied in terms of their explicit focus on injustice. In fact cohort three residents were more explicit about addressing social justice issues within the context of their content areas.

We believe this may have been for two reasons. First, we were much more transparent about the kinds of curricular issues that we deemed socially just for cohort three. More importantly, unlike cohort two residents, the cohort three residents spent three sessions in the fall immersed in the exploration of social justice in urban classrooms with Gail, one of our doctoral assistants. These interactive workshops invited them to problematize their beliefs about power and difference within the context of public education in U.S. society. Our goal for these was to gain some understanding of the ways in which they made meaning of institutional power and group privilege in their own lives as well as in urban schools. Secondly, we were interested in helping residents, in an immediate way, bring to the fore the reality that they already possessed some level of critical consciousness about issues of power and difference, even if they would not explicitly call it a "social justice" orientation. Accordingly, when asked to develop an ICE project with their students the following spring, most of the cohort three residents selected topics that addressed injustice. For example, one resident chose to draw connections between high school physics and poverty. He developed an ICE project that invited students to examine the concept of energy poverty and analyze the global distribution of energy. By asking students to research and design a poster that illustrated the social implications of living in energy poverty, he hoped that students would understand that living with clean energy is a human right, and not a privilege. We believe that these sorts of workshops are incredibly valuable for preservice teachers as they begin to think about their stance in the classroom.

4. *Should a socially just stance be one of the admissions criteria for urban teaching?* What is the extent of our responsibility in preparing individuals who are themselves diverse in political orientation and commitment to social justice? How does any social justice teacher preparation program address a preservice teacher admitted for her potential, but who has not committed to the social justice mission of the program in practice? Should that resident be pushed to become an agent of change? What implications does this have for admissions into any programs that prepare urban teachers? Although we used the Haberman (1995) protocol to assist in our acceptance decision- making, there was not consensus across the stakeholders of what a social justice stance entails. Are we responsible to educate our residents with "potential" at all costs, for social justice? Over the years we have determined that given the short time span we have for engaging in work with residents, even with the most intensive social justice work, we may be able to "move" them only so far. We have found that there are some future teachers who are either not capable in twelve months, or not willing, to view themselves as social justice educators, or agents of change at all—key principles in the NMUTR. Given this, over the years we worked to develop richer admissions protocols to help us better understand who we could support in this work and who we cannot (see Chapter Three).

NOTE

[1] Katie and Gail, two doctoral assistants involved in the NMUTR, also helped to compose this chapter.

REFERENCES

All Stars Project, Inc. (2007). *Helping youth to grow*. New York, NY.

Apple, M., & Beane, J. (1995). *Democratic schools*. Alexandria, VA: Association for Supervision and Curriculum Development.

Au, W., Karp, S., & Bigelow, B. (2007). *Rethinking our classrooms: Teaching for equity and justice* (Rev. ed.). Milwaukee, WI: Rethinking Schools.

Ayers, W. (2009). Teaching in and for democracy. *Kappa Delta Pi Record, 12*(1–2), 3–10.

Ayers, W., Hunt, J. A., & Quinn, T. (1998). *Teaching for social justice: A democracy and education reader*. New York, NY: New Press.

Banks, J. A., & McGee Banks, C. A. (2010). *Multicultural education: Issues and perspectives* (7th ed.). New York, NY: Wiley.

Bhabha, H. K. (1994). *The location of culture*. London, UK: Routledge.

Bigelow, B., Harvey, B., Karp, S., & Miller, L. (Eds.). (2001). *Rethinking our classrooms: Teaching for equity and justice* (Vol. 2). Milwaukee, WI: Rethinking Schools.

Bourdieu, P. (1973). *Knowledge, education, and cultural change*. London, UK: Harper & Row Publishers.

Bourdieu, P. (1977). *Outline of a theory of practice* (R. Nice, Trans.). Cambridge, UK: Cambridge University Press.

Bronfenbrenner, U. (1989). Ecological systems theory. In R. Vasta (Ed.), *Annals of child development* (pp. 187–249). Boston, MA: JAI Press.

Bruner, J. S. (1965). *The process of education.* Cambridge, MA: Harvard University Press.
Buck, P., & Sylvester, P. S. (2005). Preservice teachers enter urban communities: Coupling funds of knowledge research and critical pedagogy in teacher education. In N. Gonzalez, L. C. Moll, & C. Amanti (Eds.), *Funds of knowledge: Theorizing practices in households, communities, and classrooms* (pp. 213–232). New York, NY: Routledge.
Chu, M. (2014). Preparing tomorrow's early childhood educators: Observe and reflect about culturally responsive teaching. *Young Children, 69*(2), 82–87.
Cochran-Smith, M. (2004). *Walking the road: Race, diversity, and social justice in teacher education.* New York, NY: Teachers College Press.
Cochran-Smith, M., & Lytle, S. (2009). *Inquiry as stance: Practitioner research in the next generation.* New York, NY: Teachers College Press.
Cochran-Smith, M., Shakman, K., Jong, C., Terrell, D., Barnatt, J., & McQuillan, P. (2009). Good and just teaching: The case for social justice in education. *Journal of American Education, 115*(3), 347–377.
Coia, L., & Taylor, M. (2013). Uncovering feminist pedagogy: A co/autoethnography. *Studying Teacher Education: A Journal of Self-Study of Teacher Education Practices, 9*(1), 3–17.
Coia, L., & Taylor, M. (2014). A Co/autoethnography of feminist teaching: Nomadic jamming into the unpredictable. In M. Taylor & L. Coia (Eds.), *Gender, feminism, and queer theory in the self-study of teacher education practices* (pp. 157–169). Rotterdam, The Netherlands: Sense Publishers.
Crawford-Garrett, K. (2013). *Teach for America and the struggle for urban school reform: Searching for agency in an era of standardization.* New York, NY: Peter Lang.
Crenshaw, K. (1991). Mapping the margins: Intersectionality, identity politics, and violence against women of color. *Stanford Law Review, 43*, 1241–1299.
Darling-Hammond, L. (1994). Who will speak for the children? How "teach for America" hurts urban schools and students. *Phi Delta Kappan, 76*, 21–34.
Delpit, L. (2006). *Other people's children: Cultural conflict in the classroom.* New York, NY: The New Press.
Dewey, J. (1902). *The child and the curriculum and the school and society.* Chicago, IL: Phoenix Books.
Dewey, J. (1916). *Democracy and education: An introduction to the philosophy of Education.* New York, NY: Free Press.
Dudley-Marling, C. (2013). Overcoming deficit thinking through interpretive discussion. In P. C. Gorski, K. Zenkov, N. Osei-Kofi, & J. Sapp (Eds.), *Cultivating social justice teachers: How teacher educators have helped students overcome cognitive bottlenecks and learn critical social justice concepts* (pp. 68–83). Sterling, VA: Stylus.
Ellsworth, E. (1989). Why doesn't this feel empowering? Working through repressive myths of critical pedagogy. *Harvard Educational Review, 59*(3), 297–324.
Foucault, M. (1980). Truth and power. In C. Gordon (Ed.), *Power/Knowledge: Selected interviews and other writings, 1972–1977.* New York, NY: Pantheon Books.
Freire, P. (1970). *Pedagogy of the oppressed.* New York, NY: Seabury Press.
Freire, P., & Macedo, D. (1987). *Literacy: Reading the word and the world.* Westport, CT: Bergin & Garvey.
Gay, G. (2000). *Culturally responsive teaching.* New York, NY: Teachers College Press.
Giroux, H. A. (1988). *Teachers as intellectuals: Toward a critical pedagogy of learning.* Westport, CT: Greenwood Publishers.
Giroux, H. A. (1992). *Border crossings: Cultural workers and the politics of education.* New York, NY: Routledge.
Gonzalez, N. (2005). Beyond culture: The hybridity of funds of knowledge. In N. Gonzalez, L. C. Moll, & C. Amanti (Eds.), *Funds of knowledge: Theorizing practices in households, communities, and classrooms* (pp. 29–46). New York, NY: Routledge.
Gonzalez, N., Moll, L., & Amanti, C. (2005). Introduction: Theorizing practice. In N. Gonzalez, L. C. Moll, & C. Amanti (Eds.), *Funds of knowledge: Theorizing practices in households, communities, and classrooms* (pp. 1–24). New York, NY: Routledge.
Haberman, M. (1995). *Star teachers of children in poverty.* West Lafayette, IN: Kappa Delta Pi.
Harste, J. (2001). What education is and isn't. In S. Boran & B. Comber (Eds.), *Critiquing whole language and classroom inquiry* (pp. 1–17). Urbana, IL: National Council for Teachers of English.

Hinchey, P. (2001). *Finding freedom in the classroom: A practical introduction to critical theory*. New York, NY: Peter Lang.

Ladson-Billings, G. (1995). Toward a theory of culturally relevant pedagogy. *American Educational Research Journal, 32*(3), 465–491.

Lather, P. (2006). *(Post)Feminist methodology: Getting lost OR a scientificity we can bear to learn from*. Paper presented at the Research Methods Festival, Oxford, England, 2006, October.

Moje, E., Ciechanowski, K. M., Kramer, K., Ellis, L., Carrillo, R., & Collazo, T. (2004). Working toward third space in content area literacy: An examination of everyday funds of knowledge and Discourse. *Reading Research Quarterly, 39*(1), 38–70.

Moll, L., & González, N. (1997). Teachers as social scientists: Learning about culture from household research. In P. Hall (Ed.), *Race, ethnicity and multiculturalism: Missouri symposium on and educational policy* (Vol. 1, pp. 89–114). New York, NY: Garland.

Moore, D. W., Bean, T. W., Birdyshaw, D., & Rycik, J. A. (1999) Adolescent literacy: A position statement. *Journal of Adolescent & Adult Literacy, 43*, 97–111.

Nieto, S. (2007). *Affirming diversity: The sociopolitical context of multicultural education* (3rd ed.). Boston, MA: Allyn and Bacon.

Peterson, R. E. (2009). Teaching how to read the world and change it: Critical pedagogy in the intermediate grades. In A. Darder, M. P. Bartodano, & R. D. Torres (Eds.), *The critical pedagogy reader* (2nd ed., pp. 305–323). New York, NY: Routledge.

Popkewitz, T. (1998). *Struggling for the soul: What's wrong with humanitarian aid?* London, UK: Picador.

Schultz, K. (2003). *Listening to teach: Responding to the demands of teaching in a pluralistic democracy*. New York, NY: Teachers College Press.

Schwarzenbach, B., Bauermeister, C., & Pfahler, A. (2003). Save your generation [Recorded by Fall Out Boy]. *On Bad Scene, Everyone's Fault: Jawbreaker tribute* [album]. Brooklyn, New York, NY: Dying Wish Records.

Shor, I. (1992). *Empowering education: Critical teaching for social change*. Chicago, IL: University of Chicago Press.

Short, K. G., & Harste, J. C., with Burke, C. (Eds.). (1996). *Creating classrooms for authors and inquirers*. Portsmouth, NH: Heinemann.

St. Pierre, E. A. (2000). Poststructural feminism in education: An overview. *Qualitative studies in education, 13*(5), 477–515.

Suskind, R. (1999). *A hope in the unseen*. New York, NY: Broadway Books.

Taylor, M., & Otinsky, G. (2007). Becoming whole language teachers and social justice agents: Pre service teachers inquire with sixth graders. *International Journal of Progressive Education, 3*(2) 59–71.

Veltri, B. T. (2010). *Learning on other people's kids: Becoming a teach for America teacher*. Charlotte, NC: Information Age Publishing.

Villegas, A. M., & Lucas, T. (2002). *Culturally responsive teaching: A coherent approach*. Albany, NY: State University of New York Press.

Villegas, A. M., & Lucas, T. (2011). A framework for linguistically responsive teaching. In T. Lucas (Ed.), *Teacher preparation for linguistically diverse classrooms: A resource for teacher educators* (pp. 55–72). New York, NY: Routledge.

Vygotsky, L. S. (1978). *Mind in society: The development of higher psychological processes*. Cambridge, MA: Harvard University Press.

Wiggins, G., & McTighe, J. (2005). *Understanding by design*. Alexandria, VA: Association for Supervision and Curriculum Development.

Monica Taylor
Department of Secondary and Special Education
Montclair State University
Montclair, New Jersey

Alexander Diaz
Eastside High School
Newark, New Jersey

Janae Taylor
Arts High School
Newark, New Jersey

Kathryn Strom
Department of Educational Leadership
California State University, East Bay
Hayward, California

Gail Perry-Ryder
Teacher Education and Teacher Development
Montclair State University
Montclair, New Jersey

APPENDIX

Week 1 Inquiry Cycle Graphic Organizer

Knowns: What do you already know, assume, or believe about this?	*Unknowns:* What would you want or need to know more about?

Week 2 Inquiry Cycle Graphic Organizer

Question:

How you will investigate:

Plan: *Roles and Responsibilities for Group Members*

MEET THE AUTHORS FROM CHAPTER FIVE

Antonio Iglesias, I was born in Manhattan to a Colombian mother and Cuban father and was raised in northern New Jersey in a highly homogeneous (96% white) and relatively wealthy (median family income of $80k+) town. I attended public school in a moderately successful district and I was a high school student with strong academics, multiple extracurricular activities, and a job after school. High school was where I truly fell in love with math. Building on an obsessive love of counting and searching for patterns, high school was where I welcomed the relentless math challenges, in particular from Mr. Moloughney, my math teacher of three years. His expectations were high, his demands were infinite, and he accepted no excuses. As I completed one problem, another one appeared twice as difficult as the previous one. Strangely, it was never a very personal relationship (he was rather hated by the general student body), but I surely identified him as a mentor that kept me on my toes and was invested in my growth.

High school was also where I learned that I could be independent. Granted, it wasn't by choice. It was my junior year, and I was taking AP Chemistry. A couple weeks into the school year, our teacher abandoned us for a high profile administrative job in the district (we never got the full story but to us it was abandonment). We cycled through a handful of substitutes; one infamously endangered us as one student was instructed to pick up a hot and broken crucible from the ground barehanded and another was burned after being instructed to put a stopper on a test tube that contained boiling liquids. Another substitute was endearing but clueless. As the months passed and the testing day approached, my bitterness and fear of doing poorly fueled me to take matters into my own hands. I got my parents to buy me a prep book. I outlined the textbook and limited social activities. This situation made me realize that many great teachers gave me the strategies I needed to be able to handle the challenge by myself. As I look towards the kind of teacher I continue to strive to be, my number one priority is to leave students with basic essential skills that allow them to tackle their problems independently.

From there I entered my undergraduate years with the intention of being a math major. I was very undecided throughout and changed my major multiple times, but I eventually decided on Earth and Planetary Sciences. When I left college, I took a gap year. My boyfriend's sister, an English professor at MSU, helped me by getting me a temp job in her department. She then put me in contact with two of her colleagues, Emily Klein and Monica Taylor, who were running the NMUTR. After visiting the previous cohort and going through the program's interview process, it was then that I realized that education was where I wanted to be.

The whole process allowed me to reflect on where I had come from in terms of education and how lucky I was given the circumstances that should have been working against me. After all, I was part of a Hispanic family with a modest income, and it hit me that education shouldn't be about luck and probabilities. There should exist a security regardless of origins. However, the ideals of education require decades before they can be achieved, and, in the meantime, I focus my teaching practices on the most essential skills needed in the meantime, namely, resiliency and self-sufficiency when challenged by situations with few to no resources provided.

Erin Mooney, I have had a passion for the sciences my whole life. I have also been passionate as a learner my entire life; I am a curious individual that loves to experience new phenomenon. I studied biology in college, initially with the intention of becoming a medical doctor. About halfway through college, I needed to fulfill a nonwestern requirement, and on a whim I took an anthropology course, and fell in love with the discipline. I was inspired in particular by critical theory and the concept of social justice. I liked it so much that I decided to major in it as well. After college, I began working in a lab, the next logical step when considering my biology degree and my newfound indecisiveness about what I wanted to do with my career. I knew I wanted to serve and help people, but completing a medical program was something that I was no longer interested in or motivated to pursue.

At heart, and in the back of my head throughout my college career, I always knew that I would deeply enjoy being a teacher. I love learning myself, and also love helping others and having meaningful interactions with them. Becoming an educator was a way to use my skills and my passion for science in order to serve and empower people in their communities in a concrete way. I did some research, and was recommended through a friend to the MSU Prudential Teaching Scholars program that aimed to recruit math and science professionals into Newark classrooms, a precursor to the NMUTR.

I plunged head first into the program and fell in love with the work. Upon completing the program and receiving my teaching certificate, I was hired at Arts High School in Newark to teach biology. Teaching science at a high school for the arts presents its challenges. Many of my students lacked confidence, experience, and at times motivation in the science classroom. Often, students were pulled from class for performances and rehearsals even though academically they could not afford to miss another minute of class time. As the teacher, despite extenuating circumstances, my task was to provide students with real, meaningful experiences in the biology classroom that equip them with a biological lens through which they can interpret the world.

At the end of my first year teaching, I was introduced to, and met with, staff from the NMUTR to discuss the possibility of being a mentor in the following year. I was very interested in working with the program because I was excited and passionate about helping to train new teachers. I also knew that I would be surrounding myself with a supportive community of educators that would help to nurture me as an educator as well. I participated in the interviewing and selection process for the new cohort of residents for the NMUTR and also decided that I would be a biology mentor for the upcoming school year. Over the summer I learned that I would be mentoring Suzanne, someone I had actually gotten to meet and talk with over the course of the interview process. It was very exciting to know that I had another mind/ brain to bounce thoughts and ideas back and forth with, as well as a whole other pair of eyes, ears, and hands. Teaching is intimate in that for the majority of our lessons, we are alone in our critique and reflection of the lesson. More often than not there is no one to debrief with after each of our lessons, and we must rely on our instincts and past experience in moving forward. Now there would be two to experience as well as rehash each lesson. I was excited because I would also be able to try out different co-teaching models and strategies with my resident. I was excited to learn and grow in my own practice from having Suzanne in my classroom. I also was a little hesitant in that I had no idea what to expect from the experience. I had only just finished my first year of teaching and was learning the ropes myself.

Suzanne Poole, my story begins with my career path coming to a major halt. After years of preparation, I realized I no longer wanted to go into the medical field. This was a dream I had envisioned for myself since the second grade after watching an "operation smile" commercial. My interest in science had actually begun long before as I loved to be outside with animals and insects. Some of my earliest memories include trying to figure out how lightning bugs glowed, something which resulted in many deaths since I tried to use the chemical inside them to draw on the sidewalk and on paper hoping I could identify the key to their beauty. During my final year of undergraduate work I realized that I did not want to go to dental school, but my love for biology was still very strong. I had thought that the best, and possibly only way for me to make a change in the world and incorporate my love of science was medicine. However, my view was about to change completely.

Upon graduation I traveled to Tanzania for four months to work in the field of wildlife ecology and human disturbance. I loved every minute of it, including the opportunity I had to communicate with children in nearby villages as well as learn about their culture and the vast social injustices they had to live through. Not only had I always had a passion for science, but I have always been interested in social justice. After returning, I spent my time and paid my bills by working countless customer service jobs and recognized that I truly had a talent for communication (though I did not want to be doing it over the phone or in a maternity store). I began searching out careers in science and social justice. I had been told since I was younger that I would be a great teacher and, until then, I had thought that would in no way be of interest to me. But then I stumbled upon a unique opportunity at MSU.

The NMUTR highlighted both of these areas—teaching and social justice—and seemed like it might be a good fit. I had many doubts about how much I would like it and if this was something I could do for the long run. Nevertheless, with the encouragement of much of my family and friends, I pursued the opportunity. I can remember being completely honest in my interviews and expressing that education was never part of my original plan. I did however explain that it was my pursuit of a meaningful career in science and social justice that brought me there. I am not sure how I made the cut, but I did, and I am so very grateful.

I was so nervous going into that first summer. I had so many fears that I would be awful and that I would hate it. I think my humility allowed me to grow and gain a new understanding for the profession. I never understood what went into being a teacher (that is a good teacher). I had no idea how much time and effort as well as creativity and intellect were involved. I have to say that prior to this experience I also had the false view that "those who can't do, teach." However, now I hold that statement as the highest insult. I truly think it should go more like, "those who can do and who want to see others do just as well or better, teach." Being an educator is so much more that being mediocre in a particular content area. It is having a passion for that content area, knowing it so well you do not have to think about it, and wanting others to be passionate about it as well. Then, on top of all of that, you must able to create an experience in that content area so that others actually do become passionate and gain an understanding. This is what I have come to love to do and why I am so glad I have become an educator.

EMILY J. KLEIN, ANTONIO IGLESIAS, SUZANNE POOLE
AND ERIN MOONEY

5. THE MISSING VOICE

*Using Action Research to Bring Students into
Third Space Preservice Education*

INTRODUCTION

It was time for dismissal. I did my best, organizing my class of 23 1st graders into a line with partners. It's what I was taught to do. Some of them stood still and quiet, listening, while others bounced around, chatting and giggling with each other.

I led them in two lines across the schoolyard to the dismissal area, where they would shake my hand before leaving for the day. I stopped at our "spot" and turned around, expecting to see 23 pairs of eyes focused upon me. But I did not.

The front of the line was intact, as was the back. But the middle chunk was gone. It looked like someone had scooped up a group of my students and thrown them around the yard. They were everywhere, running, playing tag, or rolling around on the concrete in fits of laughter, backpacks tossed midstride. Frustrated and embarrassed, I yelled after them, but my voice landed on deaf ears. I abandoned the line of kids who had walked with me and ran across the yard to chase the others back over.

By the time I returned—my shirt unbuttoned, undershirt damp—my other students had dismissed themselves. What had gone wrong? My principal looked at me, half laughing, half serious, and said, "You'll get the hang of it." (http://www.edweek.org/ew/articles/2013/06/12/35kriegel_ep.h32.html?r= 119741986)

Emily

Recently I read the above article in *Education Week*, and the content struck me as hauntingly familiar, both to me and, I imagined, to many of those in teacher education. In it, the author relayed the challenge he describes above, one for which he felt his teacher education program had failed to adequately prepare him, or even

119

come close to preparing him. In all his semesters of educational theory and lesson plan writing, nobody had helped him think through what he would do when, as he lined up his students for dismissal, he turned around to discover half the line had disappeared into the school playground. How is it, he asked, that he hadn't learned this skill? How could theory and practice better align? While the piece revealed a notion of teacher as technician that did not, perhaps, do justice to the complex craft of teaching, the author speaks to an oft voiced complaint by novice teachers that the messiness of daily practice and the needs that arise from it are rarely the central inquiries of teacher education (Smith & Sela, 2005). My own recollection of my first year of teaching in an urban public school is that while I had a wonderful toolkit of pedagogical strategies, I had no idea how to implement them in my 9th period class of 30 students of enormously varied abilities, specifically when most of the school got out during 8th period and they all congregated outside my classroom waiting for my students to be dismissed. How did I implement sustained silent reading when 25 out of 30 students refused to sit in their chairs at all? All of my teacher education had been taught in isolation: pedagogical strategies, classroom management, and diversity in the classroom. How many of us as new teachers felt like we weren't well prepared by our teacher education programs? When and how *did* we learn the messy intricacies of teaching?

Antonio

In contrast to the article above, soon after Emily read this piece, I, by then a resident graduate, posted a comment on my personal Facebook site about frustration with first period lateness to my class and how it was affecting my earth science students. "How exciting that last year's action research on attendance is reemerging," I noted ruefully. While my action research project, described within this chapter, did not "solve" the problem of lateness for the eternity of my teaching career, it eased an entry into teaching by empowering me with some of the tools to solve those conundrums of teaching that can be so daunting to new teachers and often their deepest concerns (as described in Ginns, Heirdsfield, Atweh, & Watters, 2001). It also helped me to re-focus these questions within a larger frame of social justice and equity for students. I had listed the following as reasons for preservice teachers to engage in action research: it emphasizes the multivariable nature of teaching and the need for teachers to develop problem solving skills; it provides a general, skeletal structure that can be applied to any classroom for any given period of time; it allows for teachers to collaborate and share ideas; and it formalizes all the above processes at an early stage. Teacher education will never satisfactorily create a curriculum that sates the new teachers' desire for practical skills—"How do I best organize my classroom?" "How do I meet the needs of all learners?" "How do I manage the issue of lateness in my first period classroom?" What it can do is provide tools that support them in engaging in those questions with confidence and help to bridge the dichotomy between theory and practice that has so often plagued teacher education.

It can help them answer questions of genuine concern to their practice, even as those questions may lead to larger and deeper questions about issues of power and justice in schools. This chapter is the story of one of the ways in which the NMUTR faculty, mentors, and residents have done that. It is also one of the ways we have tried to reframe the debate between preservice teachers and their faculty about what kind of preparation is most valuable.

PURPOSE/CONTEXT

Emily

After a brief respite from the hard work during winter break, in January 2012, residents gathered in Karina's room over homemade muffins and coffee to begin their action research cycle on what is often a dreaded professional development day. January often marks the most difficult month in the residency program. After six months, the gleam of the program has worn off. Residents are tired from the summer and fall work and right after residents teach their fall curricular unit, faculty and mentors require they begin to take over the class where they implemented that unit. This marks their first day-to-day teaching responsibility and while they are usually only teaching one class, many are daunted by daily teaching responsibilities. Others beginning to take on even more teaching responsibility (this may vary with some taking on the entire teaching load of their mentors as early as December and others not doing so until February or March). Additionally, over winter break, residents reflect on their fall learning goals and then meet individually with the faculty to discuss their progress; sometimes these are difficult conversations where we focus heavily on areas for growth that need to happen in the following months. Every year, by January, one or two residents are struggling so much that they are on "probation" at this point, meaning we have put together a contract of non-negotiable goals they need to meet in order to continue on in the program. In our first session as a cohort the residents see the span of projects they will engage in for the spring: discourse tools, action research, inquiry cycle experience (ICE), instructional rounds, weekly reflective logs, as well as their additional teaching load. The terminology is new and they know enough to know everything will have to be done again and again until we believe it has met our standard. A full day to work together is a luxury, but when we walked into Karina's classroom that winter morning the mood was still serious. Monica and I brought food (with a gluten free breakfast for Suzanne and a kosher one for Marc). Food always helps and we never forget the coffee.

Monica often introduces action research to teams she works with by assuring them that it is a formal version of what they do as teacher researchers and kidwatchers every day. Like McNiff and Whitehead (2006), we took an emancipatory perspective towards action research. They write:

> Action research can be a powerful and liberating form of professional enquiry
> because it means that practitioners themselves investigate their own practice

as they find ways of living more fully in the direction of their educational values. They are not told what to do. They decide for themselves what to do, in negotiation with others. This can work in relation to individual and also collective enquiries. (p. 8)

In that way, action research was also well aligned with our understanding of the third space and as a means of disrupting the hierarchy of university and classroom knowledge.

Since Price's work in 2001 detailing his exploration of using action research in preservice teacher education courses, there has been some increase in using action research as a tool to support the formal learning of students in teacher education programs (such as the work of Cochran-Smith, Barnatt, Friedman, & Pine, 2012; Everett, Luera, & Otto, 2007; Levin & Rock, 2003; Smith & Sela, 2005). Although, action research has been used for over 50 years with teachers internationally for multiple purposes from advancing the knowledge of teaching, to forwarding a reform education agenda (Robinson & Meerkotter, 2003; Smith & Sela, 2005; Somekh & Zeichner, 2009) overall, it still remains largely underused in the area of preservice education. As Price (2001) and others point out, action research at the preservice level has its own unique challenges. While the process always requires large inputs of time, resources, and commitment required on the part of the facilitators and teachers, the student teaching semester is often a stage where the cognitive demands on preservice teachers are already overwhelming and it may seem, therefore, an inopportune moment to choose to engage them in a complex and demanding process (Smith & Sela, 2005). And yet, of course, we also believed based on the literature, that this was an opportunity to help shape their identities as teacher researchers, leaders, and inquirers, and that "entering in" at this moment was an ideal one, something Goodnough, (2010) also found in his work. Some research findings even indicate that it is in the earliest stages of teachers' careers that they are most likely to want to engage in this kind of educational research (Vogrinc & Valencic Zuljan, 2009). We envisioned that action research could help grow their "*possible selves*" (Goodnough, 2010), especially as we did so in a third space construct where theory and practice—the academy and the space of the practitioner—were both valued.

When the residents first heard about the action research project, reactions were mixed, as faculty knew it would be. One of the earliest challenges faculty faced was helping our math and science mentors and residents move from a purely experimental/quantitative view of research to a qualitative, holistic one. This was not unexpected. Every year when Monica advises school teams around their action research through a Dodge grant, she encounters such resistance, but by the end of the year after working with the teachers they learn to distinguish it from scientific research and begin to see its usefulness. Action research struck the residents as being the exact opposite of what scientists hope to learn from undergoing experiments— the test subjects were never the same, the variables were plentiful and could not be controlled, and the data acquisition seemed inexact at best. To some it was a "bogus" form of research that would not provide any accurate data and therefore no actual results or useful information; Dave even questioned how it was possible action research could be valid. Another resident felt it came off as "trying too hard" and Antonio was sure that he was averse to it. But, when hearing the term triangulation, he first thought of how seismologists take earthquake data from various stations to triangulate an earthquake's epicenter, a tried and true measure of exactness.

The literature on action research suggests engaging in the process has a number of important benefits for teachers. Some researchers such as Ginns, Heirdsfield, Atweh, and Watters (2001) and Smith and Sela (2005) suggest action research can been used as a means to engage new teachers in becoming more reflective and analytical about their practice while others, such as Ginns, Heidsfield, Atwey, and Watters (2001), Gitlin, Barlow, Brubank, Kauchak, and Stevens (1999), Price, (2001), and Somekh and Ziechner (2009) believe it can be used to make connections between theoretical and practice based knowledge. Goodnoough, (2010) and Mertler (2011) believe that we grow teachers' sense of themselves as professionals by providing them with tools to systematically examine their own practice, while adding to the knowledge base of teaching through sharing that knowledge.

THE PURPOSE OF ACTION RESEARCH IN THE RESIDENCY

Like Price (2001), we wanted our residents' action research projects to be "'authentic', in that the teacher candidates would explore issues and ideas that they puzzled about in their day-to-day teaching" (p. 45). We knew it was important they have time to be deeply engaged in questions that were of urgent importance to them as that would drive the meaning making and help make theory more significant. And yet as other university partners have so successfully done (Ginns, Heirdsfield, Atweh, & Watters, 2001; Robertson, 2005; Robinson & Meerkotter, 2003), we also wanted to "widen" the lens to encourage them to ask bigger questions about teaching and learning, equity and social justice

Cochran-Smith, Barnatt, Friedman, and Pine's (2012) study of preservice action research examined how their cornerstone project might directly focus action research towards improving the learning outcomes for students in the classrooms of preservice teachers. Their research revealed that students focused not only on increasing student knowledge, but also on creating and building student relationships, something that was extremely important to us as well. Similarly, Levin and Rock's (2003) research on learning outcomes for preservice teachers doing action research found increased "insights into their students' perspectives and an increased awareness of their students' needs" (p. 140). Although our summer experience had focused significantly on building relationships with students, we saw the action research project as part of our spiral curriculum; now residents could return to focus on those relationships, but within the classroom context. The purpose of doing action research in a residency program becomes one of many experiences to build "inquiry as stance," which "refers to a long-term and consistent positioning or way of seeing rather than a single point in time or an activity. This concept is intended to capture the lenses through which teachers see and how they generate knowledge that guides practice" (Cochran-Smith, Barnatt, Friedman, & Pine, 2012, p. 28).

Acknowledging that there are a variety of definitions, for our purposes action research involves a series of inquiry cycles: planning, acting, observing, and reflecting (Goodnough, 2010) which are, as Price (2001) writes, "systematic, intentional, collaborative, and democratic in intent and process" (p. 43). Echoing Hubbard and Power (2003), we agree that action research provides teachers with ownership of their professional learning and development. Conducting action research that relied on "classrooms as laboratories" and "students as collaborators" (Hubbard & Power, 2003, p. xiii) allowed residents to change how they worked with students and systematically examine their practices. Action research involves what McNiff (2010) calls "finding ways to improve your practice and then explaining how and why you have done so" (p. 6). The focus is on "How do I improve my practice?" (Whitehead, 1989). In addition, it engages them as reflective practitioners based on actual data and not just on their perceptions and feelings about why they think something is the way it is. For preservice teacher educators all this builds a notion of teacher as teacher researcher from their earliest classroom experiences.

CREATING A THIRD SPACE THROUGH ACTION RESEARCH

Struggling in the Third Space

Year one we floundered. Monica had worked with teams of teachers doing action research in schools for years, and in designing the residency faculty were confident that they could build collaboration between mentors and residents and initiate school-wide change efforts by having them co-construct action research projects. In general, we struggled to bring the mentors into the curriculum. At first we asked them to participate in weekly class meetings, but soon recognized that this was an enormous time burden for them. They seemed reluctant to step on our toes, and had enough to do guiding the residents through the daily work of navigating their own classrooms. We were trying both to build relationships with them and simultaneously figuring out whether or not we even shared the same values about teaching and learning. Although our challenges of doing action research in a third space construct (a space where practice and theory are both valued) were part of the larger challenge of *creating* that third space, our experience year one *also* mirrored some of the research on preservice teachers and action research.

The Mentor Teacher

One of the main challenges Price (2001) identified in doing preservice action research is that of doing it in another teacher's classroom: "Sometimes, their experimentation was conducted within the confines and parameters of relationships and representations of knowledge established by the mentor-teachers" (pp. 55–56). Mentor teachers, while supportive, often set limitations as well for what was possible and what was legitimate to study: "The action research experience occurs at a time when the teacher candidates are beginning to shape and mold their teaching practice, and, although the mentor's classroom may be an important site for this development, it can also unwittingly stifle and impinge upon development" (p. 58). Throughout his and other research studies, (Gitlin, Barlow, Brubank, Kauchak, & Stevens, 1999), it is clear that tensions between the mentor and preservice student engaging in action research as they navigated doing research in their classrooms can be a significant stumbling block.

Other research studies (Levin & Rock, 2003; Valli, 2000) indicate issues were less about tension between the preservice teacher and the mentor teacher than about the role of the mentor: was she a support person simply there to offer advice? Or a full collaborative partner? Levin and Rock (2003), in their study of preservice/mentor collaborative action research, found that mentors seemed to believe that the action research project was "ultimately the responsibility of the pre-service teacher" (p. 245). Thus, even when action research is done by preservice teachers, it is usually conducted in isolation as a coursework assignment with a mentor teacher acquiescing to the project rather than with mentors who are authentically and deeply engaged in the process. Simultaneously other data indicate there is potential for action research to support building relationships between the mentor and the mentee, and to disrupt the traditional hierarchical dynamic between the mentor as knower and mentee as doer (Levin & Rock, 2003). In addition, beliefs of mentor teachers are often contextualized within schools that may have different value systems than the preservice teachers' teacher education programs. As Gitlin, Barlow, Brubank, Kauchak, and Stevens (1999) write, "…much of what may be accomplished within the university classroom is washed out if student teachers are not able to take part in an alternative socialization process in the schools that places value on an inclusive, broad-based approach to knowledge production and decision making" (p. 768).

Part of the challenge was that in that first year we had not yet developed the relationships needed to truly engage in third space work; we found that to simply say "the hierarchies are dismissed!" was not enough. Without relationships in place, we struggled to figure out how to bring the mentors into the curriculum. Only one of the mentors had any experience with action research herself and they were overwhelmed with other responsibilities with the residency and as general teacher leaders in their departments and schools. Shortly, they left data collection and analysis to the residents and became sideline coaches in the process. Faculty were discouraged by their seeming lack of engagement and in the midst of this project and half a dozen others we struggled to be reactive and find ways to provide scaffolding for the mentors to become more engaged. Overestimating the amount of time we should spend on the action research cycle, the process dragged on and the residents felt frustrated by the project. The work quickly reverted to a traditional academic hierarchy with university faculty in charge of leading the knowledge making and faculty realized that they needed to re-think the way we were using action research in the residency. This was part of our larger thinking about how to better bring the mentors into the curriculum as a whole, with action research as one piece of that. With a year of relationship building and good will developed, we all seemed more willing to engage in joint work and build our community of practice.

The Teacher Educators Do Action Research Together

In planning for year two, Monica and I made a significant shift. Central to this shift was the assumption that in order for mentors to take ownership in the third space they would have to experience doing action research on their own. Monica and I felt we needed to do something to actively disrupt the customary hierarchies between faculty and mentors and find a way to engage the mentors as different kinds of knowledge generators. Traditionally mentor teachers hold practitioner knowledge and faculty—theoretical knowledge. While faculty wanted to highlight mentors' practitioner knowledge, they also wanted to blur the lines between boundaries of practitioner and theoretical, and maker and enactor of knowledge (Cochran-Smith & Lytle, 1993). In the fall, Monica and I asked all mentor teachers to enroll in a 3-credit course for self-study and action research, paid for by the university.

Over the course of the semester, mentors and faculty from both the elementary and secondary cohorts worked together on exploring self-study and action research projects. We read together, wrote reflections about our work as mentors and teacher educators, responded to each other on a weekly basis in small groups, created action research questions and plans, collected data, analyzed our data, and wrote up final papers which we shared with each other. Many of us also presented reflections on our work together at a number of national and international conferences (Klein, Taylor, Monteiro, & Romney, 2013; Taylor et al., 2012). We believed it was critical to this process that Monica and I were equally engaged in self-study and action research both as a means of modeling the process, but also as a way of shifting towards being co-learners. They also developed in their roles as teacher leaders in their schools. As a group, even though the time period for the research had ended, most mentors felt as if the research had not and continued to carry out their action in the classroom.

Erin

Initially, I was not really sure what action research entailed, but I was excited about being able to take a closer look at my own practice, something not always afforded to the mentors. Prior to conducting action research, as a relatively new teacher myself (I had only been teaching for one and a half years when I began as a mentor), I was still learning to balance the workload that being a newer teacher involved. I had not had a chance to take a step back or look more closely at an aspect of my practice besides what is required to be a successful teacher day-to-day. As we began to work together I wondered, "Okay, so what does that actually look like in the classroom?"

as well as how I would have enough time to teach five classes, simultaneously conduct research, all the while being a supportive, available mentor to Suzanne. At first, the process seemed a bit overwhelming.

Once we started discussing how to conduct action research, what constitutes data, as well as the broad range of topics, themes, practices, and methods for collecting data in the classroom, I started to feel like there was a long list of things about which I was curious, all of which were fascinating and worthy of an investigation. While working at Arts High School, a magnet school for students of the arts, Kim (another mentor) and I noticed many students felt that from the get go they were not cut out for math or science, and approached the course with an attitude that they were doomed to fail because they just "weren't good" in these subjects. We decided to collaborate on investigating the role of science and math in the lives of Arts High School students. The goal was to then design more appealing, interdisciplinary lessons in math and science that would incorporate the arts and better serve our talented student body.

Through Kim and my investigations and work with our students, we ended up creating a two-day, cross curricular lesson on the Fibonacci sequence that covered math, biology, and also involved aspects of music and drawing. The lessons included a hands-on activity that allowed students to investigate flowers and pineapples for the Fibonacci sequence or ratio. After these lessons, we used surveys to get students' opinions on the lessons and also to check for understanding of the learning objectives. We were interested in understanding whether students were learning or not learning in this new type of lesson and were internalizing the content and skills embedded within the lessons. As our research came to a close, Kim and I decided that we needed better professional development on interdisciplinary lesson design and decided to use our research results to apply for a grant to receive funds for just that.

On a concrete level, the experience of doing the action research cycle also allowed the mentor teachers to become the facilitators of the process for the residents in the spring semester. By the time we met in January, all the mentor teachers were prepared to lead the cycle with the residents, much as faculty had facilitated it with them in the fall. Mentors led the monthly day long working sessions that introduced residents to new aspects of the cycle, helped them work through their questions, action research plans, data, and writing process. Faculty served as secondary guides and sounding boards about what came next, but it became the first time during the year when the faculty and mentors co-taught and mentor teachers took on a new kind of teacher educator role in the program.

Bringing Action Research to the Residents

Each monthly session introduced a new piece of the cycle. As a group, mentors decided to present their research projects informally to the group so that they had some idea of the varied topics possible as well as the different methods of collecting

127

and analyzing data. Once the residents heard about a lot of the work the mentors had done, they were set to the task, just as the mentors had been, of brainstorming a list of questions/topics that they had about their own teaching. In the following sessions we introduced and used a graphic organizer that we used in our faculty/mentor research as well. The template helped residents to organize their ideas and complete a framework for conducting their research (See Appendix). Would they use journaling with students, test scores, interviews, videotaping, etc. to gather their data? The method of data collection was directly dependent on the research question being asked. The other key piece to designing the action research plan was to make sure that the amount of work needed to be done by the teacher was both doable and if possible a part of normal classroom routine. If the action research itself were too cumbersome and time consuming, it would not be a practical tool for teachers to use to study their practice. All of these decisions were made in collaboration with their mentors, who were able to bring to bear their own recent experiences designing and implementing action research with residents who had observed them do so in the fall semester. However, even as they supported the residents, over the course of their projects, the residents took ownership of these projects.

I found this stage of the process interesting and challenging for me as a mentor in that I did not want my own opinions to influence the process; rather I wanted to help scaffold and support Suzanne in making the best choice. I wanted Suzanne to feel ownership over her topic and choose it based on what she was genuinely curious about. I did, however, also need to have a voice in helping her choose a topic that would be most meaningful to her in terms of where she was in her practice. As her mentor I had insight into that, and as well, we shared students and a classroom.

I found that the best strategy to use was one of asking questions and really having Suzanne talk out what she was thinking about. We discussed what some of her wonderings were about the class with which she was working. I was deeply aware of what she was saying and really tried to ask questions rather than offer her an opinion, a strategy I had learned to use often as a mentor when debriefing. The mentor/resident dialogue, I felt, worked best was when it was supportive, yet challenging and forced the resident /mentor to critically reflect and talk about what they think. In supporting Suzanne to choose a meaningful topic, I needed to get her to think and talk aloud about what was on her mind. We discussed the biology class that she had been preparing lessons for and teaching and also talked about what she felt her strengths and weaknesses were.

We brainstormed a list of several different topics, including things like how to increase homework submission, how to help students develop study skills, and also how to have students reflect upon their own learning. In particular, the last topic seemed to be the most salient as Suzanne and I asked each other these types of questions in part of our discussion: what do students think/feel about learning biology and how can we use student reflection and feedback effectively? We talked about possible strategies for gathering data for each of the topics that were brainstormed. For example, if Suzanne decided to choose the topic of homework completion/

submission how would she gather and collect data? What would she do? We agreed that the best way for her to select a topic was to look at what was most relevant at that particular point for her as a resident on her journey to becoming a teacher as well as what data methods would be feasible and not overburden her.

NEGOTIATING THE RESEARCH PROCESS: TWO CASES

Conflicting Aims

Emily. One of the challenges we faced in expanding our work in building the third space to including the residents in that dialogue was in having conflicting aims between the faculty, mentors, and residents. As revealed in the *Ed Week* story opening this chapter, new and developing teachers are often overwhelmed with concerns about the "practicalities of teaching." One study of a university/school partnership using action research found that while the university wanted teachers to engage deeply in projects of social justice and change, the teachers were, at least initially, interested in focusing on "practical problems" (Ginns, Heirdsfield, Atweh, & Watters, 2001); or what Nieme (2002) calls "wholeness in teaching" (p. 771). Similarly, we knew that if we were committed to the questions and concerns that were of genuine interest to our residents, and through our third space framework we were committed to making them co-constructors of the curriculum, then we would have to allow space for these problems. The challenge became how we could bridge their inquiries within the context of the greater concerns of our program.

But making connections between individual practice and school change can be extremely difficult for preservice teachers at such an early moment in their career. Valli's (2000) work on preservice teachers doing action research projects made explicit attempts to influence them to engage in more school change projects, but she found, "Because teachers continue to function as isolated practitioners, with institutional change efforts set in motion without them, they do not simultaneously learn about professional community and teaching. Lessons about teaching are learned through individual reflection rather than collegial dialogue" (p. 723). The traditional structures of schools do not lend themselves well to supporting both an individual and a school change focus. As we thought about how to develop action research as a piece of the residency we approached this in a slightly different way. Because we work with the residents over the course of twelve months (and then for three years of induction), we saw this particular project as building the initial skills that would facilitate institutional change. Key to helping them envision this "possible self" was the leadership role the mentors took in facilitating the action research cycle.

Owning the Question

We found that the challenges in the literature resonated in the experiences of our residents. It was, in fact, a difficult time for residents to figure out how and what to study, given the enormity and newness of their teaching worlds. Teachers face the challenge of "owning the question" at a time when their own understandings and beliefs about teaching and learning are developing and shifting. Price (2001) suggests that, "to encourage students' understandings of the connections among research and teaching in the daily lives of teachers, a framework to help them pursue a research focus seems important. They might follow an inquiry process, but the focus of the inquiry might shift and change" (p. 56). In this way, emphasizing the emergent and fluid nature of the action research process is important; students need opportunities to allow for shifting questions as their own needs and learning shifts. Some university partners engaging in action research with first year teachers found that teachers very early in their careers wanted the university faculty to take a greater lead in providing "expert advice" and resisted ownership of the research questions (Ginns, Heidsfield, Atwey, & Watters, 2001).

Similarly, Cochran-Smith, Barnatt, Friedman, and Pine's (2012) study of pre-service action research found that students,

> experienced significant angst as they struggled to negotiate the messiness of learning to teach while attempting to inquire into practice in a systematic and effective way. They did not see the natural connections between teaching and inquiry, and they regarded these as two disparate entities. Those who were most successful had real ownership of their questions. (p. 29)

The Challenges

Antonio. I found the biggest challenge that came from doing action research was not having a full grasp of what it was, and that not being as open as I ought to have been to the practice (i.e., being too judgmental) I did not engage as freely I should have with it. As such, when I began to think about what I would do, I hit a wall. My thoughts either failed to capture an action, did not provide a suitable setup to acquire data, or both. Also, there were so many challenges from the residency year that prioritizing one focus of my action research was difficult. My class was an Earth Science class held on B-days during first block. The group of students were from various graduating classes but were predominantly juniors and seniors. There were nineteen total with the majority of them being boys and five girls; they came from a variety of backgrounds with roughly half being Hispanic, a quarter African-American, and a quarter Brazilian/Portuguese. Most of the students did not need the course to graduate, having already accumulated all the science credits they needed to graduate (then three years, today, incoming graduating classes require four years). The majority did not do extra-curriculars within the school; however, roughly half did have jobs outside of school.

The main problem and challenge I faced was a combination of low attendance and high lateness. Often, the first bell of the day would ring and a quarter of students would be present (with numbers as low as two of nineteen). Chatting with other teachers, it appeared that was not a unique situation/challenge but an epidemic in the school. To me, it seemed mind boggling, both because I had had parents that had emphasized timeliness and also because graduation was legally contingent on good attendance.

Suzanne.   My research grew out of a note a student wrote to me prior to winter break while I was out. It said that, although they liked me, they were moving too quickly through the material and they were struggling to understand the content. While at Arts High School for my residency, I had a variety of students at different levels including students with IEPs. Each of the students was involved in one of the performing arts and they were therefore very passionate and dramatic, which I found could be a good or bad thing when it came to the classroom. Students sat in groups of four, according to the results of a survey that determined what type of learner they were. The groups included students with different learning styles: either audio, visual, or tactile. This way the groupings were left up to "destiny" and not just what I wanted.

Although they were very well behaved and had few attendance issues, I was struggling to teach meaningful lessons that really captured their attention. As the spring semester began and I opened up my classroom for feedback from students, more suggested that I slow down when teaching and go over topics more thoroughly. This feedback, although disappointing, was not surprising. If I was able to detect this need for change in myself, I realized it was inevitable that my students would feel the same way. This encouraged me to transform this idea from just a personal goal for the spring to the impetus for my action research.

I also realized that the very fact that my students suggested I slow down my teaching and cover material more thoroughly was a representation of the investment my students were making in their own learning. If I were to ignore their request, it would be as if I was neglecting their desire to learn and the conditions in which they needed to do so. As I began to write and talk about this, Emily, Monica, and Erin saw a shift in my relationship with my students and my thinking about my teaching; it became more than just a research project, but a way of approaching teaching and learning that was inquiry based, and student-centered.

Navigating the Research Process

Antonio and Suzanne.   Learning to navigate the action research process was a theme that emerged for both of us; we found it to be neither straightforward nor linear. One of the important pieces for many of our residents was returning to engaging with their students as partners with their students, something that had fallen by the wayside since their summer internship experience. As Whitehead and Fitzgerald (2006) point out "pupils are frequently the 'forgotten partners', the recipients of pedagogical practices rather than seen as integral to their construction and success" (p. 44). This was the case in both of our research projects.

Antonio. I asked a series of questions in my action research that began with the following: "How can the teacher actively encourage students to become more reflective and accountable when considering their own daily promptness?" To be able to encourage certain behaviors is not a process that occurs overnight: the first step was to understand the students' motives before a course of action could be taken. The guiding supporting question was: "What do students think about attendance and promptness?" I expected that the responses to this would be incredibly diverse, though I hoped to see certain trends emerge.

To that, it became important to realize that the purpose of this action research was to foster better habits and therefore I considered a supporting question: "Does a space for students to reflect about their attendance build the value of good attendance and promptness?" I asked students to reflect often, so that they had multiple opportunities to share their voice and had time to refine their opinions. Furthermore, I wanted to see if the repetition was able to have any effect on the students' opinions (whether positive or negative).

I acknowledged that the students were not in a vacuum; their decision-making skills were not entirely organic but are impressionable to the opinions of their family, friends, school, teenage culture, etc. The question that most intrigued me was "How do the school culture and faculty contribute to student opinions of promptness?" I knew that the administration and faculty have tremendous power to set many of the beliefs and the tone present in a school, and a school's success or perpetual challenges could be traced back to how students perceive such a tone.

Once I could understand what the students' initial opinions of the students were, I then delved more deeply into understanding how students perceive their own actions or inactions both in terms of the academic sphere and elsewhere. Understanding this was guided by the supporting question of: "Do students identify a connection between their grades and their promptness/attendance?" Conversely, I wondered "Do students associate any consequences (not just academically) with strong and poor promptness/attendance?" I hoped students would explore explicitly how their actions have consequences, and that they would see opportunities for actions that might bring about more positive consequences. Finally I committed to the question: "How can teacher interventions improve student promptness/attendance?" I engaged in the principle of cause and effect, to set up multiple junctures at which the students could reevaluate personal belief systems, and to trace the development of all of the supporting questions above as my actions served to bring about student reactions.

Throughout the research cycle, I often wondered if I should change certain aspects of my teaching. After all, having conversations about attendance could only convince the students so much; I wondered if they needed to experience the consequences of good and poor attendance habits. Enough students could make it to class in time without much learning being lost and recognizing this habit, I wondered if I should increase the content in a day's instruction. However, evaluating this idea proved that the expected results would be more harmful than helpful: I worried there would be decreased learning and assessment results would decline.

Another approach I considered was to have students that arrived particularly late (forty minutes into the eighty minute block) not be allowed to engage in the current learning activity but instead read an assigned text and answer questions that were parallel to the day's content. However, I dismissed this approach because I felt it could suggest that the textbook was something negative, a punishment instead of a consequence. Furthermore, students that are frequently late and, particularly, those that benefit most from differentiation could possibly learn less from reading than from joining the class with whatever time remained as well as become fatigued and bored from always having to read. Accordingly, I decided that I would maintain my current teaching practices, highlight the conversations on attendance, and seek student reflections constantly. I include this extensive explanation of both my question development and action plan (and rejection of plans) because it is integral to my development as a reflective practitioner who thinks deeply and carefully about the implications of my questions and practices.

Over the following six weeks, I engaged in a series of reflective semi-structured conversations with my students built around question prompts and youtube videos (about issues of teens, sleep, and lateness) as well as survey data, responses from parents, and attendance data. As students engaged in dialogue with me and my mentor teacher I kept track of attendance rates and strove to better understand the issues influencing attendance and lateness.

I felt the conversations I had with students were among the most enlightening of my year as a resident. They revolved around two main themes: the value of school and accountability. Students who took earth science generally fell in the bottom percentage of the school academically. The students were aware of their academic performance in school and had reacted to it in two ways. First, as upperclassmen, they saw no value in trying very hard when a few years of trying left them with little success. Second, the school had failed to meet their needs. Many had already taken career paths that showed no connection to their studies at school. They identified that they would have benefited from attending a trade/technical school, but they saw no reason to make the switch since they were so deep into school and near graduation. And as for accountability, all of them were well aware that the consequence of multiple absences was an empty threat. All of them knew someone who had absences totaling 20+, who was still permitted to graduate or move on to the next grade. As a result, if on a given day they just did not feel like going to school, they felt no need to push themselves to attend. My experience highlights the twists and turns of navigating action research and negotiating with students and responding to their needs. There were rarely clear and easy solutions to my questions and I was constantly attempting and revising strategies, a responsive approach that would serve me well as a new teacher.

Suzanne. I similarly engaged my students as co-collaborators in my research project. Using the feedback of my students as well as my own daily written self-reflections to shape my lessons, I began to identify ways I could achieve my goal of helping to deepen student understanding. I collaborated with Erin on ways to collect my data, which included exit tickets from students asking them to critique each lesson, for example: "Which part of the lesson did you feel helped you understand the information the most (video, hands on activity, guided notes, etc.) and which helped the least? How could Ms. Poole improve the next lesson?" I also began completing a self-reflection chart after each lesson that included what my lesson design looked like, how I felt the lesson went, how I could improve the lesson, which activities students learned the most from, and which they did not learn from (after reviewing students responses). I had hoped to compare the student responses with actual assessment scores. My hope was to plan lessons and exit tickets that assessed what students were learning and how they learned it best in order to create assessments that specifically matched the objectives on the exit tickets. This would provide quantitative data that measured how each student learned best and which types of lessons and activities should be utilized in future lessons. However, at the time, this was too large of a task to complete and I was unable to track student responses on exit tickets to how they scored on their actual tests. Again, navigating the process of action research was often half the challenge involved, but preparing residents to become responsive and reflective about how to manage the challenges of teaching, design answers to their questions (and when those designs were too ambitious figuring out how to quickly regroup and create new designs).

Ultimately it was the *process* of engaging with students that proved to be more powerful than the pedagogy of finding new learning activities. Although I had planned to learn how to improve my pedagogy from my final results, I ended up learning much more from the process. From the very moment I began providing my students with the opportunity to not only participate, but to help actually shape the class lessons, they began to take more of an interest in the lessons. This gave the students a feeling of ownership in the classroom and therefore helped to create a learning environment they wanted to be a part of. This environment inevitably increased student participation in the lesson, which then led to an improvement in student grades. Although I was unable to make a link to specific lesson activities I did see an overall improvement in the students.

IMPLICATIONS

Meeting Theory and Practice: Building Reflective Practitioners

Antonio. In preparing to write for this chapter, I journaled,

> In that moment, I don't think I knew what action research meant to me. I think our action research work came at a time when the program was most chaotic, so, admittedly, I don't think I processed it as deeply as I could/should have. With that said, I think I could at least value action research as being a cornerstone to improving my own practice as well as a continuation of all the reflection

the program valued. I think the biggest shift from anything prior, though, was that action research was the first time we really invested in the before, during, and after of an action, whereas everything before tended to focus more on the during and the after. Personally, action research allowed me to be reflective of some components of my teaching that I normally wouldn't have addressed otherwise. After all, the reasons students don't value education comes strongly from the adults in their lives with the teachers being a major component. If I can't provide them with a classroom that is relevant and valuable, then why do they even need me to be there?

I think this reflection speaks to the role of action research as one of the more valuable programmatic experiences of connecting theory. For me, the focus on tying our program's theoretical focus on reflection with tangible tools for improving practice was a distinct shift in thinking about classroom dynamics. I found that over the course of my first year of teaching I consistently used the principles of action research. Namely, whenever I had a problem or challenge in the classroom, I would chat with one of my fellow teachers. The conversations that would ensue would very much mimic many of the steps undertaken in action research: What's the problem? How did you address the problem? What happened as a result of your actions? How do you know? Should you keep doing that? What else can you do? Even though my original concerns were that action research was unscientific, I came to believe that after all, if there is something a classroom is not it is reproducible. Even if I continue with this delusion that I can recreate the same action again and again, the students, the day of the week, the weather, will never all align the same way twice. So, what action research forced me to reconcile is that teaching does not equal science.

Building Residents As Teacher Leaders

Emily.   One of our goals for engaging with the mentors in action research in the semester prior to working with the residents and having them take the lead, was to use this as a means of developing leadership capacity. We see teacher leadership as a relational process "that mobilizes other people to improve their practice" (Taylor, Goeke, Klein, Onore, & Geist, 2011, p. 921). It is "motivated by a desire to help students and support their fellow teachers, not to enforce a new policy or evaluate others' competencies. Thus, a key asset of teacher leadership is mobilization of naturally occurring and informal collaborations among teachers" (p. 921). Goodnough's (2010) research on action research has demonstrated its potential for building broader initiatives by supporting coordination of efforts, and we believed that this would help lay foundation for the mentor teachers in their departmental work as we prepared more and more peers to work with them in the years to come. The mentors' continuing work on their own action research project created a vision for the residents of the potential for such work as a means of classroom and school change.

Antonio.   I quickly realized that to have significant impact, I would have to broaden my action research to work with others in my department. Ultimately, I found that for one to be able to achieve success, a larger team of teachers would need to collaborate to achieve success (such as the notable improvements seen at Arts High School that I have witnessed and Emily has seen described by other residents). My research suggested that students, craving structure, needed consistency across multiple classroom settings and that without consistency and high expectations, the students feel little need to embrace positive habits, and, appropriately, will only work towards doing the least required possible, especially when the bar is set so low in terms of attendance.

At the time, my action research spurred a realization that in looking ahead, the lateness problem would not find a magical resolution, as I did not see some external force that had identified attendance as a priority (something I believed would probably hold true as long as students were frightened into being on time during testing while all other days fell by the wayside). Thus, my thought was that change should start with me and involve building collaboration between a group of likeminded colleagues concerned with the severity of the issue. Although aware that entering the teaching world as a first-year teacher would make this difficult to achieve, my hope was that starting with younger teachers and working towards the veterans, or networking well with one particular veteran to convince my other colleagues through the veteran, could help to create the necessary community. It was then my hope to implement a plan of consequences for missed time that would involve all teachers engaging with their students in a transparent conversation about the plan, and an organizational system that would involve teachers staying after to work with students who were late for school.

Suzanne.   For me, teacher leadership came in the form of developing my work as an inquiry based teacher; it helped me gain a better understanding of my developing teaching practice as well as shape my emerging identity as a collaborative teacher. Building on this experience into my first year of teaching I found myself trying to create a classroom that belonged to, and was influenced by, both teacher and student. I wanted to allow students to make contributions to the lessons from the very start. This played out as negotiating almost everything in the classroom. Although I knew some might view this as an easy way out in order to try and get kids to be your friend as well as not having a controlled or managed classroom, in actuality, this allowed me to have even more management than many other teachers I saw around myself. The fact that I wanted my students' participation to guide my practice meant that I was able to build deeply respectful relationships with my students, something evidenced by my strong teaching evaluations throughout the year as well as a follow up study of some of the residents. I felt this well of respect inevitably allowed me to hold my students to high standards both academically and behaviorally, and has become the cornerstone for my teaching philosophy.

Growing the Third Space

Emily. For the residency program as a whole, building in action research where the mentors took leadership of the process became central towards supporting development of the third space, by privileging a methodology grounded in teacher knowledge, classroom practice, and the work of teachers. Monica and I felt the shift as we began to work with the mentors as peers in the fall, to share our own questions, vulnerabilities, and open ourselves up in the process of engaging in self-study and action research. We increasingly turned to the mentors for both feedback and direction about both the residents and the program. As the mentors took on facilitating this project for the residents, it helped to reinforce their role as teacher educators in the program. As we look back, one of the most powerful lessons we have learned about working with schools is that there have to be opportunities for university faculty and teachers to co-learn. Our experience in the program shows that through researching together we were all able to make significant identity shifts.

At the level of the residents, because through action research the questions our residents pursued often engaged their students as co-collaborators, they were able to begin to understand how our definition of co-constructed curriculum might transfer to their own practice in the classroom. Because our notion of the third space was broader than just the university, the schools, and the community, it was important to us that we find spaces that included the students' voices. Although we had continued to push our residents via discussions, assignments, and instructional rounds to include student voices in their instructional planning, reflection, and curriculum, action research proved to be a powerful means for opening the third space in their own classrooms. Yet even so, we still felt that some of them were capable of taking greater risks in their classrooms and with that in mind, faculty and a doctoral student developed a new project designed to push even our "safest" of residents.

REFERENCES

Cochran-Smith, M., & Lytle, S. L. (1993). *Inside/outside: Teacher research and knowledge.* New York, NY: Teachers College Press.

Cochran-Smith, M., Barnatt, J., Friedman, A., & Pine, G. (2012). Inquiry on inquiry: Practitioner research and student learning. *Action in Teacher Education, 31*(2), 17–32.

Everett, S. A., Luera, G. R., & Otto, C. A. (2007). Pre-service elementary teachers bridge the gap between research and practice. *International Journal of Science and Mathematics Education, 6,* 1–17.

Ginns, I., Heirdsfield, A., Atweh, B., & Watters, J. J. (2001). Beginning teachers becoming professionals through action research. *Educational Action Research, 9*(1), 111–133.

Gitlin, A., Barlow, L., Brubank, M. D., Kauchak, D., & Stevens, T. (1999). Pre-service teachers' thinking on research: Implications for inquiry oriented teacher education. *Teaching and Teacher Education, 15,* 753–769.

Goodnough, K. (2010). The role of action research in transforming teacher identity: Modes of belonging and ecological perspectives. *Educational Action Research, 18*(2), 167–182.

Hubbard, R. S., & Power, B. M. (2003). *The art of classroom inquiry: A handbook for teacher-researchers.* Portsmouth, NH: Heinemann.

Klein, E. J., Taylor, M., Monteiro, A. K., & Romney, W. (2013). Making the leap to teacher: Pre-service residents, faculty, and school mentors taking on action research together in an urban teacher residency program. In M. Taylor & K. Strom (Chairs.). *Building systemic and sustainable educational change in a third space: A multi-dimensional view of an urban teaching residency.* Paper presented at the American Educational Research Association, San Francisco, CA.

Kriegel, O. (2013, June 10). What teacher education programs don't tell you? *Education Week.* Retrieved from http://www.edweek.org/ew/articles/2013/06/12/35kriegel_ep.h32.html?r=119741986

Levin, B. B., & Rock, T. C. (2003). The effects of collaborative action research on preservice and experienced teacher partners in professional development schools. *Journal of Teacher Education, 54*(2), 135–149.

McNiff, J. (2010). *Action research for professional development: Concise advice for new and experienced action researchers.* Dorset, England: September Books.

McNiff, J., & Whitehead, J. (2006). *All you need to know about action research.* London, UK: Sage Press.

Mertler, C. A. (2011). *Action research: Improving schools and empowering educators.* New York, NY: Sage.

Niemi, H. (2002). Active learning – a cultural change needed in teacher education and schools. *Teaching and Teacher Education, 18*(7), 763–780.

Price, J. (2001). Action research, pedagogy and change: The transformative potential of action research in pre-service teacher education. *Journal of Curriculum Studies, 33*(1), 43–74.

Robertson, J. (2005). Teacher research, communities of learners, and change in schools. *Education Today, 4*(4), 13–14.

Robinson, M., & Meerkotter, D. (2003). Fifteen years of action research for political and educational emancipation at a South African university. *Educational Action Research, 11*(3), 447–466.

Smith, K., & Sela, O. (2005). Action research as a bridge between pre-service teacher education and in-service professional development for students and teacher educators. *European Journal of Teacher Education, 28*(3), 293–310.

Somekh, B., & Zeichner, K. (2009). Action research for educational reform: remodeling action research theories and practices in local contexts. *Educational Action Research, 17*(1), 5–21.

Taylor, M., Goeke, J., Klein, E. J., Onore, C., & Geist, K. (2011). Changing leadership: Teachers lead the way for schools that learn. *Teaching and Teacher Education, 27*(5), 920–929.

Taylor, M., Abrams, L., Klein, E., Wray, S., Cordero, E., Silva, J., & Rincon, R. (2012). Shape shifting or becoming third space teacher educators: A co/autoethnographic self-study of mentors and faculty. In L. B. Erickson, J. R. Young, & S. Pinnegar (Eds.), *Proceedings of the 9th International Conference on Self Study of Teacher Education Practices* (pp. 15–16), East Sussex, England. Provo, UT: Brigham Young University.

Vall, L. (2000). Connecting teacher development and school improvement: Ironic consequences of a preservice action research course. *Teaching and Teacher Education, 16*(7), 715–730.

Vogrinc, J., & Valencic Zuljan, M. (2009). Action research in schools – an important factor in teachers' professional development. *Educational Studies, 35*(1), 53–63.

Whitehead, J. (1989). Creating a living educational theory from questions of the kind, "How do I improve my practice?" *Cambridge Journal of Education, 19*(1), 137–153.

Whitehead, J., & Fitzgerald, B. (2006). Professional learning through a generative approach to mentoring: lessons from a training school partnership and their wider implications. *Journal of Education for Teaching, 32*(1), 37–52.

Emily J. Klein
Department of Secondary and Special Education
Montclair State University
Montclair, New Jersey

Antonio Iglesias
East Side High School
Newark, New Jersey

Suzanne Poole
Science Park High School
Newark, New Jersey

Erin Mooney
Spotswood High School
Spotswood, New Jersey

APPENDIX

Action Research/Self-Study Framework

Questions	
What? What is the inquiry? What is (are) the research-able question(s) /puzzle here? What are the *supporting questions/ puzzles*?	
Why? What is the background or rationale of the research? Why are you interested in the question? What motivates you?	

(Continued)

Questions	
Who? Who will be the participants in the study? What role if any will colleagues play in the study?	
Teaching How? What will you do differently? What actions will you take?	

(Continued)

E. J. KLEIN ET AL.

Questions	
Research How? What data are relevant to the research questions? How will you collect them?	
So What? Why will the research matter? To whom might it make a difference? What might you understand differently as a result?	

142

MEET THE AUTHORS FROM CHAPTER SIX

Fernando Naiditch, education has been my life and my passion as far as I can remember. Growing up, I was always amazed at how much information there was around me; everything was a source of knowledge and everyone had something to teach me. I thought there were no end and no limit to how much one could learn and how much they could do with all that they had learned.

I was born and raised in Brazil, and like so many of my fellow Brazilian educators, I grew up influenced by the work of Paulo Freire. Freire used to say that education either functions as an instrument which is used to facilitate integration of the younger generation into the logic of the present system and bring about conformity, or that it becomes the practice of freedom, the means by which men and women deal critically and creatively with reality and discover how to participate in the transformation of their world.

I have chosen to abide by the latter. I believe in education as a means of empowering. Growing up in a dictatorship, I strongly believe not only in the principle of a public education system, but in the role public schools serve in a democratic society.

I left Brazil as a young adult and went to see as much of the world as I could. I have lived and worked in a number of international contexts – from South America, through the Middle East, to Europe, and now, the United States. I started out teaching English as a foreign language and then became an ESL teacher. Multiculturalism and multilingualism have been part of my life since I was a child. Being exposed to many different languages and cultures throughout my life has shaped my identity, both personally and professionally.

I came to the United States to pursue my Ph.D. at New York University. While working on my doctoral degree, I specialized in the areas of sociolinguistics, cross-cultural pragmatics, and intercultural communication.

At MSU, I teach courses on topics that directly affect the education of culturally and linguistically diverse student populations, such as equity and diversity, culturally responsive teaching, and educating English language learners.

The NMUTR is an example of the kind of collaborative work that inspires and motivates me to continue to search for new approaches to preparing teachers and educators for the challenges and rewards of teaching in urban settings.

FERNANDO NAIDITCH AND ALEXANDER DIAZ[1]

6. PREPARING RESIDENTS TO TEACH ENGLISH LANGUAGE LEARNERS IN THE THIRD SPACE

INTRODUCTION

After a year as a resident in the NMUTR, Alex was given his first teaching assignment at East Side High School in Newark as a biology teacher. He was placed in a bilingual earth sciences classroom where Spanish was the medium of instruction. I spent the first year of Alex's experience—his induction period—at East Side visiting and studying his classroom in order to follow his progress as a bilingual teacher and his approach to addressing the needs of English language learners (ELLs). As I engaged in the research process, students got to know me and I also became a language resource in the classroom.

During one of my visits, students were studying reptiles. I sat next to a group that was actively engaged in a discussion about the crocodile being a carnivore and the kinds of animals they feed on. Suddenly, one of the students, Pablo, came across a sentence with a reflexive form in it: *El crocodilo se alimenta de antílopes.*

Pablo immediately started wondering how he could say this sentence in English. He definitely knew the verb "to eat," but quickly realized that it did not fit in this context. Was there another verb he hadn't been introduced to? Because students were sitting in round tables, it was easy for him to reach out to a classmate and ask for help. All students were Spanish speakers, but none of them could help him translate the sentence in a way that made sense in English. Pablo couldn't let it go. He even challenged his classmates to come up with an appropriate translation using humor to convince them: "I may still be in the ESL class, but I can see that I am not alone," he joked in Spanish. That seemed to have been enough to bring his classmates back into the conversation. The students started coming up with sentences that did not really mean what Pablo had intended. He was not happy with what his classmates had to offer: "*The crocodile eats the antelope.*"

But "*se alimentar,*" Pablo insisted, has an additional meaning that "eat" alone does not convey. Suddenly, the topic at his table had expanded from the food chain and reptiles to the difficulty they were having in trying to convey that idea to the teacher, Mr. Diaz. The content of the lesson motivated them to engage in a conversation about language, and the need to be able to express themselves and convey the right idea to the teacher and the other classmates prevailed. Language was at the foreground of that group discussion.

145

F. NAIDITCH & A. DIAZ

Students were alternating between their first language (L1), Spanish, and the second language (L2), English, to consider possible ways of making meaning of the sentence. More specifically, they were using language to discuss language use. They were speaking mostly in Spanish, but the need to use English in the conversation became clear to them when they realized that they found themselves translating every part of the sentence, and even creating new ones to see how it "sounded" in English and to test out their hypotheses: "Maybe this way is better" or "What if we say it like this?" and even "No, that doesn't sound right."

Because of my physical location and the fact that I had been following their group dynamics from the beginning, the students invited me to join their discussion: "How do you say *se alimenta* in English?" Pablo asked me hoping to put an end to their heated debate. Without thinking much, I said, "feeds itself." Pablo looked at his team and said: *The crocodile feeds itself the antelope.*

That did not sound right, either. My answer lacked the larger context and even made the sentence more complicated. I knew the content of the lesson and soon understood what the students were trying to say. Without planning, mine was also a calculated answer. I was enjoying seeing students so eloquently discuss language use and argue about their communicative needs to convey meaning adequately and appropriately in the second language: *The crocodile feeds the antelope,* and *The crocodile feeds with the antelope.* They kept trying—even with a version in the passive voice: *The crocodile is fed with the antelope.* It took a while, but the students finally came up with a sentence they all approved of: *Crocodiles feed on antelopes.*

I need to admit that my help aided them getting to a satisfactory version in English. As students asked me to participate in their discussion, I also used it as an opportunity to prompt them to think further about language and content, not by "giving" them the answer, but by engaging in their activity of testing out possible versions of the sentence. After all, I was witnessing students genuinely engaging in group discussions about language. They had engaged in a meaningful interaction on the intersection of content and language. Students were creatively and intensely discussing how to best convey an idea in the second language accurately and precisely, which is exactly what scientific discourse requires. Students listened to each other's contributions attentively, tested out hypotheses, and made changes to the sentence at every new attempt. They were playing with the words and their meanings in order to achieve precision, which is conveyed through the use of language.

When Alex and I talked about this class later, we were both pleased to see that a classroom activity that focused on content had motivated students to think about language in an academic way, and had organically engaged them in a conversation about language use and its purpose in developing scientific discourse. During his teacher preparation in the NMUTR, we had discussed the need to integrate language and content when teaching English language learners and the importance of talking explicitly about language uses in the classroom. Alex's students were doing just that. Perhaps due to the nature of a bilingual class that prompts students to address

146

language in a more direct and explicit way, the students were able to demonstrate their understanding of the role of language in producing meaning and in promoting learning.

TEACHING SECOND LANGUAGE LEARNERS FOR
SOCIAL JUSTICE IN THE THIRD SPACE

Social justice was a major theme that permeated all the work we did in the NMUTR. When one learns to recognize inequalities and inequities in the larger society and realize that access and opportunity are still far from a reality for many of America's school children, it is easier to understand why social justice is the ultimate goal of education.

We immersed residents in the life and the reality of an urban community to help them identify and understand how socio-economic factors affect the daily lives of the students in their classrooms, so that they could use teaching practices geared towards a more socially just and equitable society. Interacting with immigrant families and delving into their world where language and culture are concrete barriers to equity, access, and achievement gave residents a more realistic perspective of the importance of their work as educators and prepared them as advocates for their students.

Teaching ELLs is a civil rights endeavor, and in the NMUTR, residents learned that in order for ELLs to achieve their full potential, they needed to be empowered and given opportunities to develop socially, emotionally, cognitively, and academically. Learning to teach ELLs is truly about becoming agents of change, by developing the tools and attitudes required to participate fully in the life of the community.

Teaching ELLs requires the knowledge developed from being in the community and from interacting with its members. Our work was informed by the experiences residents engaged in throughout their yearlong preparation. Due to its linguistic, cultural, and socio-economic diversity, Newark was a perfect setting for residents to develop the skills, knowledge, and dispositions needed to teach ELLs. The Ironbound, for example, is an area that has traditionally welcomed Portuguese immigrants. They were followed by Brazilians, and more recently by a large number of Spanish-speaking immigrants. Our residents often went into the stores, bakeries, and other local businesses and engaged in a conversation in Portuguese or Spanish. Even if they did not speak any of these languages, it was still possible to learn about communication patterns just by observing the way community members interact with one another, the paralinguistic features, the tone of the conversation, and the prosodic features.

Our residents learned about the community by sitting at a coffee shop, by reading local newspapers, by shopping in local businesses and by engaging in conversation. In fact, we believe that the only way to learn about a community of practice (Eckert & McConnell-Ginet, 1999) is by immersing yourself in that space in order to learn about shared practices, linguistic codes, and cultural expressions.

147

One of the residents, Antonio, described his experience with a Brazilian-born student who was the kind of student with whom NMUTR residents interacted during their program:

> Donna ... is a member of a four-person family, which includes her biological mother, her stepfather, and her half-brother. Only Portuguese is spoken at home. Born abroad, Donna emigrated to the U.S.A. in the late 1990s. Living in Newark since then, she had very few encounters with anything written (whether in English or Portuguese). Essentially, her day-to-day encounters during her toddler and young child years were reduced to spoken exchanges.

In describing Donna's language experiences in Brazil and in Newark, Antonio came to realize that life in the community and before coming to the U.S. shaped her relationship to literacy and could even serve as a predictor of her journey into learning the language of schooling:

> My various one-on-one interactions have led me to believe that her difficulties with reading (less so writing) are rooted in never having a grasp of any language (let alone in an academic setting).

BUILDING ON FUNDS OF KNOWLEDGE TO TEACH ELLS IN THE THIRD SPACE

Taking an active role in the life of the community and working with the youth as an integral part of the NMUTR also provided residents with a unique opportunity to develop what the program envisioned as the third space, a new approach to educating youth that includes redesigning what counts as teaching and learning. In her discussion of a "collective Third Space," Gutierrez (2008) lays out a vision of new educative spaces,

> in which students begin to reconceive who they are and what they might be able to accomplish academically and beyond, [a space] characterized by the ideals and practices of a shared humanity, a profound obligation to others, boundary crossing, and intercultural exchange in which difference is celebrated without being romanticized. (pp. 148–149)

While interacting with Newark youth in different contexts at the Newark Museum, at La Casa de Don Pedro, and with the All Stars Program, residents were given extended opportunities as a community to reorganize learning spaces and activities and engage in rich and ongoing zones of innovation and expanded learning (Gutiérrez et al., 1999).

The third space is a hybrid space where funds of knowledge (Moll et al., 1992), home languages and linguistic varieties, and socio-cultural practices come together and interact with one another to create an in-between space (Bhabha, 1996) where new cultural, social, and linguistic forms may emerge. Situating residents within this new space that brings together the knowledge of schools, families, communities, and teacher education programs helped to create a broader and more informed idea of what teaching is and a more realistic view of what it entails.

For example, residents learned to make connections between home life and school experiences of their students by researching the history and the elements that characterized and were essential to the households in the community. Our approach was one that looked at ELLs not from that inaccurate perspective of deficit, but from one that aimed to recognize and value the knowledge that they bring from the home to the classroom. Residents learned about funds of knowledge—historically developed and accumulated cultural practices and norms that constitute knowledge within different populations (Moll et al., 1992; Veléz-Ibáñez & Greenberg, 1992) and how to incorporate them in their teaching.

In one of my classroom observations, Alex displayed this disposition and demonstrated how these funds of knowledge can promote meaningful learning and can enable students to make sense of their lived experiences within an academic context. One of the students, Maria, may not have known before that moment about the morphology of a mushroom or its classification as a fungus, but what she shared in the class about her experiences growing up in rural Ecuador and learning how to identify different types of mushrooms and their medicinal and nutritional properties informed much of the lesson that Alex had planned for that day.

In class, Maria told her classmates about her experiences in the field. Her colorful descriptions of experimenting with mushrooms of different shapes and sizes and her vivid memories of colors, smells and textures enriched the class conversation and motivated everyone to want to know more about mushrooms. The classroom provided Maria with another level of knowledge. She learned how to describe and talk about this fungus using academic language and specific terms and more specialized technical vocabulary that was appropriate for the school environment, but that was only possible because she was first given the opportunity to talk about the class content freely and to display and share her personal experiences and knowledge about mushrooms. This was the factor that contributed to her successful participation in class. Her hands-on experiences informed much of the class discussion and she met the expectations set up by Alex as part of his class objectives. In fact, they went beyond what was planned for that day by including a discussion on the economic effects of mushrooms in the lives of farmers that cultivate and sell them for a living. Its social impact in the life of the community the student was from was also part of the lesson.

This smooth transition from lived experiences to more academic ones is only made possible by valuing students' contributions and by looking at their funds of knowledge as an asset to the learning environment. Learning to tap into students' knowledge values their identity and gives them a sense of purpose in the classroom. By encouraging students to share their knowledge, experiences, and home lives, Alex managed to keep students engaged and motivated, and they were able to successfully accomplish the class goals. Moreover, he developed an inquiry-based lesson with students extending the conversation by asking additional questions and going to the Internet to look for more pictures and information.

The anecdote from Alex's classroom exemplifies our approach to ELLs as one of self-affirmation and validation. Residents learned to identify the strengths of their ELLs and to build on them. In doing so, they approached ELLs as assets to the class; as students who came from many parts of the world and walks of life and who brought these aspects of their lives with them to the classroom. As I have said elsewhere,

> giving [students] a voice and an opportunity is just a simple strategy that helps foster and strengthen the partnership between schools and the families that they serve... [Students learn to make] meaningful connections and [...] to respect and appreciate how much English language learners have to contribute to a more linguistically and culturally diverse classroom environment [...] Educating English language learners is dependent on the knowledge that comes from the community, from crossing the street and getting to know a parent, a life story, a different way of defining and practicing literacy. (Naiditch, 2013, p. 29)

Ultimately, this anecdote from Alex's class reflects one of the main concerns and aims of our ELL course, which was to integrate the lived experiences of the English learners with the curriculum by learning about what they already bring to school and by building on their strengths. Using students' funds of knowledge as part of the curriculum and class activities is not only an effective strategy in motivating and engaging students, but also in ensuring that their voices and histories are validated in the classroom.

The best way to learn about a community's funds of knowledge is to engage in meaningful interactions with community members. From the beginning of the program, when the residents were doing their internships in the museum, or in youth programs, they were learning how to become ethnographers by observing the community attentively, by developing relationships with its members and by engaging in meaningful conversations in different settings in Newark. Residents were encouraged to explore different areas in the community in order to learn about its ways of knowing. Our assignments asked students to take the role of participant observers and also to engage with students and their parents in some form of open-ended conversation to learn about the funds of knowledge in the households.

In our classes, we discussed the information that residents had gathered about their students' lives, households, and literacy levels and worked to transform this body of knowledge into curriculum. Learning about funds of knowledge needs to be an intentional and guided practice. It is a complex process which involves developing skills and dispositions that help teachers make meaning out of every aspect in the life of a community; an artifact, a place, a conversation, a person, an interaction.

UNDERSTANDING LANGUAGE USES IN THE COMMUNITY

From the beginning of their teacher preparation in the NMUTR, residents learned about the communication patterns, language styles, and even about people's preferred language structures and lexical choices in the community. By being exposed to the languages and the cultures of the community, how they are used and how they sustain or prevent interactions, residents gained a deep understanding of the important role that language plays in establishing relationships and in defining the members of a group. One of the residents, Marc, commented on his learning just by going to a local bakery for lunch:

> I don't speak Portuguese, but when I sit at *Princesa*, I can feel the rhythm of the language and how it brings these people together.

Alex also expressed his understanding of the role of language in creating a sense of community and identity. He used his own personal experience growing up in a bilingual home to make sense of the experiences of others in the Newark community. The exposure to an environment where language mediates relationships prompted him to want to rescue his own sense of identity through language:

> For years, although I always appreciated the culture, the food, I couldn't speak and all my older relatives only spoke Spanish ... So I decided that I wanted to learn Spanish ... It also helps that my girlfriend and her family speak Spanish and they only speak Spanish at home entirely. So I wanted to learn, so what I started doing was I started buying books.

After the residency year, determined to develop his language skills further, Alex immersed himself in the language as a way of rescuing his identity and helping him become part of the community of which he was going to become a member:

> What I would do over the summer, I spoke nothing but Spanish to my family and to [my girlfriend's] family ... I really just tried to immerse myself in it as much as humanly possible.

Understanding that language has the power to bring people together and create a sense of community was essential for residents who, during the course of their program, learned not only how to address the linguistic needs of students or how to incorporate their culture into the class curriculum, but most importantly, learned to advocate for them.

My contact with the residents started at the beginning of their program. As one of their supervisors during their summer internships, I visited them in all the sites and met with them both individually and as a group to make sense of their experiences. Our group seminars gave residents a chance to systematically debrief important aspects of their experiences in the community. Because of the large number of ELLs in Newark, I also asked residents to start paying attention to the linguistic features and discursive elements of the different speech patterns to which they were being exposed. Through the lens of the learning theories we read at the beginning of the summer, I asked them to observe how language mediates relationships and defines communication patterns in the different sites and with the different people around the community.

Janae used the experiences and knowledge gained in the summer to continue her close observation of ELLs during the academic year. She described how much observing the life of a community and interacting with its members affected her ability to read between the lines of not just linguistic clues, but also paralinguistic features, such as nodding. She described the case of a student who used nodding as a communication strategy, as a way to prevent engaging in dialogue by just pretending to understand what was being said:

> [A] Dominican American student ... first captured my attention due to how quiet she was. She would always nod her head and tell me that she understood the material ... but she didn't.

After spending some time in the community and being able to develop a relationship with students by demonstrating an understanding of the cultural rules that affect discourse patterns, Janae noticed that the Dominican girl changed her own patterns of communication:

> When talking to her, I noticed that she would pause to find the appropriate words to make communication between the two of us effective.

One of my aims was for residents to start observing ELLs and looking at language as an object of study. It was not an easy task to ask prospective math and science teachers to start paying attention to language as an object, especially because this was not traditionally part of their undergraduate experience. However, from the moment they understood how powerful language is in the identity of a community, they also started seeing language as content.

Marc, who worked closely with a student named John, described how difficult it was for the student to transition to English because his native language was his comfort zone:

> John was born and raised in Newark. His parents do not know English, and communicate with him solely in Spanish... John uses Spanish as a language of comfort. He seems much more comfortable speaking in Spanish, though his basic interpersonal communication skills in English are good.

As a consequence of her early interactions with Newark youth, Suzanne described how she soon came to understand the role of language in establishing youth as language brokers for parents and elderly in the community:

> When I had the pleasure of meeting Sam's father at a parent-teacher conference, Sam played the role of interpreter between his father and me. This event

opened my eyes to the many roles, appropriate or not, that Sam has to play in and out of school.

Language brokering is a communicative practice that often involves children of immigrant families who mediate interactions between family members who do not speak English and individuals from the larger community. What is interesting for residents in recognizing this communication practice is that they also learn to understand the socio-psychological aspects of this activity that means much more than simply a translation practice. Brokering is an opportunity for the youth to serve as mediators who, while assisting family members, are in fact negotiating language and culture.

As Hall and Robinson (1999) put it: "in such situations children are not simply constructing the world for themselves but are playing principal roles in constructing versions of the new world for other family members" (p. 4). They go on to say that "being a language broker makes complex linguistic and cognitive demands upon children but it also offers them positions of power and responsibility within the family, a position which is often at odds with their more general role as children in a family as well as one which might generate some difficulties for parents" (p. 4).

Moreover, many are ELLs themselves and the fact that they may have some knowledge of English does not guarantee the success of these interactions. Alex's statement below summarizes the growing understanding residents develop of how hard it is for the youth in the community to take on this role of language broker, of having to speak on behalf of their parents. This adds another layer of complexity to the work of ELL teachers who will be developing personal relationships with students and families:

> I definitely know that to translate something from one language to another, especially if you're doing it for the first time, if you have no experience doing it, it's a very difficult task … [This student] is in ESL 1, but she tries and she works hard. And her mom tells her "yes, you have to practice your English. We're going to try practicing your English more," but she acts as a somewhat translator too for her parents, so I don't know what her level is.

Alex referred to the student's level both in terms of linguistic as well as cultural knowledge. The fact that the student can communicate in "basic" English puts her in a position that she has not chosen for herself and one that may have serious consequences for the family. On numerous occasions residents reported situations involving multiple uses of language and the outcomes they may have for the families in the community. As Alex said:

> I have to wait for them to test her because she acts as a translator for her parents to some extent. Because they said something about court, I don't want to pry, but they said something about a court so she may need to help translate things in court.

WORKING WITH ELLS IN THE CLASSROOM

My work with the residents during the academic year was integrated into the other courses. I developed a series of workshops and additional time was also built in for me to observe and work with the residents in their classrooms. As residents came to know their students and learned to identify those who were ELLs and who were struggling with the content because of the language barrier, they also learned how to relate to the students and develop appropriate instructional interventions. This was done through a hands-on individualized approach, which allowed for me to work with each resident in his or her classroom.

My main aim was to expose students to the central issues in the education of ELLs in US schools, particularly in urban settings, and help them learn about best practices in educating them. Residents heightened their awareness and sensitivity both to the resources that ELLs bring to learning and to the challenges they face in school.

Our objectives for the residents can be summarized in three main domains: understanding who ELLs are and the basic principles of second language acquisition (SLA), investigating school responses to dealing with ELLs, and learning best practices for teaching and assessing ELLs. Each domain focused on specific aspects that affect the performance and success of ELLs at school.

Even though there is a body of knowledge residents needed to understand in order to address the ELLs' needs, many topics for the workshops came from the actual work residents were doing in the classroom or as a result of interactions with a parent or even a person at a local business or community center. This emergent curriculum was informed by the experiences residents had during their residency and by their personal anecdotes or examples, and was consistent with the third space framework of the entire program.

Often times we found ourselves starting the workshop by discussing a story or trying to understand the cultural and linguistic meanings behind an attitude, a gesture, or even a communication style. The following comments exemplify the kinds of concerns residents expressed in dealing with the reality of the day-to-day life of a linguistically diverse classroom and reflected issues of comprehension and expression:

- *I have a student who insists on leaving the subject out of his sentences.*
- *Why is it that they can't seem to be able to pronounce these sounds in English?*
- *Sometimes I feel like they are listening to me, but can't understand a word of what I'm saying.*
- *The vocabulary is already difficult for the students who speak English. How do I teach these words to the ELLs?*
- *I don't speak Spanish and I can't understand what he is trying to say.*

These statements demonstrate the residents' level of anxiety and their concern in trying to integrate content and language when they did not feel that secure about language in the first place. This is not uncommon, particularly given the emphasis on content and the lack of awareness towards language in traditional teacher education programs. One of the advantages of working in the third space was the fact that residents understood that language and content are inseparable and that content can be found everywhere and is informed by students' lived experiences, not only by textbooks or school curricula.

During the NMUTR, residents learned to understand, identify, address, and assess the needs of ELLs at the same time that they developed the skills and dispositions to become culturally and linguistically responsive teachers (Gay, 2010; Godley et al., 2006; Ladson-Billings, 2009; Lucas, 2011). The work was built on the premise that this collaboration between the stakeholders and the residents helps teachers to understand and develop the necessary skills to become teachers of ELLs (Valdés, 2001).

The strategies developed with the residents echoed those of sheltered instruction (Echevarria et al., 2012) and encompassed instructional practices and pedagogical dispositions that helped teachers of ELLs in terms of content and literacy skills while at the same time providing academic support for ELLs to learn content in English (Brinton et al., 2003).

Sheltered English Instruction (SEI) has been used by content area teachers since the 1980s to help make content comprehensible for ELLs. Although the meaning of the term has changed over the years, especially because most ELLs are no longer sheltered in separate classes, SEI remains an effective instructional approach by providing developmental language support for students in learning both the English language and content. Because ELLs are placed with native English speaking children in mainstream classes, the need to support their learning with a well designed framework for teachers to prepare and deliver sheltered lessons in all content areas is even more critical.

School success lies in the development of academic literacy in English (Cummins, 2000). Students need to develop appropriate language skills in order to achieve the goals of every grade and to perform according to state standards in terms of content and knowledge. Without being academically proficient, students will lack the resources to succeed in school and will lag behind—not performing at grade level and not being able to further their education. In order to understand mathematical concepts, scientific experiments or historical periods, for example, one needs to perform academically in both spoken and written English.

Short (2002) describes three knowledge bases as the major components of academic literacy: knowledge of English, knowledge of the content topic, and knowledge of how classroom tasks are to be accomplished. Cummins (2000) expands on his distinction between BICS (basic interpersonal communicative skills) and CALP (cognitive academic language proficiency) to draw attention to the three components of academic language that should be addressed as part of an instructional program for ELLs: cognitive (instruction should be cognitively challenging and require higher-order thinking skills), academic (academic content should be integrated with language instruction), and language (students should be given ample opportunities to develop projects investigating their own and their community's language uses, practices, and assumptions).

In the NMUTR, we discussed the means and the strategies to help ELLs develop academic language proficiency and did so by focusing on three main components so that the residents could have a better understanding of the relationships between language/literacy and content area knowledge and the pedagogical approaches to bring them together: how to integrate language into the content area curriculum, how to adapt and modify language and instruction, and how to develop culturally responsive pedagogy.

From the beginning, our residents understood that modifying instruction reflects a disposition that teachers need to have when dealing with a diverse group of students. The term "accommodation" has typically been used to refer to the practices and procedures used by teachers to make sure every student has an equal opportunity to learn. Traditionally, teachers learn to develop accommodations focusing on the materials they use and on classroom procedures, which involves aspects of teaching such as how they present material, how students are to respond to tasks, and even elements in the classroom setting itself (like seating arrangements, visual displays and grouping of students). Issues of timing and scheduling are also considered part of accommodations—anything that can potentially affect the learner's ability to understand and demonstrate knowledge. Strategies such as translating directions, signs, and explanations into the students' native languages, providing additional time for the completion of tasks, paraphrasing and repeating classroom language in different ways, learning to ask questions in different formats, and using linguistic and non-linguistic aids, for example, are all seen as resources in teaching ELLs.

Any adaptation, modification, or accommodation has the ultimate aim of providing access to knowledge for all students and this is particularly relevant when the student is an ELL who is expected to "perform within the required academic standards while also struggling to make sense of the American language and culture" (Naiditch, 2013, p. 28).

PORTRAIT OF AN ELL

One of our initial assignments was the portrait of an ELL. Residents needed to identify an ELL and develop a case study about this particular student. Case studies are powerful pedagogical tools which helped residents develop an ability to look closely, observe attentively, record information, and process it while trying to make sense of what they had observed.

Residents' choices of ELL students were justified by their observation and by our workshop discussions. Pri, for example, decided to study a student that would challenge the assumption that ELLs lack content knowledge. In fact, as he recognized below, many ELLs are at advanced levels in the content area, but their language needs prevent them from fully participating in class and demonstrating their knowledge:

[P.J.] stood out from the rest of the class due to her talent in the subject matter. She is a very smart girl and is able to grasp the material faster and with a better understanding than most of her peers. I chose her because she is not afraid to ask questions and challenge our methods. I know many bilingual students who are afraid to speak up or ask questions because they do not want to be embarrassed or made fun of due to their linguistic skills, but not P.J..

Through the case study, residents were able to understand the learning process of a particular learner and identify specific aspects that may have contributed or hindered progress. Case studies were highly descriptive, but also exploratory. Residents were encouraged to make hypotheses, understand causation, explore possibilities, identify underlying principles, and develop specific strategies for improving teaching and learning.

In the example below, Dave described how his ELL seemed to be also learning the strategies used with him in the classroom and how he incorporated them in his discourse. He even wondered about the long-term effects of using this strategy:

He will often pause before he speaks to make sure he is communicating effectively. This is especially true when the conversation is highly academic. This can be misinterpreted as he doesn't understand the topic or is slow. Adults who are in a hurry, for example robotics coaches from other schools, may be short with him because they think he doesn't get something, when the reality is quite the opposite. The fact that Lewis does not speak English as a first language does not seem to impact his academic performance in an obvious way. Although he might not understand a term or phrase, he knows enough English to still derive meaning or find an alternative explanation. This shows his adaptability as a person and is a trait that will serve him well later in life.

Because residents observed the ELL in his/her educational setting, the task was also realistic and more meaningful, as they interacted with the particular student, the classmates, and the teachers to get a wider perspective of the learner and the language acquisition process. Janae was able to pinpoint specific issues that were affecting her math student and her case study ended up revolving around methods or approaches that may be suitable for ELLs' specific content area needs:

This student has difficulties in understanding particular concepts and methods used in mathematics. When she figures out a way to do things through her own method, she does it well. She really understands the basic concept of numbers and operations, however when it comes to understanding methods for solving problems, she gets steps and procedures mixed up. Her difficulties are really impeding on her mathematical skills and finding a way to use her skills to her future benefit.

The demographic information about the learner included aspects such as age, time in the US, family background, language spoken at home, literacy in the L1, and information about his/her socialization process (with whom the learner interacted, how much time the learner spent speaking L1 and L2 during the school day, and situations in which each language was used). This initial information was crucial in helping residents understand the contexts and the purposes for each language use and how much investment (Norton, 2000, 2013) there is in learning the second language. Focusing on students' life stories and histories helped residents develop a broader and more comprehensive understanding of who ELLs are and their language development and socialization processes, as can be seen in Suzanne's description of Sam:

> An English Language learner may not be a student who has emigrated from another country; instead the title includes all who have a poor understanding of the English language due to a variety of different circumstances. This is the case with my student Sam. Although he was born and raised in the United States, his parents were not. Being the son of immigrant parents, his understanding of the English language has had a major influence on his learning ... Sam is a student in my 10th grade honors biology class. Although he is not classified as an English Language Learner, he informed me that his first language was Spanish ... Although Sam has an accent when he speaks, it does not appear to restrict him in non-academic conversation. However, I have noticed that his misconceptions of certain English words have played a role in his understanding of biology content.

Residents used the information collected from observing the ELL closely to connect it to our class content. The information about the learner's culture and literacy skills in the first and second languages was used to develop an action plan to address the needs they identified, to adapt their lessons to accommodate those needs, and to differentiate instruction. Suzanne's approach to Sam provided an example:

> There have been several instances where I have provided Sam with a definition or example of a non-vocabulary word in order for him to better grasp a concept. This is a tool I use with all of the students when introducing new biology vocabulary. After providing him with the correct meaning, it was surprising to see him actually understanding the topic. Not only does he seem to gain understanding, he becomes more vocal and participatory during class discussion. This shows that the reason a student might be struggling with the class material, could be due to their inability to recognize the meaning of everyday English vocabulary.

The concern with a humanistic approach, i.e., a way to reach out to and relate to the learner on a more personal level was something residents needed to develop from the very beginning of their program when they started their summer internships in local and community organizations. Again, residents needed to understand how to relate theory and practice and think of both a methodological strategy to address the linguistic needs of the ELL, but also a cognitive and emotional approach to relate to the learner so that they could develop a rapport with their students and lower any anxiety the ELL may have experienced. Suzanne's choice of Sam was an example of that disposition:

> I chose Sam for my ELL student because I truly wanted to develop lessons that meet his needs as a learner. I think that he has the potential to be a critical thinking and self-sufficient student if he is provided with the right tools. Once Sam understands the vocabulary, he shows critical thinking ability that surpasses many of my other students.

In the NMUTR, the academic aspect of teaching and learning went hand-in-hand with the socio-emotional aspects involved in teaching and learning. Moreover, in learning a second language, the affective state of the learner can directly affect the rate and the route of acquisition (Krashen, 2003; Moskowitz, 1991). Barbara's case study was a good example of how residents struggled as they tried to make meaning of the ELL and the issues surrounding language acquisition and socialization. On the one hand, it was easy to identify language and grammatical problems. On the other hand, any student can make grammatical mistakes. This made the job of the residents more complex, as they needed to learn to see what is not on the surface. Barbara's example of CS2 illustrated her anxiety and her journey, as she tried to understand the issues that affected CS2's performance in biology and as she learned to walk on that fine line that separates emotion from reality. In the following description, she was able to demonstrate how her demeanor changed as she learned about CS2's struggles while she learned to recognize, identify, and build on her student's strengths:

> After examining CS2's work, I have noticed a pattern of errors in simple and content-based language. I believe that there may be some misconceptions resulting from these small, often overlooked, misinterpretations. CS2 is a smart young man with an interest in going to college. I feel that these seemingly minor miscues of the English language, mostly on paper but occasionally in speech, may be keeping CS2 from fully understanding the course material. If this is not recognized and addressed now, it could have a permanent effect on his performance, and success, in high school. He is doing well in all of his classes and I have gotten testimonials to his performance from Mr. Lewis, the history teacher ... Many of the words that CS2 has trouble with, he replaces with sound-alike words that often do not fit into the context of the sentence. His handwritten work is very messy, but it is full of grammatical errors even when typed ... I hope to work with CS2 and modify a lesson to help him improve his proficiency in written language. I would also like to identify whether he needs further help to improve his overall literacy and maintain his outstanding academic performance. CS2 has a bright future, but in order to test well and succeed in high school he needs to have a better understanding of English, both written and spoken... He struggles writing the answers to open-ended questions in my class, even when I am sure he knows the concept.

The strategies that I use to help CS2 could be beneficial to the majority of my students, many of whom struggle to express themselves clearly.

This example also highlighted our departure from that nonsensical deficit approach that looks at ELLs as lacking knowledge and language. Rather, we looked at ELLs as assets to the classroom; students whose diverse life and language experiences contribute to group learning and extend classroom content and activities by bringing in different perspectives and various funds of knowledge.

MODIFYING LESSONS FOR ELLS

When writing lesson plans, residents were asked to modify or adapt instruction and assessment for ELLs based on the needs identified as part of classroom observations and instruction. Residents developed multiple ways of assessing linguistic and content literacy (Gottlieb, 2006). They also collaborated in order to develop appropriate linguistic aims for their lessons and content objectives that were meaningful, realistic, and supported literacy development.

Learning to develop language objectives on top of the content objectives for a lesson was a challenging task for content area residents, but it was essential in making sure the lessons supported literacy development in the second language. Language objectives focused on specific linguistic aspects as parts of the lesson, but also more integrated uses of language within the larger academic discourse. Because we dealt with language and content as organically integrated in the lesson, residents always had to be reminded of this integration and were encouraged to create opportunities for learners to use language related to their content in meaningful and appropriate ways.

The following examples were all from different lesson plans developed by the residents. I divided them into four categories: knowledge of language skills, language functions, lexical items associated with resident's content area, and a combination of all of them.

When developing language objectives related to the four basic language skills (reading, writing, speaking, and listening), residents wrote:

- Students will talk about the planets and the galaxy while answering questions and listening to each other's explanations during group work.
- Students will skim the text for gist and then scan it for specific information.

Language objectives also referred to particular language functions (discussing, negotiating, reaching a conclusion, etc.), as in:

- Students will be able to negotiate designs for building a DNA structure.
- Students will make predictions based on the genetic information of the parents.

One of the most discussed topics in our sessions was that of vocabulary and how important it was for second language development, particularly in the academic discourse, where precision and clarity are achieved through the use of specific lexical items in particular contexts. Some of the language objectives residents developed that focus on the use of specific lexical items related to the content were:

- Students will be able define and use the following vocabulary during the lesson: centripetal force, centripetal acceleration, radius, tangential velocity, perpendicular, and kinetic energy.
- Students will be able to use the word "potential" within the context of energy, and the word "conservation" within the context of the energy conservation theory.
- Students will be able to use the word "work" in the context of energy and will need to differentiate from its use in everyday language.

As they progressed in the program, residents became more confident in writing language objectives and strove to integrate them more fully with the content of the lesson within the larger academic discourse, as in:

- Students will use key vocabulary while reporting on their group experiment: first, second, then, plus, and finally.
- Students will participate in a close article reading to identify the benefits of increased amounts of carbon dioxide in the atmosphere.

Adapting their lesson plans to meet the specific needs of ELLs was also part of the assignment, and, in doing so, residents needed to demonstrate their understanding of the particular demands of second language learners and an ability to identify appropriate instructional strategies that may help in each situation. Some adaptations the residents designed in their lesson plans included:

- ELLs will be placed in cooperative groups with bilingual peers. Students will be given more wait time, and terms will be repeated often during the lesson. All writing on the board will be in print and the first term will be modeled. Language skills of listening, speaking, writing, and reading will all be used during group discussion and in the construction of the concept map.
- The teacher will provide students with visual aids in every station. The ELLs will be able to draw, play with play dough, and explore computer simulated labs. Every student will be provided with a packet of questions so that ELLs can work at their own pace and can have the written instructions in front of them. In the computer simulated labs, there will be the option to "click" on certain words to get a visual example of the meaning of the word.
- Students will be in groups throughout class, so ELLs can benefit from skills of native/fluent speakers; high percentage of student-student talk in class; frequent use of academic vocabulary is stressed, orally and in writing. Key vocabulary will be written on the board for their reference.
- Graphic organizers will be used for all note-taking. Students will have the option of replaying the video clips and asking peers in their groups if they missed information from the video clips. The teacher is also available as a resource during lunch and after school.

If lessons were being adapted or modified to meet the needs of ELLs, the same needed to be true about the ways ELLs were being assessed. Because of the way we integrated our curriculum, modifying instruction referred to a larger set of knowledge and skills that residents needed to be able to have and display in their teaching, and this also included making sure that the same accommodations they identified for teaching ELLs were used when assessing the students.

One of the advantages of working in the third space was that it provided us with a unique opportunity to truly develop work that was collaborative and cooperative in nature. I observed and worked with the residents in their classrooms and encouraged them to observe one another. In feedback sessions, we discussed how successful different strategies and approaches were or not, and what could be done to improve their teaching of ELLs. Ongoing and thorough feedback sessions also provided a venue for residents to share their questions and uncertainties, and to relate to me and each other on more personal levels.

CONCLUSION

Learning to teach ELLs for many is about learning different and varied instructional strategies and how to use them. However, teaching ELLs is not only a matter of learning a repertoire of instructional strategies and approaches. It is about understanding the psychological, cognitive, and social processes a learner is experiencing as he/she navigates life in a new country, a new language, and a new culture. It is about being able to relate to learners on a personal level and create a system of support within a caring environment. It is about being able to see life from someone else's perspective. It is about embodying the role of a culturally and linguistically responsive teacher.

This kind of teacher preparation program—a third space residency model— has the potential of bringing about educational change by preparing teachers who are able to identify and address the needs of ELLs as they develop relationships with them and their communities, and understand the factors that affect teaching and learning students who come from various linguistic and cultural backgrounds from a more personal, yet informed perspective. By developing strong ties with the community and learning about the students and their families from various perspectives, the residents, ultimately, learned to become advocates for their ELLs. As they empowered their students through teaching them content and language, they were also empowering themselves as educators who understood their place and their role in the fabric of the larger society.

Not all residents developed their knowledge and skills in the same way or at the same pace. Like teaching in general, learning to teach ELLs is a third space process and its practice will improve and refine as residents continue to teach and engage with students, families, and the communities that they serve. As the instructor of the course, I hoped that their classroom practices would continue to be informed by our workshop discussions, the activities we developed, the projects they engaged in during their year long preparation, and the work we did together as part of their classroom observations and interactions with community members. I also hoped I had instilled in them a curiosity about language, culture, and the many variables that directly affect the process of learning a second language, socializing in a different culture, and integrating in a new society.

This chapter illustrates one particular collaborative endeavor between Alex and me. Alex comes from a home where English is not the primary language. He grew up surrounded by heritage language speakers and by a culture that embodied different traditions and ways of seeing and relating to the world. This may have been the reason why he decided to teach bilingual classes and further his education by pursuing a bilingual certification. Not every resident comes from a similar background or similar experiences, and not all of them may have had the same level of engagement or connection to a particular issue or situation we encountered along the way. However, as a program, we aimed at giving the residents the necessary tools to be able to teach all children across the lines of language, culture, and socio-economic status.

Of all the lessons learned during my work in the NMUTR and in the third space, the most important one as far as teaching ELLs was that learning with ELLs is different from learning about ELLs. If traditional teacher education programs could find ways of bringing prospective students into classrooms and communities and expose them to the types of language uses, communication patterns, community practices, and the daily lives of immigrant families, teacher candidates would develop a more informed and realistic view of what it means to educate ELLs and what it entails.

The third space provided a perfect venue for residents to engage in lived experiences both inside and outside the school setting. These experiences were meaningful, realistic, and had practical consequences to the work in the schools, as residents learned to translate what they saw and lived in the community into pedagogical approaches in their classrooms. A walk in the park sometimes is more than just a walk in park, as it reveals how community members go about their lives, what affects them, what they talk about, and how they communicate. Residents learned about the purposes of language and its many meanings in the real contexts it was being used. The third space taught them how to navigate a foreign universe and how to make sense of it.

Moreover, our work with ELLs engaged residents in the social justice lens through which our curriculum was developed and helped them become advocates for their students and the larger community. Residents were not just visiting or spending time in the community; they were a part of it—they were with, not about.

NOTE

¹ In this chapter, Fernando creates multivocality by integrating narratives from the residents' assignments and artifacts rather than co-writing. Because Alex Diaz, one of the residents, is primarily cited throughout the chapter, he is included as an author "with" Fernando.

REFERENCES

Bhabha, H. K. (1996). Culture's in-between. In S. Hall & P. Du Gay (Eds.), *Questions of cultural identity* (pp. 53–60). London, UK: Sage Publications.
Brinton, D., Wesche, M., & Snow, A. (2003). *Content-based second language instruction.* Ann Arbor, MI: University of Michigan Press.
Cummins, J. (2000). *Language, power and pedagogy: Bilingual children in the crossfire.* Clevedon, England: Multilingual Matters.
Echevarria, J., Vogt, M. J., & Short, D. (2012). *Making content comprehensible for English learners: The SIOP model* (4th ed.). Boston, MA: Allyn & Bacon.
Eckert, P., & McConnell-Ginet, S. (1999). New generalizations and explanations in language and gender research. *Language in Society, 28*(2), 185–201.
Gay, G. (2010). *Culturally responsive teaching: Theory, research, and practice* (2nd ed.). New York, NY: Teachers College Press.
Godley, A. J., Sweetland, J., Wheeler, R. S., Minnici, A., & Carpenter, B. D. (2006). Preparing teachers for dialectally diverse classrooms. *Educational Researcher, 35*(8), 30–37.
Gottlieb, M. (2006). *Assessing English language learners: Bridges from language proficiency to academic achievement.* New York, NY: Corwin Press.
Gutiérrez, K. (2008). Developing a sociocritical literacy in the third space. *Reading Research Quarterly, 43*, 148–164.
Gutiérrez, K., Berlin, D., Crosland, K., & Razfar, A. (1999). *Social organization of learning classroom observation protocol.* Los Angeles, CA: Center for the Study of Urban Literacies, Graduate School of Education and Information Studies, University of California, Los Angeles.
Hall, N., & Robinson, A. (1999). *The language brokering activity of children in Pakistani families in the U.K.* (Unpublished research report).
Krashen, S. (2003). *Explorations in language acquisition and use.* Portsmouth, NH: Heinemann.
Ladson-Billings, G. (2009). *The dreamkeepers: Successful teachers of African American children* (2nd ed.). San Francisco, CA: Jossey-Bass.
Lucas, T. (Ed.). (2011). *Teacher preparation for linguistically diverse classrooms: A resource for teacher educators.* New York, NY: Routledge.
Moll, L. C., Amanti, C., Neff, D., & Gonzalez, N. (1992). Funds of knowledge for teaching: Using a qualitative approach to connect homes and classrooms. *Theory Into Practice, 31*(2), 132–141.
Moskowitz, G. (1991). *Caring and sharing in the foreign language class.* New York, NY: Harper Collins Publishers.
Naiditch, F. (2013). Cross the street to a new world. *Phi Delta Kappan, 94*(6), 26–29.
Norton, B. (2000). *Identity and language learning.* New York, NY: Pearson.
Norton, B. (2013). *Identity and language learning: Extending the conversation.* London, UK: Multilingual Matters.
Short, D. (2002). Language learning in sheltered social studies classes. *TESOL Journal, 11*(1), 18–24.
Valdés, G. (2001). *Learning and not learning English: Latino students in American schools.* New York, NY: Teachers College Press.
Veléz-Ibáñez, C., & Greenberg, J. (1992). Formation and transformation of funds of knowledge among U.S. Mexican households. *Anthropology and Education Quarterly, 23*(4), 313–335.

Fernando Naiditch
Department of Secondary and Special Education
Montclair State University
Montclair, New Jersey

Alexander Diaz
Eastside High School
Newark, New Jersey

MEET THE AUTHORS FROM CHAPTER SEVEN

Anna Karina Monteiro, growing up in a family of educators, I tried very hard to go against the grain by pursuing other degrees. However, after obtaining an undergraduate degree in biology and faced with the challenge of finding a job, my mother, also a teacher, introduced me to a program called "Transition to Teaching" that placed science, math, and technology teachers in urban schools. Within a month of graduation I was doing my student teaching experience during summer school at Barringer High School in Newark. It was on my first day that I realized I would have to give into my true passion, a passion I had tried to ignore for so long—teaching. Immediately, I knew that my place was not only in a science classroom, but in an urban science classroom. My connection with the students and more specifically, my role in helping connect them to the content drove me to learn more about science teaching. I quickly enrolled in a Master's program in curriculum and instruction and focused on science education.

My student teaching experience did not really prepare me to take on a regular teaching load in September. The faculty and my mentor teacher, although very nice people, did not help in understanding pedagogy let alone any of the key principles in science education like teaching through inquiry. This made transitioning in the fall into a full time teaching position very difficult. On my first day of school, I felt utterly unprepared and quite shocked that "the system" would allow someone as ill prepared as me to be responsible for students only a few years younger than me. One particular student was only three years younger than me.

I was assigned a mentor teacher through the district who was helpful, but was herself unsupported and not prepared to be a mentor teacher. My unofficial mentors were the key factors in making me the teacher I am today. There were about four science teachers that immediately took me under their wing during my first years. They supported, encouraged, and guided me as I learned to be a teacher but most importantly showed me the value of a professional community. That critical network during my first years teaching was vital to not only my development as a teacher but also a factor in wanting to make teaching a lifelong commitment.

During my graduate work I met many other teachers and quickly learned my experiences at East Side were uncommon and many of my peers were leaving the field. I then realized that a key component in teacher retention, especially in urban schools, is the establishment of a strong and supportive community of teacher learners. I wanted to be a mentor teacher to support new teachers in the capacity that I had been supported.

During the spring semester of my third year teaching, I was approached by Dr. Santos, my school principal, and asked if I would be interested in becoming a mentor teacher in the NMUTR. Dr. Santos was very excited about this opportunity and was eager to have me participate. His interest encouraged me to seek more information about the program's mission and vision. I quickly learned that this program was very different from the traditional teacher education program when I was introduced to the rigorous mentor selection process. I was first observed by Monica and Cindy, two of the lead faculty for the secondary cohort, followed by a debrief, and elaborate interview with the professors and Jennifer Robinson. During this interview I was asked to bring artifacts, assessments, and other student work that would help to support my philosophy of teaching. It was during this selection process that I realized the dedication the faculty and staff had towards preparing new science and math teachers for NPS. I knew this was a program I wanted to be a part of and help provide the necessary support to preservice teachers.

Unfortunately I was not able to attend the cohort two resident interviews but when I first met Alex and Dave, I could see that they had very different personalities that would end up greatly complementing each other and myself. Alex was a young and eager new teacher. He was full of energy, ideas, and enthusiasm when it came to teaching and working with students. His passion for the content and for teaching was evident from day one. Having worked in a special needs school prior to his residency, Dave came into the program with a slightly different and more realistic perspective than Alex. Dave was excited to use the skills and understandings he learned in his prior experiences as he began his residency.

As the school year progressed, these differences in personalities had positive and negative consequences, but most importantly served as an essential balance to the relationship between Alex and Dave and also the relationship between the three of us. Alex's enthusiasm was always encouraging and added a sense of urgency and eagerness to my own practice and was contagious for Dave as he planned and implemented his lessons. Dave's more at ease approach helped ground Alex during his lesson design and implementation and encouraged me as the mentor to be more flexible in my own expectations. There was a balance that I think provided a critical factor in the success of our relationship and our success as team teachers.

Kimberly Scott Kallai, I decided to become a NMUTR mentor because of my own experiences of being mentored during my first years of teaching. My mentor was magnificent at demonstrating what a good mentor is not. He was great at pointing out my flaws, showing absolutely no signs of compassion or understanding, singing his own praises and generally just not "being there" for me. I really thought long at hard at the end of that school year about whether or not to continue teaching especially since I was so deficient, according to him. I tried to fight my feelings of inadequacy by moving on to another school, which I had hoped would provide me with some glimmer of hope, motivation, and inspiration. I was sadly disappointed.

My second school consisted of an enormous student population, around 3000 students, where I immediately felt lost in the madness. I was given four different classes to teach, which were all the lowest level classes. I was teaching in three different rooms on three different floors and didn't know if I was coming or going half the time. I looked to my supervisor and department colleagues for advice and guidance but to no avail and I was left to navigate on my own. I remained at the school for two years and they were the toughest teaching years in my career. I was resolute in my decision to leave the profession.

After having spent the last few months at my school preparing for a career change, I found myself confiding in a friend, who was also a teacher, about my decision to leave the profession. She spent a good amount of time trying to convince me that I was a good teacher and that I was making the wrong decision. She also informed me about a vacancy at her school and that I should interview for the position. After adamantly rationalizing my reasons for not wanting to go, she told me that she was going to let the principal know to expect me for an interview. I agreed only to appease her, and showed up to the interview at the specified date and time. I proceeded to meet with the principal and one of the first questions that she asked me was why I wanted to teach. I responded with, "I don't." After the shock left her face, she replied, "Why you are here?" to which I admitted that I was doing it to appease a friend. Her next response took me by surprise. She said, "Describe to me your experiences thus far as a teacher." Well, I let loose, and began to describe every horrible thing that had happened to me over the last three years. Probably not the best way to go about an interview, but I was honest and felt that I had nothing to lose. After finishing my rant, I waited for the courteous, yet generic response of "Thank you for coming", "We'll be in touch." To my utter disbelief, her response was, "Kim, I am so sorry that you have been treated that way and I promise never to treat you like that." I couldn't believe what I was hearing. "Is she for real?"

Yes, in fact she was for real. Not only did she convince me to give this teaching thing another try, she salvaged my career. She kept her promise and treated me with nothing but respect and professionalism. She was everything I believe a great mentor is supposed to be. She was supportive, caring, knowledgeable, empathetic and someone who listens. Her actions shaped my perceptions as an educator and instilled a desire for personal and professional growth.

I am now currently a math teacher at Arts High School and cannot imagine teaching anywhere else. Do I have those days where I think I can't possibly deal another day with the emotional, mental, and physical strains of the political bureaucracy found in an urban school district? Absolutely! But I always manage to overcome those feelings and I can always attribute it to one compelling factor—my amazing students! Growing up myself in a somewhat affluent community, I used to hear the stories about Newark and the schools that existed there. Usually all negative. But most of those conversations did not revolve around how resilient, creative, loving, and insightful the students truly are. I have to admit, I was not planning on sustaining my career within NPS, but here I am, fourteen years later and still amazed by my students. Do most of the students come to us grossly below skill level? Unfortunately they do, but where can the blame be placed? Many would say on the students. I don't agree. It is however, my responsibility to right that wrong the best way I can and that begins in my classroom. Teaching and learning in a math classroom or should I say MY math classroom may not be what someone would expect. Yes there are conversations surrounding mathematical content, but more often than not, the dialogue often takes on unconventional forms. It is from those conversations that trust is developed, fear is alleviated, courage is enacted, and critical thought begins to take shape.

My journey to the NMUTR, in many ways, was deliberate and I believe destined. I have been employed at my school for the past fourteen years and have taken on a mentoring role in various capacities over the last eight years. Many of those opportunities have involved working with multiple programs through MSU so the NMUTR was a natural progression for me. When I heard about it, I knew that this was something I had to be a part of because I deeply believed in its mission.

I remember meeting Janae Taylor, a resident from cohort 2, for the first time at her interview. Ultimately I became her mentor during the 2011–2012 school year, but I vividly remember thinking how young I thought she was. Interviewing her with Monica, I remember how nervous she was, tripping over her words at times and nervously giggling through awkward pauses. I remember talking to her and trying to ease her mind and calm her with my words. It was completely obvious to me that Janae wanted this more than anything, but could she handle it? She confided in me later that she was so happy that I was assigned as her mentor. She talked about her interview and how she was in fact so nervous. She told me that I was a comfort to her during that process and how appreciative she was that I had been there. I knew after that interview that I had to mentor Janae. I knew that she needed to be nurtured and I was just the one to do it. And so it began, in September of 2011, our journey. Being a Newark native, Janae had so much to offer the students, but even more to offer me. It was so much more than a mentor/resident relationship. It was more like family. Her experience, her life, her journey was all-inspiring and sparked in me a new found motivation for teaching. Not just for teaching students but for teaching teachers.

William Romney, throughout my young adult life I developed a passion for social justice through working to improve the quality of the educational atmosphere—in terms of bullying and microagressions—for young queer and questioning youth in NYC including myself. This passion followed me into college where I began to see that education in general was also a source of inequity. In the final two years of college I did peer mentoring for freshman and saw the huge discrepancy in preparedness overall and especially when it came to STEM subjects. I began reflecting on my own educational upbringing and how my family struggled to ensure I did not have to go to the public schools in my city. I began to research more to uncover and understand why a single mother of three earning less than 45,000 a year would choose to pay tuition instead of sending me to the public schools. I still have no idea how that worked. Knowledge became power and fueled my entrance into teaching. I was not just angry that students were under-served but also that the lecture style of education, the teacher who dumps information into a child's brain, was still prevalent regardless of the historic records of what good teaching should be. I began to branch out in efforts to be a better teacher for my students.

Eventually, I found the NMUTR. Honestly, the program was a beacon of light that was sorely needed. I fully believed in inquiry based learning across the curriculum, that it can be rigorous, and that it is a great way to engage, invest, and build knowledge with students at all levels. With the NMUTR, I was able to do more than just practice in isolation, which never works all that well, and instead gained an entire community of people that practiced, was not afraid to fail, and was fully collaborative and very thoughtful. I was able to work with newer teachers that really had that same fire to change what education looked like for the children I so loved to teach. One of the best things about the NMUTR, in addition to the amount of heart and clarity of vision, is that each and every teacher in that program not only becomes a better teacher but a leader. Leaders are innovative, collaborative, reflective, critical of their own work and ready to take the leap and if they fail they regroup and try again, they persist and they do so smartly through research and asking tough questions to the right people. That insight was the turning point of my career and I will always be thankful. Teaching is the greatest profession. Education is the light at the end of the tunnel for humanity. I am happy to be part of the movement towards getting the formula for education right, for each and every person.

Linda Abrams, at the time of this cohort's program, I was a second year doctoral student assistant. My interest in working with mentor teachers grew out of my own mentored experience. My mentor (back in 1984!) was a true teacher educator. We met every Friday to discuss our week and we usually read something during the week, like Dewey, which we would discuss and relate to what happened in school. This experience fundamentally shaped my teaching and later my approach to supervising my department and then in my last job as I worked with teachers in writing curriculum.

Joining the NMUTR as a doc assistant was a great learning experience for me because I had a front row seat in a program that valued the mentors and worked hard at building their capacity as teacher educators. I could see the cooperation and the collegiality developing between the faculty and mentors with both groups tapping into each other's expertise. At first this was done informally during the mentor meetings. But later, especially when the video project took off, there were occasions when the mentors' knowledge of teaching practices became the focus. (Before that time, this knowledge was applied but not discussed as explicitly. I would say that their "insider" knowledge of how the school functioned, knowledge about the students, and knowledge about how the resident was doing was most frequently and explicitly shared.)

From a very personal perspective, I thought the UTR faculty's value for teachers' practice knowledge matched my own, which was so important to me. I believe teachers know a lot that just goes unarticulated and unexamined because it is so embedded in what they do. I have read so much that is critical of teachers that spending time in the NMUTR and feeling the respect for teachers were just inspiring for me and my work.

171

EMILY J. KLEIN, ANNA KARINA MONTEIRO, KIMBERLY SCOTT
KALLAI, WILLIAM ROMNEY AND LINDA ABRAMS

7. ARTICULATING THE INTIMATE KNOWLEDGE
OF TEACHING

Mentors and Faculty Design Protocols to Explore
Video Artifacts of Teaching

INTRODUCTION

In the spring of 2012, Linda, one of the two doctoral assistants in the program, sat down with Kim and Erin, the mentors at Arts High School, who were beginning to "practice" using a series of video protocols (described within) that she, faculty, and mentors had recently co-created.

Kim: I was imagining myself working with one of the residents and how would I be able to get them engaged in the conversation because I mean I don't know how you guys feel about it. But I know it's very hard to talk about my teaching practices. I don't know how to talk about them.

Erin: Yeah.

Kim: I can't even verbalize sometimes why I've done something. It feels like it's natural. I think I've just been teaching for so long and I've had so many student teachers that, for me, it isn't difficult 'cause I've had to do it so often for so many years.

Erin: You have to question her to get her to think about things and have her question you back kind of, which–

Kim: Yeah. I'm interested in using it to watch the video of myself teaching versus her. I feel like she misses a lot of the things that I do. And I guess it's my job to point them out. But then like I'm like, "Oh, and did you see that? Did you see when I did that?"

The dilemmas of creating a strong mentoring program in the third space are multiple. As described above, for all mentors, the prospect of trying to explain the intimate knowledge of teaching and practice can be daunting and isolating. For universities, the tendency is to create a false dichotomy where the university "holds" the theoretical knowledge and the schools, the tacit or practice based knowledge. Part of our work in the third space was finding ways to blend these conventional assumptions about knowledge. In early 2012 the faculty and mentors developed a series of video protocols that tried to support teachers in making the tacit, explicit. Knowing the research that suggests mentors may need support using such protocols (Borko & Mayfield, 1995), Linda, Kim, and Erin selected a random clip from one of their videos, role-played using the protocols, and then debriefed the process. Linda audiotaped the meeting and later transcribed the recording. As these practices unfolded throughout the semester, we began to realize the power of video in supporting a variety of aspects of our practices as teacher educators.

Later in their conversation that day, they began to realize that one clip could be discussed through multiple lenses. At first they talked about using the clip they watched to discuss the link between classroom management and lesson organization, but finally Kim suggested that what they were noticing was Suzanne's ability to communicate effectively and to create a culture of respect with her students.

Kim: So it's like, how do you create and enforce expectations but also then how do you communicate those expectations? Or teacher as culture agent, establishing a culture of respect and rapport, you know? Democratic ideals that, you know, that you're respecting each other 'cause they were—they talk over each other, you know?

Linda: Yeah, yeah they do.

Erin: Right. And it's not to be disrespectful but it is and they don't even—they don't even realize that it is disrespectful, so like how do you establish that culture?

Linda later reflected that this was when she and the mentors began to develop a mentoring language. For Monica and Emily it was also the beginning of an important, but significant shift in the third space collaborative work. In this chapter, Emily, along with two of the mentors, Karina and Kim, and one of the two doctoral assistants, Linda, narrate the process by which videos emerged as a vehicle to unpack and communicate practice.

PURPOSE/CONTEXT

In February 2012, the faculty and mentors completed the official course in self-study and action research, but we knew as a team that we wanted to build on the momentum and maximize the benefits of the community we were creating. In our first meeting after that course, Linda, wrote in her journal,

This afternoon the mentors decided to study their own and their residents' teaching practices in a way that reminds me of lesson study. The structure of their studies will be different, but they are directed at developing a line of communication for talking about learning teaching. Learning *teaching* is different from learning how to teach because the assumption is that both the mentor and the resident will be learning. I think this process will be fascinating, so I hope to observe and record at least two meetings when they meet to talk about their lesson videos. I would like to see how they work through the learning by critiquing process.

We saw the seeds of our third space taking root, but we were not sure what to do next. We were starting to see a shift in who was creating the agenda and doing the knowledge making; it was no longer the university faculty only, and through our self studies, the mentor teachers seemed to appreciate that the faculty were willing to be open to sharing these spaces with them. As we wrote and reflected about this time together each of us expressed concerns about program needs. For Karina and Kim the issue of video came about as a way to manage a concern they were seeing related to "tunnel vision." Karina reminded us that as teachers, we often think of our teaching through our own eyes and experiences. What we see, what we think we do, and how we react can be one-dimensional. The use of video provides an additional perspective, an objective one that is critical to our development. When an observer, like a supervisor, administrator, or mentor provide feedback to a lesson it can be easy to think the observer is being subjective and not truly accept what they say is true or simply not "see" what they are talking about. Video can provide an "objective" perspective that can support an observer's feedback. Much of the literature supported the mentors' beliefs that the use of video increases reflection for preservice teachers (most notable among that research is the work of: Charles, Ria, Bertone, Trohel, & Durhand, 2004; Masats & Dooly, 2011; Rosaen, Lundenerg, Cooper, Fritzen, & Terpstra, 2008; Schepens, Aelterman, & Van Keer, 2007).

As mentors observing a lesson, Kim and Karina felt they could tell their residents over and over again that they needed to pay attention to a particular component in their lesson, but to no avail. Video can serve as a critical and factual representation of the resident's movement throughout the room. The struggle to find novel ways to give feedback to the residents was one of the reasons we first came to the idea of using video. Often times Kim and Karina would find themselves repeating feedback to residents but it continuously was not "clicking" for them. It was the use of video protocols that helped to solidify feedback and provide an avenue for those "aha!" moments.

The faculty continued to be concerned with how best to build a third space and support the mentor teachers in emerging as teacher educators; they knew they needed to continually provide a means for mentors to have a legitimized space for teacher knowledge. As the group transitioned out of the self-study and action research course, we came together in January to think about what might be next for us. Although Monica and Emily had ideas, they knew that they had begun to create a more genuine, but still fragile democratic professional community, where the problems of practice drove all of our learning. They also knew that the next steps needed to be negotiated by all members of this third space community. As we sat together during that January afternoon, one of the concerns the faculty, Linda, and the mentors articulated together was, as we mention earlier, how the mentors might be more explicit in discussing their practices with their residents. This concern came specifically, in part, from observing (on the part of Monica, Emily, and Linda) and participating in (on the part of faculty and mentors) several debriefing and planning sessions where the mentors did not have the language to express what they intended to convey. Kim later wrote about her memories of that day:

> Karina's room is always inviting, which helps to make for a great place to vent and share positive and negative experiences. I remember feeling so tired and it was so dark outside. It felt like there was a small group of us that day—a very intimate group. We started out by sharing our recent resident experiences as we always did... someone was talking about a RTOP and giving feedback and discussion continued about how to relay feedback to our residents... Erin mentioned that she was having some difficulty giving feedback to Suzanne... There was discussion as to what she could do differently to possibly counteract that outcome from Suzanne. I can't remember who initially brought up the idea of video, but I remember we ran with the idea and began brainstorming about it. Someone asked, "How should we do it?" "Should we videotape the residents? ... the final consensus was something along the lines of ... well let's just do it and see how it goes. We can make adjustments as we move through the process.

Their knowledge of what they did in the classroom every day was so tacit that they did not seem to recognize it as knowledge that could be conveyed, as opposed to just modeling a practice or skill. What we want to emphasize was that while Linda and the faculty were familiar with the literature about video (and soon to become more familiar), this was a messy, non-linear process, where we sought a number of specific methods to support each other in the goal of both meeting the authentic concerns of the mentors and faculty, while also nurturing our third space community. The process evolved over time.

This chapter explores what happens when faculty and mentors co-construct a process for using video artifacts as a means of helping them articulate their instructional moves with their residents, and more importantly, the conditions that need to be in place for this to be an effective tool. We argue that the tool, devoid of a third space construction, is far less effective as a means of knowledge construction. Kim, one of the co-authors, uses her work with Janae as a lens to describe how mentors and residents use the protocols and how they experienced them in terms of reflecting on and developing their practice.

BUILDING THE PROTOCOLS

The literature on the use of video supports a variety of purposes and as Sherin's (2004) historical reading of video use in teacher education makes clear, "video has proved itself to be a flexible medium, adaptable in both form and function ... driven to a large extent by changes in leading theoretical frameworks in education" (p. 9). Thus, a behaviorist model of education will largely use video to deconstruct teaching into bits and pieces that can be analyzed and taught. Conversely, underlying our video use was a conception of teaching as inquiry based, constructivist, complex, dynamic, and relational. When we first began to explore video use in the residency it was without a single clear pedagogical purpose, but as Sherin suggests, video affords teachers a "new set of practices ... based on repeated viewings and reorganizations of video" based on such things as time, providing access to others' practices, and the opportunity to hone in on smaller sized pieces of practice (p. 14). Sherin (2009b) suggests video can be used both to exhibit best practices in teaching and to help us see other possibilities in teaching but can also be used as a means to reflect on one's own practice. When we initiated our use of video we hoped to be able to navigate across these domains: identifying best practices, discovering new strategies, and improving our teaching through reflection.

Similar to Whitehead and Fitzgerald (2006), Emily and Monica were particularly interested in video as a tool that would help expand our third space enterprise. Whitehead and Fitzgerald (2006) noticed that they had re-created a traditional top-down hierarchical teacher education model, and were seeking ways to create a "new and democratic" model that would emphasize the value of practitioner, teacher generated knowledge, as well as value pupil and preservice teacher knowledge (p. 46). Using videos of mentor teacher practice, they invited both preservice teachers and students in classrooms to engage in dialogue and reflection about effective practice, making significant inroads against the "traditional hierarchy" between faculty, mentors, preservice teachers, and students (p. 47). The faculty too wondered if it would support our own attempts at pushing back against this hierarchy, by creating a "text" where teacher knowledge was valued as a significant source for learning and growth.

After the first meeting when we tentatively decided we might move forward with video, Emily contacted Joseph P. McDonald at New York University, whose work with protocols is well known, (McDonald, Mohr, Dichter, & McDonald, 2003) to ask for guidance in developing a protocol for viewing videos in our next mentor-resident meeting. He shared the "Text Rendering Protocol—Video Version" (private email, 3/12/12) as a model we could tailor to our needs. Given that we had a clear understanding of the mentor and resident needs and a growing understanding of how we might be able to use video to meet them, Linda, Monica, and Emily emailed before the meeting about how to modify the protocol. Monica was clear from the start, that rather than come in with a protocol, that this had to emerge from our co-constructed knowledge. In her email she wrote,

> Ok—so now that I have had a moment to think—I think we need to do this differently. We need to be generative and not imposing so... I think we first ask what their goals and objectives are for the protocol. Then we say that we found this McDonald protocol and we would like to try it out—may not be exactly what we want as a group—but we could get some ideas from it. We watch video (preferably of Karina not the residents) and do one round of the protocol.

> Then we pause to see what people are thinking—if it meets their needs—do we
> need to alter it, add to it, etc. What did we like about it? And then create our
> own protocol—What do you think?

It was in these frantic moments of thinking through agendas, where the faculty and
doctoral assistants would push back on each other, and often Monica would remind
the team not to re-create the very dynamic that needed to be disrupted. It would have
been simple for the faculty to take the lead, but they were consciously trying to resist
the traditional hierarchy between university and school faculty, and the difference
between generating motifs and presenting them to mentors proved to be a crucial
one.

Prior to the meeting, Linda asked Karina to videotape a lesson where students
were giving a presentation they had designed regarding a specific body system. The
lesson consisted of Karina and a student co-teaching a mini lesson. When the group
came together to discuss the process we first began by brainstorming how we could
use videos with residents. During this meeting, we initially thought to only use the
video as a means of providing feedback to the residents after a lesson but we worried
that it might be too overwhelming for them if it focused on the entire lesson. So
instead we decided to brainstorm some motifs or themes as viewing lenses. First, we
watched the 10-minute video of Karina's lesson. Then, in pairs, mentors and faculty
came up with some motifs on which we could concentrate during the second watch.
Some examples that we came up with were "teacher as facilitator," "classroom
culture," and "student engagement," etc. Each team selected a motif on which to
focus for the second viewing. As we watched, we wrote down observations on post-
it notes that supported or did not support the particular motif. We then came together
and discussed the evidence of each motif in a large group. We knew that figuring out
what to pay attention to was one of the crucial challenges for new teachers and so that
became a particularly useful part of the protocol. As well, the motifs connected to
salient issues the mentors and faculty were confronting with the residents. Using the
motif and the evidence showed promise in mediating conversations about teaching,
although we wanted to create a number of other options about how we might work
with the video and also add to the motifs. The group agreed that Linda should re-
work the protocol and we worked collaboratively to think about how to build upon it.

Linda wrote-up the group's suggestions and developed specific protocols for
viewing mentor and resident videos differently (see Appendix). The protocols are
aimed at eliciting tacit teaching knowledge and answering questions about what,
how, and why the teacher and/or students are doing what they are during a segment
of a lesson. Like McDonald's protocol, these ask the viewer to identify a motif in the
video, however what differs are the extension of the observation and conversation
into inquiry.

During our first attempt at using the modified protocols version, we struggled to
name teaching motifs. To address this barrier, we turned to the work of Danielson
(2009), Hollins (2011), Ball and Forzani (2009), and Grossman (2011) to help us

identify teaching practices that could be clustered into teaching motifs. Linda added a list of 11 motifs, co-developed by faculty and mentors, and associated practices to the new video protocols so that mentors and residents could more easily name what they observed and wanted to discuss. Drawing from our brainstorming discussion, she noted that where the camera was placed in the room and where it was focused, would have an influence on what was observed, and she offered two suggestions for gathering evidence of practices while viewing.

USING THE PROTOCOLS

Differentiated Use and Co-constructed Practice

The spring allowed for some initial experimentation with the video protocols, and below we describe how those played out with a number of our teams, highlighting the most significant themes that arose from those earliest experiments. This beginning analysis would later lay the groundwork for how we would further develop our video protocols use.

When Kim and Janae were placed together, the faculty knew that the mentoring and mentee relationship would be a powerful one. They thought Janae might particularly connect with Kim, an older woman of color who was nurturing and had worked with student teachers for years. Janae, a young African American woman (she tells her story in the section before chapter four), had recently graduated from high school and college in Newark, and often the issue of gaining perspective on herself and her teaching was her greatest challenge. The faculty wanted a mentor who would help her through that transition in the gentlest way possible, and Kim was one of their most experienced, nurturing mentors. We thought that cultural match might be helpful as well so that Janae would have a mentor who understood some of the issues of navigating a teaching job where her personal identity as a black woman would play a crucial role in her relationships with her students. Kim's years of urban teaching experience (with students very much like Janae) helped her to foster a productive mentoring relationship.

But she was unprepared for how difficult Janae would find the process of examining videos of herself. Initially Kim presented two clips of video, one of herself teaching a segment of a lesson, and next of Janae teaching a similar segment. Immediately Janae "crumbled" as Kim described it. Rather than being able to dissect the video using the motifs laid out together in the protocol, Janae was overwhelmed by what she saw were the massive differences in their skills and teaching abilities. Quickly Kim realized that she would need to re-think her use of the protocols. She realized that as Borko, Jacobs, Eiteljorg, and Pittman (2008) suggest in their work with inservice teachers, she needed to create a safe space for Janae to learn from video. Sharpe et al.'s (2003) research also confirmed that because preservice teachers feel uneasy and self-conscious engaging with video, mentors sometimes withheld criticism to avoid any hurt feelings. We all needed to figure out a way to use this tool productively and it underscored the importance of *differentiated use* in how we approached this process.

In Kim and Janae's second use with the protocols, they paired up with another mentor/resident team in their school, Erin and Suzanne, and the two mentors led two cycles of reflection. In the first, the mentors each picked a segment of the video to analyze, and in the second, the residents picked a segment and a motif on which they wanted to focus. Kim theorized that Janae needed more ownership of the process. In a planning meeting with Linda and Erin, she identified which protocol would be best for them to use:

> I think the second one would be more beneficial for her because she just tends to never ask me questions of why I did what I did or how, or what. She just sort of lets me teach and she just sort of mirrors in some way, and she doesn't really ever stop to say, 'Well, why did you do this?' or 'Why did you do that?' So she needs to learn to do that. So I think this is probably more beneficial for her.

In addition she repeatedly emphasized the importance of Janae picking the clips to watch, coming up with the question, and driving the process because it "gives her the power, puts her in the driver's seat, and that's something that kind of would push her … " This was an essential strategy that Kim became acutely aware of during her own reflections on her mentoring. Early on in their work together, Kim remarked: "I still feel like I'm doing too much talking, too much direct instruction almost. In particular working with Janae who is very quiet I felt like I dominated the conversation instead of eliciting her understanding and knowledge."

She also hoped that it would be useful for Janae to see another resident (Suzanne) share her video. Although the residents had multiple opportunities to see each other teach, and therefore had multiple representations of novice practice, there seemed to be something about the video artifact that made the experience particularly challenging in a one-on-one interaction with their mentors. Therefore Kim, in collaboration with other mentors and faculty, experimented with using the video protocols in a small group community, a community with which Janae had worked throughout the year. She told us:

> I did that (RTOP) different ways with her. The first time I did it, I just observed her and wrote down comments and just filled it out that way. I went over it with her and she thought it was helpful. The second time I scripted her and she felt that was more helpful than the previous observation, she was like "Wow, did I say that?!" The third one I took her video and I sat there with headphones on and I took my time and scripted the lesson from the video and even though she had seen herself on video, when she read what I wrote, she was like "Did I say that?" And I was like "Yes, it's in the video." And she was like "Wow, I didn't even know I said that." She thought for me to have the video and to script it was the most helpful. It took me a long time and it was kind of tedious, and to do it once I think was enough but I think I would do it again because it was the most helpful.

One of the many things we learned from Kim and Janae's early experimentation with the protocols was that unlike much of the research with structured protocols, we needed to engage with our protocols more flexibly. Part of this was helping the mentors and residents articulate their purpose in using the protocol. Although there is research suggesting that using video with teachers provides them with space to reflect on their practice (particularly the work of Sherin, Linsenmeier, & Van Es, 2009a; Sherin & Van Es, 2009b), there is less research on what happens when they are afforded the opportunity to co-construct this process either as researchers or with preservice teachers (Clarke, 2006; Muir, Beswick, & Williamson, 2010). Clarke's study uses a modified stimulated recall—where the mentor has the opportunity to choose what portions of the video to return to again and again. This research provides evidence that when mentors are empowered to make decisions about their own professional development and growth they make more significant reflections about their own practice, (although any work with a student teacher does give opportunities to think more deeply about practice). Other studies where teachers have made decisions about what video clips to use and how to use them, have found that it allows for greater co-construction of knowledge, where preservice and inservice teachers collaborated on problems together and jointly constructed knowledge of teaching practice in collaboration (Cartaut & Bertone, 2009; Charles, Ria, Bertone, Trohel, & Durand, 2004).

As faculty and mentors, we were attempting to build relationships and meet the needs of a variety of different partnerships, to grow teachers in very different contexts, in different subjects, with different backgrounds and experiences. We were not engaged, primarily, in a research project. The use of video *grew out of* our work with residents, rather than something we created and then brought into the work. Thus, *differentiation* was one of the emergent themes from this work.

We saw this as well in Antonio's work with Will. Will and Antonio chose to focus the camera on the students rather than on either the mentor teacher or the resident; they realized that the focus of their practice as a team at that point in the year was on how they were impacting student learning and student behaviors. This was a unique interpretation of video use in their work together, and we later found out that Will had struggled to help Antonio feel comfortable using video at all, "I definitely learned that everyone has different comfort levels, and even though it's a good strategy, sometimes you have to know when to back off, or to change strategies—differentiate mentorship. And so learning different ways to use videotapes because it depends on comfort levels." Given Antonio's discomfort, they adapted the use of video protocols to afford them other opportunities to learn about classroom practice. For his partnership, video had to be used in a particular way to support the needs of his mentee.

Specifically, during a social justice, inquiry based, unit on environmental science, Will and Antonio documented students' reactions to building a garden in Newark and the unit around that. While they were interested in teaching behaviors, too often they noticed that despite beautifully planned and implemented lessons, there were many aspects of student learning they were missing. Thus, for a period of time they focused the lens on groups of students, so that they could pay attention to those aspects of classroom learning that they felt they were not attending to in the midst of the chaos of class time: "…we don't always remember everything or see what the children are doing, their facial expressions and everything like that, so to just be able to pinpoint …. To see how they respond to whatever's going on…" One discovery Will made in this process was that despite creating what they considered to be inquiry based lessons, the lessons still tended to be teacher centered—something that was most sharply revealed through video: "… he definitely asks great questions, it's just that a lot of the inquiry classes, it's still him leading it and not enough conversation and participation from the kids."

Articulated Practice

Janae and Kim also confirmed for us that one of the most important aspects of using video was that it supported *articulation of practice* for the mentors and the residents. Consistently, mentors found that video encouraged their own professional development and articulated "reflection on action" (Schon, 1983). One mentor spoke about it as follows,

> …the program kind of forces us as mentors to be really reflective and to pay attention to our own practice so that what we do positively reflects what we see in our mentors … You have to be—not perfect, but just be confident in what you're doing, and be able to reflect and be able to share and be able to process— metacognitively process what you're doing so that you can teach someone else.

The work of Clark (2006), Ethell and McMeniman, (2000), and that of Schepens, Aelterman, and Van Keer (2007) speak to one of the main purposes of using video in teacher education; it allows for teachers to articulate features of practice that often go unspoken. The mentors had articulated, and faculty had observed that this was crucial in supporting mentor development as teacher educators in the program; in order to be able to become teacher educators they needed to be able to make explicit the tacit "moves" within their day-to-day work. Carroll's (2005) study about a school-based mentor study group used artifacts of practice like video to collaboratively "develop both their understanding of learning to teach and their repertoire of practice for mentoring novice teachers" (p. 457). He examined these artifacts and their discourse to unpack the "mentoring moves" within (p. 460) and understand how their work led to "new ideas and commitments about mentoring practice" (p. 460). He emphasized the ways in which mentors negotiate and represent meaning in their work together around artifacts, which was significant for our work using video. He writes:

> The idea of 'thinking out loud' is a basic strategy for helping a novice learn in the context of an experienced teacher's practice, whether it be in the context of planning, teaching, or reflecting after teaching. Unless the experienced teacher takes deliberate steps to reveal her thinking to the novice, important aspects of

the decision making and other intellectual work involved in these fundamental tasks of teaching remain invisible. (p. 464)

What video allows us to do is offer another opportunity for mentors to do this "thinking aloud" in a way that is often hard to do in the moment of practice.

Another finding of Carroll's (2005) relates to the joint construction of learning that occurred in the group through "re-voicing moves"—moves that get built upon, reflected back again and again, that are further developed and re-thought as they gain credibility throughout the group. This leads to the creation of "joint work", and ultimately helped to construct the group's identity as a community of practice, suggesting again, that there was potential for the use of video to support the continual creation of a third space.

Meijer, Zanting, and Verloop (2002) also confront the challenge of how mentors reveal their instructional moves to preservice teachers, and how they can "unearth" what they refer to as teacher's "practical knowledge." Their study looked at stimulated recall and concept mapping as two tools in this process. In stimulated recall, teachers "explicate their interactive thinking while watching a videotape of a lesson they have just been given" (p. 410), and the video serves as a memory prompt for the lesson taught. When preservice teachers conduct stimulated recalls with their mentors they are often able to uncover the reasoning behind split second decisions that may not seem highly reasoned, but often "teachers' interactive cognitions reveal thoughts beyond the "how" of teaching and into the 'why'" (p. 411). Kim would later reflect:

I think one of the major issues/challenges is trying to make the invisible visible to our residents. There are so many nuances to our teaching and at times it was difficult to describe them to our residents. We as mentor teachers paradoxically perform so many deliberate things in the classroom that are also done subconsciously that we are almost unaware that we are doing them. Being able to videotape a lesson that was taught by both mentor and resident allowed for rich discussions where we compared and contrasted behaviors, body language, spatial sense, along with many others. I think this aided in bringing the invisible to the forefront for Janae. Explaining to our residents why we do the things we do was one aspect, but actually being able to show them explicitly using the video was quite another.

Since school structures do not support mentor and resident reflection time, they often moved throughout the day so quickly that by the time school was over, even the most immediate reflection on a lesson had slipped their memory. Mentors often wished residents would ask different questions about practice, but felt uncomfortable just "telling" them what they wanted them to pay attention to. They also worried residents made assumptions that mentor teaching practices like facilitating group work, closing a lesson, or checking homework were relatively random. And often residents "missed" these very instances for learning, focusing instead on those things that were their *own* greatest concerns—curriculum, major instances of classroom management, and organization.

Some mentors worried that the residents were not even sure what questions to ask, despite extensive work on supporting the residents on how to ask good questions. The structure and use of the protocols gave them an additional structure to support the "culture of inquiry" we were trying to develop throughout the residency and supported the residents in asking more reflective questions. In a planning meeting around using video, Erin said "I don't think she thinks about why I'm doing the things I'm doing or that I'm even doing them for a reason. I think she kind of takes that at face value as—like she'll be like 'Oh, you were so good at questioning during that part.' But she doesn't wonder—like why did I ask the questions I did." Kim agreed, suggesting that the video protocols were "a way of getting them to do their own inquiry… Start getting them to think about, you know, why. That's so important for them to do that next year when they're on their own."

In an audiotaped meeting between Kim, Janae, Erin, and Suzanne, we listened to Kim speak about why she used extensive repetition, "… but I wanted to be clear that they knew what they were doing and what they were putting in the third column. That it was actually y divided by x. And it's about reiterating over and over what we're doing. So that's why I like to repeat myself and reiterate." Janae probed her thinking by asking, "Well I don't know, that kind of ties into my second question—since you said you like to repeat yourself, like, why did you repeat back like a student's explanation in a different way 'cause the student explained like, a pattern they saw that was incorrect and you repeated it back in a different way. Why did you do that?" Kim pointed to parts of the video, so that they could reflect on actual classroom data that otherwise might have been extremely hard to remember or was otherwise subjective. In the transcript of their conversation Kim indicates when a student actually says something "backwards":

> … so I wanted to clarify that's why I said it out loud to her and I gave an analogy to make it clear—I wanted to make sure she was clear on what she was saying and that all the other students were clear on what she was asking, what statement she was making, because then as a group we can go back and discuss is that true- what she said? So I try to, when a student's saying something, I try to repeat it back. In other words, "Is this what I'm hearing from you?" "Is this what I'm understanding?" So they either agree or disagree. And usually it's, yes, this is what I'm saying or no Ms. S you misunderstood me.

Following up on this Erin says, "cause also I think it makes the students think about what they're saying more slowly; actually think about the words, 'cause a lot of times they just say stuff." The conversation continues on with the residents asking questions of the mentors about their practices.

Connecting Theory to Practice

Emerging from our initial work with video, was a recurring theme that residents needed to be *"primed" for reflection*; some were not ready to coolly reflect upon their practice or were not initially prepared with the analytical tools to engage in video analysis. When describing her first challenging experience with Janae, Kim described how early in the school year, Janae assumed a mistake meant, "I suck as a teacher":

> She didn't want to watch herself because she beats herself up and she had to learn. And that was a really important lesson for her to learn, the most important, that she has to be able to look at herself, watch herself make mistakes, and say I made a mistake, and I recognize that and I'm going to do better the next time. Not say, I made a mistake and I suck as a teacher. And that's what she was doing at the beginning of the year, so to undo that I had to force her to keep watching herself … against her will, but she got used to it. So I think that was the most helpful for her because that was what she struggled with the most.

Sometimes this meant we had to engage in hard or difficult conversations.

Similar to action research, the use of video afforded us another opportunity to connect theory and practice (Ethell & McMeniman, 2000; Koc, 2011; Masats & Dooly, 2011). Because video allows for the dissection of classroom practice, freezing moments in time, and deep analysis and review of particular classroom moments, both mentors and residents can re-visit aspects of practice to move behind tacit understandings and assumptions about what happened in a classroom. Ethell & McMenamin (2000) found that student teachers were able to reconcile "propositional and procedural knowledge and [video] was identified by them as a catalyst in their development as reflective practitioners" (p. 98). For inservice teachers, Sherin's (2004) work in video clubs encouraged "a stance of inquiry" (p. 167). The body of her work on video clubs suggests that professional development work for math teachers using video helps them re-think the nature of students' ideas about mathematical thinking influencing teachers' classroom practices (Sherin & van Es, 2009b). Also, Rhine and Bryant (2007) found that the use of video encouraged teachers to explore moments of "incongruence" in practice, helping them to learn "reflection-in-action," something often so difficult for new and developing teachers. However, Masats and Dooly (2011) caution that critical viewing is not automatic, the reflective skills that need to be brought to the table to take advantage of the possibilities of video will not happen without support and coaching from the mentor teacher or university faculty. Many researchers use some form of stimulated recall, modified stimulated recall, concept mapping, or a combination of all three in order to support the kinds of reflection needed to make video more than just "re-watching" a class, something noted by any number of additional researchers (Ethell & McMenamin, 2000; Meijer, Zanting, & Verloop, 2002; Santagata & Angelici, 2010; Sharpe et al., 2003).

Building the reflective capacity of the resident was another way that video supported our work, as it provided the means for *connecting theory to practice*. The use of video gave the opportunity for the mentors to reinforce theoretical principles that the faculty emphasized but in real time or literally in practice. The faculty could talk about differentiation for example but it was much more powerful to discuss it in the thick of teaching. They often spoke about issues of differentiation, connecting with individual students, working with small groups, and managing large groups. They asked questions about what engagement looks like, about how you know students are learning, and about how a teacher meets the needs of all learners. For residents these questions often felt highly theoretical. This was frequently the case with Karina and Alex. Often times before we began using videos, Karina would give Alex feedback on a lesson and make mention that although it was critical he work in small groups, it was also important that he was aware of his surroundings and the actions of the students with whom he was not directly working. It was difficult to explain to him not to put his back to the rest of the class, or kneel down in a way that would block his vision of the remainder of the class. It was when Karina used the video protocol that Alex had an "aha!" moment. While watching a clip of Alex speaking with a small group of students they could both see that another group of students were off task and disengaged. Despite months of discussion with Karina, Alex had no idea this was going on during the lesson, but with the use of the video protocol he was able to see how important it was to have a broad lens at all times while teaching. Karina found the video process helped to solidify and provide evidence for the feedback she gave the residents. It was one thing to give a resident verbal feedback but a completely different story to support that feedback with video evidence. From her experiences with this protocol, using the video brought out many "aha!" moments similar to Alex's. It was after the residents saw their actions on video that they really made the connection between the feedback and their actions as teachers.

Overall the stories reveal that the use of video was grounded in conversations about mentoring and reflective practice but these conversations did not always come naturally. Analysis of data helped reveal the need for both multiple instances of the video protocol use to establish trust, and the ability to turn the lens on oneself, as well as some scaffolding or models of how to have deep and productive dialogue around both the "what" of teaching, the use of pedagogical and organizational strategies, as well as the "why" of teaching, the rationale behind instructional moves. Additionally, the mentors and faculty saw the impact of these reflective conversations when they developed out of specific needs to support residents with weaker practices. As we discuss below, the faculty continued to add a variety of reflective assignments into the everyday curriculum to prime the residents for reflection. Some examples of these assignments include weekly critical blogging, video blogging, and the use of other protocols to encourage warm and cool feedback (Klein, Taylor, Onore, Strom, & Abrams, 2013).

IMPLICATIONS – GROWING TEACHER LEADERS AND EDUCATORS IN A THIRD SPACE

While the protocols themselves were designed to help mentors articulate their instructional moves and residents learn to better "see" elements of their own practice, there was a secondary level of purpose behind the work together, which was to support the development of the mentors as teacher leaders and continue the construction of a third space urban teacher residency; delicate work often happening within a more fragile space than perhaps conveyed in the past tense writing about it.

Zanting, Verloop, and Vermunt (2001) write that the "missing role" for mentors is that of articulator of practical knowledge (p. 407). In developing that "role" it was the faculty's hope that mentors would develop as teacher leaders, a key facet of the residency work. Certainly the literature suggested that groups of teachers reviewing video together could build communities of practice (Borko, Jacobs, Eiteljorg, & Pittman, 2008; Sherin, 2004) and build their knowledge even as they worked with preservice teachers (Charles, Ria, Bertone, Trohel, & Durhand, 2004). And also the role of mentors in working with preservice teachers in unpacking video was key in helping them best make sense of what they saw (Rich & Hannafin, 2008). Most importantly using video as a tool for professional learning validates practitioner knowledge (Parker-Katz & Bay, 2007). Parker-Katz and Bay's study (2007) as well as others (Clarke, 2006; Korinek, 1989; Zimpher & Sherrill, 1996), showed that mentors saw their role as assisting teacher candidates through the lens of collaborative work and they appreciated the opportunity to contribute to the profession through their work with preservice educators

Examining videos with the video protocols during mentor meetings served to give them an opportunity to "practice" the protocols with other mentors and faculty and it provided another means of feedback on their own practice. In doing so, the mentors and faculty often struggled to move beyond the "nice" community norms Grossman, Wineburg, and Woolworth (2001) describe. However, a number of the mentors mentioned this as an opportunity for their own professional growth and learning. Kim was particularly struck by the impact of watching herself on video:

> Just seeing myself on video, too. I had never done that before. Watching myself on video made me more aware of how I behave physically, my facial expressions, and I know she sees that, and I'm a mentor, so I was definitely more critical of myself. More mindful. After I saw myself on video, the next day I was actually trying to watch this facial expression or this action.

Karina found that she began to use video of herself teaching to model particular methods or strategies for her residents. She felt this contributed to her own growth as an educator, as it helped to point out particular strengths and weaknesses in her strategies. In turn the use of video during her own lessons modeled for the residents the benefits and importance of self-reflection and the value in critical feedback when improving your practice. By demonstrating how to take feedback and being reflective, her residents were able to become more comfortable when it was their turn. Through making her work transparent and being vulnerable she exhibited more qualities as a teacher leader, as did others who found new opportunities to speak with authority about their professional expertise. Monica and Emily knew from past work in teacher leadership, "that teachers who are leaders of their own learning can support students in taking charge of their learning, thus, affecting student engagement in learning" (Taylor, Goeke, Klein, Onore, & Geist, 2011, p. 928). For many teachers in Newark, a space that historically has not always been supportive of teachers engaging in leadership work, this had the potential to be the beginning step of teacher leadership as well: "teacher leaders shifted from being receivers of knowledge to meaning makers as they identified and amplified their professional voices" (Taylor et al., p. 923). This first step, of becoming "meaning makers" in their own work, was something the faculty felt they could not push in year one of the program, but became a more urgent priority during the course of year two. This was the case for several reasons: most of their energies were devoted to launching the curriculum and routines with the residents and in truth their relationships with mentors were still too tentative. It was only after the first year and then doing the action research/self-study alongside the mentors that they felt they had developed a solid trusting collaborative community where they could name the work together. Teachers began to see leadership as something that was not a "role" named by an external office, but rather as something they named for themselves.

Emily and Monica felt the work, building upon the semester of action research and self-study and the leadership mentors took in facilitator residents' action research, continued to build the mentors as co-teacher educators and teacher leaders. Recognizing that we had different knowledge bases became another concrete and tangible means of accessing practitioner knowledge. And yet, as faculty, they often struggled to know how far they could push critical feedback and conversations with mentors, whose good will they relied deeply upon in the work. In becoming mentors, they had all agreed they wanted to grow as teachers, but the faculty often felt they needed to tread carefully in how they gave feedback. Below such a conversation is highlighted, where the video gave the faculty an entry into an honest and potentially critical conversation about practice, but where they were unsure of how to proceed.

Monica: Were there moments when you saw something you wanted to work on for yourself?

Kim: I know I wasn't completely happy with the lesson but I was being observed too—the way that I was asking the questions. I wish I had layered them better—sometimes this was in the sequence of questioning—sometimes hindsight is 20/20—the video helps me to be clearer about what I could improve.

Monica: The resident used the think/pair/share a lot since you suggested it— when a student asks a question, he re-posed it the group instead of answering it myself.

As evidenced from the conversation above, the discussion tiptoes into Kim's analysis of her practice, but rather than delve deeply into her questioning, it veers back into the practice of her resident. Part of this stems from the faculty's own hesitation to seem "critical" of mentor practice and some of it may stem from a lack of clarity about the purpose of video protocol use. The tool vacillated between one where mentors used it to help reveal their own teaching purposes, to one where they helped residents' examine their practice. But it was never identified as a tool specifically for mentor growth, instead it might inadvertently support their own learning as a secondary purpose. This left faculty feeling unsure about how far to engage mentors in reflection about their teaching practice in any way that might be perceived as negative. They were often highly aware of how fragile the third space was and how dependent they were upon the good will of the mentors. Also, the mentors had not signed up as "students" or even for a professional development program. They had signed up to be mentors and as such, had taken on an even stronger identity of "knowers" than even the average teacher, a position the faculty respected deeply. In many ways, the faculty felt they needed to validate the mentors' knowledge and experience, before they could begin to suggest the mentors examine their work in a way that might make them feel vulnerable.

Similarly, mentors were cautious to be critical of the amount of time the protocols were taking for them. They were gentle and slow in sharing with the faculty how much of a burden video use was becoming on them. Through some of the informal conversations and formal interviews, the faculty came to realize that in the following year, they would have to build video work into the curriculum in a way that would spread the work across faculty and mentors so that mentors were not left with the bulk of the responsibility for working with this tool. Because the third space is a delicate space, the faculty and mentors cautiously offered suggestions, showing concern not to do damage to their relationships. We all respected the nature of our work together and wanted to be careful to nurture that.

With reflection, a number of recommendations occur to the chapter authors in the building of this rather fragile, yet clearly rich third space with the mentors. While, we cannot guarantee that these would have advanced the community quicker or more effectively, still we make them in mind with the idea that even organically evolving partnerships require deliberate strategizing.

1. *Co-develop protocols to build professional voice:* One of the most effective strategies used in the process with the mentors was pulling back from imposing our own vision for what the protocols had to look like and do. Although they were grounded in research and in the faculty's vision, they very much emerged from the needs and ideas of the mentors. We cannot strongly enough emphasize how important the moment was when Monica urged Emily and Linda to ensure that they were not imposed from the university; it was a turning point for how they emerged and in their ultimate success. This was an important piece of developing the "professional voice" Taylor et al. (2011) discuss in their work on teacher leadership.

2. *Be clearer about asking mentors to videotape to use video both as professional learning for themselves as well as their residents*: We very quickly moved towards using video solely for the use of the residents. Upon reflection, the faculty might

have made a stronger push for some of the time and energy of the protocol use to be focused solely on the professional learning of the mentors. This might have created some discomfort amongst the mentors who would have wondered why they needed to engage in this work, but it would also have led to some important conversations about why we all need to continue to grow in our teaching.

3. *Faculty should engage in the professional learning as well:* As one means of addressing this discomfort, faculty might also consider both modeling and engaging in this work. Too often, faculty ask mentors to do the same work as their residents, but a real shift in the dynamics between university and school based faculty can occur when they jointly do work together. When school based faculty see university faculty present a video of their own teaching, struggle with a concept, ask hard questions, and invite cool feedback, they may be more open to the process. It is not always feasible, but as the faculty reflected back, they believed they might have done well to attempt this as a means of both modeling the practice and building trust in the group.

The fragility of the third space is not to be underestimated and Monica and Emily found themselves more likely to err on the side of careful rather than on the side of too aggressive, particularly with the mentors, who, they believed were the linchpin of a residency program. Slowly, and with care, those nurtured relationships formed the foundation for a stronger third space, but the process seems far more linear upon reflection than it did in the moment of creation. Similarly, they wanted to find ways to encourage the professional voice and actions of those who have largely been silenced in a system that fails to recognize the role of teachers as leaders in school change. For teachers who have largely been discouraged from any community level change initiatives, it has been important to the process to be respectful of the mentors' professional identity. Faculty's role is to find multiple ways to do this, while still urging everyone out of their traditional roles and comfort zones.

REFERENCES

Ball, D., & Forzani, F. (2009). The work of teaching and the challenge for teacher education. *Journal of Teacher Education, 60*(5), 497–511.

Borko, H., & Mayfield V. (1995). The roles of the cooperating teacher and university supervisor in learning to teach. *Teaching and Teacher Education, 11*(5), 501–518.

Borko, H., Jacobs, J., Eiteljorg, E., & Pittman, M. E. (2008). Video as a tool for fostering productive discussions in mathematics professional development. *Teaching and Teacher Education, 24*(2), 417–436.

Carroll, D. (2005). Learning through interactive talk: A school-based mentor teacher study group as a context for professional learning. *Teaching and Teacher Education, 21*(5), 457–473.

Cartaut, S., & Bertone, S. (2009). Co-analysis of work in the triadic supervision of preservice teachers based on neo-Vygostkian activity theory; Case study from a French University Institute of Teacher Training. *Teaching and Teacher Education, 25*(8), 1086–1094.

Charles, S., Ria, L., Bertone, S., Trohel, J., & Durand, M. (2004). Interactions between preservice and cooperating teachers and knowledge construction during post-lesson interviews. *Teaching and Teacher Education, 20*(8), 765–781.

Clarke, A. (2006). The nature and substance of cooperating teacher reflection. *Teaching and Teacher Education, 22*(7), 910–921.

Danielson, C. (2009). *Talk about teaching! Leading professional conversations.* Thousand Oakes, CA: Corwin Press.

Ethell, R. G., & McMeniman, M. M. (2000). Unlocking the knowledge in action of an expert practitioner. *Journal of Teacher Education, 51*(2), 87–101.

Grossman, P. (2011). Framework for teaching practice: A brief history of an idea. *Teachers College Record, 113*(12), 2836–2843.

Grossman, P., Wineburg, S., & Woolworth, S. (2001). Toward a theory of teacher community. *The Teachers College Record, 103*(6), 942–1012.

Hollins, E. (2011). Teacher preparation for quality teaching. *Journal of Teacher Education, 62*(4), 395–407.

Klein, E. J., Taylor, M., Onore, C., Strom, K., & Abrams, L. (2013). Finding a third space in teacher education: Creating an urban teacher residency. *Teaching Education, 24*(1), 27–57.

Koc, M. (2011). Let's make a movie: Investigating pre-service teachers' reflections on using video-recorded role playing cases in Turkey. *Teaching and Teacher Education, 27*(1), 95–106.

Korinek, L. A. (1989). Teacher preferences for training and compensation for field supervison. *Journal of Teacher Education, 40*(6), 46–51.

Masats, D., & Dooly, M. (2011). Rethinking the use of video in teacher education: A holistic approach. *Teaching and Teacher Education, 27*(7), 1151–1162.

McDonald, J., Mohr, N., Dichter, A., & McDonald, E. (2003). *The power of protocols: An educator's guide to better practice* (1st ed.). New York, NY: Teachers College Press.

Meijer, P. C., Zanting, A., & Verloop, N. (2002). How can student teachers elicit experienced teachers' practical knowledge: Tools, suggestions, and significance? *Journal of Teacher Education, 53*(5), 406–419.

Muir, T., Beswick, K., & Williamson, J. (2010). Up close and personal: Teachers' responses to an individualised professional learning opportunity. *Asia-Pacific Journal of Teacher Education, 38*(2), 129–146.

Parker-Katz, M., & Bay, M. (2007). Conceptualizing mentor knowledge: Learning from insiders. *Teaching and Teacher Education, 24*(5), 1259–1269.

Rhine, S., & Bryant, J. (2007). Enhancing pre-service teachers' reflective practice with digital video based dialogue. *Reflective Practice, 8*(3), 345–358.

Rich, P., & Hannafin, M. (2008). Capturing and assessing evidence of student teacher inquiry: A case study. *Teaching and Teacher Education, 24*(6), 1426–1440.

Rosaen, C. L., Lundeberg, M., Cooper, M., Fritzen, A., & Terpstra, M. (2008). Noticing noticing: How does investigation of video records change how teachers reflect on their experiences? *Journal of Teacher Education, 59*(4), 347–360.

Santagata, R., & Angelici, G. (2010). Studying the impact of the lesson analysis framework on preservice teachers' abilities to reflect on videos of classroom teaching. *Journal of Teacher Education, 61*(4), 339–349.

Schepens, A., Aelterman, A., & Van Keer, H. (2007). Studying learning processes of student teachers with stimulated recall interviews through changes in interactive cognitions. *Teaching and Teacher Education, 23*(4), 457–472.

Sharpe, L., Hu, C., Crawford, L., Gopinathan, S., Khine, M. S., Moo, S. N., & Wong, A. (2003). Enhancing multipoint desktop video conferencing (MDVC) with lesson video clips: Recent developments in pre-service teaching practice in Singapore. *Teaching and Teacher Education, 19*(2), 429–541.

Sherin, M. G. (2004). New perspectives on the role of video in teacher education. In J. Brophy (Ed.), *Using video in teacher education* (pp. 1–27). Amsterdam, The Netherlands: Elsevier.

Sherin, M. G., & van Es, E. A. (2009). Effects of video club participation on teachers' professional vision. *Journal of Teacher Education, 60*(1), 20–37.

Sherin, M. G., Linsenmeier, K. A., & van Es, E. A. (2009). Selecting video clips to promote mathematics teachers' discussion of student thinking. *Journal of Teacher Education, 60*(3), 213–230.

Schon, D. A. (1983). *The reflective practitioner: How professionals think in action.* London, UK: Temple Smith.

Taylor, M., Klein, E. J., Onore, C., Goeke, J., & Geist, K. (2011). Changing leadership: Teachers lead the way for schools that learn. *Teaching and Teacher Education, 27*(5), 920–929.

Whitehead, J., & Fitzgerald, B. (2006). Professional learning through a generative approach to mentoring: lessons from a training school partnership and their wider implications. *Journal of Education for Teaching, 32*(1), 37–52.

Zanting, P. C., Verloop, A., & Vermunt, N. (2001). How can student teachers elicit experienced teachers' practical knowledge: Tools, suggestions, and significance? *Journal of Teacher Education, 53*(5), 406–419.

Zimpher, N., & Sherrill, J. (1996). Professors, teachers, and leaders in SCDE's. In J. Sikula (Ed.), *Handbook of research on teacher education* (2nd ed., pp. 279–305). New York, NY: MacMillan.

Emily J. Klein
Department of Secondary and Special Education
Montclair State University
Montclair, New Jersey

Anna Karina Monteiro
East Side High School
Newark, New Jersey

Kimberly Scott Kallai
Arts High School
Newark, New Jersey

William Romney
Manager of Teacher Leadership Development
Teach for America
New York, New York

Linda Abrams
Montclair State University
Montclair, New Jersey

APPENDIX: VIDEO PROTOCOLS

Using Video to Discuss Teaching

This document provides examples of protocols that may be helpful in using videos for thinking and talking about teaching. The protocols presented here are used to create a structure for viewing videos of teaching and for discussing it together. They are designed to support exploration of teaching motifs and practices, activation and sharing knowledge of pedagogy, and responding to questions about teaching. Collecting evidence, analyzing it independently and together, and reflecting on what was uncovered and learned facilitate the process.

Following the sample protocols you will find a list of suggested motifs and teaching practices that you can use to focus your viewing and discussion. You should also consider how to collect evidence of the motif or practice. Recording evidence on sticky notes will facilitate sorting it for analysis. Recording it on a sheet of paper labeled with time intervals is helpful for examining how a lesson develops or time on task. Changes in where the camera is focused (e.g., on the students or on the teacher) will also influence what you learn from the video. We encourage you to make a decision about where to place the camera before you begin recording.

Finally, we hope these protocols are helpful, but we encourage you to create your own protocol to accommodate the learning objectives of your resident-mentor team.

Mentor Video Protocol 1: Focus on Motif and Practices

Mentor selects a 10-minute clip of his/her video.
↓
Mentor and Resident watch the video together and briefly discuss what they noticed.
↓

EITHER Mentor pre-selects motif or teaching practice they will focus on.	*OR* Mentor and resident identify a motif or teaching practice they will both focus on.	*OR* Resident identifies a motif or teaching practice they will focus on.

↓
Mentor and resident watch the video again and collect evidence of the motif or teaching practice.
↓
Mentor and resident discuss the evidence. The focus of the discussion is around "what" (what the mentor does around the motif), "how" (how she does those things), and "why" (why she might make the decisions she makes based on the evidence).
↓
Resident writes a reflection about what he/she learned about the motif or practice and how the knowledge can be applied in his/her practice.

193

Mentor Video Protocol 2: Focus on Resident's Questions

Resident watches his/her video and selects a 10-minute clip.		Mentor watches the video and selects a 10-minute clip.	
↓*Either* Resident selects a motif/practice, watches the video again, gathers evidence, and writes a reflection about "what," "how," and "why" she/he did what she did.	*OR*↓ ↓*Either* Resident and mentor watch the video together and select a motif/practice.		*OR*↓ Mentor selects a motif/practice, watches the video again, gathers evidence and writes questions to the resident about "what," "how," and "why" she/he did what she did.
↓ Mentor watches the clip, gathers evidence, reads the resident's reflection, and writes questions and observations.	↓ Resident and mentor watch the video together for a second time to gather evidence of the motif/practice.		↓ Resident watches the clip, gathers evidence, and answers the mentor's questions.
↓ ↓ ↓ Resident and mentor meet to discuss the evidence, questions, and observations.			
↓ Resident writes a reflection about what he/she learned about their practice from this process and how it will influence what they do in t			

Resident Video Protocol

Resident watches the mentor's video, selects a clip, and writes 3–5 specific questions to understand "what" (what the mentor is doing in the clip), "how" (how she does those things), and "why" (why she might make the decisions she makes based on the evidence). ↓	
Either Mentor watches the clip to prepare answers to the resident's questions and to consider other observations to be discussed.	*Or* Mentor and resident watch the clip together.
↓ Mentor and resident meet to discuss questions and observations.	
↓ Resident writes a reflection about what he/she has learned in response to the original questions and discussion and how that knowledge can be applied to his/her practice.	

Examples of Motifs and Some Associated Practices

- Teacher as resource person during student presentation (extending the student lead lesson by providing information, clarification, and/or questioning)
- Teacher as facilitator of group work (establishing effective groups; establishing and monitoring routines, roles, and expectations; monitoring student understanding)
- Teacher as facilitator of discussion (questioning, guiding, engaging all students)
- Teacher as facilitator of knowledge construction (scaffolding of instruction, selection of lesson materials, eliciting student thinking during a lesson)
- Teacher as lesson manager (time management, transitions, pacing)
- Teacher as classroom manager (non-instructional routines)
- Teacher as a physical presence and space manager (movement in the classroom to monitor student behavior and/or progress/understanding; to advance instruction)
- Teacher as communicator (verbal communication such as giving directions and explaining content; non-verbal communication such as body language, positioning, classroom arrangement; written communication such as using the board, worksheets and written directions)
- Teacher as culture agent (establishing a culture of respect and rapport, academic rigor and high expectations, safety and trust, fairness and democratic ideals)
- Teacher as monitor of student conduct (creates and enforces expectations for conduct)

Options for Where to Focus the Camera:

- On the teacher
- On the students
- On the classroom
- On a student or small group of students
- On the white board

Examples Evidence Gathering

Sorting

Checking for
understanding

Monitoring behavior

Teacher visits
table 1 to
check students'
work, asks

Teacher stands
near disruptive
student

Teacher asks:
"Which of
these images
provides an
example of
mitosis?"

Time Intervals

8:30	Teacher stands near disruptive student
8:35	Teacher visits table 1 to check student work, asks questions
8:40	Teacher visits table 2, sits, does not speak to them.
8:45	Teacher asks: "Which of these images provides an example of mitosis?"

MEET THE AUTHORS FROM CHAPTER EIGHT

Doug Larkin, on my initial morning as a first-grader, I heard the teacher say that she would be taking us to the laboratory across the hall after lunchtime. I imagined a roomful of glassware, bubbling liquids, and jars of colorful chemicals stacked messily on the shelves. But after lunch, she just took us to the bathroom. I thought that she had just made a mistake, or ran out of time, and would be taking us to the laboratory soon enough. I waited all year to see that laboratory, but never did. My imagination has been fired up for science ever since.

I grew up in New Jersey, and my love of science led me into becoming a physics major in college. Attending punk rock shows at City Gardens in Trenton was my first clue that everyone did not share the suburban existence I had experienced up to that point. Eventually my curiosity about the city, and my own inklings that my future lay in education, led me to the schools where I began to work first as a volunteer, and then as a substitute teacher. I finished college as a certified physics teacher and worked in two of my hometown high schools before joining Peace Corps to teach physics and math in Kenya and Papua New Guinea. Upon returning to the U.S. to raise a family, I took a job as a physics teacher at Trenton Central High School, and with my students was able to create the engaging laboratory classroom environment I had envisioned as a six-year old student so many years prior.

I did my graduate work at the University of Wisconsin-Madison, first earning a Master's degree in Multicultural Science Education, and later returned for a Ph.D. in Teacher Education. During my time as a graduate student, I spent a great deal of time in science classrooms supervising student teachers, and even though I was there as an instructor, I could not help but learn from all of the different teaching strategies I witnessed.

Over time, I became intrigued with the challenges of learning to teach science for culturally diverse classrooms, and it has since become my major area of scholarship and teaching. In addition to preparing with preservice secondary science and mathematics teachers in the NMUTR, I also work with undergraduates who are preparing to be teachers, and doctoral students in MSU's Teacher Education and Teacher Development program.

DOUG LARKIN, ANNA KARINA MONTEIRO
AND SUZANNE POOLE

8. SCIENCE PEDAGOGICAL CONTENT KNOWLEDGE DEVELOPMENT IN AN URBAN TEACHER RESIDENCY

INTRODUCTION

Doug was a few months into his first year as an assistant professor when one of his MSU colleagues, Monica, invited him to lunch. Not one to decline such offers, they met off campus at Raymond's, a restaurant in the town of Montclair, on a snowy day shortly thereafter. Over the course of the afternoon—remaining long after the meal—they talked a great deal about science and math education. Doug shared his experiences teaching a science methods class and supervising secondary science teachers at the University of Wisconsin, and Monica told him about the NMUTR, where teachers were being prepared in a one-year intensive program situated in NPS. Monica was the lead faculty for the secondary program, which included residents in math and science. Doug was intrigued, and they talked about whether or not he might play a role in the NMUTR somehow. It was only later that Doug realized that had been the point of being invited to lunch, and that this sort of cultivated relationship-building was characteristic of what he would experience over the coming years with the program.

In this chapter, a university faculty member, Doug Larkin, a biology teacher, Karina Monteiro, and a graduate of the residency, Suzanne Poole, discuss our experiences in developing residents' pedagogical content knowledge within the NMUTR. Commonly referred to as "methods," this aspect of the NMUTR curriculum concerns the preparation of residents to teach science content within their chosen subject areas.[1] In particular, we discuss the design, implementation, and outcomes of the methods course taught during the fall of 2011 with the second cohort of residents, which included Suzanne as a resident at Arts High School, her mentor Erin, and Karina, a mentor at East Side High School with two residents of her own.

Our expectations and experiences with this methods course were informed by our own positions in the program. For Doug, a seasoned physics and chemistry teacher who had previously taught university science methods courses, the main task was adapting the content of science methods courses to the context of the residency, in a way that was coherent with the program as a whole. As a classroom teacher with five years of experience and involvement as a mentor with the NMUTR from the beginning, Karina viewed herself as an equal partner in the education and preparation of her residents, whose role was to nurture the connection between theory and practice. From her perspective, the science methods course was the place where residents were able to explore the ideas that they would then implement in the classroom. For Suzanne, the methods course was one of many components of her program, because she also learned a great deal about teaching specific topics in biology from her mentor teacher, Erin.

We begin the chapter with a discussion on the purpose and significance of methods to preservice teacher education, after which we elaborate on the ways in which our science and math methods course in the NMUTR contrasts with more traditional methods courses. We then discuss the construction, implementation, and integration of the methods course within the larger context of the third space residency program, and reflect upon some of the lessons learned along the way. This is followed by an examination of the methods class curriculum that focuses on three of its core components: the teaching of inquiry, assessment, and teaching with a focus on "big ideas," as they pertained to our roles in the program. We conclude with a description of the methods course in action, as seen from each of our perspectives, and discuss the lessons learned about developing pedagogical content knowledge within the context of an urban teacher residency.

CRAFTING A SCIENCE AND MATH METHODS COURSE FOR AN URBAN TEACHER RESIDENCY CONTEXT

In the spring of 2011, Doug ran a series of workshops in the NMUTR with the first cohort of residents, and it is important at the outset to state that this was made possible by the relationship-building efforts of both the university and partner school faculty. The workshops were held on site at East Side High School, in a professional development room above the media center, a room that proved to be both a metaphorical and literal third space in our work. One of the ideas that residents and faculty alike wished to target with these workshops was the topic of inquiry, so Doug prepared some self-contained lessons on different types of inquiry teaching by drawing upon resources developed by the Exploratorium in San Francisco, materials from the University of Washington's "Tools for Ambitious Science Teaching" project, as well as his previous science methods classes.[2]

Over the summer, Doug joined Monica and Emily as NMUTR secondary faculty and together they planned for the fall. One initial idea for methods was to develop a set of independent modules that could be completed by the residents over the course of the semester. As planning continued, it became clear that methods instruction had to be integrated with everything else that was happening in the NMUTR. This is worth exploring because it is an issue that emerges from the third space structure and nature of the residency model. Though the NMUTR had substantial resources in terms of faculty load (3 full-time faculty for 8 residents), university support (a program director and graduate assistants), partner district contributions (mentors, access to schools, and principal support), and a budget to pay for all of this, the one thing that these resources could not do is wedge more time into the week. Doug describes the dilemma, "We knew that we could ask more of the residents in terms of assignments—especially in the fall when the in-class load was a little lighter—but we were hesitant about pulling them out of class more than a few times each week." Karina and the other mentors in the program did worry about the amount of time the residents would miss from their practical experiences, and what impact these classroom absences would have on the residents' immersion experiences.

To be consistent with our vision for a program that was coherent and unified, the three secondary faculty crafted a plan to co-teach a single class for 2½ hours each week, with the methods instruction interwoven with other teacher preparation content for the course. We wanted the residents to begin to understand the connections between these different components of teaching; we intended for them to experience how science and math pedagogy, planning, and assessment all worked together to produce teaching and learning, in addition to the practical dimensions of linking all of this with experiences in the classroom. These goals required further relationship-building between MSU faculty and the mentor teachers in order to ensure that the methods course did not impose unreasonable demands on the curriculum or the teaching. In this way, the third space dynamic of the methods course entailed reconciling the needs of both interest groups without ceding excessive power to either. An important component to this work is what Doug called a "hello visit," which was simply a visit to a mentor's classroom in which the only agenda is simply to introduce oneself. (He can clearly recall his hello visit to Karina's biology class on the day of a lab.) Though it seems like such a simple action, the impact of these hello visits is important theoretically in terms of the third space because the absence of demands on one another allows for an equitable establishment of power in the relationship.

As might be expected, such an effort took quite a bit of coordinating, yet by September's first meeting there was a solid plan in place to incorporate math and science methods instruction into the residency. Understanding this plan requires a brief detour into understanding the role of methods instruction in teacher education generally, a topic to which we now turn.

THE NATURE OF METHODS IN THE RESIDENCY

Methods courses across various teacher preparation programs differ in length, scope, and structure, but in the NMUTR it could be difficult for an outside observer to tease apart what program components are "methods" and which are not. For the purposes of this chapter, we loosely define the purpose of methods instruction in teacher preparation as the development of candidates' pedagogical content knowledge, or simply, PCK (Abell, 2007; Shulman, 1986). Included in this vision of methods instruction are skills—such as lesson planning and the use of instructional technology—needed to enact PCK into teaching.

There is hardly consensus in the field of teacher education regarding the specific components of a methods course, or even how many methods courses are necessary and appropriate in given content areas. Currently, a wide variety of approaches to methods courses in science teacher education are in use (Larkin, 2014; Smith & Gess-Newsome, 2004). Many programs require either one or two science teaching methods courses (each for 3 credits) applicable to all secondary science subject areas. Other methods courses are tailored to a specific science discipline, as is the practice in a Methods of Teaching Biology class taught at another state university in New Jersey. Conversely, a number of fast-track alternate route programs across the country offer only a general methods course that is not specific to secondary science or mathematics. Karina describes her own experiences in learning to teach as a series of components detached from actual practice. She recalls, "Methods was totally separate from student teaching. I was often asked to create unit and lesson plans that I was never able to actually use." Doug described a similar experience in learning to teach, "None of the various people responsible for my teacher preparation were in communication with each other. In order to be certified, I just had to satisfy each individual requirement. There was never a sense of a coherent whole the way there is in the NMUTR."

In many university-based teacher education programs, the methods course is also a place where prospective teachers learn about disciplinary curricula and state teaching standards, as well as receive support in strengthening content knowledge (Clift & Brady, 2005). The hybrid nature of coursework and fieldwork in the NMUTR and the shared roles for university and practitioner expertise created both opportunities and challenges in terms of providing residents with the requisite methods instruction. The process of defining and working within a third space perpetually under construction in a residency program has shaped this methods course content in new and unexpected ways.

In the secondary NMUTR, our science and math methods instruction was integrated throughout the year in various respects, and an important feature of the program was that methods instruction was not a stand-alone component. One obvious drawback for this arrangement was that the time structure—so clear in traditional university courses scheduled for a certain place and time—required continuous attention. Of course, the residency classrooms and mentor teachers were also a valued source for learning the PCK goals of methods instruction. While in some ways these might differ little from "student teaching" experiences in other teacher preparation efforts, the close working relationships formed by our carefully selected mentors and their residents over the course of a full year allowed for deep discussions of PCK in these sites. The whole idea of a third space residency is that the residents' learning to teach occurs primarily with the mentor in the classroom, in a much more intensive way than traditional student teaching, and lasts for an entire school year.

Suzanne characterized her year-long trajectory this way:

At the start, I just sat in the back and observed, but it quickly became a co-teaching situation where both of us were considered the teachers in the room.

Our roles were fluid, and the students were unable to tell who was the mentor and who was the resident. Knowing that I was going to be in the classroom for entire year allowed my mentor to invest time in me because I wouldn't be leaving anytime soon. I really was able to make one class completely my own. My mentor was not just a resource in planning lessons, but also someone with whom to reflect and from whom to take advice. We were able to learn from each other. Continuously having someone with whom to reflect and collaborate was probably the most useful part of the program. I was able to constantly ask for feedback both positive and critical in order to improve my abilities as an educator. I was able to see what an entire year as a teacher looks like, but with genuine support.

Karina's perspective as a mentor encompasses this whole support system:

As a mentor teacher to a resident, my role is not only to directly work with residents on a one-on-one basis but also to have an open line of communication with the other individuals who are involved in their learning, primarily the faculty. An example of this collaborative process occurred during my first year as a mentor. My resident at the time had a difficult time with creating and using questions during her presentations. Once I reached out to the faculty about this, we worked together on improving her ability to ask higher order questions within the lesson. The faculty included readings and discussions in their curriculum, while I had the opportunity to work with her during the lessons and help her to create questions relevant to what she was teaching. With this cooperative framework that supported her in various settings, we were able to help the resident improve on this critical teaching skill. As a cooperating teacher, my student teacher would only get my perspective on this topic and not be exposed to the various methods of learning such a skill and without such a strong support network.

A tremendous benefit of the residency program is the opportunity it affords residents to apply their theoretical understandings from coursework to their practice, as well as to reflect upon them with their mentor. In fact, this learning in the classroom between the resident and mentor is a crucial aspect of the residency. As a mentor, Karina often had the opportunity to model and help her residents put pedagogical theory into practice. This provided her with a unique perspective on how preservice teachers learned within the NMUTR, an expertise that was valuable later as the NMUTR secondary faculty met with the mentors as a group over the summer to map the curricular expectations for the residents throughout the year. Karina remembers:

Having this curricular map developed by our group of NMUTR mentors was useful because it enabled us to not only have insight and a voice as stakeholders in the residents' development but also provided us an opportunity to identify key school year functions such as testing, breaks, and content curriculum and discuss how they may influence the residents' curriculum. Although this map was flexible and dependent on each individual mentor-resident relationship, it served as a guideline and overall progression resource for each mentor. I believe this was especially useful to first year mentors as many were often hesitant about when and how to mentor their residents.

One outcome of this planning was to solidify the goals for the methods instruction, and the NMUTR secondary faculty decided that the methods instruction would work in support of three main goals:

- Teaching with a focus on "big ideas"
- Using robust assessment practices
- Developing an inquiry approach to teaching

There were other goals as well, such as learning to connect with professional communities, leveraging instructional technology for teaching, and understanding the nature of scientific practice, but the main focus of methods was on those three goals.

In planning the methods course, the intention was that the residents would develop proficiency in the process of designing lessons and unit plans. The Understanding by Design (UBD) framework (Wiggins & McTighe, 1998) was a useful scaffold for this work because of the way it organized this task, and all of the secondary faculty were involved in teaching residents how to plan lessons and units. The sequence of the UBD framework aligned nicely with the main goals of our methods instruction. In UBD, teachers first set goals for students' learning (the big ideas), then determine what would be acceptable evidence of learning (robust assessment). Next came designing the learning experiences that would prepare students to be able to provide that evidence of learning (an inquiry approach to teaching). Karina and the other mentors worked with their respective residents in applying this framework to ensure each lesson was appropriate and applicable with their own students.

The role of the mentors in this work was to assist in this planning, as well as to model aspects of teaching practice emphasized in the program. As the year progressed, the resident would gradually assume more of the responsibility for planning and teaching all parts of a lesson. During this transition, the mentors provided detailed ongoing feedback to residents about the design and implementation of lesson components.

As Karina's residents assumed more responsibility in the classroom, she tried to make the transition as smooth as possible. She reflected:

From the first day in the classroom, I considered my resident as an equally valued teacher in the classroom and demanded this same respect of my students towards the resident. As the resident slowly transitioned to lead teacher during lessons, our roles would switch. For example, during the beginning of the year I would lead most of the lesson, while the resident practiced more of a support role, like the "one teach, one support model." By the end of the year our classroom looked very similar to what it looked like in the beginning of the year with the one teach one support model, except I was the support while the resident was the teacher.

Suzanne recalls that when she began the NMUTR, she had no understanding of what it meant to be a teacher, never mind a good one. "When our UTR professors first described inquiry teaching," Suzanne said, "I thought maybe it just meant having students re-discover things that scientists already knew, but I was puzzled as to how this could work in a classroom." She had even less understanding of what it meant to teach using big ideas and inquiry. Looking back on her own education, she noted that it was not common for her to learn science through the lens of an exciting topic, and hands-on labs were even more rare. Instead, she perceived her science classes as lengthy and wordy because they were taught to her through lectures and notes on the board, with maybe a lab at the end of the week. Inquiry as a type of lesson design was brand new to her, but became something that she seized upon immediately.

Now that she has students of her own, Suzanne finds it strange that her teaching could be anything other than inquiry-based:

> Now I understand that using inquiry in the classroom means allowing students to investigate some phenomena (which can include images, data, models, etc.) in order to make meaningful explanations that build upon their prior knowledge. Depending on the topic of the lesson and the level of the student, this may take on different forms from class to class. The point is for students to be confronted with something that requires exploration and explanation, and giving them the opportunity to make meaning of it on their own. Inquiry allows students to be a part of the lesson and to be involved in the actual development of learning.

She compares her experiences in the NMUTR with those of the other new teachers at her school, and states that she has a much clearer understanding of how inquiry lessons should be designed, how to teach with big ideas in mind, and how to create assessments that actually measure what she wants her students to learn. Though she admits she may not have mastered these skills perfectly, she recognizes the importance of these three components in creating meaningful lessons.

In the following section we discuss the development of residents' pedagogical content knowledge from our different vantage points, and do so in terms of the three goals for methods described above.

TEACHING WITH A FOCUS ON BIG IDEAS

Methods courses in secondary science commonly focus on developing candidates' pedagogical content knowledge in directions consistent with current math and science education reforms (Achieve Inc., 2013; National Research Council, 2012). One of the major goals of these standards efforts is to identify the central topics for each study in each grade level and high school discipline, though they are not prescriptive documents for daily use. We know that good teachers know how to design lessons that ensure their students have the opportunity to learn these organizing concepts of their subject matter. Connecting each lesson to these "big ideas" is important in order to ensure that students are able to develop a connected and coherent understanding of phenomena and their explanations, as opposed to a fragmented collection of science concepts. Windschitl, Thompson, Braaten, and Stroupe (2012) define big ideas as "substantive relationships between concepts in the form of scientific models that help learners understand, explain, and predict a variety of important phenomena in the natural world" (p. 888).[3]

Using the UBD framework, one of the first tasks that residents encounter is writing a rationale for their unit. While they also identify the learning goals for the unit, being able to articulate the big idea is a crucial step in the rationale. In September 2011, Suzanne was developing a unit on chemical reactions. Initially, her reasons for having students learn about chemical reactions involved detailed lists of other chemistry and biology topics that depended on chemical reactions, but after some feedback from her instructors and peers in methods class, she submitted this rationale:

> Without them first gaining a working knowledge and feeling comfortable with the idea of a chemical reaction, when one or more substances are changed into one or more substances, [students] will be unable to understand what is actually happening within every living being, the majority of processes discussed in life sciences, and also the origin of existence.

The big idea—namely that chemical reactions underlie all of life—is indeed a central organizing concept that she would be able to point to again and again throughout her unit.

Karina also uses big ideas regularly in her planning and teaching. As she designs her lessons, she constantly asks herself, "Does this help my students understand the big idea? Is this relevant to the big idea?" If the answer is yes, then the teacher is teaching to the big idea. Without a big idea holding the lessons together, students may be able to remember a few "whats" from the year, but they will be less likely to remember the "whys." For example, in her biology classes Suzanne often uses the big idea of *form follows function*. She reinforces this idea throughout the year, from evolution to cell biology to the structure of DNA. As one of the central concepts in biology, she shows her students its connection to each topic, with the hope that they will recognize it in nature for the rest of their lives.

One of the most significant challenges science mentors face is trying to get the resident to plan lessons with the big idea in mind. Most residents still think about teaching their subjects from the perspective of their own college coursework, and it can be very difficult for them to reorganize their knowledge of the content for their students' learning. We also press our residents to align the content to the needs and interest of the student, which is easier said than done for new teachers. Perhaps more importantly, it is challenging to remember what it was like to learn difficult science concepts for the first time. Working closely with their mentor teacher helps resident teachers better grasp the need for the big idea focus. "This is a common challenge for every resident I have," Karina notes, "which is why it is imperative to be part of the planning process with my residents."

An additional perspective is offered by research on teacher learning, which states that one of the primary tasks of learning to teach is organizing one's own knowledge for teaching (Shulman, 1986), and points to research that new teachers often feel more confident in their subject matter knowledge than is warranted (Hewson, Tabachnick, Zeichner, & Lemberger, 1999). "Developing an understanding of big ideas is a way of accomplishing this work of reorganization," Doug says, "and the time spent doing this on the teachers' part pays off in a more focused kind of teaching."

As a mentor, Karina puts a strong emphasis on this in the beginning of the year as she plans with residents and other biology teachers in her department. There is an overarching big idea for each unit, which is then broken down to create an essential question for each lesson. The content within the lesson, then, is aimed to answer the essential question. As the residents slowly take over the lesson planning, it is important for them to continually ask themselves, "does this essential question speak to my big idea" and "does this content help my student answer my essential question?"

ASSESSMENT

At its core, the practice of assessment in teaching is figuring out what students are thinking, and one of our goals in the NMUTR is to move our residents beyond the simple notion of assessments as synonyms for tests and quizzes. Assessments have many purposes: they may be used to elicit student ideas about science topics prior to instruction, inform teachers' actions as instruction proceeds, and identify students' knowledge of content and skills to measure learning outcomes (Black & Wiliam, 1998; Wiliam, 2011). Multiple forms of assessments are necessary to provide different perspectives on students' ideas and understandings. In the NMUTR, we feel it is important that residents be able to develop and use a variety of assessment practices in order to get a well-rounded representation of what their learners do and do not yet know in terms of the learning goals and big ideas.

To introduce the idea of assessment in the methods class, Doug chose the film "A Private Universe," (Schneps, Sadler, & Harvard-Smithsonian Center for Astrophysics, 1987). The film includes a case study of a student named Heather, and explores the nature of her misconceptions about the phases of the moon and the seasons of the year. In science teacher education, the use of this recording has become a signature pedagogy (Shulman, 2005) because of the way it highlights the alternate scientific conceptions that even the brightest students can develop from instruction.[4] Part of the purpose of showing the film is to demonstrate that a detailed one-on-one probing conversation with a student is one of the most valid and reliable forms of assessment because it allows the teacher to fully elicit student thinking about a given idea. "I was very shocked when I saw this," said Suzanne. "I never really had thought about how prior knowledge—accurate or inaccurate—could shape the way students would interpret information for the rest of their life. To see Harvard graduates still hold misconceptions about the Earth's orbit and seasons was astounding and eye-opening. This made me rethink and be more aware of how I convey material to my students."

Learning to develop usable assessments for everyday practice in classrooms that reach high levels of validity and reliability is one goal of our focus on assessment in methods. As residents learn about assessment in the methods course, the mentors model assessment practices and support the residents in the creation and use of all forms of assessment. The mentors seek a balance between the types of assessment that are currently emphasized in their own schools—usually those that resemble standardized exams—and other forms such as "authentic assessments" that have real world applications and audiences as well as provide rich portraits of student thinking. It is critical then, that the resident learn to incorporate both forms of assessment equally throughout a unit in order to best assess students' learning from multiple perspectives. Navigating this issue is a real source of tension that forces faculty, mentors, and residents alike to continually find solutions that work for everyone. It is worth pointing out that such an issue is precisely the sort of thing that would be glossed over or ignored in traditional teacher education: a professor might assign one thing that the cooperating teacher could say wouldn't work, leaving the student teacher stuck in the middle just trying to survive.

During the early part of the school year, the mentor generally takes the lead in designing assessments, particularly those that are summative (i.e. reflected in recorded grades). When creating a summative assessment, mentors and residents discuss and practice methods in creating a valid assessment that will directly align to the learning goals and course objectives. As the year progresses, the resident slowly transitions into the role of designing these forms of assessment independently, though they are still reviewed by the mentor. By the end of the residency they are self-designing a wide variety of both formative and summative assessments.

Karina notes that residents often struggle most with the design of "alternative assessments," that is, assessments that are not straightforward tests or quizzes. Residents often need convincing of the value in creating alternative assessments because they are simply unfamiliar with their use. Moreover, they find it difficult to design assessments that are both authentic, data rich, and valid. Concept maps, lab design, informal questioning, and portfolios are just a few that Karina and Suzanne use in their classroom throughout the year, all of which aid in giving a clearer picture to both mentor and resident of what their students know. As her residents take the lead in designing these assessments, including rubrics for scoring, Karina ensures that they are given detailed feedback on each draft until their item meets the assessment goal. When the resident has completed a few alternative assessments and has scored them, they are generally more at ease with the process mainly because they see the robust and in-depth perspective evident in their students' understandings that they may not have otherwise obtained from a traditional test or quiz.

As a resident, Suzanne underwent a conceptual shift from thinking about assessments as inert documents used to rate students' abilities, to viewing them as tools to inform her instruction in the classroom. She was able to put this new understanding into action when she was put in charge of developing her department's monthly common assessments. She showed her colleagues how the validity of the first common assessment could be improved by aligning the objectives of the unit to the test. Several others just trusted that since the test had nice format and was created by a praised teacher in the past, that it must be good. Suzanne recalls, "It was then that I realized that it still is easy for good teachers to create an assessment that fails to measure what students are supposed to learn."

This understanding was hard-won, as Suzanne remembers it. She notes that completing the Assessment Analysis project (detailed below) was probably the most difficult and arduous task she had as a resident in the program. At first, she created an assessment that probed what she wanted her students to be able to know and communicate, but none of them were able to answer correctly. She was unsure whether the assessment question was appropriate or if she simply had not taught the material in a meaningful way. The truth was the latter. As she interviewed her students (a requirement of the project), it was easy to see that they understood what the assessment was asking, but they simply did not know the answer. "This is when I realized that I needed to go back and reteach the material in a way that my students would understand," Suzanne noted. She also began to see that the topic in which she had found so important—the evolution of eukaryotic cells—was difficult because students had a limited understanding of evolution itself. This led to the insight that she had not provided her students with the conceptual supports that they needed in order to successfully complete the assessment that she had given.

Of course, assessment was not just for the students. Their mentors and university faculty assessed the residents' teaching regularly. Suzanne remembers this process well. "My mentor, Erin, was very good at respectfully providing both warm and cool feedback after nearly every lesson to let me know what I did well and what could be improved upon in the future." Erin was adept at anticipating upcoming issues with particular students and planning the necessary day-to-day details, skills that are notoriously hard to learn in a methods class. In sharing these insights with Suzanne, Erin's feedback was of immediate use. As instructors of the methods course, Doug and the other faculty also modeled good assessment practices regularly. For example, rubrics and samples were provided for major assignments, and different techniques for eliciting student ideas were demonstrated in every class.

The culminating project for the methods component of the NMUTR in the fall of 2011 was the Assessment Analysis, a sprawling and comprehensive task that made use of the multiple strands of both the discipline-specific methods and more general pedagogy that had been the substance of our weekly class meetings. The assignment was as follows:[5]

D. LARKIN ET AL.

Assessment Module

The goal of this project is to examine assessment structure of a lesson in light of the intended learning outcomes (ILOs). After teaching a lesson, assessing the students, and collecting interview data, you will revise a specific assessment task in ways that take advantage of your in-depth analysis of student learning.

1. *Lesson Plan:* Select a lesson from your unit. Make sure it consists of multiple assessment strategies so that you'll have something to analyze (formal and informal).
2. *Lesson Assessment Analysis:* Complete a written assessment analysis of the lesson. This should include an identification of *all* the "assessment points" in the lesson. For each assessment point describe the nature of the assessment (how are you gathering insight/information from the students), whether it's formal or informal, and what sort of information you expect the students to generate.
3. *Specific Assessment Analysis:* Choose *one* formal assessment task (or part of a larger assessment task) in the lesson plan that is designed to demonstrate achievement of one of the lesson's ILOs. Use a more in-depth analysis to describe this specific assessment task.
4. *Teach the Lesson.*
5. *Student Interviews:* Now that the lesson is taught and the students have been assessed it is interesting to find out if they really did achieve true understanding of the ILOs. Choose two students to interview. Make sure you (audio or video) tape record the interviews. Use the original assessment questions as a starting point for your interview. Your goal is to probe student understanding at a deep level. You could have students perform a task to determine what they really know or talk them through the process. Be sure to just focus on the *one* specific ILO you are analyzing. Do not include questions involving whether the student enjoyed the experience or not. Interviews should last around 20 minutes.
6. *Student Interview Summary:* Compose a brief summary (approximately 600 words each) of two 20-minute student interviews (audio or video tape recorded, which should be available for review if needed, but need not be turned in). Include brief descriptions of the students as learners and as individuals. This should consist of a narrative summary of how the students performed during the interview with respect to the one specific ILO and their depth of understanding. It is not expected to be a transcript of the interview itself.
7. *Analytical Comparison:* This section compares the interview data to the formal assessment data. The comparison should focus on the question of 'validity'. That is, to what extent did the original assessment task accurately measure student understanding of the concept in question?
8. *Revised Assessment Task:* Provide detailed suggestions for revision of the assessment task, or for the creation of a new task altogether. This should be based on both your findings during the student interview and the readings from your course work.

210

Completing this assignment required residents to focus on student thinking from beginning to end, and offered them the opportunity to redefine what it means to "teach" a lesson. "I remember one of the discussions that took place at the end of the semester," Doug recounted, "when each resident shared his or her assessment analysis project. It was remarkable in the way that the conversation centered on the relationship between teaching and learning, and how one of the residents asked 'If the students aren't learning, can we really call it teaching?' The fact that our residents were at such a point only six months into their teacher preparation program spoke volumes to me about their future as teachers in the NPS."

Karina watched her residents really struggle with this assignment, as it required the residents to push themselves creatively. "I found that the process caused the residents to not only be more creative but also be reflective in the *why* behind what they teach and what the connection is to the big idea. "For one of my residents," Karina said, "the assignment led to a really nice 'Aha! moment' when all the concepts discussed throughout the course fell into place."

Suzanne recalls that this assignment exemplified the third space approach, in which the teacher and student inhabit both roles simultaneously and encourage a collaborative teacher preparation experience. She recalls that her particular teaching situation led to questions that Doug needed to act upon, subsequently readjusting the goals of the assignment to meet her classroom needs. This led to his own learning about new pathways for teacher learning about assessment.

DEVELOPING AN INQUIRY APPROACH TO TEACHING

In science education, the term "inquiry" is often used without clear definition, and frequently assumes multiple meanings among teachers and administrators (Crawford, 2007; Lawson, 2005; Windschitl, 2004). In the NMUTR methods course, we sought to represent two particular views on inquiry. First, inquiry was presented as a component of a constructivist approach to teaching, and diametrically opposed to a transmissionist view of teaching, in which the teacher simply delivers information into the receiving brain of the learner. This view is not only consistent with both historical and current theories about learning (Bransford & Donovan, 2005; Dewey, 1910), but exemplifies the type of active and engaged science teaching our program sought to foster. At the core of this view of inquiry is the necessity of classroom teachers to elicit and build upon the existing knowledge of learners. In our experiences as science educators, all of us have found that students best understand and retain science content if they have the opportunities to construct it themselves.

The second view of inquiry was as a continuum representing teacher and/or student *control* over the questions that are investigated, the methods for investigating, and the presentation of the findings. Such a conceptualization of inquiry leads to a wide variety of classroom activities that might reasonably be categorized as inquiry, some more student-driven or teacher directed than others. Windschitl's (2003) definition of *structured* inquiry "in which the teacher presents a question for which the students do not know the answer, and students are given a procedure to follow in order to complete the inquiry" (p. 114) was helpful as a starting point, but pushing residents to go beyond this to have the questions and procedures determined with input from students was key in the effort for developing an inquiry approach to teaching. Later in the spring, after residents came to view an inquiry approach as a crucial aspect of teaching, the focus of methods shifted to classroom discourse as the essential element in inquiry-based teaching (Windschitl, 2003).

"Throughout the residency year," Karina notes, "it is common to hear my residents ask me to show them what inquiry looks like. What many are looking for is a clean cut example, but the use of inquiry in the science classroom has multiple forms and is highly dependent on the types of learners in our classrooms, the content we are teaching, and the format of a lesson. As a mentor teacher I try to first explain to my residents that there is no single right way to create an inquiry lesson. Often times the residents come in with the belief that inquiry is this enormous phenomenon that overwhelmingly takes over every lesson. I try to teach them otherwise, that inquiry happens at all levels and in all forms." She adds that in the current schooling climate, with the current curricular and standardized test pressures that exist, it is difficult to do a lesson for every new science concept from an inquiry-based perspective.

Karina tries to teach the residents that there are different levels and means of implementing inquiry within a lesson, each of which can help to balance the need to get through content and support students as they build upon their own understandings. For example, she may model a lesson that includes an overarching PowerPoint that covers several key concepts. However, within that PowerPoint there are embedded inquiry-like tasks, activities, and questions that help the students to draw conclusions and build understandings of such concepts. Again, this is another aspect of the bridges being built between theory and practice in the NMUTR.

Suzanne's initial uncertainty about the nature of inquiry science teaching gave way to understanding that such an approach entailed allowing students to investigate some phenomena, in order to make meaningful explanations that build upon their prior knowledge. Suzanne explains her insight: "The point is for students to be confronted with something that requires exploration and explanation, and to give them an opportunity to make meaning of it on their own. Inquiry allows students to be a part of the lesson and to be involved in the actual development of learning." Depending on the topic of the lesson and the level of the student, this may take on different forms from class to class. "I found that doing things this way consistently leads to greater student investment in the lesson," Suzanne adds.

Suzanne's growth in developing an inquiry approach to teaching was reaffirmed during her first year of teaching. "My department chair asked that I lead a common planning session on inquiry-based lessons," she recalled, "I may not have been the best at inquiry-based teaching, but I was using inquiry in almost every lesson, and was able to lead this session and utilize all of the concepts and skills sets that I had been provided through the UTR. Something that my UTR professors often did when teaching a new concept was to teach it to us using that very concept, so I designed the session in an inquiry format."

It is worth considering that Suzanne's development of this concept was supported by a philosophically coherent group of faculty and mentors in regular communication with one another. This is quite different from other programs where the student teaching experience entails learning methods one semester with faculty, then implementing it separately with a mentor teacher who might never meet that methods professor! Doug points out that the faculty made sure to let the questions and concerns of the residents help drive the methods curriculum, "It was just as important for us to walk-the-talk as teacher educators," he said. "That's really at the heart of what it means to be doing teacher education in the third space. It's not a situation where we as professors are simply imposing our agenda on the mentors and residents. The goals and priorities of everyone in this partnership matter a great deal."

THE METHODS COURSE IN ACTION

This section describes the components of the methods course curriculum while attending to the program's guiding programmatic construct of teaching in a third space. In a typical university teacher preparation program, the question of where to hold class is usually a perfunctory bureaucratic issue, but in the residency this task was deeply intertwined with the philosophical orientation of the NMUTR. The locations of the various components of the residency had important implications for the nature of resident learning in the program. While the university and school classroom settings remained important anchors for methods instruction, the third spaces (Bhabha, 1994; Zeichner, 2010) in which this instruction occurred were equally important for the ways in which they helped to equalize power relations among all of the residency participants. In the first year of the NMUTR all of the residents had been at the same school, but beginning with the second cohort, our residents were spread over three different sites. As a result, the locations of each class meeting changed regularly. In the beginning of the fall, we met at the Marion Bolden Student Center on the north side of the city. Later, we rotated our class between the different schools where our residents worked.

Logistically, this arrangement for holding class in different places presented us with both benefits and difficulties. Certainly it was convenient for the residents to just drive across town or walk down the hall to class, rather than drive thirty minutes to a crowded campus with parking issues. Yet, the major benefit in rotating classes at different school sites was that it facilitated communication and instructional coherence with our partners in those buildings. In this age of instant digital communication, there is still great value in simply showing up. Even just brief moments of face-to-face contact with mentors, administrators, and students allowed for communication that helped answer questions, reinforce relationships, and address emerging issues to keep the whole NMUTR running smoothly.

Gaining access to the Internet and using audiovisual technology was a challenge in the schools (though the district attempted to help us in this regard) and so at times when we wished to watch a video clip we had to assign it to the residents ahead of time to watch at home or find a mentor with a classroom that we could use. Being able to bring materials (such as science supplies, or even water), or even having a place to store class items from week to week, was sometimes an issue. Doug felt this keenly, "I was always lugging whiteboards, plastic containers of inquiry materials, and large wooden black boxes from my distantly parked car up to whatever room hosted our methods class that week."[6]

One of the obvious drawbacks to this arrangement of timing for the methods instruction of residents is the complicated logistics of making it work. While such an approach is consistent with the focus on emergent and negotiated curriculum in the NMUTR, it took more maintenance and schedule flexibility than would a traditional three-credit methods course that meets in the same place at the same time every week. Part of the sustainability challenge of such a model is making sure that the methods component of a residency does not exceed reasonable bounds —at least in terms of faculty time.

If this were the only time for methods, it would certainly not be sufficient. Yet the NMUTR had other components that served the goals of the methods instruction, and with three tenured or tenure-track faculty assigned to the program, we had the flexibility to carve out time throughout the residency to ensure that our residents met the methods goals we had set. Our residents visited classrooms in other schools, attended instructional technology workshops on campus and in Newark, spent an overnight in the woods at the New Jersey School of Conservation, did a summer internship at the Newark Museum, conducted instructional rounds (City, 2011) in each others' classrooms, and attended the NJ Science Conference and/or NJ Math Teachers Convention. In separate sessions outside of class, we read and discussed books such as "The Golem: What You Should Know About Science" (Collins & Pinch, 1998), "Making Sense" (Hiebert, 1997), and "What's Math Got to do With It?" (Boaler, 2009).

The feedback that residents received from mentors and faculty was structured by a tool introduced in the methods class, and helped to reinforce the learning goals we had for their science and math teaching. Over the year, each resident received at least six observations using the Reformed Teaching Observation Protocol (RTOP) (Piburn et al., 2000; Sawada et al., 2010) from university faculty and their mentors, which is an observation protocol designed specifically for inquiry teaching in science and mathematics. The 25 observation categories on the RTOP include ratings on items such as:

- The instructional strategies respected students' prior knowledge and the preconceptions inherent within.
- The lesson promoted strong coherent conceptual understanding.

- There was a high proportion of student talk and a significant amount of it occurred between and among students.
- Students were encouraged to generate conjectures, alternative solution strategies, and ways of interpreting evidence. (Piburn et al., 2000, p. 31)

The RTOP reinforced many of the central themes of the methods course, and as a result, the residents' own practice (as well as that of peers and mentors in the instructional rounds) became the raw material for discussions both in methods class and in the post-observation conferences.

CONCLUSION

Many of the challenges commonly faced by novice secondary science and math teachers (Davis, Petish, & Smithey, 2006) were encountered by our residents as well, particularly as most were prepared to teach their subjects in ways that differed significantly from the way they themselves learned math and science. Yet it is our firm belief that the unique structure of methods instruction in the NMUTR has prepared them well to be fantastic science and mathematics teachers for the young people of Newark, as well as to become active leaders for reformed teaching practices in their professional communities.

In many ways, the structure for methods in the NMUTR was a product of its larger context, but there are still some lessons learned that may benefit more traditional science methods courses. First and foremost is the value of integrating methods instruction with the field experience, which was made possible by the overall coherence of all of the program components. Traditional teacher education programs may not be able to replicate the intensive program of the NMUTR, but certainly greater efforts can be made between universities and school districts to better integrate these experiences.

Another insight from this work concerns the value of the mentors' input. In many teacher education programs, it is unheard of for teachers who host preservice teachers in their classrooms to exert an influence over the curriculum of a university teacher education course. Yet in our program we continually sought out the input of mentors, and the resulting conversations undoubtedly contributed to the professional growth of all involved and strengthened the program. Certainly traditional programs can do more to make practitioner voices carry more weight.

Lastly, in this program we sought to take the goals we set for our residents and put them into practice for ourselves. Rather than subject residents to a survey course about science teaching methods, the secondary faculty focused on a small number of topics for deep mastery. Doug shared his lesson plans for methods class with the residents. Karina modeled the type of teaching she wished to see, and worked patiently with her residents to get them there. And we all applied the lessons of inquiry to our own practice as teachers, examining our teaching continuously for ways to improve. The different perspectives of faculty and mentors in this effort served to enrich the experience of the residents.

It is clear that the third space teacher residency model is a powerful approach to teacher education. Yet it is also resource-intensive and dependent upon the expertise of the faculty and mentors, and thus depends heavily on the cultivation of personal relationships necessary for this type of interdependent work. Our residency program started small and continues to grow along with the relationships of the individuals in the third space of the residency—faculty, mentors, graduates, and residents alike.

NOTES

[1] While there was much overlap between the science and math methods course in the NMUTR, due to space limitations we limit this chapter to discussing only the science methods.
[2] These science teacher education resources are available currently at http://www.exploratorium.edu/education and http://ambitiousscienceteaching.org/
[3] In our methods work, we used the "Big Idea Tool" developed at the University of Washington-Seattle, which may be found on the Ambitious Science Teaching website: http://ambitiousscienceteaching.org/
[4] Heather received a standing ovation from hundreds of science educators at a 2008 National Science Teachers Convention celebration marking the 20th Anniversary of the film.
[5] This assignment is used with permission from John Rudolph from the University of Wisconsin-Madison, who initially created it for a science teaching methods course there. It was then modified by Brian Zoellner from the University of North Florida and Doug Larkin from Montclair State University.
[6] The "black boxes" for were used for developing models of phenomena, and were developed as part of the Modeling Understanding in Science Education project at the University of Wisconsin-Madison. (Stewart, Cartier, & Passmore, 2005).

REFERENCES

Abell, S. K. (2007). Research on science teacher knowledge. In S. K. Abell & N. G. Lederman (Eds.), *Handbook of research on science education* (pp. 1105–1150). Mahwah, NJ: Lawrence Erlbaum Associates.

Achieve Inc. (2013). *Next generation science standards: For states, by states.* Washington (DC), WA: National Academies Press.

Bhabha, H. K. (1994). *The location of culture.* New York, NY: Routledge.

Black, P., & Wiliam, D. (1998). Inside the black box: Raising standards through classroom assessment. *Phi Delta Kappan, 80*(2), 139–148.

Boaler, J. (2009). *What's math got to do with it?* New York, NY: Penguin Books.

Bransford, J. D., & Donovan, S. (2005). Scientific inquiry and how people learn. In National Research Council (U.S.). Committee on How People Learn A Targeted Report for Teachers (Ed.), *How students learn: History, mathematics, and science in the classroom* (pp. 397–420). Washington (DC), WA: National Academies Press.

City, E. A. (2011). Learning from instructional rounds. *Educational Leadership, 69*(2), 36–41.

Clift, R., & Brady, P. (2005). Research on methods courses and field experiences. In AERA Panel on Research and Teacher Education, M. Cochran-Smith, & K. M. Zeichner (Eds.), *Studying teacher education: The report of the AERA panel on research and teacher education* (pp. 309–424). Mahwah, NJ: Published for the American Educational Research Association by Lawrence Erlbaum Associates.

Collins, H. M., & Pinch, T. J. (1998). *The golem: What you should know about science* (2nd ed.). New York, NY: Cambridge University Press.

Crawford, B. A. (2007). Learning to teach science as inquiry in the rough and tumble of practice. *Journal of Research in Science Teaching, 44*(4), 613–642.

Davis, E. A., Petish, D., & Smithey, J. (2006). Challenges new science teachers face. *Review of Educational Research, 76*(4), 607–651.

Dewey, J. (1910). Science as subject-matter and as method. *Science, 31*(787), 121–127.

Hewson, P. W., Tabachnick, B. R., Zeichner, K. M., & Lemberger, J. (1999). Educating prospective teachers of biology: Findings, limitations, and recommendations. *Science Education, 83*(3), 373–384.

Hiebert, J. (1997). *Making sense: Teaching and learning mathematics with understanding.* Portsmouth, NH: Heinemann.

Larkin, D. B. (2014). Structures and strategies for science teacher education in the 21st century. *Teacher Education & Practice, 27*(2).

Lawson, A. E. (2005). What is the role of induction and deduction in reasoning and scientific inquiry? *Journal of Research in Science Teaching, 42*(6), 617–740.

National Research Council. (2012). *A framework for k-12 science education: Practices, crosscutting concepts, and core ideas.* Washington (DC), WA: The National Academies Press.

Piburn, M., Sawada, D., Turley, J., Falconer, K., Benford, R., Bloom, I., & Judson, E. (2000). *Reformed teaching observation protocol (RTOP) reference manual.* Tempe, AZ: Arizona Collaborative for Excellence in the Preparation of Teachers.

Sawada, D., Piburn, M. D., Judson, E., Turley, J., Falconer, K., Benford, R., & Bloom, I. (2010). Measuring reform practices in science and mathematics classrooms: The reformed teaching observation protocol. *School Science and Mathematics, 102*(6), 245–253.

Schneps, M. H., Sadler, P. M., & Harvard-Smithsonian Center for Astrophysics. (1987). *A private universe* [video recording]. Washington (DC), WA: Annenberg/CPB.

Shulman, L. S. (1986). Those who understand: Knowledge growth in teaching. *Educational Researcher, 15*(2), 4–14.

Shulman, L. S. (2005). Signature pedagogies in the professions. *Daedalus, 134*(3), 52–59.

Smith, L. K., & Gess-Newsome, J. (2004). Elementary science methods courses and the national science education standards: Are we adequately preparing teachers? *Journal of Science Teacher Education, 15*(2), 91–110.

Stewart, J. H., Cartier, J. L., & Passmore, C. M. (2005). Developing understanding through model based inquiry. In National Research Council (U.S.). Committee on How People Learn A Targeted Report for Teachers (Ed.), *How students learn: History, mathematics, and science in the classroom* (pp. 515–565). Washington (DC), WA: National Academies Press.

Wiggins, G. P., & McTighe, J. (1998). *Understanding by design.* Alexandria, VA: Association for Supervision and Curriculum Development.

Wiliam, D. (2011). *Embedded formative assessment.* Bloomington, IN: Solution Tree Press.

Windschitl, M. (2003). Inquiry projects in science teacher education: What can investigative experiences reveal about teacher thinking and eventual classroom practice? *Science Education, 87*(1), 112.

Windschitl, M. (2004). Folk theories of "inquiry": How preservice teachers reproduce the discourse and practices of an atheoretical scientific method. *Journal of Research in Science Teaching, 41*(5), 481–512.

Windschitl, M. (2008). What is inquiry? A framework for thinking about authentic scientific practice in the classroom. In J. Luft, R. L. Bell, & J. Gess-Newsome (Eds.), *Science as inquiry in the secondary setting* (pp. 1–20). Arlington, VA: NSTA Press.

Windschitl, M., Thompson, J., Braaten, M., & Stroupe, D. (2012). Proposing a core set of instructional practices and tools for teachers of science. *Science Education, 96*(5), 878–903. doi:10.1002/sce.21027

Zeichner, K. (2010). Rethinking the connections between campus courses and field experiences in college- and university-based teacher education. *Journal of Teacher Education, 61*(1/2), 89–99. doi:10.1177/0022487109347671

Douglas Larkin
Montclair State University
Montclair, New Jersey

Anna Karina Monteiro
East Side High School
Newark, New Jersey

Suzanne Poole
Science Park High School
Newark, New Jersey

MEET THE AUTHORS FROM CHAPTER NINE

Priyank Bhatt, my story began in a place where education was deemed highly valuable and of upmost importance in any society. However, it wasn't for everyone. I grew up in a low middle class family in India, a place that taught me the importance of having a good education and the consequences of not being able to afford it. My grandfather, for example, only completed school up to 6th grade and then had to drop out due to financial reasons. Even though he could not complete school he made sure my father excelled at it. He saw how limited he was due to a lack of education and wanted to make sure his two sons did not follow in his footsteps. My father ended up graduating with two degrees, one in chemistry and the other in law, while his younger brother excelled in accounting and was hired at a firm in the United States.

My father remained in India while his younger brother and his wife came to the United States to start a new life. Growing up in India and going to school there was an experience like none other. We did not have video games or board games and the only thing we could do for fun was go out and explore the world around us. Even though I enjoyed helping my peers with their learning and helping my brother/sisters with their homework, I never envisioned myself as a teacher. And I never saw myself as a mathematician. But that all changed when my parents informed us that we were leaving all this behind to start a new life in the United States with my uncle and his family.

The first day of school in this country was not easy. I was placed in a school that was predominately white and the person that was supposed to look out for us, my niece, was too embarrassed to be seen around us. I barely spoke English and was wearing clothes that were not cool at all. But the most memorable experience of that day was my math class. I was able to communicate using the language of math. I did not need to speak or understand English because I knew the numbers, the operations, and the symbols. I could solve the problems and show what I was doing on the board. The teacher was as excited as I was because he was able to connect with me and accomplish something with me. But he still was not the one who put me on the path to teaching. This difficult task was accomplished by my ESL teacher.

The only other class I enjoyed as much as my math class was my ESL class. It was a class full of a bunch of misfits who were not easy to deal with. We were all from different backgrounds and we could not communicate with one other. We spoke broken English and used that as a way to communicate with each other. But the biggest challenge rested on the shoulders of our teacher, Mrs. Boutin. She was not only there to teach us English but also there to help us survive high school. Many of us would come to class angry, upset, or frustrated due to being picked on for our inability to stand up for ourselves because of the language barrier. She was there to comfort us and help us find our voice. Her compassion towards us and dedication to our success had a huge impact on me. I chose math as my major in college because it gave me a voice that I did not have and Mrs. Boutin's teaching methods fueled the passion in me to become a teacher.

During my final years of college I volunteered for programs that focused on bringing social justice to many urban areas. I wanted to continue working with young urban youth and help them see the value of education. As part of the second cohort of the NMUTR, I met professors that were as passionate about education and social justice as I was. The professors focused on teaching methods that were student centered and used inquire to engage and motivate students. For the next two years I was a member of a program that focused on impacting urban youth and helped me to achieve my goal as an educator and a community member.

The work I did at the All Stars Project focused on being an active member of the community. How could I be an effective teacher and create a culture of achievement with my students if I do not take an active role in the community in which they live? The professors that I worked with at the NMUTR were all experts in their own fields and had a vast knowledge to share. Our cohort engaged in pedagogy that centered on motivating and engaging students as well as using reflective practices to improve our teaching.

My experiences growing up and coming to this country have had a huge impact on me as an educator. I believe that I have gone through multiple transformations since beginning this journey and continue to transform as an educator even today. Through the NMUTR I have learned how to engage not only myself but also my students in reflective learning. As an urban educator I am responsible for finding ways to connect with my students just like my high school math teacher did, even though I did not speak English, and invoke the passion for learning just like my ESL teacher did. Success in my classroom means more than just learning math; I want my students to reflect on their experiences and use their educations to become advocates for themselves and their communities.

MONICA TAYLOR, EMILY J. KLEIN, PRIYANK BHATT,
ALEXANDER DIAZ AND SUZANNE POOLE

9. BEYOND SCHOOL WALLS

Engaging in Curriculum, Community, and the Complex World

MONICA AND EMILY

When you remove the school environment or the expectation of having
to succeed in a specific way or having to achieve to some sort of standard,
amazing things can occur!

Suzanne shared this as she reflected about her summer experience in the NMUTR.
At the end of their first year of teaching, she and her cohort two colleagues, Alex
and Pri, participated in a focus group discussion with Bonnie Gildin of the All Stars
Project and Cindy Onore, our MSU colleague who helped us to write and design the
NMUTR secondary cohort program.[1] Bonnie and Cindy facilitated this conversation
in order to generate resident narratives about the impact of the summer community
experience on the residents. Interestingly, what emerged was a rich reflective
dialogue about what Suzanne, Alex, and Pri had learned during their summer
internships at the All Stars Talent Show Network and La Casa De Don Pedro, two
Newark community organizations (described in detail within) and more importantly
how these principles of teaching and learning manifested in their challenging first
year of teaching. When we planned the summer curriculum we had hoped that it
would lay a foundation for how they perceived and related to their Newark students,
how they conceptualized authentic learning and inquiry, and how they developed
collaborative relationships with their peers, yet we were still surprised when we saw
just how much these experiences had influenced, and also supported, their instincts
to build strong relationships with their students, demand highly engaged classroom
interactions, and nurture strong partnerships with their colleagues. It is as if their
internships created a third space home for them, and any time that they began to lose
their way during their first year of teaching, they only had to return to the memory
of these experiences and they quickly found their inner compass back to their most
profound beliefs about teaching and learning. They were reminded that they were not
alone nor were they without a safety net of peers who could provide intellectual and
emotional support. This mattered deeply at the most challenging teaching moments,
as their rich descriptive narratives illustrate throughout this chapter.

Suzanne's insightful observation above clearly captures our intentions for the residents' summer experiences. Integrating a community based field experience into a preservice teacher education program is not a new concept (Adams et al., 2005; Cristol & Gimbert, 2002; Zeichner & Melnick, 1996). Similar to our model, many programs use these experiences as part of their initial coursework (Szente, 2008/2009; Weber, 1998) with the intentions of helping preservice teachers gain understandings about diverse populations and how to communicate and engage with these communities (Hollins & Guzman, 2005; Koerner & Abdul-Tawwab, 2006; Lenski et al., 2005). However, most of the research from these models does not make a clear connection between these experiences and the program's goals or the influence on these teachers once they are in the classroom.

We constructed work with community organizations that would further contribute to the third space framework, providing another perspective about Newark youth and their potential, and the strengths and needs of their communities. We hoped the residents would become the intersecting agent between the students' lives, their school experiences, and the communities (Gonzalez, 2005). We believed the residents would build strong relationships with Newark youth that would illuminate the complexities of their identities and the "funds of knowledge" of their families, homes, and communities (Moll & Gonzalez, 2004). We also predicted that working with these organizations would help them grow to know Newark in a deeper way and begin to recognize its many community resources. The residents in their capacity as "community teachers," as Onore and Gildin (2013) call them, "might align themselves more closely with other, more transformative purposes such as cultivating civic virtue in the young. In doing so, they would be engaging in shared responsibility for community betterment" (p. 153). They might transform their concepts of what it means to be a teacher to include the notion of teaching as a "public profession," a term that Onore and Gildin (2013) borrow from Yinger (2005). In doing so, their work would be "a form of social activism in which teachers engage in collaborative exploration of educational issues, identify mutually valuable social projects, and commit to core values, all of which would simultaneously serve educational purposes" (p. 154).

Additionally, within settings like the All Stars Project and La Casa De Don Pedro, there would be plenty of inquiry and authentic learning taking place without the constraints of the curriculum, standards, and testing. We expected that our residents would be asked to facilitate learning that was meaningful, engaging, and relevant to the Newark students. For example, at La Casa De Don Pedro, as we detail in this chapter, our residents had freedom to design curriculum for students with absolutely no pedagogical or content constraints. They could design experiments, go on field trips, write skits, or make models (they would do all of those and more). We knew that these demands would be challenging but reflective of our own teaching paradigms and therefore worthwhile. Our residents needed the experience of planning and carrying out teaching practices in a safe and relatively stress-free environment without the heavy hand of testing or content standards (Schultz, 2008).

We predicted that these settings would invite them to take risks, collaborate with one another, experience trial and error, and formulate some beliefs about teaching and learning. After all, these were what we considered the steps for the learning cycle. Finally, we hoped that the residents would begin to consider curriculum as a means to "read the word and read the world" (Macedo & Freire, 1987) where learning involved bridging the students and the classroom to the local and global community. These experiences had the potential to activate a curriculum that involved "a series of occasions for individuals to articulate the themes of their existence and reflect on those themes until they know themselves to be in the world and can name what has been up to then obscure" (Greene, 1978, pp. 18–19).

Using the narratives from their focus group discussion, in this chapter, Monica and Emily, as MSU faculty, and Suzanne, Alex, and Pri, cohort two residents, share insights into the summer internships and then examine and discuss how these learning principles manifest in the residents' first year of teaching and beyond. For the purposes of this chapter, we focus primarily on the residents' summer internship participation in the All Stars Talent Show Network and the summer enrichment camp at La Casa De Don Pedro. A more in depth discussion of the mentoring that residents did with All Stars Project youth is provided in chapter four.

ALL STARS TALENT SHOW NETWORK AND BROWNEYES

Monica and Emily

The All Stars Talent Show Network (ASTSN) is an afterschool and summer enrichment program for inner city youth ages 5–25. Youth participate in a variety of events including auditions, rehearsals, talent shows, and performance workshops in auditoriums in local schools at their theater in New York City (http://allstars.org/content/all-stars-talent-show-network). The program envisions that all youth are "stars" and "is designed to reach the vast majority of 'ordinary' kids from the poorest neighborhoods—the young people who typically do not make it into 'special' programs" (para. 3). They bring kids into the program through flyers passed out by youth and adult volunteers, presentations at community centers and schools, and in person at "tables on street corners in the neighborhoods where the performance is to take place" (para. 4) The organization holds auditions at auditoriums in the local high schools and "every young person who auditions makes it." The ASTSN provides urban young people opportunities to perform and to learn production skills necessary for a live, stage performance. The young people do everything from dance, to synchronized step, singing (R&B or rap), skits, and instrumentals in groups or as solo performers. Besides performing, they "with the support of staff and trained volunteers—manage all aspects of the event including the lights, sound, security, ticket sales, outreach and publicity. The events take place in the community, often at local high schools, giving the young people a chance to perform before family, friends and neighbors" (para. 4).

Suzanne and Pri had the unique opportunity of working with ASTSN. As described above, in the summer of 2011 they were the adult volunteers who handed out flyers on the street in various neighborhoods in Newark, attempted to get youth and adults to join the talent show network, and helped to organize and produce a talent show. They were mentored by Nichele Brown, a rapper also known as "Browneyes." A young single mom, on welfare, from Far Rockaway, Queens, Browneyes is "a talented artist and a dynamic organizer who grew up with the program; she is equally at home on stage and on the street" (para. 6). She has been involved with the All Stars for over twenty years as a performer and volunteer (http://allstars.org/content/browneyes-announcement). Suzanne and Pri both found Browneyes to be an inspirational role model; certainly she was a non-traditional teacher educator, but as such, she was able to provide alternative ways of thinking about how to connect and work with kids. By positioning her as a teacher educator, the NMUTR sent a message about the nature and values of the program and who was "allowed" to do the work of teacher education.

Below Suzanne and Pri describe the ways in which participating in the ASTSN influenced their process of becoming urban teachers. They highlight how this internship expanded their knowledge of Newark and its various neighborhoods. They reflect on how soliciting volunteers, an action rarely associated with teaching, provided them with opportunities to build their confidence, take risks, and learn how to talk to urban youth. Finally, they examine the Talent Show production as a parallel to authentic learning and contrast it to the ways in which teaching and learning are confined in schools.

Suzanne

The teaching aspect was only one part of what I learned from being involved in the Talent Show. But there was so much more. Going into it, I already had significant assumptions about Newark. And in truth I really had done nothing but wait at Penn Station before, even though I grew up in New Jersey all my life. A big part of it for me was being on the streets of Newark and talking to people and seeing someone like Browneyes communicate with everybody. I appreciated her perspective, which was totally different from mine, considering I am a white woman who grew up in a suburban environment and Browneyes is an African American woman with an urban background. Watching her engage with people on the streets helped give me insight into her perspective. Even if I did not relate the experience necessarily to teaching, getting used to being in Newark and being someplace that I was going to be for a significant amount of time was really important.

Pri

I struggled to determine how the ASTSN was helping me become a better teacher. But the more time I spent working there with Browneyes and Suzanne and everybody, the more I realized that it was about us experimenting with different things and going out there, introducing ourselves, and building up the confidence and different ways to talk to the urban youth. This was helpful since my own background as an immigrant from India set me apart from Newark youth.

A key moment for me with the ASTSN was the first time that we went out to get people to volunteer or sign up. It had been a while since I had to solicit from strangers and I was not clear how it related to me becoming a teacher. The first time that Browneyes worked with us, she started going over our speeches. I was a little taken aback because I had had no idea we were actually going to go into the streets and start talking to people randomly. She told us to give the speeches we prepared, and the whole time I had no idea what we were doing at ASTSN. They never directly explained to us how this would impact us as teachers—they just asked us to go out there and have the experience. So it was definitely a key moment when we got out there in the streets and Browneyes said, "Alright I need you to go and start getting people to sign up or volunteer." It was a little intimidating at first. I did not think that it would build my confidence, but if you just start talking to people randomly, start having a conversation with them like, "Oh, do you want to sign up?"—that does build your confidence because you are not used to doing something like that with complete strangers. So that was definitely a key moment for me. I thought I would be bad at it but the more I did it the easier it became. I would just bring ASTSN into the conversation and then ask young people to sign up. So that was definitely fun and scary at first and an interesting experience all at the same time.

Monica and Emily

We were struck by the continued references to "confidence" that Suzanne and Pri made when they reflected on this summer experience. Much as the ASTSN asks kids to "perform" we were asking our residents to "perform" as well, something they would refer back to, as they would later take on the role of teacher (Sarason, 1999). Both Suzanne and Pri were clearly puzzled by the relationship between their work at the ASTSN and that of the NMUTR, but also were quickly struck by the task of "getting out there" to talk to youth and ask things of them. They realized that the act of doing so made them more confident in working with young people. In many ways the discomfort and disequilibrium of the task would mirror the nature of putting on their teacher hat the coming September. Rather than the metaphor of teacher as entertainer, the work in ASTSN was preparing teachers for "teaching as performance art"—the unexpected performance that occurs when the prepared script comes to life in a moment of interactions (Reardon & Mollin, 2009; Sarason, 1999). As Sarason (1999) points out, most teacher education programs ill prepare future teachers for this kind of performance; the majority of teachers have few worries about "whether the audience will return" (p. 50). The relationship in performance art involves a different kind of performer, one "in which the teacher defines and seeks *to appear* in his or her role..." This role "...contains a 'picture' of what the members of that audience needs, thinks, feels, hopes for, expects, deserves, and that constitutes and

225

defines what a teacher understands" (p. 51). Our residents were beginning to develop their performances as teachers.

Suzanne

Besides getting young people to sign up and volunteer at ASTSN, I was also so moved by the Talent Show production. I remember almost tearing up when we watched the first one. It was something that we had worked on for the whole summer. I had not realized how emotionally attached I had gotten to it. So watching the kids and seeing them have this experience from the minute we first met them on the street to seeing them having to come in and perfect their performance was incredible. Actually seeing everyone perform well and in particular viewing those students about whom, to be honest, we had our doubts, was so rewarding. They performed so well and received so many applauses. I just had no idea that something so amazing was happening in Newark. So I do not really know how to describe how the ASTSN affected my teaching or affected me in any specific way, but I just remember being really affected by it and feeling really connected to the performers and a part of their community.

Pri

That was the first time that I had ever been a part of putting something like that together. We actually helped to not only bring these performers to ASTSN but we helped in the process of making the talent show happen. We distributed the flyers, constructed and set up the stage, and made sure that everything was ready. We helped usher the audience. We were all part of creating that talent show. It was such a great moment for all of us. The young people even brought their parents who were so excited to see their kids perform. We had kids from all over Newark, from all different places and with all different backgrounds. Our time and efforts contributed to their amazing performance, which they enjoyed and about which they felt proud.

Suzanne

At the Talent Show, the young people just came and performed. They did not have to be perfect. They did not have to sound like Mariah Carey even though some people did. They were just invited to come and perform. Students actually started to achieve when they were able to experience a feeling of success. So we were moving barriers and pulling down walls, and I think that was something that we were able to already start to understand in the summer internships. I know I wanted to emulate that in my classroom.

Monica and Emily

The concept of classroom and curriculum as performance was a metaphor we would refer to throughout the year. Pineau (1994) calls this "educational play" and emphasizes, "The concept of play, with its attendant implications of experimentation, innovation, critique, and subversion, breaks open conventionalized classroom practices...performance creates a play space of possibility removed from the culpabilities of everyday life ..." (p. 15). In many ways we were asking students to think of their curriculum as a performance that their students would construct and in which they would engage, much as they did with the talent show; scripted and yet also improvisational, structured and yet, dialogic. Education became a "performative experience" (Pineau, 1994, p. 9) and the residents were there to draw out, construct, and help create a backdrop for achievement. The feeling of "success" that they first noticed in their interactions with youth at ASTSN, was what we wanted them to bring to the Newark classrooms in the months to follow. This kind of experience is powerful in dislodging the deeply entrenched notions of what teaching and learning look like.

LA CASA DE DON PEDRO AND THE ZOMBIE CURRICULUM

Monica and Emily

Our residents also had the opportunity to do summer internships at La Casa De Don Pedro (LCDDP), "a community based development corporation and provider of comprehensive services that has been working with and serving residents of greater Newark, New Jersey for more than 40 years" (para. 1). Their mission involves fostering "self-sufficiency empowerment, and neighborhood revitalization" (http://www.lacasanwk.org, para. 2). Among many other programs, LCDDP offers a summer enrichment camp for children between the ages of five and twelve during July and August. Each day involves different activities, which stem from the students' interests. These could involve arts and crafts, games and activities, art, drama, and scientific explorations. Intending to bridge the school year, this camp "provides a fun learning experience to help sustain their basic skills in reading and writing" (http://www.lacasanwk.org/programs-and-services/youth-enrichment/elementary-school/, para. 3).

To understand what inquiry looks like we have to, as Short, Harste, with Burke (1996) point out, look at how "learners actually go about inquiry in their lives outside of school" (p. 257). Authentic inquiry emerges when learners explore and engage in the world around them and develop real burning questions that they then can pursue to construct meaning for themselves. It tends to work from a concept that "knowledge is dynamic, ever changing, and multiple, and not static, does not reside in textbooks or with experts, and cannot be simply transmitted to students" (Taylor & Otinsky, 2007, p. 71). Using inquiry as a curricular framework, "students," according to Wells (2001), "need to be given the opportunity to develop personal initiatives and responsibility, adaptable problem-posing and -solving skills, and the ability to work collaboratively with others" (p. 173). To do this, teachers and students must participate in a dialogical community where ideas are shared, discussed, examined, and reformulated (Stock, 1995) and new understandings about the world are constructed.

Below Alex elaborately describes the "zombie" inquiry curriculum that he developed with Marc during their internship at LCDDP. Of particular note is the deep student engagement that stemmed from this creative approach they took to curriculum development with the children at the camp. Because of the authentic nature of the learning and its relevance to the children's lives and interests, Alex and Marc were able to experience first hand and early on in their teacher preparation, the impact of developing a curriculum that was owned, in part, by the learners. Then, reflecting on their first years of teaching, Alex and Suzanne analyze the challenges of using a curriculum as inquiry model in their classrooms as first year teachers in increasingly pressured school cultures where testing and standards dominate.

Alex

I was interning at LCDDP and the staff there did not give us a set role. They said, "Just get some of the students, and if you have an idea, kind of run with it." That statement scared me because I did not even know what that meant. And then I thought, "I'm in this program to learn how to teach…" I remember sitting down with students initially (I was working with Marc), just talking to them, getting to know their interests and playing games. They were very young, between the ages of 6 to 12. I remember taking one of their interests—because I remember one of them saying to Marc, "Oh I really like zombies!" Marc has the most wonderful imagination so he proposed, "Let's make zombie skits!" I thought, "That sounds great! Why not, right?" So we kind of ran with it, and he started making skits and having the students write skits, and I did biology lessons on how zombies take over the brain and all the different parts of the organs and all that. I just remember thinking to myself, "I never thought I could generate interest like this, especially in biological topics," like how a virus could possibly take over the brain because we tried to imagine what would be the best way for a zombie virus to actually make people into zombies. It was really ridiculous but amazing at the same time.

While we were doing the activities the kids were so excited to participate that they were lining up to work with us. When we came in in the mornings, the students would say excitedly, "Oh my God we're gonna do the zombie skits!" We explored zombie symptoms through a series of recordings and documents of people who were undergoing the zombie apocalypse that I had created. I made these ridiculous recordings of pretend people who were becoming zombies. I tried to sound like I was losing my mind. And I made fake journal entries too. I asked the children to read the documents and then listen to the recordings and see if they could figure out the symptoms of zombie infection and what eventually would happen. I asked them about the time frame too. At first, they just grabbed the papers and read them without thinking about identifying a disease or synthesizing information. They were so into the material.

Marc worked with other students to write the skits and then act them out. When he was teaching them how to act, they really wanted to get it right. They said things like, "Oh, so I have to give it more emotion!" He even tried to show them how to be the "bad cop" at one point. He said, "No, you really have to get into it!" and then to demonstrate he slammed the table and threw the cup. The students were so into it that they did not hesitate trying different things. I think it is because it was such a low-stress learning environment. It did not feel high-stakes at all. They were learning at the pace that they needed to learn. They learned a lot in that time frame and I do not think they felt shy about it because there was not this idea of a classroom and a school and them being tested on it. And even though we subversively used informal assessments, we never focused on whether or not they were learning something. There was no right or wrong answer. They were engaged because it felt real to them. They knew to some extent that there was progress being made, but they didn't associate it with a school environment. Also the students knew that these projects were theirs. We tried to build off of their interests, no matter what it was.

I accomplished more in that summer internship at LCDDP than I did the whole of my first year of teaching. The combination of our excitement about their interests with helping them produce something from these interests really shaped my teaching. In my first year of teaching, I was not helping the students do something that they wanted to do. I did not build a sense of interest in the topic. That summer experience set the bar for what I hope to achieve as a teacher. Because during that summer, the kids did not even know they were learning. When they stopped worrying about the learning and just had the experience, a whole barrier was removed. I did not achieve that my first year of teaching. That really bothers me, but I think that bother is good because it gives me a healthy sense of what I hope to accomplish and what I want students to accomplish for themselves.

I was not alone in making this realization either. I noticed, at the end of my first year of teaching that many of my colleagues talked about how tired the students were of learning in their classrooms. This is not a comment on the students as much as it is the kind of teaching that we do and the kind of things we try to generate. I understand we are a public school, and we try to make students more rounded and we have goals, and I understand what we try to achieve, but I think there is something missing.

Suzanne

I felt exactly the same way in my first year at North High School.[2] There was more testing done than actually having teaching time. I am sure that was happening in other places. Kids felt the pressure, and so this idea of learning, by default, was now learning for the tests whether we wanted it to be or not. It did not matter if I said something completely different or told them I was not even grading the tests, which is what I started to do towards the end. This is the context in which we teach and one that the students have gotten used to from the time they are little. Newark is a testing culture where nothing makes sense from an administrative standpoint. And in response, the kids are always fighting this approach because they never get a glimpse of the possibility of something else. There is always a battle. And even if the teacher tries to do something outside of the box and tries to generate curriculum with the students, she also has to confront obstacles. If the teacher uses an innovative curriculum then her department chair may criticize her for not meeting the learning objective or not aligning with the NJ standards by her department chair. Then the teacher is also battling and in the midst of that battle, the nature of true engagement and true learning is lost.

Alex

There is a component missing in our push for student achievement. Perhaps we need to research student engagement and emotional learning to advocate for a different approach to teaching for our students with our department chairs and principals. This would help us to justify why we are using more student-centered inquiry. Newark is a pretty exciting place right now with a lot of pressure to succeed. Because of that, I think we have generated a lot of interest in the community around us, and I think there are a lot of resources from which we can pull. With that said, the challenges of being a first year teacher make it difficult to focus on those areas of my teaching. I know there is a better way of fulfilling both the district's wants and needs and the students' wants and needs, and building something from that. But it is going to take a big push, and will involve researching and finding what we are looking for to support the kind of things that we want to do.

Suzanne

I do not think it is just first year teachers. I think all teachers are feeling these pressures. I talked to a lot of veterans at my school, teachers who were not necessarily jaded, but really great and motivated ones. They said that in the past few years they feel so monitored either through the excessive testing or being observed every week. At North High School, I was observed every week. So there was really very little room for creating new spaces for inquiry. The administration has been taking away our freedom in the classroom. This probably depends on the school in which you are teaching. In particular North High School was being monitored because of some grants that it had. It is awful that they are taking away the little spaces that a teacher has to break free, build on the curriculum in an interesting way, or meet a learning objective in a more innovative way.

Monica and Emily

It was important for our residents to construct inquiry based curriculum during the summer internship because it meant that our residents had tangible experiences of what that felt and looked like when they returned to more traditional and constrained classroom settings. Bridging those experiences to much more complex contexts given the constraints of testing and standards has been complicated, but the influence of the summer experience was obviously something that we wanted our residents to understand because it provided the impetus for further learning and experimentation. In the years to come all of them would work to return to that kind of teaching. Continuing to support a third space construct, our intentions were not to dictate specifically how our graduates would negotiate the complexities of testing and standards. Rather we hoped that their experiences of teaching through inquiry would provide them with a guiding pedagogical framework. How they balanced the curricular constraints in light of their emerging knowledge about teaching and learning was often discussed and problematized but we never presented them with clear cut solutions. We acknowledged that this sort of socially just inquiry based teaching manifests in unique and organic ways and cannot be prescribed. We felt strongly that their first experience in the residency be one that reflected the kind of teaching and learning that we wanted them to emulate as we knew they had much to "unlearn" from their own school experiences (Lortie, 1975). Many new teachers are trying to engage in inquiry having had few, if any, experiences themselves of this kind of teaching. Over the course of their year in the residency, we would offer a variety of inquiry based teaching and learning experiences, but we were struck again and again, by how potent this first one, interestingly one outside of a school, was for them.

GETTNG TO KNOW STUDENTS AS PEOPLE AND BUILDING THIRD SPACE CLASSROOMS

To teach in a manner that respects and cares for the souls of our students is essential if we are to provide the necessary conditions where learning can most deeply and intimately begin. (hooks, 1994, p. 13)

Our priority for the summer experience was to provide our residents with a chance to build relationships with Newark's young people. We hoped that through their summer internships they would learn strategies that could later be used to develop a similar type of rapport with their students in their classrooms. For us, this was one of the most important aspects of teaching in urban schools. Nieto (2003) notes that effective teachers focus on: "respecting and affirming students' identities and demonstrating care and respect for students" (p. 39). They also came to believe in the capacity of their students to learn and to hold them to high standards of learning. Effective urban teachers "see" their students holistically, and "learn to look and listen carefully and nonjudgmentally in order to understand who students really are, what they think, and how they make decisions about how they behave" (Darling-Hammond, 2002, p. 210). Gathering this kind of information about their students moves them away from teaching generically to a more third space orientation where they tailor the curriculum to their students' interests and needs. It also encourages a more fluid understanding of their students that is not limited to labels, assessments, or even initial assumptions. When teachers relate to students as people, they realize that they have complex multiple identities, which manifest in different contexts. They are not penalized or limited because they have special needs, are below grade level, or curse. These characteristics, in a third space classroom, can exist next to talent, ambition, politeness, or even care.

For this section, Pri and Suzanne share how they built significant relationships with their students during the beginning of their first year of teaching. We see the impact of the summer curriculum on their first year of teaching and they describe how beneficial this was in the long run for their students and how these deep connections created an honest and open community. Students were more willing to take risks and at least try innovative learning methods like inquiry, which were so different from the worksheets to which they were accustomed from their own schooling experiences. Pri and Suzanne were better able to differentiate instruction because their students became comfortable voicing their need for extra help or new explanations of concepts. There was a mutual commitment by students and teachers, which empowered everyone and propelled learning within their classrooms.

Additionally, Alex very honestly provides another perspective as he shares his challenges of teaching a new content area, in a bilingual classroom, with a department chair who is emphasizing a focus on academics rather relationships with students. As many new urban teachers can relate, Alex describes his realization a month into the school year that effective teaching relies on knowing one's students. He shares how he was able to back track and re-focus his energy on his students' needs and wants. Interestingly, this is something that we too have been thinking about within our own teacher education practices.

Pri

Even though I felt pressure to get to the academics from my principal, she also reminded me to make sure to get to know my students. This was especially important because our students came from so many different schools. They were bussed from all over Newark, and a lot of them had troubled backgrounds, so she wanted to make sure that we were actually getting to know them, from where they come and what their family life was like. During the first couple of days of school all I did was talk to my students. We sat down. I had them fill out cards and we talked about what they wrote down. We did surveys together. We sat in a circle and just talked. It was important for me as a teacher to know what their likes and dislikes were. They were honest about hating math and feeling like they did not have good math teachers in the past. It helped me to determine what kind of teacher I needed to be for them. I had to think about what I wanted to do that was different from their past teachers and how I could meet them where they were.

I realized that I did have to start a little bit behind the curriculum to catch them up. For the 8th graders, I had to work on some of the 7th grade concepts. In the end, this was a worthwhile strategy. In general in Newark there are many students who are not on grade level. So it is the teacher's job to accommodate their students but also push them to perform on grade level and beyond. In math especially this meant motivating and engaging them. I had to increase their curiosity and teach differently than how I was taught or how I learned.

The students were always brutally honest with me and would stop me in the middle of a lesson and say, "This is not working for me. You need to do something because I'm not getting it." I would literally stop what I was doing and I would say, "Ok, let's try a different way." It was amazing how aware the students became about their learning. They would be able to explain which method of learning they preferred. They would actually come up and write down what they thought their process was and then compare it with one another. My teaching moved from me coming up with a way to solve a problem for the class to the entire class community working on a plan to solve a problem together.

They did not want me to just give them worksheets even though that is what they were used to. I definitely observed some classrooms in my school where students were working on worksheets at their desks, while the teacher was on the computer. My students were tired of that. They expected something more from me. The first day built trust between us and they wanted me to teach in a more authentic way. Our open communication helped me realize I did not want to be that teacher that gives worksheets. I wanted them to explore and become interested in math. They said things like, "I don't like math but the fact that you are teaching it is at least a little better for me. At least I understand it and I'm able to pass the subject." All those factors put together have helped me to become the teacher that I want to be for the next 10, 15, 20, or 25 years.

Suzanne

Despite my criticisms, because there was a lot of chaos at North High School, I was able to stay off the radar and do what I wanted to do in the classroom. I was able to take the curriculum where I wanted it to go. So the first few weeks of school there was no pressure. I used that time to completely build relationships with my students and get to know them as people and as learners. I had really small class sizes as a special educator so it was easier to create a really comfortable atmosphere. Building those relationships with my students empowered them.

But I had almost the exact opposite situation as Pri. I went in full force trying to do inquiry lessons and trying to make science different from what they experienced in the past. I had complete resistance at the beginning because they were so used to following a worksheet, especially as students with special needs. They had a reputation of only being able to complete a worksheet. The students themselves believed that the only way they could be successful was when they were filling the blanks on a guided worksheet.

So any time I tried to break free from that, it was really difficult. I jumped into inquiry too fast and then I had to back track and provide them with scaffolded structures to support them in a more gradual transition from worksheets to inquiry. If I had had the foresight then I could have started off with guided notes and then slowly taken away supports in order for them to become more investigative and independent. But by the end of the year they were used to inquiry and expected it. They realized that whatever we were doing I was not going to just give them the answer. They were required to use some brain power and critical thinking skills.

Initially I worked really hard to create a Socratic seminar with my students. It went really well and it was successful, and then I planned another one. I sent emails to all of the teachers about the seminar because it required that I pull them out of different classes to participate. Then without any notice, I had to completely cancel the seminar because the school decided they were having this random assembly during that time. They did not even inform the teachers. They did not tell anybody about it. The kids had to be pulled from my seminar. I requested that they be able to go to the assembly late so that they could at least have the seminar for a shortened amount of time. My students came with me to my department chair and said, "We really want to stay in this seminar." I realized that forcing the students to go to the assembly instead of my seminar was not my department chair's decision and that she could have been reprimanded if the administration knew that one of her teachers had held back 25 kids from going to this assembly. I was pleased that she saw how dedicated the students were to wanting to be in the seminar. So all in all, the whole process was really meaningful. I was especially happy to see them taking a stake in my classroom and wanting to learn. Even though we were not able to negotiate getting them out of the assembly, it was important that they were fighting to be in the seminar and be a part of non-traditional learning. I realized that I really had built significant relationships with each one of my students. They were committed to learning in my classroom because of these real relationships but also because I was completely honest with them.

There was a huge stigma attached to teaching students with special needs at North High School. It seemed like there was an unspoken message that teachers did not have to push students with special needs and that they were not going to be successful or able to achieve basically what other students could. One teacher said: "You should just give them a lot of coloring." So I was completely honest with my students. I would tell them "I'm not changing your grade unless you do work, and I'm not giving you less work. So if you want to actually get a good grade in my class, you're going to have to come on your own time and complete it." And even though they tried to challenge me about that in the first month, they saw that I was not budging. As a result, I had herds of students coming in to complete assignments because they actually wanted to see their grades change. I not only built a relationship with them as a friend or as a not-teacher, but I also tried to build a relationship with them as a teacher who saw them as capable learners and students.

Alex

I wish I had focused on building relationships that first week or so. At East Side High School, my department chair kept saying that we had to immediately start with the academics, to start doing work from the very first day. I felt so much pressure because I was teaching bilingual classes for the first time this year, which was a completely new kind of teaching for me. I was also teaching environmental science, which I had not taught the previous year so in the first month or so I was just trying to tread water. I was just so focused on the tasks that I had to do and so overwhelmed by them, that I did not do enough to establish those important student relationships that would have really helped the students learn.

Slowly throughout the year, I began to realize how important it was for me to talk about myself to my students so they knew who was teaching them. No one wants to be taught by a random face. I also needed to get to know them and so I started doing that more and more throughout the year and spending time with them after class if they were willing. I started incorporating topics that allowed them to talk about themselves. I wanted them to write about an experience they had with either a family member or friend who might have had some sort of genetic disease, and most of them were able to either talk about something that was personal to them in regards to that or talk about something that wasn't necessarily genetic but was very serious. I shared my own personal story too. This kind of personal narrative sharing humanized all of us. The students were more human in the sense that I knew a lot more about them. They had so much more depth. And they knew more about me, which made it so much easier for us to talk and connect. But I think having that time to get to know them at the beginning was just so critical, and I missed that this year. It was a catch-up game for me for the rest of the year.

TEACHING FOR SOCIAL JUSTICE: CONNECTING STUDENTS TO THE CURRICULUM, COMMUNITY, AND BEYOND

Monica and Emily

> Teachers can create classrooms that are places of hope, where students and teachers gain glimpses of the kind of society we could live in and where students learn the academic and critical skills needed to make it a reality. (Au, Bigelow, & Karp, 1994)

As we developed the summer curriculum, we had a clear vision that their internships would begin to build the foundation for our residents' socially just teaching stance. But with each cohort, we worried that we were not being explicit enough about our focus. As a result, we added the ICE project to cohort two's spring curriculum and a series of social justice workshops to cohort three's fall curriculum, as we describe in chapter four. We share our teaching and curricular reflections here to illustrate the context in which we later read Alex, Pri, and Suzanne's narratives about the impact of their summer experiences on them as teachers. Although they do not explicitly name themselves as social justice teachers, they describe the tenets of socially just teaching and the ways in which, through their third space experiences, they question the boundaries of the classroom and begin to re-envision the community as an extended classroom.

These tenets echo the social and pedagogical vision illustrated in the introduction to *Rethinking Schools Volume 2* (Bigelow, Harvey, Karp, & Miller, 2001), a reading that we share with the residents in the spring semester. We too believe that curriculum should be "grounded in the lives of our students," "should probe the ways their lives connect to the broader society, and are often limited by society," and should "equip students to 'talk back' to the world" (p. 2). This sort of teaching involves asking students to think about issues of power and privilege and construct possible alternatives that are more just. If students are to become "truth-tellers and change-makers" (p. 3), they need to understand how they are connected to their communities and that they have great potential to make change locally, regionally, and beyond. These objectives are neither easy nor automatic and they are not always shared by school administrations. But they are attainable if teachers learn to work collaboratively towards these goals both with their peers but also with community organizers.

The stories below from Alex and Pri give life and illustrate what social justice teaching looks like in real Newark classrooms when students, teachers, and community organizations work together. Alex poignantly shares how difficult the beginning of his first year of teaching was and how his teaching compass led him to find ways to engage his students and connect them to their communities and most importantly re-connect him with other teachers and with community organizers. Pri recounts his involvement with Math Olympics, an extracurricular endeavor, which provided him with a community where he could collaborate with other math teachers but also as a vehicle for his students to engage with a larger world beyond Newark. He reminds us that teaching is about helping our students to dream big and actualize their dreams.

Alex

My students kept asking me: "Why is this important to study?" I tried to remind them that what we were studying was relevant to their lives. It seemed like there was no engagement because nothing was really relevant to them. This was so frustrating because I see myself as a teacher who connects the content of what I am teaching to the real world and prepares my students for their futures in that real world. I worry that if they are not informed, other people will make decisions for them.

In my first year of teaching, I did not do enough to provide them with a different perspective of the world, which would prevent them from just accepting everything that happens to them. I did not help them to build their own voices and engage with something in a deep analytical way to ask the big questions like: "Do I believe this is right or do I believe this is wrong? Why?" I interpreted their questions of why the content was relevant as resistance rather than their real authentic questions. I should have given them opportunities to explore these questions themselves through inquiry.

Those first three months of teaching were a total blur. I think I cried more that year than I have in my entire life. I was trying so hard to do my job. I just did not have enough hours in the day to do more. Part of the problem was that I chose to only rely on myself and not reach out to my school community around me. Being a new teacher and teaching transitionally bilingual students was really hard. I was trying to figure out how to push my students to learn English even though some of them had only been in the country for a month. I had very few bilingual teaching strategies and was feeling very clueless. I was shocked and overwhelmed by all of these new pressures and truly I felt the repercussions of that all year.

I began to realize that it is about getting these students engaged in something that is not just their immediate world, but involves the world around them. I hoped to broaden their world through seeing it through different lenses in all its depth. I hear so many students say that, "There's nothing to do" or "There's nothing to see," and I'm just like, "There's a whole world out there! You barely touched the tip. You are in this small space and the world is just so large and so interconnected and there's so much depth and richness to it."

Once I regrouped in about December, I realized there were many resources available to teachers at any given point. In some ways, I realized this because I was feeling so desperate and I knew that I needed support. The summer experiences that we had taught me that there are a lot of players in Newark who are willing and interested in being involved with students in schools. It was time to ask for help. So I asked myself: "What are the things that I need?" Then, mid-year, I started going to professional development workshops and conferences. I went to a school gardening conference about NJ food. I just started getting more involved. It helped my sanity because I could talk to people, but it also helped me open up my world a bit more, realizing that there are all these resources. So, in a way, what I learned during that first summer in the residency emerged half way through my first year of teaching. I was finally ready to take advantage of all that the Newark community had to offer my students and me.

I started to become a community teacher whether intentionally or unintentionally. For example, I became a club adviser by accident. The previous one with whom I had worked during the residency, moved and so I became more involved in the environmental science club. Antonio and I started going to conferences and we realized how interconnected this club could be to our classes and how it could be a community hub and a center for generating interests, not only for students, but different players that are involved in Newark. So we started learning about a lot of community organizations like the Newark Tree Foundation, and we really started getting involved with them. This helped me feel more invested in what I was doing which made me feel better. I felt like I was doing something.

When we started talking to the students about these different projects through the environmental science club and asking them for their suggestions and feedback, they also really got much more invested in everything we were doing. Some of our students, for instance, worked over the next summer to plant trees. They did something for the community, and made connections, and got some life skills. They were paid for planting trees but at the same time, they increased their involvement in the community.

Working on this project made me realize that the community is really important to my teaching and that my students' learning can be interconnected to the broader context or society. When students are involved in the community with us and we are all receiving training together, then we are on equal ground. They also had opportunities to meet so many different people and be treated as equal players in part of this larger world. It really just started to get at what we are trying to achieve in our teaching around connecting them to the world. It gave the students a chance to be invested in something, to engage in the world, and do something that was meaningful and context-driven.

Also my community partners have given me immense support. This has really helped me to think outside of the box as a teacher. Instead of thinking that we are confined to our school classroom, I have begun to think that the park could be the classroom or the farm we visited. Maybe the park could be part of our classroom on a daily basis. Maybe the idea of a "classroom" is null and void, meaning it can be something much more rich and something that lets you forget that you're learning.

Pri

I got involved in a different way outside of my classroom but it was also by accident. I became part of the Math Olympics Committee even though I was a first year teacher. At first, this was definitely difficult because I wanted to spend as much time in the classroom as possible and I would be pulled into these meetings with the other math teachers. Our charge was to develop the questions for the district's Math Olympics. Although I knew it was important, it was hard to be involved because I had to miss class to work on this committee. I would be thinking to myself: "I'm missing my students who are probably sitting there doing worksheets instead of learning something, and I'm just here writing questions."

As I continued to participate on the committee, I knew that it was a worthy endeavor and I appreciated getting to know the other math teachers in the district. The most important meetings were when we actually got to talk about math. We talked about: What is Math Olympics? How do we engage and motivate the students to be part of Math Olympics? How do we make it so that students who are not so good at math still get to come and see the competition and view the Math Olympics at NJIT and Essex County College?

That year I was able to take some students to Math Olympics to compete. It was the first time they actually made it and they placed. We came in third place. It was an extremely big deal both for them and for me. I appreciated meeting and getting to know all these different math teachers, as well as educators from different colleges.

My students were excited to meet professors from colleges where they hoped to one day apply and visit campuses like Rutgers.

In the end, we are trying to prepare our students for their futures after high school. We each teach a specific subject, but we are also teaching them how to be responsible, respectful, and active in their communities, and how to survive in the world. For example, my 8th graders did not know how to be respectful. I took politeness for granted but when I said to the students, "It's very rude when you curse in front of adults," they looked at me like I was crazy. One student replied, "But that's normal." So even though I was primarily teaching them math, at the same time, I was teaching them social and organizational skills because I want them to be ready when they leave high school and go to college, technical school, the military or wherever they end up going. I want my students to be academically capable but also socially and physically capable. We have lots of responsibilities as teachers because technically we are their second parents. There are so many things that we could teach them that, sometimes we do feel pressured, but that's why I try to make sure that every day I'm teaching them something that's important and useful to *them*.

For example, when I taught my students the quadratic equations, one of them said, "I'm never going to use this in my life," and I replied, "Do you want to live your life or do you want to just get by? Because if you want to just get by, then whatever. You don't have to come tomorrow. You can drop out of school. But if you want to actually live your life and enjoy your life, then trust me, you need to pass high school; you need to do something with your life." These conversations helped my students to realize that they want to do something with their lives in the end. A lot of my students have these dreams and aspirations to be doctors or lawyers, or whatever they want to be. They think about what they want for the long-term future but they do not think about the steps to get there. I try to remind them that they do need to pass high school in order to pursue these dreams because most of them say, "Well, I don't really need math to do all that." But I tell them, "You cannot just be a doctor next year. You need to go through high school." As a teacher, I want to invite my students to dream big, but I also want to make sure that they are ready to accept the responsibilities necessary for dreaming big.

REFLECTING BACK, LOOKING FORWARD: WHAT WE HAVE LEARNED

Monica and Emily

In many ways when we created the summer internships, we hoped we knew what we were doing—that residents would build relationships with kids outside of school, that they would collaborate with one another, and that they would think about curriculum, learning, and their content area outside of school learning. We wanted them to come to know the community in different ways. There was, and continued to be, lots of pressure to do something else. Colleagues, schools, and residents pushed for us to give them summer teaching opportunities in NPS high schools as many other programs do. They wanted students to practice traditional teaching in traditional schools. We pushed back and we believe that the experiences and voices of our residents speak to the pedagogical significance of community based experiences in a preservice teacher education program. Below we detail some of the key learning we have taken away from this work.

1. *Authentically engaging with young people nurtures a "pedagogy of possibility" and inquiry.* It is essential that preservice teachers have an opportunity to work with young people who are involved in real projects of which they have ownership, audience, and purpose. We firmly believed when we designed the summer curriculum that the internships would give the residents a chance to see and experience what learning outside of the constraints of school would look like. We purposely did not prescribe to our community partners what we thought the roles of the residents would be. We wanted them to have a chance to invent or co-construct curriculum as Alex shared and to witness what real engagement in learning looked and felt like. We hoped that this would encourage them to adopt what Simon (1987) calls "a pedagogy of possibility," through which they facilitate learning in the classroom that is relevant to the students' interests and invites them to problematize the world around them.

   By participating in such activities as the ASTSN, they began to understand that all young people are "stars" and can achieve and that some of the obstacles to learning and succeeding involve how teachers organize and control learning in the classroom. Engaging with young people in "performative play" (Pineau, 1994) during the summer allowed them to imagine these types of experiences could happen during the school year too. Other ways preservice teachers might engage in such work could be participating in after school or extra curricular activities where they are able to witness what can happen when students lead their own learning through artistic performances, team sports, school newspapers, academic clubs, community service, peer mentor groups, or even hosting school events. Ideally these activities are facilitated in partnership with or through the support of community organizations, where there are opportunities for other teacher educators to take the lead in guiding the learning.

2. *Partnering with community organizations in a third space involves trusting and being open to their ideas for the internships, which may not directly correlate to teaching.* We realized how fortunate we were to partner with community organizations that had a deep commitment to the youth of Newark but we were not always completely sure we understood the connections between parts of the internships and becoming teachers. It was our deep respect for one another and our commitment to fostering a third space that helped us to trust that our community partners had insights into the process that we did not envision. For example, we had worked with the All Stars Project before but never with the ASTSN and Browneyes. We were not clear how the tasks required for the Talent Show would pay off for our residents as teachers but we were willing to take a risk. In fact,

originally we assigned Janae to intern there with Pri but perhaps no more than 30 minutes into soliciting on the street, she asked to switch internships. She felt, because of her upbringing in Newark, that asking for volunteers on the street, which to her felt like begging, was something that she could never do. Suzanne quickly replaced her and she and Pri made an excellent team. As they shared, although there were no explicit connections to teaching, they learned a tremendous amount about the learning and achievement potentials of their Newark students from their participation in the ASTSN. They also felt their confidence grew and they began to understand Newark in a much different way. Teaching entails a whole range of skills and abilities that can emerge from soliciting participation from strangers on the street, making phone calls, or organizing a production. We recommend that teacher educators look for community partners who share similar visions of youth first and foremost. Connecting the activities of these organizations to teaching may feel strange, not deliberate enough or unorthodox at first but more explicit connections will emerge. Building the third space with community organizations involves some risk taking and imagination on the part of the teacher educator.

3. *Becoming a socially just teacher who encourages students to "read the world" is risky business that takes time.* It takes experience, confidence, and a trusting community to support this kind of subversive teaching. When we interviewed our residents right after the summer experience and then at the end of the program, they were not ready or able to share the ways these internships had impacted them. It was only after having a year in the classroom on their own that they were able to describe how the seeds of the teaching and learning principles sown during the summer blossomed into practices in their classrooms. For some these manifested themselves from the opening of the school year. For others, like Alex, they became part of a teaching compass that helped him to find his way back to what he knew and believed was important to teaching. Within a third space teacher preparation framework, we recognize that becoming a teacher is a non-linear process that fluctuates depending on a variety of factors including the complexities of the context as well as the individual's multiple identities (Strom, 2014). We suggest that teacher educators break away from the notion that learning to teach starts and ends during the teacher preparation program. Our complex and rigorous objectives of becoming socially just teachers who are public professionals (Yinger, 2005) cannot be attained over night. These tenets require time, experience, and reflection to percolate and develop in the hearts and minds of teachers.

NOTES

[1] We are so grateful to Cindy Onore and Bonnie Gildin for facilitating and transcribing this powerful focus group discussion. This chapter is dedicated to them and their pioneering of the collaborations between MSU and the Newark All Stars.
[2] North is a pseudonym.

REFERENCES

Adams, A., Bondy, E., & Kuhel, K. (2005, Spring). Preservice teacher learning in an unfamiliar setting. *Teacher Education Quarterly, 32*(2), 41–62.

All Stars Projects Inc. (n.d.). Retrieved from http://allstars.org/programs http://allstars.org/content/all-stars-talent-show-network http://allstars.org/content/browneyes-announcement

Au, W., Bigelow, B., & Karp, S. (1994). *Rethinking our classrooms: Teaching for equity and justice* (Vol. 1). Milwaukee, WI: Rethinking Schools.

Bigelow, B., Harvey, B., Karp, S., & Miller, L. (Eds.). (2001). *Rethinking our classrooms: Teaching for equity and justice* (Vol. 2). Milwaukee, WI: Rethinking Schools.

Cristol, D. S., & Gimbert, B. G. (2002, Fall). A case study of an urban school-university partnership: Designing and implementing curriculum for contextual teaching and learning. *The Professional Educator, 15*(1), 43–54.

Darling-Hammond, L. (2002). Educating a profession for professional practice. In L. Darling-Hammond, J. French, & S. P. Garcia-Lopez (Eds.), *Learning to teach for social justice* (pp. 201–212). New York, NY: Teachers College Press.

Elementary School « La Casa de Don Pedro. (n.d.). Retrieved from http://www.lacasanwk.org/programs-and-services/youth-enrichment/elementary-school/

Gonzalez, N. (2005). Beyond culture: The hybridity of the funds of knowledge. In N. Gonzalez, L. C. Moll, & C. Amanti (Eds.), *Funds of knowledge: Theorizing practices in households, communities, and classrooms* (pp. 29–46). New York, NY: Routledge.

Greene, M. (1978). *Landscapes of learning.* New York, NY: Teachers College Press.

Hollins, E. R., & Guzman, J. T. (2005). Research on preparing teachers for diverse populations. In M. Cochran-Smith & K. M. Zeichner (Eds.), *Studying teacher education: The report of the AERA panel on research and teacher education* (pp. 477–548). Mahwah, NJ: Lawrence Erlbaum Associates, Inc.

Hooks, b. (1994). *Teaching to transgress: Education as the practice of freedom.* New York, NY: Routledge.

Koerner, M. E., & Abdul-Tawwab, N. (2006). Using community as a resource for teacher education: A case study. *Equity & Excellence in Education, 39*, 37–46.

La Casa de Don Pedro. (n.d.). Retrieved from http://www.lacasanwk.org/

Lenski, S. D., Crumpler, T. P., Stallworth, C., & Crawford, K. M. (2005, Spring). Preparing culturally responsive preservice teachers. *Teacher Education Quarterly, 32*(2), 85–100.

Lortie, D. (1975). *Schoolteacher: A sociological study.* Chicago, IL: University of Chicago Press.

Macedo, D., & Freire, P. (1987). *Literacy: Reading the word and the world.* South Hadley, MA: Bergin & Garvey Publishers.

Moll, L. C., & Gonzalez, N. (2004). Engaging life: A funds of knowledge approach to multicultural education. In J. A. Banks & C. A. M. Banks (Eds.), *Handbook of research on multicultural education* (2nd ed., pp. 699–715). San Francisco, CA: Jossey-Bass.

Nieto, S. (2003). *What keeps teachers going?* New York, NY: Teachers College Press.

Onore, C., & Gildin, B. L. (2013). A community-university partnership to develop urban teachers as public professionals. In J. Noel (Ed.), *Moving teacher education into urban schools and communities* (pp. 152–167). New York, NY: Routledge.

Pineau, E. L. (1994). Teaching is performance: Reconceptualizing a problematic metaphor. *American Educational Research Journal, 31*(1), 3–25.

Reardon, J., & Mollin, D. (2009). *Ch-ch-ch-changes: Artists talk about teaching.* London, UK: Ridinghouse.

Sarason, S. B. (1999). *Teaching as a performing art.* New York, NY: Teachers College Press.

Schultz, B. D. (2008). *Spectacular things happen along the way.* New York, NY: Teachers College Press.

Short, K. G., & Harste, J. C., with Burke, C. (1996). *Creating classrooms for authors and inquirers.* Portsmouth, NH: Heinemann.

Simon, R. I. (1987). Empowerment as a pedagogy of possibility. *Language Arts, 64*, 370–382.

Stock, P. L. (1995). *The dialogic curriculum: Teaching and learning in a multicultural society.* Portsmouth, NH: Heinemann.

Strom, K. (2014). *Becoming-teacher: The negotiation of teaching practice of first-year secondary science teachers prepared in a hybrid urban teacher education program* (Unpublished dissertation). Montclair, NJ: Montclair State University.

Szente, J. (2008/2009, Winter). Academic enrichment programs for culturally and linguistically diverse children. *Childhood Education, 85*(2), 113–117.

Taylor, M., & Otinsky, G. (2007). Becoming whole language teachers and social justice agents: Pre-service teachers inquire with sixth graders. *International Journal of Progressive Education, 3*(2), 59–71.

Weber, C. (1998, Winter). Preservice teacher preparation for character and citizenship: An integrated approach. *Action in Teacher Education, 20*(4), 85–95.

Wells, G. (2001). *Action, talk, & text: Learning and teaching through inquiry.* New York, NY: Teachers College Press.

Yinger, R. (2005). A public politics for a public professional. *Journal of Teacher Education, 56*(3), 285–290.

Zeichner, K., & Melnick, S. (1996). The role of community field experiences in preparing teachers for cultural diversity. In K. Zeichner, S. Melnick, & M. L. Gomez (Eds.), *Currents of reform in preservice teacher education* (pp. 176–196). New York, NY: Teachers College Press.

Monica Taylor
Department of Secondary and Special Education
Montclair State University
Montclair, New Jersey

Emily J. Klein
Department of Secondary and Special Education
Montclair State University
Montclair, New Jersey

Priyank Bhatt
Newark Early College High School
Newark, New Jersey

Alexander Diaz
Eastside High School
Newark, New Jersey

Suzanne Poole
Science Park High School
Newark, New Jersey

MEET THE AUTHORS FROM CHAPTER TEN

Rosiane Lesperance-Goss, I am a second generation Haitian/Cuban-American who was initially pursuing a career in dentistry. However, after spending some time in the classroom, I realized that I had a passion for teaching science and was able to connect to urban youth, which I felt stemmed from my own experiences as an urban student. Early in my college experience, I realized that there were discrepancies in my foundational education, which I felt led to subsequent struggle to catch up to my peers, who had attended schools in more affluent areas. This realization fueled interest and passion in uncovering those discrepancies as a high school teacher in an urban setting, and providing adequate educational experiences to remedy them.

As part of the first cohort of the NMUTR secondary cohort, I engaged in pedagogy and learning that focused on teaching for social justice, inquiry as a form of learning, and reflective practice. This learning resulted in multiple ongoing transformations of how I see my role as an educator and community member. For example, as a product of urban education herself, I was culturally unaware of many institutionalized ideas of members and outsiders of urban communities. My experience mentoring teens from the Newark All Stars Project, correlating those experiences to readings, and constant reflection raised my own cultural consciousness. This realization transformed and continues to impact what I views is my role as a citizen to my community. I also feel that developing reflective practice—a metacognitive process that allows for an individual to evaluate and identify indicators, strategies, and procedures for future instructional action—has been one of the main contributors to my accomplishments and successes as a teacher. For an urban educator during this particular time in history, I believe, it is imperative that he/she be able to reflect on experiences to learn, develop, and strategize ways of being successful in the classroom.

10. INQUIRY AND INDUCTION IN THE THIRD SPACE

INTRODUCTION

Rosie

The beginning of my first year of teaching was filled with energy and excitement as I learned all about my students, their abilities, and how best to support their academic needs. Like most first year teachers, I struggled to find my niche as an educator. However, no struggle has been as difficult, nor as important, as bridging my students' educational experiences to the demands of my biology curriculum. This challenge became apparent during a particular sequence of lessons focused on the structure and function of the cell membrane and cell transport. Although the students seemed interested and were participating in the activities and discussions, they scored dismally on the test that concluded the set of lessons.

I was so confused. I was so sure that if I made the learning fun, interesting, and connected to their experiences, students would do well on their assessments. I designed my "Do Now" questions to spark interest and build on familiar ideas as we began class, posing questions like "Why would the cell membrane be considered the security guard of the cell?"—asking them to connect their ideas about the role of security guards to a new concept in a non-threatening way. From these types of questions, I bridged into active learning experiences like labs, station activities, research investigations, and projects that used familiar analogies while moving them toward autonomy. During all of these assignments, students engaged in discourse that seemed to demonstrate understanding; they led discussions, corrected, or built upon each other's ideas about biology concepts, and made their own analogies about content. However, when the time came to apply their learning on a test, they performed well on the multiple choice recall questions, but poorly on more open-ended items.

One particular incident was instrumental in helping me uncover the problem. During class one morning, I was reviewing the role of the cell membrane in the four types of cell transport. I asked the class, "Who can explain the difference between osmosis and diffusion?"

About four students raised their hands. I called on a male student, Kamal, who does not often comment in class. He answered, "Osmosis is the movement of water,

K. STROM & R. LESPERANCE-GOSS

from where there is a lot, to a little bit. And then diffusion is the movement of solute from where there is a lot to a little bit."

I nodded. "Great answer! Osmosis and diffusion both move things from a higher concentration to a lower concentration. Excellent!"

With a big smile, Kamal exclaimed, "Y'all see, that's right!"

Another student, Lisbeth, called out, "I don't know why you guys are getting happy, because once we get the test, none of this will be on it."

Her comment took me aback. "What do you mean it won't be on the test? OF COURSE it will be on the test—why do you think I'm going over it so many times?"

"Well, it might be on the test but you won't ask us easy questions like this. You ask us some other type of questions that be mad hard," she responded.

"Yuuuuuup," concurred Kamal. As I looked around in surprise, I saw that nearly every other student in the room was nodding and laughing in agreement.

"What makes them so hard?" I asked.

Another student, Jasmine, replied, "They're not hard. They're just worded stupid."

"Well, I can't just give you the definitions of words. I have to see if you really understand them," I told the class.

Lisbeth shot back, "Well I guess I don't understand them, then."

After this exchange, I took a closer look at the tests and my students' answers. I began to see that students did not lack the content knowledge. They needed to develop the skills to answer questions requiring them to apply and/or extend their knowledge. From that point on, I began offering my students the option to choose one or two of multiple open-ended questions. After each test, I would note the questions students avoided, and I would incorporate questions with similar features into my Do-Now to help students practice in a supported environment.

It was this type of cyclical teacher inquiry that the secondary NMUTR induction program hoped to deepen and foster within a community, supplemented by inquiry-into-practice endeavors like the artifact package project. In this chapter, Katie, a doctoral fellow who worked with the secondary resident graduates as an induction coach in 2011–2012, and Rosie, a first-year tenth grade biology and twelfth grade forensic science teacher, describe the design of the secondary induction program and discuss in detail the spring artifact package project. We conclude the chapter with reflections of and implications for the project, a teacher inquiry project completed during and offer an appendix with practical tools and artifacts that might be used to recreate a similar learning opportunity.

DESIGNING AN INDUCTION PROGRAM IN THE THIRD SPACE

Katie

The opportunity to support the first cohort of graduates from the secondary NMUTR program came at a fortuitous time in my doctoral studies. I had just begun to narrow my research interests to the first year of teaching in urban schools, and had recently completed an independent study in which I set out to identify patterns in the research about new teachers. What I found would not surprise anyone who has worked in a school setting for any length of time. The theme of "survival" runs throughout the novice literature (see specifically the work of Chubbock et al., 2001; Eldar et al., 2003; Feiman-Nemser, 2001; Sabar, 2004), with new teachers facing multiple institutional and pedagogical challenges that affect retention and influence their teaching methods to become more traditional (Ingersoll & Smith, 2004). For example, multiple studies, such as the work of Sherff (2008) and Tait (2008) showed that institutional challenges often serve as a barrier to enacting learner-centered practices, as new teachers often are assigned the most challenging classes. As well, Fantilli and McDougal (2009), Flores and Day (2006), and Griffin, Kilgore, and Winn (2009) all detail examples of how this often happens in isolated environments with a lack of consistent and appropriate instructional support. Working in tandem with the secondary NMUTR faculty, I used the findings from this literature to shape the induction program for the three secondary resident graduates with whom I was working.

I knew that classroom observations would be a key strategy for providing induction support. From reading about the development of beginning teachers, including Wang, Odell, and Schwille's review of the literature on beginning teachers, I had learned that pedagogical challenges tend to arise as they continue to learn to teach while having to take on the same responsibilities as veteran teachers. As Feiman-Nemser (2001) writes, "Charged with the same responsibilities as their more experienced colleagues, beginning teachers are expected to perform and be effective" (p. 1028). By regularly observing their lessons and discussing both their preparation for lessons and instructional enactment, I hoped to help them navigate the struggles new teachers often experience organizing and planning lessons (Beck, Kosnik, & Rowsell, 2007; Grossman & Thompson, 2008), differentiating instruction (Tait, 2008), assessing student learning (He & Cooper, 2011; Watson, 2006), and enacting inquiry-based lessons (Bianchini & Cazavos, 2007).

I also sought to continue one of the core attributes of the NMUTR program: the supportive, collegial, and dialogic community that had been established during the residents' apprenticeship. As the school year began, I asked the three teachers if they would be willing to participate in bi-monthly meetings to sustain and grow the community that had been created with the residents, their mentors, and the faculty the year before. Within these meetings, I envisioned continuing critical discussions of the residents' experiences, investigating problems of inquiry-based practice, and assisting each other in honing their lesson plans via the tuning protocol they had used in their preservice year. I hoped that this kind of community would lessen the isolation and reality-shock that first year teachers tend to feel, providing a forum where the residents could affirm their relationships, discuss commonalities, and understand the layers of support they had, including and above all, each other.

We made the decision early on that meeting topics, and any readings, would need to organically arise out of our co-constructed dialogues, and problems of practice would focus our work. By approximating the emergent curriculum model from the previous year (Klein, Taylor, Onore, Strom, & Abrams, 2013), this type of learning community worked to continue constructing a third space—a hybrid "in-between" induction space that was neither completely the district nor the university. The fact that I was a doctoral student, not faculty, may have also assisted in the creation of a safe space where we could be vulnerable together as we worked through the tensions of first-year teaching. Rosie commented that our weekly meetings were even "counseling-like," while at the same time resulting in developing ways to either solve a problem and/or improve something.

Rosie

As my first year of teaching began, I was so excited to get started with my students. My mentor, Karina, and I met before the school year started and mapped out most of the curriculum for the first few months, and we did it in a way that made sense for *our* students—not necessarily according to what the district recommends. We structured everything around problems and questions I thought the students would find interesting; every day I was going to try to do something hands-on. But the very first week, something happened that I had not expected, and it really made me think about the kind of teacher I wanted to be. During my second period class, I had a lab planned that reviewed the scientific method. The students were being so loud, yelling out and walking around, I could not get through the directions. I gave them several warnings and, still, I could not get them to listen to me. I got really angry. Finally, I got Biology books out and assigned them to read a chapter and complete the questions at the end, rather than do the lab.

After school that day, I met with Katie and the other two cohort one graduates, Rob and Cristina. I told them about what happened. I could not believe that just like that, I could revert back to being so traditional, even though I know it happens often to new teachers; as they deal with the reality of colleagues, students, and school experiences. The tendency to adopt transmission methods, despite being prepared otherwise, is described in a good deal of the literature on the first year of teaching. For example Allen (2009) writes that "Upon entry to the workplace, graduates come to associate good practice with that of the veteran teacher, whose practice and cache of resources they seek to emulate" (p. 647). Zeichner and Tabachnik, (1981) also found that pre-service teacher education can be "washed out" by school experiences (p. 7). But it was comforting to be able to talk to others who were in the same situation, having the same problems with classroom management, and hearing what they were doing in their classrooms. Meeting every other week also helped me keep my focus on inquiry. Although it was very important to me to design my lessons around questions, the set curriculum and testing pressures made it hard sometimes NOT to lecture.

Near the end of the first semester, data and testing were on our minds a lot. It was frustrating because my lessons took much longer than I expected, and I needed to have my students on the same pacing schedule as the other Biology teachers' classes, so we could collect data and compare it across classes. There were also certain standards that we needed to include, and planning became difficult. If I had to hit five standards, for example, it did not really leave room for an open, generative discussion. We also found out that our district was going to be taking part in a pilot project that would base my evaluation on my students' test scores, and that was in addition to the system my school already had in place. At East Side High School, we have a database that assesses every student on the common Biology assessments and provides an average score for the teacher based on her students' scores. Those scores are used to informally evaluate teachers.

This spoke to a familiar tension, one I had been grappling with since nearly the beginning of my residency year. If I taught my lessons in an inquiry-based way, with students posing questions and exploring them in open discussions, I would not get through all the topics that would be covered on the test. That would mean my students would score lower on the assessments, and I would most likely receive a poor evaluation. On the other hand, just getting through the curriculum meant that I had to teach in ways that contradicted my NMUTR learning. It was extremely challenging to try to find a balance between teaching all the concepts I knew would appear on the test and infusing what I have learned to be good teaching into the classroom, especially when I have all these outside forces telling me, "You are not doing this, and you are not doing this." In a third space, there is no either/or, only both/and/also. Yet this is easier said than done—how do I meet the demands of the district while also pushing the boundaries of teaching and learning in inquiry-based ways?

THE ARTIFACT PACKAGE PROJECT

Katie

I was distressed by the discussions with the three teachers. At the same time as I was serving as an induction coach, I was in a doctoral class learning about the national policy focus on "accountability," which was taking shape—as Rosie was experiencing—through the evaluation of teachers via their student test scores (Baker, 2012; Karp, 2012). The conversations with Rosie, Rob, and Cristina were doubly frustrating because, as the teachers and I recognized, these policies and the resulting testing focus contradicted their learning from the NMUTR. Rather than nurturing a learner-focused model of teaching organically and democratically, negotiated through student questioning and discourse, the test-driven culture of the district seemed to encourage top-down, teacher-led "filling" of students with tested content, an echo of the "banking" model of education (Freire, 1970).

Within the NMUTR program, residents had also practiced inquiry into their own teaching as a type of assessment, which meant reflecting on problems of practice and generating rich information from multiple sources about student progress to guide their own practices. Yet the district's obvious privileging of summative measures for students—which yielded little or no applicable knowledge for the resident graduates for their teaching—triggered residents to voice questions to each other in our meetings. *Shouldn't assessment practices be authentic and multi-faceted? Shouldn't assessment provide you with information to inform your instruction so you can tailor it to your students' needs?* These questions, of course, eventually led to the most upsetting question of all: *If the system in which we are working doesn't support inquiry-based teaching, and we will be punished for doing it, then why should we bother?* While this last question was asked rhetorically, this comment showed their peaking frustration with the constraints imposed upon them by so-called "measures of teacher quality" that seemed to be punitive in nature rather than in any way informative for their practice. Again, although the issues had been raised in the residency year, now that the teachers had their own classrooms, the conflicts seemed to be felt even more acutely.

While I stewed on this tension, I happened to read an article in my doctoral course that made me begin to think about alternate measures of assessing teacher quality which would be useful to the teachers in their ongoing processes of development and becoming. The article presented an idea known as an "Artifact Package" (Borko, Stecher, Alonzo, Moncure, & McClam, 2005), a means of analyzing and evaluating classroom practice by collecting various artifacts related to teaching via a tool called the scoop notebook. The authors had piloted the measurement as a "characterization of classroom practice" (p. 76) that they felt would be a richer source of descriptive information than available protocols or surveys. Their idea for the artifact package stemmed from scientific exploration of the unfamiliar. They explained, "Just as scientists may scoop up a sample of materials from the place they are studying...we planned to 'scoop' materials from classrooms for *ex situ* examination" (p. 79).

When introduced to teachers, the notebooks were framed by the question, "What is it like to learn science/mathematics in your classroom?" (p. 79). Teachers were asked to collect three types of artifacts: handouts, lesson plans, and other materials teachers created prior to their lessons; student work and other artifacts created during class; and materials produced after class, such as homework. In addition to these artifacts, teachers used disposable cameras to take pictures of their classroom arrangements and materials that were not transferrable to the notebook. For each class, teachers also wrote brief summaries and answered reflective questions about how the lesson went. As I read through the article—which validated the scoop notebook as a measure of assessing teaching practice—I began to think of ways to adapt the project for our residents, as a way to inquire into their instruction that would allow them to self-evaluate while generating useful data to inform their practices.

The next week, I brought a proposal to Monica for an inquiry-into-practice induction project based on Borko et al.'s (2005) research. I hoped the project would support the three resident graduates' continuing development of an "inquiry-as-stance" (Cochran-Smith & Lytle, 1999) mentality as well as encourage deeper reflection, improvement of instructional efforts, and dialogue regarding their current classroom practices and related challenges. The process of this project, which would simulate an inquiry cycle, such as the process described by Taylor and Otinsky (2007), and involved the identification of an issue or challenge, the collection and analysis of data, self-assessment, and presentation. Monica and I agreed that the three teachers would find this to be a familiar structure, as it approximated the inquiry cycles in which they had engaged with students the previous year in their residency classrooms. Further, because the cycles arose from the needs of the residents themselves and would involve collaborative, inductive problem-solving, the project would operate well within our third-space framework.

At our next induction meeting, I brought the idea to Rosie, Rob, and Cristina. While I was excited about the potential project, I was very worried that they might find it too cumbersome, given their already hugely heavy workloads. On the one hand, I knew that like most new teachers, the resident graduates were overwhelmed with the combination of planning, instructional, and administrative tasks they were still learning (Hargreaves & Jacka, 1995; Hong, 2010), and I did not want the activity to feel burdensome. Yet, to lead to growth, we needed to push beyond mere "venting" and engage in productive problem-solving around these issues. I brought my concerns to the teachers, and after some discussion, they agreed they would feel comfortable collecting artifacts that addressed planning, in-class activities, and reflection over a period of three classes. With their approval, I then moved into a conversation about quality indicators. I posed a question to them—what do you consider to be the components of quality teaching practice in math and science, and what do those look like? For inspiration, we read over the rubric that Borko et al. (2005) had created, and the teachers collaboratively identified five areas of teacher practice they felt strongly about:

- *Connections:* Relationships are clearly established between concepts, the real world, and students' experiences.
- *Cognitive Depth:* Lessons require and support the development of complex, higher-learning skills, and understandings.
- *Multiple Representations:* Content/concepts are illustrated in varying, sophisticated ways.
- *Structure of Instruction:* Lesson is structured coherently and has an inquiry focus, is highly interactive, and is student-centered.
- *Authentic Assessment:* Student learning is measured by a variety of formal and informal assessments allowing meaningful demonstration of learning.

Using these indicators, we co-constructed a rubric that detailed what each of these categories would look like at a beginning, developing, accomplished, and exemplary stage. Each teacher received a three ring binder that was divided into three sections for lesson plans, student work samples and in-class materials, and a summary and reflection. We agreed that during a week in February, each teacher would collect these artifacts for three consecutive class sections. Afterward, using a self-assessment graphic organizer that corresponded to the rubric, they would assess their practices with specific examples, assign themselves a stage of development, and cite evidence to support their evaluation. At the following meeting, each teacher would share her notebook and self-assessment with the group.

Rosie

When I was initially presented with the idea of the artifact package, I thought it was going to be a burden. As a first year teacher, just getting familiar with all the teaching and administrative duties was overwhelming (Stanulis, Fallona, & Pearson, 2002). I wanted to focus my time and energy on doing those things the best that I could. As Katie reviewed the different parts of the artifact package and the pieces we would need to complete, I remember thinking, "Oh God, where am I going to find the time to do this?" But, seeming to sense my worries, Katie assured us that the process would be done in steps that would allow for minimal interference with our planning, classroom teaching, and all the bureaucratic responsibilities that come with being a teacher.

Although I was worried about timing, I looked forward to discussing my experiences and hearing about the experiences of my fellow grads—the induction meetings had already become valuable opportunities for me to discuss and develop strategies to improve teaching, learning, and even relationships with students. As I had already realized, our experiences with induction were different from those that new teachers normally received in Newark. Not only did we meet more frequently, but we ourselves created the topics of discussion, ensuring they were specific to the topics that we wanted to improve on in our classrooms, instead of a set sequence of generic conversations about things like classroom management. Because we were all struggling with different problems of practice at different times, the meetings resulted in different outcomes and methods of improvement for all of us, making it possible to discuss and come up with ways of addressing current issues. Since our induction meetings had been so useful up to that point, I thought the artifact package project would continue along the same lines.

For my package, I collected artifacts from three classes on molecular genetics. In the first class, I wanted students to understand DNA structure and function. After a "do-now" question that activated their prior knowledge about what "extraction" meant and where the DNA in a cell is located, we had a mini-review about cell structures, followed by a lab where students extracted DNA from strawberries. In the following lesson, students applied their understanding of DNA structure and learned about how DNA replicate. After reviewing the different roles of DNA, students engaged in an activity where they used colored pieces of paper to create and model the process of DNA replication. In the third lesson, students used their cumulative knowledge about DNA and cells to analyze the process of protein synthesis. We reviewed the concepts of protein synthesis, transcription, and translation, and then students took part in a "quick lab" meant to demonstrate how cells interpret DNA.

The process of putting together the artifact package provided a focus for my lessons and an awareness of my students' thinking and feelings. In particular, the reflections helped me to ask myself questions about the ways that students responded to the different activities and probe their reactions more deeply, as well as think about the ways their responses could guide me in future planning. For example, in my third lesson, my students were able to easily complete the first two tasks, comparing and contrasting DNA and RNA and defining three key concepts in their own words. But when we moved into the activity where they had to transfer that knowledge and use it to understand protein synthesis, I could tell I was losing them. In response to the confused looks, I started asking different kinds of questions. Rather than asking very specific questions ("How does tRNA act with rRNA to produce a polypeptide chain?") I moved to more general questions about the two important processes. Suddenly, I noticed that students' body language had changed from staring into space to waiting for the next sentence to come out of my mouth. Thinking about this shift as I wrote my reflection, I realized that I could not get caught up in the details—I had to make sure that students were really deeply understanding the big ideas first.

When we got together at the next meeting to share, we used a modified form of the tuning protocol used in the NMUTR (see Klein, Taylor, Onore, Strom, & Abrams, 2013, for a more detailed description of tuning protocol) to share our packages and summarize our self-reflection. I talked about the "aha's" I had from analyzing the student work, taking the time to write reflections, and then looking at the package as a whole to assess my practice. I was happy to share that in three categories I had given myself an "accomplished." My lessons were full of connections to prior knowledge as well as their lives and the real world, such as the question: "Is there DNA in your food? How do you know?" I thought that my lessons reflected cognitive depth as well, since they were executed with a variety of activities that promoted interaction, sharing of ideas, and a mix of higher order and general questions that I used to gauge student understandings. I also made sure students had opportunities to engage in activities with a variety of representations of concepts to demonstrate their learning such as labs, models, and texts. On the final two categories of the rubric, I gave myself a developing/accomplished score. Although my lessons incorporated aspects of inquiry, I also used direct instruction for reviews. While I had a variety of summative and formative assessments to check student progress, I wanted to work on involving students in their creation.

Besides actually putting together and sharing the notebook, receiving feedback from Rob, Cristina, and Katie also extended my own learning. In particular, I learned a lot from our discussion stemming from my reflection on my first lesson, where I planned a lab that was more structured than usual. Normally, I require my students to create their own lab procedures in pairs or groups, which means they have to decide which materials to use and what steps to take for the actual experiment. In the strawberry DNA lab, the students got detailed procedures that walked them through each step. I saw that students were really enjoying themselves as they mushed up strawberries and dripped the mess into a test tube. At the end of the lesson, nearly everyone was able to make a connection to the "big idea" on the exit slip.

I shared my reflection with Cristina and Rob, where I wrote that "students felt a sense of relief" and seemed to have more fun because they did not have to worry about getting something wrong. I honestly had not realized how "stressed out" designing their own labs made my students. Not only was it challenging to create the procedures, but if a step were incorrect, students sometimes did not end up with a product, which they found frustrating. I was conflicted about this realization, because on the one hand, I did not want to cause my students stress or anguish, but on the other, I felt it was really important for students to learn scientific ways of thinking and to independently conduct experiments using those. Talking with the group, I came to the realization that perhaps I had started the students out at a level that was too autonomous, and my students needed scaffolds to reach the level of designing their own labs.

Katie

Much of the literature on the development of first year teachers follows stage-based theories of teacher development proceeding from novice to expert (Fuller, 1969; Berliner, 1988). Generally, these frameworks describe new teachers as being mainly concerned with routines and procedural tasks of teaching (Kagan, 1992) and tending to focus on maintaining "control" of their classes (Chubbock, 2008; Cook, 2009; Farrell, 2003; Stanulis, Fallona, & Pearson, 2002). These inclinations might explain why many first year teachers return to the methods of their apprenticeship of observation (Lortie, 1975), adopting teacher-led methods that allow them to feel more "in control" of their instruction. Over time, according to stage-based perspectives, new teachers will become more comfortable through practice and thus move from apprenticeship to appropriation, from novice to expert (Berliner, 1988)— although the dominant pattern of transmission instruction that largely continues to characterize teaching, especially in urban areas, suggests that this type of sequential development does not necessarily apply consistently.

Moreover, the learning exhibited by the residents does not follow this teacher-focused pattern, nor were their learning trajectories linear ones. For example, Rosie had situated her inquiry squarely on her students from the beginning—as she noted in the first vignette, she felt one of her main responsibilities in planning instruction was to pay close attention to what her students were producing so as to tease out the areas that needed to be better emphasized. As she collected data and analyzed them for the artifact project, she even began recognizing that the most important information resided *in-between* her and her students—those responses and reactions that students had to questions and activities during instruction were ways that she could gauge learning and adjust as needed. In addition, the learning was not necessarily linear steps or progressions to a more "expert" stage, but rather spiraling to become more complex over time (Vygotsky, 1978). This non-linear development is illustrated through her refining of her knowledge of processes of inquiry. Through observing, analyzing, and reflecting on her students' responses to her lab, as well as dialoguing with the other resident graduates, she began to understand that inquiry may take multiple forms, and that her support of students to gain the confidence to work more autonomously does not necessarily compromise her teaching.

THE ARTIFACT PACKAGE PROJECT: REFLECTIONS AND IMPLICATIONS

Rosie

The artifact package gave me a chance to reflect on my lessons and talk with others, which helped me identify specific aspects of my teaching that could be improved. I also developed specific steps in terms of what and how to move forward with my pedagogical development. Although I know reflection is important and critical, sometimes I forget because of all the other responsibilities that seem to come first (something I would later find in the literature on novice teachers to be common—see Kagan, 1992; Wideen, Moon, & Meyer-Smith, 1998). The artifact package forced me to reflect in the moment and I learned things that would have just passed me by if I did not take the time to examine my practice. Another helpful component was the summary of how I started and ended the lesson. I had to think carefully about what happened, and in our busy lives, you often do not have time to sit back and think about that. In the moment, you constantly make adjustments based on students' needs, but you rarely revisit that after class and write out, step-by-step, how you responded with those minute changes during class. This process provides a perspective not only of your teaching methods, but also of your students' take-aways from the lesson. Within induction programs, this emphasis on reflection and insight into your actual classroom practice is extremely unusual. Most induction operates via "workshop model," presenting pre-determined topics in infrequent, one-time seminars that do not necessarily correspond with any of our actual classroom needs (Wang, Odell, & Schwille, 2008).

As a bigger implication, this project has given me long-term guidance and focus for my own professional development. Coming up with this rubric together helped me put into perspective the actual changes that were happening with my teaching practices and my students' learning—outside of "the data" on which administrators and educational leaders are so focused. It allowed me to track my progress toward meeting my instructional goals and provided multiple avenues for me to gather data and unpack that data, so as to discover the strengths and weaknesses of certain strategies in the classroom.

By making me aware of a method by which I can influence and track educational outcomes for my students in a way that does not compartmentalize their educational experiences to formalized assessments, this rubric became my blueprint for developing transformative educational practices in a third space. After the project, I started using the indicators from the rubric, at first unconsciously, to self-assess my own lessons and understand the relationship between my teaching and my students' learning in a more useful way. The group-generated rubric gave me a sense of autonomy in designing a pedagogical and professional plan that spoke to the values and capabilities of what I believe a good teacher should be doing.

The rubric also gave me a type of positive, alternative assessment of teaching to the one that my department and district used. Instead of focusing only on numerical student test scores, this method of assessment concentrates on what actually happens between teachers and students in the classroom—which gives me information that multiple-choice tests may not show. When I go through this rubric I am able to see more than just the quantitative student outcome. I ask myself, "Are connections made? Is there cognitive depth?" Being able to track my own progress in developing my teaching through a variety of methods gives me confidence and conviction. It helps me look past the pressure to cover curriculum and focus on test scores, and brings a different perspective. Perhaps my students scored a fifty on their summative assessments, but if they made connections and engaged in analysis, I consider that a success. Unlike many first year teachers, who spent their initial year focused on classroom management at the expense of pedagogy, I started my second year on different footing and have had enhanced psychological endurance throughout the year.

Katie

This project has implications for teachers themselves as well as for induction, mentoring, and professional development programs. First, we deliberately sought to create a third space induction experience, one that broke with the traditional experiences afforded new teachers that often result in teacher socialization into traditional patterns of transmission teaching, collegial isolation, and ultimately, a reproduction of societal power imbalances (Zeichner & Gore, 1990). The structure of the artifact project provided opportunities for focused reflection and dialogue, which in turn pushed teacher thinking and development in new directions. Our joint effort also moved beyond the traditional induction supports that are normally offered to novice educators, such as individual mentoring, lesson observation, and topic-specific workshops (Wang, Odell, & Schwille, 2008). Instead, a learning community was forged and continually constructed through collaborative, context-specific inquiry and reflection.

For new teachers, this type of methodical reflection offers a framework for ongoing assessment of practice, based on indicators of quality that contribute to meaningful opportunities for professional growth. As Rosie's narrative above shows, this type of qualitative, multifaceted self-assessment of practice also can be empowering and affirmative for new teachers. In this era of narrowly-defined accountability, teachers often see professional assessment as burdensome at best, and at worst, punitive and/or degrading. Perhaps this type of collaboratively generated assessment, which yields rich data speaking to far more than student "outcomes," can be offered to teachers as a way to re-appropriate and reclaim the notion of "accountability" as a positive activity.

The structure and process of the artifact process also served as a facilitating aspect for reflection and dialogue that produced new learning and development. We realize that the constituent parts of the artifact package—the lesson plans, the student materials, and so on—are merely tools to focus the activities in which learning can be constructed, either during self-talk (reflection) or group conversations. Rosie's "aha's"—for example, that her students required her to actively support them to develop the skills needed over time to complete labs autonomously—began to be built through interacting with the different pieces of the artifact project, but were solidified and articulated through her own reflections on her students' responses and in conversation with Katie, Rob, and Cristina. This reminds us that the structure of learning, whether an artifact package, a lesson tuning protocol, or other task, is there as a support and enabling condition for the *dialogic interaction* that ultimately produces new understandings and subsequent action (Freire, 1970).

As a professional development initiative, the artifact project continues the efforts of inquiry-based teacher learning in a third space (Klein et al., 2013). This type of professional learning is quite different from not only those commonly offered by induction programs, but also usual inservice teacher development opportunities, which tend to be presented as one-time or short-term workshops, handing prescriptive and often decontextualized information to teachers from outside experts (Ball, 1994; Stein, Smith, & Silver, 1999). In contrast, projects like the artifact package provide extended opportunities to inquire into one's own practice, thus tightly connecting professional learning outside the classroom to teaching activity and making it immediately relevant, as recommended in the work on professional learning by Borko and Putnam (1997), Darling-Hammond and McLaughlin (1999), and Hawley and Valli (1999). The teachers are the architects of the inquiry focus, collaboratively generating the parameters based on their own questions and challenges of practice. While perhaps an "expert other" is present (in this case, me), I was a facilitator and co-learner rather than the leader or authority. This type of activity, then, flattens traditional hierarchies in professional development and makes the teacher and her particular problems of practice the central focus rather than the "expert knowledge" to be handed down from an outside source.

Certainly this is an activity that is adaptable to a variety of professional learning contexts and offers multiple benefits. To successfully implement such a task, however, is predicated on a fundamental shift in perspective for teachers, and those working in conjunction with them to provide professional learning opportunities. Such a shift will entail viewing teachers, even very new ones, from an affirming stance. We must see them not as novices to be inducted and socialized into particular knowledge or ways of thinking in schools, but as individuals both possessing valuable knowledge and expertise, and inherently capable of serving in multiple roles simultaneously: as teachers, as researchers, and as professional developers.

REFERENCES

Allen, J. (2009). Valuing practice over theory: How beginning teachers reorient their practice in the transition from university to workplace. *Teaching and Teacher Education, 25*(5), 647–654.

Baker, B. (2012). *Take your SGPs and VAM it, damn it!* Retrieved from http://schoolfinance101.wordpress.com/2011/09/02/take-your-sgp-and-vamit-damn-it/

Ball, D. L. (1994). *Developing mathematics reform: What don't we know about teacher learning—but would make good working hypotheses?* Paper presented at Conference on Teacher Enhancement in Mathematics K-6, Arlington, VA.

Beck, C., Kosnik, C., & Roswell, J. (2007). Preparation for the first year of teaching: Beginning teachers' views about their needs. *The New Educator, 3*(1), 51–73.

Berliner, D. (1988). Teacher expertise. In B. Moon & A. Mayes (Eds.), *Teaching and learning in the secondary school* (pp. 107–113). New York, NY: Routledge.

Bianchini, J., & Cazavos, L. (2007). Learning from students, inquiry into practice, and participation in professional communities: Beginning teachers' uneven progress toward equitable science teaching. *Journal of Research in Science Teaching, 44*(4), 586–612.

Borko, H., & Putnam, R. (1997). Learning to teach. In D. C. Berliner & R. C. Calfee (Eds.), *Handbook of educational psychology* (pp. 673–708). New York, NY: Macmillan.

Borko, H., Stecher, B. M., Alonzo, A. C., Moncure, S., & McClam, S. (2005). Artifact packages for characterizing classroom practice: A pilot study. *Educational Assessment, 10*(2), 73–104.

Chubbuck, S. (2008). A novice teacher's beliefs about socially just teaching: Dialogue of many voices. *The New Educator, 4*(4), 309–329.

Chubbuck, S., Clift, R., Allard, J., & Quinlan, J. (2001). Playing it safe as a novice teacher: Implications for programs for new teachers. *Journal of Teacher Education, 52*(5), 365–376.

Cochran-Smith, M., & Lytle, S. L. (1999). Relationships of knowledge and practice: Teacher learning in communities. *Review of Research in Education, 24*, 294–305.

Cook, J. (2009). Coming into my own as a teacher: Identity, disequilibrium, and the first year of teaching. *The New Educator, 5*(4), 274–292.

Darling-Hammond, L., & McLaughlin, M. (1999). Investing in teaching as a learning profession: Policy problems and prospects. In L. Darling-Hammond & G. Sykes (Eds.), *Teaching as the learning profession*: Handbook of policy and practice (pp. 376–412). San Francisco, CA: Jossey-Bass.

Eldar, E., Nabel, N., Schechter, C., Tamor, R., & Mazin, K. (2003). Anatomy of success and failure: The story of three novice teachers. *Educational Research, 45*(1), 29–48.

Fantilli, R., & McDougal, D. (2009). A study of novice teachers: Challenges and supports in the first years. *Teaching and Teacher Education, 25*(4), 814–825.

Farrell, T. (2003). Learning to teach English during the first year: Personal influences and challenges. *Teaching and Teacher Education, 19*(1), 95–111.

Feiman-Nemser, S. (2001). From preparation to practice: Designing a continuum to support and sustain practice. *Teachers College Record, 103*(6), 1013–1055.

Flores, M., & Day, C. (2006). Contexts which shape and reshape new teachers' identities: A multi perspective study. *Teaching and Teacher Education, 22*(1), 219–232.

Freire, P. (1970). *Pedagogy of the oppressed.* New York, NY: Continuum.

Fuller, F. (1969). Concerns of teachers: A developmental conceptualization. *American Educational Research Journal, 6*(2), 207–226.

Griffin, C., Kilgore, K., & Winn, J. (2009). First-year special educators: The influence of school and classroom context factors on their accomplishments and problems. *Teacher Education and Special Education, 32*(1), 45–63.

Grossman, P., & Thompson, C. (2008). Learning from curriculum materials: Scaffolds for new teachers? *Teaching and Teacher Education, 24*(8), 2014–2026.

Hargreaves, A., & Jacka, N. (1995). Induction or seduction? Postmodern patterns of preparing to teach. *Peabody Journal of Education, 70*(3), 41–63.

Hawley, W., & Valli, L. (1999). The essentials of effective professional development: A new consensus. In G. Sykes, & L. Darling-Hammond (Eds.), *Teaching as the learning profession: Handbook of policy and practice* (pp. 127–150). San Francisco, CA: Jossey-Bass.

He, Y., & Cooper, J. (2011). Struggles and strategies in teaching: Voices of five novice secondary teachers. *Teacher Education Quarterly, 38*(2), 97–116.

Hong, J. (2010). Pre-service and beginning teachers' professional identity and its relation to dropping out of the profession. *Teaching and Teacher Education, 26*(8), 1530–1543.

Kagan, D. M. (1992). Professional growth among preservice and beginning teachers. *Review of Educational Research, 62*(2), 129–169.

Karp, S. (2012). Challenging corporate reform, and ten hopeful signs of resistance. Retrieved July 11, 2012, from http://www.rethinkingschools.org

Klein, E. J., Taylor, M., Onore, C., Strom, K., & Abrams, L. (2013). Finding a third space in teacher education: Creating an urban teacher residency with Montclair State University and the Newark public schools. *Teaching Education, 24*(1), 27–57.

Lortie, D. (1975). *Schoolteacher: A sociological study*. Chicago, IL: University of Chicago Press.

Sabar, N. (2004). From heaven to reality through crisis: Novice teachers as migrants. *Teaching and Teacher Education, 20*(1), 145–161.

Scherff, L. (2008). Disavowed: The stories of two novice teachers. *Teaching and Teacher Education, 24*(5), 1317–1332.

Smith, T. M., & Ingersoll, R. M. (2004). What are the effects of induction and mentoring on beginning teacher turnover? *American Educational Research Journal, 41*(3), 681–714.

Stanulis, R. N., Fallona, C. A., & Pearson, C. A. (2002). 'Am I doing what I am supposed to be doing?': Mentoring novice teachers through the uncertainties and challenges of their first year of teaching. *Mentoring & Tutoring, 10*(1), 71–81.

Stein, M. K., Smith, M. S., & Silver, E. A. (1999). The development of professional developers: Learning to assist teachers in new settings in new ways. *Harvard Educational Review, 69*, 237–269.

Tait, M. (2008). Resilience as a contributor to novice teacher success, commitment, and retention. *Teacher Education Quarterly, 35*(4), 57–75.

Taylor, M., & Otinsky, G. (2007). Becoming whole language teachers and social justice agents: Preservice teachers inquire with sixth graders. *International Journal of Progressive Education, 3*(2), 59–71.

Vygotsky, L. S. (1978). *Mind in society: The development of higher psychological processes*. Cambridge, MA: Harvard University Press.

Walqui, A., & van Lier, L. (2010). *Scaffolding the academic success of adolescent English language learners: A pedagogy of promise*. San Francisco, CA: WestEd.

Wang, J., Odell, S., & Schwille, S. (2008). Effects of teacher induction on beginning teachers' teaching: A critical review of the literature. *Journal of Teacher Education, 59*(2), 132–152.

Watson, S. (2006). Novice science teachers: Expectations and experiences. *Journal of Science Teacher Education, 17*(3), 279–290.

Wideen, M., Mayer-Smith, J., & Moon, B. (1998). A critical analysis of the research on learning to teach: Making the case for an ecological perspective on inquiry. *Review of Educational Research, 68*(2), 130–178.

Zeichner, K., & Gore, J. (1990). Teacher socialization. In W. R. Houston (Ed.), *Handbook of research on teacher education* (pp. 329–348). New York, NY: MacMillan.

Zeichner, K. M., & Tabachnick, B. R. (1981). Are the effects of university teacher education "washed out" by school experience? *Journal of Teacher Education, 32*(3), 7–11.

Kathryn Strom
Department of Educational Leadership
California State University, East Bay
Hayward, California

Rosianne Lesperance
Eastside High School
Newark, New Jersey

APPENDIX: ARTIFACT PACKAGE TOOLS

I. Indicators of Quality Practice

The following criteria, excerpted in part from Borko et al., 2005, pp. 81–82, served as "indicators of quality" for residents' self-assessment of teaching practice.

Indicator	Description
Authentic Assessment	The extent to which the series of lessons includes a variety of approaches to gather information about student understanding, guide instructional planning, and inform student learning.
Structure of instruction	The extent to which instruction is organized to be conceptually coherent such that activities build on one another in a logical way; extent to which instruction is organized to provide opportunities for student meaning-making, interaction, inquiry, and intellectual engagement.
Cognitive depth	The extent to which the lessons promote students' understanding of important concepts and the relationships among them and their ability to use these ideas to explain a wide range of phenomena; The extent to which the series of lessons promotes command of the central concepts or "big ideas" of the discipline and generalizes from specific instances to larger concepts or relationships.
Multiple representations	The extent to which the series of lessons promotes the use of multiple representations (pictures, graphs, symbols, words) to illustrate ideas and concepts, as well as students' selection, application, and translation among mathematical/scientific representations to solve problems.
Connections	The extent to which the series of lessons helps students connect mathematics/science to their own experience, to the world around them, and to other disciplines.

II. Rubric

	Beginning	Developing	Accomplished	Exemplary
Connections	No relationships between concepts present; no real world connections apparent.	Some relationships between concepts are established or present in students work. Some evidence of connections between content and real world.	Relationships between concepts and real world connections are clearly established in activities and/or student work.	Relationships between concepts and real world connections are clearly established in all planning materials and student work and extend beyond subject.
Cognitive Depth	Learning objectives, questioning, and activities mainly utilize recall. Information is presented in discrete pieces without attention to essential questions/ideas or conceptual understanding. Student work reflects little or no understanding of main concepts addressed.	Learning objectives, questioning, and activities mainly utilize recall and understanding, with some application. Information is presented in discrete pieces, although attempts are made to connect to essential questions and ideas and with some attention to conceptual understanding. Student work reflects some understanding of main concepts addressed.	Learning objectives, questioning, and activities utilize some recall, understanding and application, but also require analysis and evaluation. Content is connected to larger ideas and essential questions; conceptual understanding is a priority. Student work reflects understanding of main concepts addressed.	Learning objectives, questioning, and activities focus on analysis, evaluation, and synthesis rather than lower-level skills & understandings. Content is situated in a larger context of essential questions and concepts and student work demonstrates deep understanding of the main concepts addressed.

(Continued)

263

	Beginning	Developing	Accomplished	Exemplary
Multiple Representations	No attempt to use multiple representations of content or concepts.	Limited use of multiple representations by the teacher to illustrate concepts.	Varied and successful use of multiple representations by the teacher to illustrate concepts.	Varied and sophisticated use of multiple representations by both teacher and students to illustrate concepts.
Structure of Instruction	Lesson is completely lacking in coherence; no evidence of scaffolding or sequencing. Instruction is characterized by teacher-led presentation and little or no student interaction.	Some structure of activities and instruction that attempts to build concepts logically. Instruction is characterized by teacher-led presentation and activities and some student interaction, but little or no wrap up.	Coherent structure of activities and instruction that flow logically and build on previous concepts. Instruction is characterized by presentations and activities that are inquiry driven; led by both teacher and students; and high student interaction and engagement.	Clear and coherent structure of activities and instruction that incorporates student input. Instruction is characterized by presentations and activities that are inquiry driven; mainly led by students; and high student interaction and intellectual engagement.
Authentic Assessment	Student learning is measured through multiple choice tests and quizzes.	Student learning is measured through some informal probes, a few projects, but mostly multiple choice tests and quizzes.	Student learning is measured by a variety of formal/ informal, summative and formative assessments, some of which are created by students.	Student learning is measured by a variety of formal and informal/ summative and formative assessments, most of which are created by students.

III. Components Of Artifact Package

Before Teaching

- Lesson Plans
- Copies of all materials, including student handouts

During Teaching

- Student work samples of high, medium, and low quality

After Teaching

- Summary of how the lesson unfolded, including any in-the-moment adjustments made
- Reflection on teaching, student response, problems of practice

IV. Self-Assessment

Indicator	Rating	Evidence
Connections		
Cognitive Depth		

(Continued)

Indicator	Rating	Evidence
Multiple Representations		
Structure of Instruction		
Authentic Assessment		

MEET THE AUTHORS FROM CHAPTER ELEVEN

Maria Cristina Morales, the first time I was in front of a class explaining how to solve a math problem, I was 26 years old and working with incoming freshmen over the summer as a teacher's assistant for NJIT's educational opportunity program. I can clearly recall how immersed I was in explaining how to solve this problem on the board during a recitation hour. The explanation easily flowed from my mind to my mouth and to my hands as I wrote on the board without second guessing myself. For a few minutes, I felt as though I was a completely different person. My timidity, shyness, and fear of speaking in front of large groups of people suddenly disappeared. I didn't feel scared or nervous, oddly enough everything felt so natural and comfortable. However, I quickly snapped out of this "trance" when I saw my supervisor watching me from the doorway. That moment stands out to me so many years later, because I discovered I was capable of doing something I had never imagined nor considered ever doing, "teaching."

I was born in Quito, Ecuador in the late 70s, to a barely 18-year-old mother and 21-year-old father. I have very few memories of my early years in Ecuador because I only lived there for a short period of time. My parent's marriage did not last very long. After my mother left my father, and my younger sister and I came to the U.S. at the age of 3 and 5, respectively, to "temporarily" stay with our paternal grandparents, while my father settled their divorce. The temporary stay ended up being a permanent stay after my sister and I started school and any intentions of returning to Ecuador quickly disappeared as we made Newark our home.

My grandparents created a loving and structured yet strict home environment. They always stressed the importance of doing well in school and being educated. I recall my grandfather telling my sister and me that we all had jobs, his job as an auto mechanic was to earn money to provide food and shelter, my grandmother's job, a stay at-home wife, was to maintain the house, and our job was to get an education and become professionals one day. Although I was very quiet and shy in school, I felt that I could express who I was through my work and work ethic; therefore I worked and studied hard to do my very best in school in preparation for someday attending college.

By the time I graduated high school, an over-looked issue arose, that would prevent me from taking advantage of scholarship opportunities not to mention attending college at all. Since our "temporary" stay had become permanent without much thought, my father and grandparents overlooked the legalities of the immigration status of my sister and me. It was only when I needed to apply for financial aid that we realized that it was too late to do anything. My sister and I fell into a loophole that would not allow us to adjust our status without leaving the country and being barred for ten years. Everything seemed so unfair and unjust. I could not understand why such a thing was happening to us when we had always done things right. Didn't our story and circumstance matter? Couldn't there be an exception made? I fell into a dark and angry place, where I blamed everyone around me including my parents' divorce for what was happening to us.

Out of the anger and helplessness came an understanding that I was in control of my life and a resolve that I would not let anything get in my way of achieving my goal of attending college, earning a degree and becoming a professional like I had always envisioned myself doing. I found a full-time job at a local agency and with the encouragement of my boyfriend, now husband, I enrolled at my local community college and started attending classes part-time. Even though it took me longer and cost me twice as much, I achieved my goal of attending college and earning not only one degree, but several degrees over a period of 11 years. Through my educational experience, I was able to meet people that mentored and influenced me to identify and pursue my talents in mathematics. It was my math professor at Essex County College that recommended me for the summer job as a teacher assistant at NJIT and it was there that I discovered "teaching" as a possible professional option.

After graduating from MSU with my B.S. in Applied Mathematics, I started working at a retail store as a supervisor and quickly realized this was not what I wanted to do for any extended period of time. I recall my general manager telling me that I would be known for the number of credit card applications my sales force pushed through. If his statement was supposed to encourage me it did the opposite. After so much work, time, and effort I had put into my education, I didn't just want to be a number on someone's corporate spreadsheet. I needed my work to be meaningful somehow, I just didn't know how.

I began looking into graduate school and learned about the NMUTR through flyers and information sessions. I immediately thought about my TA experience and felt excited about becoming a teacher. I felt I could do something meaningful to impact young people from Newark just like some teachers had influenced me.

I didn't realize how rigorous and selective the admission process for the UTR program was until I was taking part in it. It was probably a good thing that I didn't know most of the people present because I was just being myself. When I received the news that I was one of the four residents selected for the first cohort I was thrilled and excited to get started. Looking back I really had no idea what I had just signed up for because the next four years were some of the most challenging times of my educational career.

Michael De Antonio Jr., I am a vice principal of Mathematics at East Side High School in the Ironbound section of Newark, where I was born, raised, and currently reside. I received my B.S. from MSU in Applied Mathematics and my M.A. in Supervision and Administration with a Principal's Certificate from St. Peter's College. I began my teaching career working at the high school from which I graduated. Now in my seventh year of administration, I drive mathematics instruction in my department and through the district and am a member of the National Council of Teacher of Mathematics. I took a key role as a point person in the NMUTR being housed at East Side High School. I participated in the selection of residents for each cohort. I assisted the mentors and residents by providing additional scheduled planning time to collaborate and strategies to be implemented in classes.

Mario Santos, I was born in Portugal in a small village on the outskirts of the city of Cantanhede. Just before Portugal's peaceful revolution, "Vinte Cinco de Abril", my parents made the difficult, but important decision to move to the United States in search of a better life for their children. We settled in Newark and it has since been a very fascinating experience. My educational path in the US afforded me the opportunity to attend Lafayette Street School, Wilson Avenue School, East Side High School, Rutgers University, Kean University, Saint Peter's University, and Seton Hall University.

Following my undergraduate studies in 1990, I was fortunate to work in my alma-mater, East Side High School, as a bilingual social studies teacher. As a teacher, not only did I gain important insight on what it means to be a teacher, but also what it takes to be a learner. I truly believe that teaching is bi-directional where I learned just as much from my students as I hoped they learned from me. My students presented many challenges, academic and social, but they all have made me grow intellectually and emotionally.

Upon completing a Master's degree at Kean University in the spring 1996, I was offered the position of school core team facilitator and a few years later as special assistant working with the assistant superintendent, Dr. Don Marinaro. In these two roles, I focused on implementing site base planning/management and operations in fifteen elementary schools. This experience allowed me to learn about the process of change and how difficult it is to implement. A paradigm shift in how people think is at the heart of real change. I have learned that you must start with mindset and everything else will fall into place. It comes as no surprise that I feel very fortunate to be part of such major educational initiatives in the largest school district in New Jersey.

In 2000, I left central office to become a vice principal at Wilson Avenue School. Consequently, in 2005, I became principal of East Side High School. Upon my arrival in 2005, I knew things would be in rough shape, but I did not anticipate the true magnitude of the problems. On multiple levels, our students were clearly underachieving. Our scores on the High School Proficiency Assessment (HSPA), New Jersey's state assessment, were pitiful with only 24% of students scoring proficient in Math and 39% proficient in Language Arts Literacy (LAL). We offered only 3 Advanced Proficient courses and only 2 students passed the end of course exams. Our student attendance was poor, approximately 1200 students failed one or more courses and we only had approximately 80 students on the honor roll. Culturally, the students demonstrated no investment or pride in their school by engaging in regular acts of vandalism and violence. I was astonished at the number of adults that had absolutely no sense of accountability or urgency. I quickly learned that in their eyes, student achievement rested solely on the student. If the students wanted to learn, then all was well. However, if students did not want to learn, then they were on their own. Other examples of adult dysfunctions were rampant absenteeism, not showing up to classes, stealing school resources, and even gambling on school grounds. The combination of these destructive components were all prime conditions for a failing school.

Fast forward nine years later and I am proud to say that East Side High School is a drastically different school. I take pride in knowing that I am one of the longest standing principals in the city of Newark. Through the hard work of my committed staff and exemplary partnership with MSU through the NMUTR, we have established 229% proficiency gains in Math (79%) and 112% proficiency gains in LAL (83%) on the HSPA (NJ School Report Card 2012–2013), in which we are leading the way in our district for comprehensive high schools. It is also important to note that these gains were accomplished while 18% of my student population consisted of English Language Learners (NJ School Report Card 2012–2013). We now offer 10 AP courses and as of 2011, we had 37 students pass the AP exams. We also have the International Baccalaureate Program (IB), which was implemented in the 2013–2014 school year and an early college program where 14 of our seniors graduated with an associate's degree. Additionally, we now have approximately the same number of students on the honor roll as well as failing one course or more. Last but certainly not least, I have a strong number of teachers who care deeply for their students and their craft, where 10% were rated as highly effective and 83% as effective. Our growth and success over the years was not achieved by accident nor was it done by one person. It took the efforts of my entire team and some intentional strategies and partnerships, like the NMUTR, which struck at the heart of the true transformation.

MONICA TAYLOR, ANNA KARINA MONTEIRO, CRISTINA
MORALES, MICHAEL DE ANTONIO JR. AND MARIO SANTOS

11. FOSTERING SOCIALLY JUST TEACHER LEADERSHIP FOR CHANGE IN URBAN SCHOOLS

INTRODUCTION

Monica

Opening Scene: Wednesday October 1st, 2014: Newark Professional Development Day

After my work with the residency had formally ended, I am still teaching preservice MAT students at East Side High School, bringing the elements of the NMUTR to our general teacher education program. I hold my class in Karina's classroom, one of our biology mentors, and I am trying to scale up elements of the design with 17 students there for the year. We have spent months re-designing our year-long practicum sequence to incorporate the most significant elements of the residency model.

I enter Room 482 and find Karina sitting informally with a group of her mentees, eating a rich chocolate cake and talking about biology curriculum and their teaching. It is after school hours but they are "hanging out" until Back to School night at 6:00 p.m.. I feel so touched by the scene but why I react this way doesn't hit me until I am driving home. Karina is naturally and organically acting in the role of mentor and teacher leader. Her mentees, who are mostly now hired and teaching at East Side High School, represent several cohorts of residents as well as a new teacher and one of my MAT students who is doing her fieldwork and student teaching with Karina. In an attempt to align the biology curriculum and ensure that all students, no matter the level, are focused on the same learning objectives, Karina leads the discussion with the most experience, eight years of teaching, and her perspectives of teaching honors and AP biology. Her biology team is comprised of Rosie from cohort one who is now in her 4th year of teaching general education and honors biology (she is a co-author of the induction chapter with Kathryn Strom). Liz, from cohort three, is in her second year of teaching as an inclusive biology teacher. Ariana, from cohort four, who actually attended East Side High School, has just started her first year of teaching there. Emily, a newly hired teacher who did her preservice teaching program at Rutgers, sits with the group, focused on teaching the lower level biology classes in the school, and finally Veronica joins them as a fieldwork MAT preservice teacher. Karina as mentor seems in her element. She is comfortable directing the conversation, listening to different experiences, and offering ideas. She is their friend, a resource, and a mountain of support. She knows how to describe the work of teaching in ways that make her work transparent.

Karina

When Monica came into my classroom, she witnessed a typical informal planning session with the biology teachers. These informal meetings whether over cake, lunch, or at happy hour, are when we do our most constructive work. We really try to work at planning equitable, common lessons, staying at the same pace and giving all students, no matter the ability or knowledge background, the same experiences with labs, inquiry activities, and developing their reading and writing skills. It is because of this that our collaboration has become so critical. We all have the same big idea for our lessons and then we modify it based on the needs of the students in our particular classes. For example, next week, when you walk into any biology class at East Side High School, all students will be doing some form of a pH lab investigation. The only difference between the sections is that we have differentiated instruction to meet the needs of the students. For example, the honors students in my classes may be completely designing their own pH labs, Rosie might have created an in-between version of the pH which gives her general education students opportunities to self-design the lab with some scaffolding, and finally Liz, with her inclusive biology students, may design a lesson where she and her students co-construct the lab together.

It is during these informal meeting times that we go beyond our scheduled common planning where we typically determine the learning goals, order of lessons, and common assessments. We share strategies of teaching the same content through various approaches and lenses. It is this mode of collaboration and helping my former mentees teach their students equitably that is most rewarding to me. I feel that I am in some way in each of their classrooms, making a difference in the lives of their students where regardless of class level, honors to special needs, all students are equally getting access to the best science education and learning the same material.

Monica

When Emily and I present and talk about the NMUTR, most of the time, people focus on the preservice aspect of this program, how we work with the residents, and their preparation for teaching in urban schools. Without question, these are important aspects of our program but there is much more to our mission. We emphasize that we have developed a three-pronged approach to sustainable urban school change that centers around the process of nurturing a third space community of socially just teacher leaders. What we mean is that as we prepare new teachers, we are also working closely with mentors to help them develop as teacher leaders. This happens through their participation in building the residency curriculum, being primary teacher educators, and examining their own teaching and mentoring practices through self-study and action research. In many instances, our mentors enter our third space program with a propensity for leadership and it is our responsibility to help them discover how they envision themselves as teacher leaders and what their individual goals are. Second we prepare effective urban teachers who are, from their residency days into their teaching careers, already positioning themselves as socially just teacher leaders and collective change agents. This involves a strategic social justice focus throughout the 12 month residency but also one that continues through their three years of induction and beyond. And finally we work closely with principals and department chairs to make sure that the shared vision of our third space residency of promoting sustainable change in schools is actualized.

This chapter tells the story of how resident graduates and mentors have developed as socially just teacher leaders at East Side High School, one of our partner schools in Newark, through the support of NMUTR faculty and administration. It is very much a narrative told through five voices: Monica, NMUTR faculty; Karina, biology teacher of eight years and experienced mentor (she mentored a total of six residents from the four cohorts); Cristina, resident grad from cohort one and 4th year math teacher; Mike, math department chair; and Mario, principal. Unlike the rest of this book which primarily focuses on the experiences of cohort two, this chapter is written three years later and attempts to demonstrate from a longitudinal perspective what can happen in a third space residency when the stakeholders together work and lead as socially just teacher leaders for sustainable change.

FOSTERING SOCIALLY JUST TEACHER LEADERSHIP FOR CHANGE

Monica

> The fact is that teachers do make a difference, even in difficult situations, and good teachers of all backgrounds have a crucial role to play as leaders in educational change. While it is necessary to work for equitable public schools and societies, and to change destructive societal ideologies and restrictive structural barriers, we cannot wait around for these things to happen. In the meantime, we know that teachers can help alleviate—although they certainly cannot completely solve—the low achievement of students. (Nieto, 2007, p. 303)

Having both worked in urban schools for the past twenty-five years, Emily and I were under no illusion that fostering socially just sustainable change in schools involves both macro and micro approaches over a long extended period of time. We firmly agree with Payne (2008) who writes that one of the problems with school reform is that it tends to rely on "The Solution" rather than differentiating our change approaches to the needs of a particular context with its own unique set of variables. We too struggle with Payne's dilemma of sometimes attributing the fundamental failure of urban schools to "the rigid and incompetent bureaucracies" of schools and other times worrying that it is the "deeply ingrained and deeply negative teacher attitudes" (p. 122). In fact, throughout our leadership of the residency, we repeated the mantra "Not on our time!" implying that we would do everything in our power not to accept residents in our program who had a deficit perspective of urban students or were complacent about mediocrity or failure in schools. With this in mind, being asked to develop and facilitate an urban teaching residency, with the expectation that in only four years we would see a marked change in student achievement in the vast and expansive metropolis of Newark, seemed a truly insurmountable feat.

In some ways, as we conceptualized the program, we had to think strategically about the domain of our third space and how exactly we were going to define the boundaries of our spheres of influence. We recognized that our expertise and experience bound us to focus on the role of socially just teacher leaders in urban schools and the grassroots ways they impacted their students and school communities. We were in no way thinking that the efforts of our residency would impact policy or even the local politics of the three different superintendents who governed during the four years of our residency. We did believe that, in our third space program, working collaboratively with the administrators, the principal and the math and science department chairs, at East Side High School would help to foster collaborative agency among an intergenerational cadre of teacher leaders. We agreed with Levenson (2014) who writes that, "the principal's leadership has a critical impact on school culture, including whether teacher leadership is welcomed or discouraged" (p. 137). We envisioned that leadership for change would involve what Haugh, Norenes, and Vedoy (2014) call a "mutual dependency" or "a joint enterprise involving leaders and teachers in a reciprocal activity of realising the organisation's core objectives" (p. 358). For us, this meant working strategically with the principal, the math and science chairs, and the mentor teachers. We recognized that this was only one way to approach sustainable change but we firmly believed and continue to believe that inviting teachers to be socially just leaders in schools in the current regime of standardization, high stakes testing, and public scrutiny (Margolis, 2008), is an important vehicle for empowerment and agency.

In other words, as urban teachers struggle to understand their worth in schools with cultures that perpetuate "mediocrity" (Kennedy, 2005; Opfer & Pedder, 2011; Stigler & Hiebert, 1999), teacher leadership provides a means for teachers to individually or collectively influence their colleagues, principals, and other members of the school community to improve teaching practices and impact their students' learning (York-Barr & Duke, 2004). They have opportunities to share and enhance professional learning within their school setting, generate new knowledge for themselves from action (Reason & Bradbury, 2008), and develop new socially just initiatives (Onore, Goeke, Taylor, & Klein, 2009) that can affect change in their classrooms, schools, and communities (Taylor, Goeke, Klein, Onore, & Geist, 2011). Viewed from this perspective, "teachers who are leaders lead within and beyond the classroom, identify with and contribute to a community of teacher learners and leaders, and influence others towards improved educational practice" (Katzenmeyer & Moller, 2001,

p. 5). Their actions could involve: improving their own teaching practice; mentoring preservice and inservice teachers; deepening content knowledge; developing and altering curriculum; facilitating professional development; building community; participating in school-level decision making; and challenging the status quo in schools (Danielson, 2006; Fairman & Mackenzie, 2012; Levenson, 2014; Lieberman & Miller, 2004; Stone & Cuper, 2006). These were the opportunities that we hoped to foster for our mentors and residents when we began working collaboratively at East Side High School. As Mario, the principal there will explain below, the vision we had for our residents and mentors echoed the very principles that guided the leadership and administration of the school. With the stakeholders seeing eye to eye, we were able to enter the partnership more deeply, skipping the superficial "polite" stage, and moving right into a third space where we could have honest, authentic, and at times difficult dialogue. We were committed to an equitable education for the East Side students, which meant forging change no matter the obstacles through our collective agency.

We were fortunate to be welcomed into the East Side community with open arms by all of the administrators, and we had a clear vision about supporting and nurturing our residents and mentors as teacher leaders. In other schools where the residency tried to establish itself, when the vision between the administration and the residency were not well aligned, the results were less impactful. Adding another dimension to this third space endeavor, we realized that we weren't just encouraging them to be "generic" teacher leaders but more specifically we hoped to develop socially just teacher leaders who were committed to address inequities in their schools. Interestingly, very little attention is paid to socially just teacher leadership in the literature (Jacobs, Beck, & Crowell, 2014). This is particularly surprising in the current sociopolitical context of schools in the United States where the practices and policies around issues of race, ethnicity, class, language, ability, sexual orientation, and gender of our students continue to perpetuate inequalities. How can teacher leaders be equipped to address such issues as the achievement gap, inequitable access to knowledge and resources, and poverty if they are not developing an explicit social justice lens? We see a significant emphasis on teaching for social justice in preservice teacher education programs (Gay, 2010; Ladson-Billings, 2009; Nieto & Bode, 2012; Villegas & Lucas, 2001) and yet there is significantly less research on what happens to these teachers when they become socially just leaders working with other teachers (Achinstein & Athanases, 2005; Jacobs, Beck, & Crowell, 2014).

We define socially just teacher leadership in the realm of what Theoharis (2007) calls "the daily realities of school leadership" (p. 223). These teacher leaders make "issues of race, class, gender, disability, sexual orientation, and other historically and currently marginalizing conditions in the United States central to their advocacy, leadership practice, and vision" (p. 223). Socially just teacher leaders strive to prevent "marginalization in schools" and advocate for "inclusive schooling practices for students with disabilities, English language learners (ELLs), and other students traditionally segregated in schools" (p. 223). These are the every day realities of urban schools where on a daily basis students need teacher leaders to advocate for them. They not only "identify inequities, but work as change agents to construct more equitable practices, structures and policies in schools and communities (Brown, 2006; McKenzie et al., 2008)" (Jacobs, Beck, & Crowell, 2014, p. 580). This can be accomplished through the types of more general teacher leadership strategies that Lieberman and Friedrich (2010) list such as "advocating for what's right for students; opening the classroom door and going public with teaching; working 'alongside' teachers and leading collaboratively; taking a stand; and learning and reflecting on practice as a teacher and a leader" (p. 95). We would go so far as to say that all urban teachers must be socially just teacher leaders who draw upon the same characteristics that Haberman (1988, 1995) emphasizes (see the admissions chapter for more details). These include resistance, persistence, resilience, and self-awareness; qualities, which help teacher leaders to use "their power inside and outside of the classroom" (Nieto, 2007, p. 307) to address inequities (McKenzie et al., 2008).

Nurturing socially just teacher leadership involves constructing a supportive environment where teachers can find their voices and participate in a variety of different change endeavors. In the NMUTR, using the third space framework as our guide, MSU faculty, East Side High School administrators, mentors, and resident graduates co-constructed a change community which invited all members to enter the work at their own points of readiness and grow as change agents at their own pace. Our community was driven by a shared vision of providing Newark students with the maximum educational opportunities at East Side High School. For example, during his first year of teaching chemistry at East Side High School, Rob, cohort one resident, was deeply committed to making sure that his students received their free breakfast (Mario insisted on adding this program to his school even though they are the only high school in Newark to participate). One morning Rob realized that his class had mistakenly missed breakfast. He left the classroom and ran down to the cafeteria to fetch it for his students. Upon his arrival back, he was reprimanded by one of the department chairs for leaving his students unsupervised. Fearful that Mario would also consider his actions inappropriate, he was happily relieved when instead Mario praised him for prioritizing his students' basic needs above all else. We all strove to create a space where there was "respect and support from administrators and colleagues, the time and resources to practice leadership, and the opportunity to work collaboratively with colleagues" (Nieto, 2007, p. 308).

Karina

I always get excited when someone asks me "how bad is it, working in the inner city?" I look forward to such questions because I want to share with them the successes that are happening within the commonly criticized urban school district. Too often, there are horror stories of poor student performance, lazy teachers, poorly allocated funds, and the list goes on and on, all of which paint this picture of this urban school as being a "bad" place in which to work. I look forward to these questions because I get to tell one of the many untold and often unrecognized stories of the great things happening in Newark. My response to those questions always starts the same, "It's been so exciting to be part of a school and team that is without question improving and growing." I feel much like Ayers and Ford (1996) when they write,

> An urban pedagogy must be built on the strengths of the city, the hope and the promise of city kids and families, on the capacities of city teachers ... The classroom cannot be a place where teachers bite their lips, hold their breaths, and endure. Rather urban classrooms must be places where teachers can pursue their ideas, explore their interests, follow their passions – and be engaged with students in living lives of purpose. (pp. 198–199)

As an 8th year veteran teacher of the same school, I have experienced and been part of the tremendous growth that has happened within East Side High School. This is true in terms of student performance and behavior, academic and athletic achievements, and most importantly the strengthening of the school community. This can be attributed to the strong leadership within the school, specifically Mario, the principal. His outstanding support of successful programs such as the NMUTR has helped to give the teachers within the school, such as myself, the agency to grow as educators and leaders within the urban school community. As Nieto (2007) writes,

> It is up to those who administer schools and make policy to change the conditions in schools and in the broader societal context so that teachers can take their rightful place as intellectuals, as guides for our youth, and as the inspiration for new teachers joining the profession. Until school administrators and policymakers begin to make these changes, we are bound to lose some of the best leadership that is right in front of us. (p. 308)

Mario

Since my time as principal, the vision of East Side High School has very simply been a belief in the potential of teachers and students and a commitment to doing whatever it takes to support them. In other words, I know that students and teachers can achieve their fullest potential, provided that they are given the right opportunities and support. I want my teachers to adopt a social justice stance and expect nothing short of excellence by providing all the necessary support and interventions to ensure students' success (Oakes et al., 2005; Theoharis, 2007). Although this may sound like common sense, the cold truth is it was not so common. In my early days as principal, I recall having a conversation with a few teachers about this notion of believing in the potential of students. I asked them, "What were their expectations of students and how were they the same or different from students in non-urban districts? A veteran teacher responded with firm conviction that, "students in urban schools don't value education and therefore do not perform as well as those in suburban schools!" He proceeded to tell me, "My daughter is performing at exceptional levels because as her father I demand that of her." I asked if he thought the teachers at his daughter's school had the same expectations that he had for students at East Side. Without hesitation he replied, "They better not, I will raise hell!" This sentiment strikes at the core of the problem in trying to transform East Side High School from good to great. Nothing GREAT can be accomplished without the belief that students have the ability and will be successful. Thus, the focus of transforming East Side High School was to change the hearts and minds of educators and of students. As a principal committed to social justice, my goals are similar to what McKenzie et al. (2008) describe. I am striving "to increase student achievement as evidenced, in part, by high test scores; to raise the critical consciousness among students and staff; and to accomplish these tasks by creating intentional, heterogeneous learning communities for students and staff" (p. 117).

When I was asked to be part of the partnership with MSU, I was thrilled. If change were to occur at my school, it would have to happen from within the building and the presence of an educational institution of higher learning on a daily basis would certainly be a change agent against the status quo. I know from the literature that I play a key role as principal in creating the conditions necessary for teacher leaders to flourish (Muijs & Harris, 2006; Silva et al., 2000; Taylor et al., 2011; York-Barr & Duke, 2004). I have worked collaboratively with my department chairs to strategically provide opportunities for mentors and residents to initiate new programs, design curriculum, and innovate teaching. I am a firm believer that success is driven by people, not by programs. Hence I saw the residency program as a means to develop teachers, through trusting them, empowering them, sharing responsibility with them, and ultimately acknowledging their contributions to our students' success (Barth, 2001). I knew that in collaboration with the NMUTR faculty, my chairs and I would provide a supportive learning environment where my teachers could learn, explore their own questions, and find their voices as teacher leaders (Jacobs, Beck, & Crowell, 2014).

Having myself been a student and teacher once at East Side High School, I knew what it would take to make change. I knew that this partnership would provide the opportunity and resources to move staff and students in a positive critical direction, invite residents who really wanted to make a difference, support mentors that appreciated collaboration, and cultivate administrators and teachers that engaged in effective socially just pedagogical practices.

I knew that selecting the right mentors was critical to the success of the program. It required mentors who were passionate, committed to urban kids, and open minded to sharing ideas and taking creative risks. I also realized that in order to develop this third space, mentors and residents needed time in their schedule to plan and revise their work together. Thus, the need for creative scheduling was required for this to occur. Each mentor was given a reduced teaching load and additional planning time to work with their residents. I knew that the time invested in my mentors would pay off in the long run. I relied on my department chairs, like Mike in mathematics, to help me select and find ways to support their undertaking as mentors. Below he illustrates the ways in which he engaged in the residency work by mentoring residents and supporting the adoption of new and innovative practices of the mentors.

Mike

Being a product of NPS and then working here as an urban educator since 2003, I have seen many changes in the district. I have witnessed various programs come in as the "next best thing in education" and go out without leaving much of an impact (Payne, 2008). When I was first introduced to the idea of hosting the NMUTR, it sounded like just another time-consuming student teaching program. What I would come to find out over the past years was that this would become one of the greatest educational programs in which I have had the opportunity to partake. Teaching at the high school I attended, in the community where I was born, raised, and still live, gave me the chance to give back in meaningful ways. Now, as an administrator, one of my career goals is to help teachers become highly effective in their practices and disrupt the status quo to provide a rich and meaningful education for all students. I strive to hire individuals who show this potential from the onset and this is exactly the mission of the NMUTR.

Because of the small number of mathematics residents, in the first two years of the NMUTR, only one of my mathematics teachers, Luba Lidman, mentored residents. A distinguished teacher and a MSU graduate, Luba was actually a little hesitant about mentoring because she put all of her time and effort into teaching her students. Addressing her time management concerns, I met with the scheduling vice-principal to adjust her schedule and allow for additional daily planning time for Luba and her resident, Cristina. With full buy-in from Mario, this became a continued practice for all mentors.[1]

Luba and Cristina were able to develop a co-teaching model (Friend & Cook, 1996) for their classroom that was unique to them and met the needs of their students. They collaborated together to develop extraordinary lessons by creating engaging activities that may not have been possible in other teaching environments. They experienced the challenges and successes of inquiry-based learning first hand and their students were able to think for themselves and discover learning objectives within the curriculum. Working collaboratively with residents has been an incredible learning experience, not only for residents, but for the mentors as well.

RESIDENTS AND MENTORS BUILD AN AUTHENTIC PROFESSIONAL LEARNING COMMUNITY

Cristina

My mentor, Luba, and I clicked immediately. We seemed to have a lot of things in common and Luba opened her classroom to me without hesitation. I now know that may be difficult for some teachers to do, but then again Luba was part of the committee that selected the residents for the program, so she had some say in whom she would be sharing her classroom with for the entire school year. Since Luba and I got along so well, I felt very comfortable sharing my ideas and she was more than willing to let me try them out. We experimented with co-teaching models (Friend & Cook, 1996). I remember literally dividing the class in two with a portable white board and both of us teaching our groups at the same time. Obviously, the noise level and both of us talking at the same time was a problem, but she was always willing to try new practices.

I quickly realized that the NMUTR professors were going to challenge "traditional" teaching methods that most of us may have experienced and would most likely use if it were not for the program. We were constantly asked to think outside and beyond anything we may have ever experienced because in order to engage our students we needed to not only know our content but know our students and make learning math and science relevant to their lives (Gonzalez, Moll, & Amanti, 2005). Although there were moments where the course work, while being observed, did not go very well, I feel that they were defining moments of growth for me. I realized the hard way that even though I might have put a lot of time and effort into creating what I thought was a good activity or lesson, if the students were not engaged in meaningful learning, then I had to be honest with myself and reflect on how to improve my teaching. I was learning to adopt a social justice teaching stance that valued my students' worth and abilities, set high and rigorous learning and teaching expectations, and helped to support them in gaining social and cultural capital for their success in the classroom and the world beyond (Nieto, 2007). This constant reflection and revision have been a crucial component to my continued personal and professional growth.

The pedagogy we were learning made complete sense in theory but the constant struggle was in the actual implementation (Klein, Taylor, Onore, Strom, & Abrams, 2013). This is where I feel that the support of my mentor and department chair, Mike, came into play. I recall having a very difficult time coming up with the essential questions when designing a lesson for my unit plan. I felt extremely frustrated and confused but I felt that my mentor and chairperson were readily available to help me through this process. Much like my mentor, Mike was very welcoming and made himself available at all times to share ideas for teaching strategies, lessons, and activities. Below he shares his own perspectives about the process.

Mike

One of the positive impacts spurred by hosting the NMUTR was a change in educational practices among mentors and other teachers at East Side High School, specifically in the mathematics and science departments. Traditional lessons shifted, with more of a focus on inquiry-based learning. This educationally sound practice placed more ownership of learning on the students, getting them to discover various concepts leading toward a deeper conceptual understanding of the curricular objectives.

When inquiry-based learning was first introduced to East Side teachers by the NMUTR, there were struggles to overcome. This learning paradigm was new to many of us in the fields of mathematics and science. We understood that for the program to be successful, we would all, residents, mentors, and administrators, have to be willing to experiment with inquiry-based approaches in classrooms (Taylor & Otinsky, 2007). There were emotional challenges that mentor teacher and residents had to overcome, stemming from insecurities on their implementation of inquiry-based learning. As the mathematics department chairperson, I continually supported Luba and her residents. We would pitch ideas off of each other to decide what was best for the students. I would observe their inquiry-based lessons and provide feedback for improvement. Over time, you could see growth in the teaching of residents and mentors alike. I was also able to grow as the department chairperson. From my experiences in Luba's classroom, I began to share inquiry-based lessons observed in some mathematics classes with the other teachers, and encourage the teachers to commonly plan lessons together and share best practices.

During the year of the NMUTR's cohort two, Luba and her resident, Pri, invited Mr. Nuno Duarte, another mathematics teacher at East Side High School, to attend their Honors Pre-Calculus class on a daily basis. In a very direct way, this invitation provided Nuno with an opportunity to observe and participate in inquiry-based practices that were encouraged by the NMUTR. He then utilized these strategies in his own teaching, helping him to be rated as a highly effective teacher. The following year, in his first year teaching Advanced Placement Calculus, Nuno successfully had students receive scores of 3's, 4's, and a 5. Furthermore, he coached the two East Side High School teams to win first place in both the Calculus and Pre-Calculus competitions of the Newark Math Olympics. Nuno attributes these achievements to his learning experiences with Luba and Pri. The mentor teachers also benefitted tremendously from their work in the residency. Karina describes the ways in which her mentoring participation strengthened her identity as a teacher leader.

BEING A MENTOR AND TEACHER LEADER EXPANDS SPHERES OF INFLUENCE

Karina

On a personal level, I found the NMUTR supported my growth as a socially just teacher leader and it has fortuned me the opportunity to help produce and develop outstanding teachers, most of whom work alongside of me now at East Side. Of the six residents I have mentored in the program, five have been hired within the school and it has been nothing but exciting and rewarding to watch them grow as educators. My role in the residency and watching my residents turn into such outstanding educators has forever changed my own philosophy of education, to one that is centered on the necessary support and community based efforts required to educate our urban youth. In a small way I feel as though I am not teaching only my five classes of students, but through collaborative efforts and working together, I am also reaching the students of my former residents and current peers.

Their motivation, energy, and eagerness to learn and try new things have been contagious within the school community. I truly believe that the community that exists within the school, especially within the science department, is because of the residency. The holistic approach to developing the residents aids in establishing well rounded educators that are aware and prepared to deal with the many challenges that often time burn out new teachers. It is because of this that during their first years of teaching they can devote more time and energy into creating and implementing lessons instead of just trying to survive like many of their peers.

The program has also helped me emerge as a teacher leader within the school. I have learned the valuable skills in making observations, providing feedback, and tackling sometimes difficult conversations. On occasion it was challenging to give the essential feedback to some of my residents, especially when it was a sensitive issue. For example, Alex, one of my cohort two residents, was and still is one of the most caring, compassionate, and loving teachers I have ever encountered. His strengths lie within the one-on-one genuine interactions he has with his students in every class period. Although this is an exceptional natural skill to have as an educator, it often caused Alex to focus too much on one small group of students during a lesson. It was difficult to tell him that he was focusing his attention too much on one group of students as they tried to tackle difficult content because I did not want to come off as saying "you are caring too much." As his mentor, I had to learn how to communicate that he has a skill and nature about him that is what all teachers need, but that when he pays too much attention to one student or group of students, he is disregarding the others. I did this by pointing out a few things that happened during the class period while he was focusing on the small groups; like a student from the hall walking in and out of the classroom and one of our students keeping his hand up for several minutes, both of which went unnoticed while he was focused on the small group. Mentoring residents has helped me to develop my identity as a teacher educator and has expanded my sphere of influence (Taylor, Klein, & Abrams, 2014).

A SCHOOL WIDE APPROACH TO CHANGE

Mario

The mentors' experience in the partnership has been tremendous. Karina has commented that it has been a two-way learning experience. She has learned as much from the resident teachers as she has taught them. She herself said that she could not see why anyone would pass up the opportunity to become a mentor. "You learn so much from having this other teacher in the classroom for a full year," she exclaimed. When Karina shared this with me, I thought about how fortunate we were at East Side to have a program that allowed for this type of effective and meaningful learning experiences in the classroom for teachers. After all, that is what an educational system is supposed to be—a two-way learning experience for both teacher and student. It also proves to be a critical element to move a school from good to great.

The mentor teachers, however, were not the only ones to be impacted by the work of the NMUTR. Echoing Mike's narrative above from the perspective of an administrator, both the science chairperson and the science department as a whole, were influenced by the inquiry-based vision of the residency. When Maria Queruga Pessoa became the science chairperson, she was clear that change needed to take place in her department in terms of student engagement and academic performance. She had the passion and desire to challenge the status quo in her department, but she did not have a clear road map on how to do it. Working collaboratively with the NMUTR, she supported its professional development and began to experience firsthand the positive impact it was making on her teachers. She also commented on how the residency helped push the tipping point of effective teachers. Thus, when the results were present and the number of effective and excited teachers became the majority, those who were known to be skeptical of new initiatives, changed their attitude about the residency program. What was once the tipping point now transformed into progressive momentum. All of which helped the science department to flourish over the years.

This is an interesting phenomenon because although I encouraged the science teachers and the science department as a whole to adapt an inquiry based approach to teaching and learning, it was the teachers themselves who decided to make these changes to their teaching. They took advantage of the presence of the NMUTR faculty and their focus on inquiry to improve their own teaching practices and increase their students' engagement and ultimately achievement. Rather than receiving a formal directive from me or the chair for formal pedagogical change, they were influenced by their work with the residents to try out new ways of teaching. This kind of ownership of their process offered them opportunities to become more expert as teachers, something that Guskey and Peterson (1995) point out is very rare for teachers.

The NMUTR not only mobilized the science department, but it provided much needed momentum for the other content departments. The best practices of the residents, mentors, teachers, and professors were now being championed and shared across all disciplines. Instead of teachers blaming students' for poor performances, there was a shift in terms of accountability. More and more teachers centered their conversation on how to motivate students to excel. I believe that this shift in mindset is profound and crucial to the transformation of any school that wants to go from being good to great.

There was also a long-term impact on the school because I hired as many residents as possible when teaching positions became available. This has directly transformed the science department. By having the residents in the school for the full year, I had plenty of time to see if they had the potential to become excellent teachers. Not only was I impressed that the residents spent an entire year in the classroom, but more importantly that the content of their courses was driven by what was occurring in the classroom with East Side kids. I strongly believe that learning comes from doing and I could not ask for a more effective teacher preparation program. As such, results have been astounding where I have seen a clear increased positive climate in the science department and school as a whole. For example, the resident graduates and mentors willingly collaborate with one another in planning lessons aligned to common core standards, review student work on a weekly basis, and provide professional development within the department and to the school. Their professional development initiatives have been so impressive. Most recently, this past summer, a team of science resident graduates and mentors submitted a proposal to the district to review and rewrite curriculum aligned to common core standards. The proposal was accepted and hence the summer was spent rewriting curriculum that is currently being implemented this year.

It is no accident that East Side High School has been on the move for the past ten years. Why? The focus has been on hiring passionate and committed people who believe in the potential of students. However, it does not stop at the hiring process. Professional development must be intentionally based on the needs of students and consistent (daily, weekly, and monthly) throughout the year. As it is understood, sporadic and poorly planned professional development will not work. I had a clear advantage in the hiring process because I was able to see the residents in action when I observed them in class and solicited feedback from their mentors. Therefore, when I experienced the impact of the program and was able to see residents teach first hand, the decision to hire was simple.

An essential skill set I look for in all teachers is whether they possess a growth mindset. I do not care if you are teaching for three decades, there is always room for improvement and growth. I assessed this with the feedback and coaching they received from their mentors. How residents receive feedback and put it to action gives me a clear sense of if they will be coachable. Hence, as opposed to the typical hiring process, I was able to see the development of a resident over the course of a year versus a ten minute demonstrated lesson. When it was time to make a decision about hiring a resident, I was fully confident about my decision. As a result of the partnership and knowing that the residents are being trained in one of the most stellar teacher programs in the country, I have no doubt that I have been hiring committed and well prepared teachers resulting in almost 100% retention. What a huge payoff knowing that I have been able to select socially just teacher leaders who will drive the school's success.

In the narrative that follows, Cristina shares her own experiences of transitioning from being a resident and working with Luba to becoming a mathematics teacher at East Side High School. Her story demonstrates that the process of going from resident to teacher, even with this level of support, remains bumpy. Now in her fourth year of teaching, she is able to reflect on her challenges and successes as a new urban teacher. She also shares her journey of becoming her own version of a socially just teacher leader.

FINDING WONDER WOMAN: FROM RESIDENT TO TEACHER

Cristina

During my residency, I had the opportunity to work with a diverse group of students that gave me a realistic view of what urban teaching on my own would be like. I am grateful for this because I felt more prepared for my first year of teaching than the average student teacher. After completing the residency program, I was hired by East Side High School. I was extremely excited to have my own classes and in my mind I was going to transform my students with all the things that I had learned during my residency. I felt like a superhero at the beginning of the school year, but my superhero energy and excitement quickly drained out within the first month. Like many first year teachers, classroom management, classroom management, classroom management was my daily focus. During this time, I still had the support of both Luba and Mike, the math chair, and I also had the formal support of the induction program by means of an induction coach, Chris Rennie. Chris was very helpful with class management strategies and routines and she also conducted observations and provided valuable feedback on my lesson design and implementation. However, Rosie, my cohort one colleague and friend, was my main support during my first year. We spoke on a daily basis and shared a lot of the good and bad things that were going on in our classes. It was a great stress reliever being able to talk to someone who was experiencing similar things without fear of sounding or looking incompetent.

My first year of teaching in a nutshell was an emotional and physical roller coaster ride because of the diverse learners, a handful of challenging students, and logistical changes to my teaching schedule. Specifically half way through the year I lost my classroom and had to teach in two different classrooms. With all the ups and downs of my first year, I not only learned a great deal about classroom management, teaching, and reflection but I also started to build my self-confidence and find my voice within the East Side community.

During my second year, I still felt a sense of excitement about getting a fresh new start with all the things that I had learned during my first year. Although, I still had challenging students, I was teaching the same subject, had my own classroom and the support of an inclusion teacher; therefore, I was able to spend more time refining lessons I taught the year before and less time worrying about class management. Furthermore, I started to feel more established and part of the larger school community as I got to know more teachers and students. I was also receiving formal support from the NMUTR's induction program and informal support from Katie and

Cyrene, two MSU doctoral students. Rosie and I continued to talk and support each other throughout the year. I also started to develop relationships with cohort two residents, like Alex, Antonio, and Dave, who were then working at East Side.

Mike

The NMUTR presented a unique learning opportunity for Cristina that she may not have ordinarily been provided from a traditional teacher preparation program. It allowed her to experience an entire year of what it is like in an urban classroom as a teacher before committing to her first full year of teaching. Starting her first year at East Side, she had a greater command of the classroom and was comfortable teaching inquiry-based lessons that promoted greater student learning and engagement. However, as she describes above, as with any first year teacher, she struggled with classroom management. She realized that she needed to develop stronger management skills that would more positively support in their attainment of daily objectives. She did this with Luba's help as well as some induction support from the NMUTR. Through her continuous work and unwavering perseverance (Haberman, 1988, 1995), she improved her craft tremendously. This growth became evident during her second year of teaching, when she implemented a unique management style that maintained a learning-focused environment of high expectations while promoting curricular mastery and student success.

Seeing the limitless potential in her teaching career, the administration at East Side High School scheduled Cristina for several honors-level classes for her third year of teaching. Once again, she put in an inordinate amount of time and incredible effort to drive students to be successful in these courses. In addition to all of her teaching responsibilities, she also coached the East Side High School Algebra II team for the Newark Math Olympics. Through her professional development as a teacher and as a result of the NMUTR program and associated rigorous induction, Cristina continued to develop engaging and differentiated lessons. Her efforts did not go unnoticed, as she received a "highly effective" rating during her third year of teaching, qualifying her for a merit-pay bonus as per the NPS teaching contract.

Cristina

My third year felt like my first year with respect to the time spent creating lessons since I was teaching two new courses. I still felt excited but also felt a sense of uncertainty because I did not know what to expect. Classroom management was no longer the main concern; rather I started focusing on student learning goals. I continued to receive the formal support of the induction program and department chairperson in addition to informal support from Rosie. Although Rosie and I did not talk to each other on a daily basis we still managed to get together after work along with other co-workers to reconnect. During my first three years of teaching, my self-confidence continued to grow. I really believe that it was the process of informal self-reflection that has helped me think about students' learning process more deeply and helped in my professional growth with respect to checking for understanding and anticipating students' misconceptions.

Additionally, my successful completion of the residency and the past three years has been largely due to the formal and informal NMUTR supports. Within the NMUTR community, I feel safe to speak and express myself. However outside of the NMUTR I still do not feel that same sense of comfort and freedom. This makes me think about the power of being part of a community with a shared commitment to teaching for social justice like the NMUTR. I hope that as I continue to work at East Side, I will be able to work collaboratively with my colleagues to expand my influence beyond just what I can do as a single superhero. As I begin my fourth year here I am now thinking about my role as a teacher leader.

MOVING FROM TEACHER TO TEACHER LEADER

Cristina

I do not feel like I am becoming what I would consider a "teacher leader." To me teacher leaders are very visible, sometimes outspoken, and tend to express their opinions freely and openly. You see them a lot. They are leading school committees, they are running extracurricular activities, and they are more involved in the school community as a whole. I do not see myself that way. I am also resistant to calling myself a teacher leader out of respect for the more experienced teachers. I feel like others have a lot more experience than I do since they have been teaching for far longer than I have. I feel uncomfortable overstepping and I do not want to build negative relationships with other teachers or seem like I am imposing my own opinions on others.

I am more comfortable being a teacher leader when it comes to my students and what affects their learning in my classroom. When I see certain behaviors in students like excessive absences or behaviors in class that are not productive, I do go out of my way to contact parents, contact the guidance department, to find an intervention that will help them improve. These behaviors tend to affect their performance in my class as well as others. I assume that everyone is dedicating this kind of time to our students; I know my mentor Luba always did. But sometimes we receive different messages from the school culture. For example, when we were having some contract negotiations, union representatives told us to not call parents during our prep time, and not to call parents on our cell phones because of the personal cost. These are subtle messages that go against the intuitive responsibilities of a teacher. I do not mind spending my lunchtime calling parents because who else will and I do not want my kids falling through the cracks.

I think one of my issues is that I find teaching to be very all consuming. I am always trying to improve my lessons and really listen to my students. I am consumed by my work in the classroom with my students. Does this make me selfish? Maybe a little. But I feel a huge responsibility to the students. I need to model what I expect from them – to show up every day prepared to teach, to be consistent with them, and to work really hard. I have the same expectations for them. The kids say that I am so strict and serious but I think that is okay. Education is something serious and important. I hear a lot of excuses from the kids but I expect them to work hard and be accountable for their learning. I am not here to give them the answers. Sometimes I get frustrated with them and I have to let them know that in this class they have to be learners and take responsibility for their own learning. It goes back to that whole concept of Freire (2000) not filling them with information but rather giving them opportunities to make meaning for themselves. Sometimes it is really hard to stay focused on that commitment but I think that throughout the years I have tried to be consistent in my mission and approach. I do think I am beginning to feel more confident about my teaching now after three years of experience and have agreed to do some mentoring this year. For example, I have been working with one of the other Algebra One teachers. We have been meeting on a daily basis to share where we are with our classes in teaching this new math curriculum. I have taken the lead as far as creating a lot of the lessons and materials and I am a little bit ahead of him so I can give insights into what works. He has not taught Algebra One in several years so I feel like I have more experience than he does. I am also mentoring one of the new math teachers in the Big Picture program in the school. I have only been able to have two conversations with her but of course her main struggle is classroom management. I tried to share some strategies, to help her think about engaging her students individually about their behaviors and finding ways for them to work together. I have suggested that she create a written contract that has teacher and student expectations. We were also talking about using this application called Dojo, which helps to monitor positive and negative behaviors. I will start observing her this week.

It is hard for me to mentor others because I like to be in control. I like things done my way and I worry that someone else may not be able to do it as well. I am mentoring a MSU preservice teacher and I am finding it very challenging. I am worried that my students will suffer if he does not teach them exactly as I do. For example, the couple of times that he has taught, he tends to have one-on-one conversations with a single student, and he neglects the rest of the class. I know in my head that he just needs time to practice teaching, but I worry about the consequences for the students who are my first priority.

I know myself too. I am happy to dedicate 110% to my work, but I do not want to have to spread that out over five different commitments. For my first few years, I knew that I had to focus on my teaching and now I am more ready to take on different things. I am not the type of person to act as an authority without feeling confident about my knowledge. Each year I gain more confidence.

I am a teacher leader but how I lead is different from the typical ways that you think about leadership. I lead from within my classroom and this impacts the students.

They carry with them what they have learned in my class and bring it into other classrooms. Mike also acts as a conduit for me, sharing new lessons or activities that I have created, with the other teachers. There is not one way to be a socially just teacher leader – I have learned this over and over again in my time working with the NMUTR.

SCHOOL WIDE CHANGE FROM THE BOTTOM UP

Karina

After trying to explain the success that is happening at East Side to an outsider, I often get the reply, "Well this is a special circumstance." An outsider interprets what is happening at our school as ideal and not replicable at another location. I disagree with this notion and believe that the reason the change has happened within the school is because all of the stakeholders, the university faculty, the mentor teachers, the administrators, and the students bought into the NMUTR mission. Additionally, I think because many of the residents were initially placed at East Side, the school turned into the main hub for many of the program's functions, meetings, and classes and finally, where many of the residents were eventually hired. It was this central focus on one school that truly influenced the success of the program, but more specifically influenced the growth within the whole school. I believe that frequently problems in urban districts aim to focus on breadth rather than depth in their implementation of such programs, which may be a leading cause of why most programs that are brought into the district dismantle within a few years and tend to only further the larger problems at hand. It is the fact that the NMUTR had a mission, they found a school that shared their mission, and both perspectives within the third space worked hand in hand to develop the school into what it is today and will be tomorrow. It is this focus on something that is working that is what made the program so successful. The model of transforming one school at a time has the potential to be more successful than spreading resources across many schools. In doing so you make a more meaningful and sustaining change. I hope to only participate and support programs such as the NMUTR that focus on whole school growth and change rather than simply just producing certified teachers.

A MULTI-DIMENSIONAL APPROACH TO SCHOOL CHANGE: TEACHER LEADERS, ADMINISTRATORS, AND FACULTY PARTNERS

Monica

As I wrote at the beginning of this chapter, our perspective represents an examination of our work five years into the partnership with East Side High School. Looking back at our collaboration from this longitudinal time advantage helps us to honestly reflect and see realistically the sorts of change we have made over the years. This is a powerful and triangulated account in five voices. Five third space members, all with diverse responsibilities, agendas, and expertise, share their insights about a multi-dimensional approach to school change. We do come to the table with a whole continuum of perspectives but we share the same mission: to cultivate socially just teacher leaders who believe in the potential of the students at East Side High School and are committed to providing them equitable access to knowledge and the best possible education.

Partnering together through the third space work of the NMUTR has enabled us to nurture relationships built on mutual trust, respect, open communication, and flexibility. The third space construct that has framed our collaboration reminds us to continually care for the partnership as the third space is a fragile utopian enterprise, which needs constant attention. This paradigm reminds us too of the value of having multiple perspectives and also the need to be willing to be flexible in terms of expectations and responsibilities. As you have heard throughout the book, a third space residency is guided by the principle that there is never a one fits all model— every aspect of our program involves differentiation. This is true of school change too and the roles of the teacher leader, administrator, and even the faculty. Our model meets people where they are and attempts to allow them to grow in their own way--to begin to position themselves as agents of change in ways that feel right. We are clear that up until this point the spheres of influence of the NMUTR secondary program were at the grassroots, local school level. We recognize that our partnership is unique because of its status as a residency but we believe that there are many implications from this work for all teacher educators who partner with schools to prepare teachers. Below are some of these insights.

1. *Our local grassroots approach to socially just school change is multidimensional.* This involves the collective participation of a variety of people, including Newark students, residents, mentors, teachers, administrators, and faculty. This is a multi-directional approach to change where many are committed to being open, taking risks, and changing pedagogy to provide the best learning experiences for the students of East Side High School. Too often, school change is seen as being directed by the administration. Even the distributive leadership model positions change as initiated by the principal. In our model, change could be even initiated by a resident. For example, Mike as math department chair, described learning about inquiry based teaching when he would meet and observe Cristina and Luba teaching. This experience led him to value an inquiry approach to learning and providing him with real life teaching examples that he could share with the rest of his faculty.

2. *Third space school change and teacher leadership is not a one size fits all model.* Change agents at any level of the work enter these identities at different entry points, bringing a continuum of life experiences as well as different types of leadership stances and commitments. There is no hierarchical assessment of being a better or worse teacher leader or change agent. These stances take time to develop and need to be approached authentically. This is illustrated most clearly in the case of Cristina who has gradually taken on more and more responsibility

as a teacher leader. As a fourth year teacher, she is now beginning to mentor other teachers and preservice students in her school. But for her, she had to feel confident in terms of her knowledge and expertise as a teacher before she could move outside of her classroom.

3. *Socially just teacher leaders come in all different shapes and sizes.* The obvious teacher leaders are often assertive, confident, and comfortable expressing their opinions but those are not the only potential leaders. As we mentioned in the admissions chapter, we began to realize that we had to be careful of not favoring candidates who were the loudest and most assertive ones. Leadership takes many different forms and if someone is quieter or more introspective (Cain, 2012) it does not necessarily imply that they are a follower. A socially just leader needs a variety of strategies to enact change and sometimes being a good listener or being extremely thoughtful can be equally as effective.

4. *Collective school change for social justice involves identifying participants' strengths and building partnered strategies to use these to their fullest potential.* Besides strengths or expertise, this could involve recognizing the power that one has because of their positioning in the school and using it to promote another's work. We see this in the example of the mentoring relationship that Mike has with Cristina. Aware that she is still finding her voice as a teacher leader, rather than forcing her to act in a way that makes her uncomfortable in her relationships with others in the math department, he instead opts, with her permission, to share her curriculum with the other teachers. This allows Cristina to make an impact on her department without making her feel awkward. These instances over the course of three years have strengthened her confidence and encouraged her in her fourth year of teaching to mentor several new teachers.

5. *Look for "maverick" principals who are willing to buy in to partnerships and lead creatively.* I use the term "maverick" to describe Mario because of his independent minded and free spirited way of working with his students, staff, and community. As he wrote, he attended and taught at East Side High School. His "funds of knowledge" are the same as those of his students, parents, and many of his staff. He understands the cultures of his community and he is not afraid to take risks when it comes to the safety and education of his students. He continually challenges "conventional wisdom by believing in his students and staff" and expects "the best from them in spite of societal expectations to the contrary" (Nieto, 2007, p. 304). As Karina and Mike have shared throughout the chapter, Mario was an integral part of why the NMUTR and our partnership have been successful. Without him, we are not sure if we would have been able to make the impact that we have so far. Without the principal's support, very little real socially just change can happen because teacher leaders in those environments spend most of their time trying to build healthier school cultures (Jacobs et al., 2014).

6. *Finally and most importantly we know that there is not one road to sustainable school change for social justice.* A multidimensional third space framework allows for a variety of participants with unique strengths, experiences, and

positions of power to collectively work toward this goal. Our NMUTR construct has begun to be successful because we carefully crafted it to meet the needs and the strengths of all of those involved. We continue to spend time tending to our partnership through honest dialogue and reflection. We have expanded our relationship. This year East Side High School is hosting 17 MSU students in a variety of content areas including English, Social Studies, Math, Biology, Art, Physical Education, and Health. Some of the students are preparing to be dually certified in special education. There is an energy in the building: an urgent, deep socially just commitment to the students.

NOTE

[1] It was a stand out for our residency schools, but it was these kind of administrative practices that made the residency so successful at East Side.

REFERENCES

Achinstein, B., & Athanases, S. Z. (2005). Focusing new teachers on diversity and equity: Toward a knowledge base for mentors. *Teaching and Teacher Education, 21*(7), 843–862.

Ayers, W., & Ford, P. (Eds.). (1996). Introduction. *City kids, city teachers: Reports from the front row.* New York, NY: The New Press.

Barth, R. S. (2001). Teacher leadership. *Phi Delta Kappan, 82*(6), 443–449.

Brown, K. M. (2006). Leadership for social justice and equity: Evaluating a transformative framework and andragogy. *Educational Administration Quarterly, 42*(5), 700–745.

Cain, S. (2012). *Quiet: The power of introverts in a world that can't stop talking.* New York, NY: Random House.

Danielson, C. (2006). *Teacher leadership that strengthens professional practice.* Alexandria, VA: ASCD.

Fairman, J. C., & Mackenzie, S. V. (2012). Spheres of teacher leadership action for learning. *Professional Development in Education, 38*(2), 229–246.

Freire, P. (2000). *Pedagogy of the oppressed.* New York, NY: Continuum.

Friend, M., & Cook, L. (1996). *Interactions: Collaboration skills for school professionals.* New York, NY: Allyn & Bacon.

Gay, G., (2010). *Culturally responsive teaching: Theory, research, & practice.* New York, NY: Teachers College Press.

Gonzalez, N., Moll, L. C., & Amanti, C. (2005). *Funds of knowledge: Theorizing practices in households, communities, and classrooms.* New York, NY: Routledge.

Guskey, T., & Petterson, K. (1995). The road to classroom change. *Educational Leadership, 53*, 10–15.

Haberman, M. (1988). Proposals for recruiting minority teachers: Promising practices and attractive detours. *Journal of Teacher Education, 39*(4), 38–44.

Haberman, M. (1995). *Star teachers of children in poverty.* West Lafayette, IN: Kappa Delta Pi International Honor Society in Education.

Haugh, T. E., Norenes, S. O., & Vedoy, G. (2014). School leadership and educational change: Tools and practices in shared school leadership development. *Journal of Education Change, 15*, 357–376.

Jacobs, J., Beck, B., & Crowell, L. (2014). Teacher leaders as equity centered change agents: Exploring the conditions that influence navigating change to promote educational equity. *Professional Development in Education, 40*(4), 576–596.

Katzenmeyer, M., & Moller, G. (2001). *Awakening the sleeping giant: Helping teachers develop as leaders* (2nd ed.). Thousand Oaks, CA: Corwin Press.

Kennedy, M. (2005). *Inside teaching: How classroom life undermines reform*. Cambridge, MA: Harvard University Press.

Klein, E. J., Taylor, M., Onore, C., Strom, K., & Abrams, L. W. (2013). Finding a third space in teacher education: Creating the MSU/NPS urban teacher residency. *Teaching Education, 24*(1), 27–57.

Ladson-Billings, G., (2009). *The dreamkeepers: Successful teachers of African American students*. San Francisco, CA: Jossey-Bass.

Levenson, M. R. (2014). *Pathways to teacher leadership: Emerging models, changing roles*. Cambridge, MA: Harvard Education Press.

Lieberman, A., & Friedrich, L. D. (2010). *How teachers become leaders: Learning from practice and research*. New York, NY: Teachers College Press.

Lieberman, A., & Miller, L. (2004). *Teacher leadership*. San Francisco, CA: Jossey-Bass.

Margolis, J. (2008). What will keep today's teachers teaching? Looking for a hook as a new career cycle emerges. *Teachers College Record, 110*(1), 160–194.

McKenzie, K. B., Christman, D. E., Hernandez, F., Fierro, E., Capper, C. A., Dantley, M., … Scheurich, J. J. (2008). From the field: A proposal for educating leaders for social justice. *Educational Administration Quarterly, 44*(1), 111–138.

Muijs, D., & Harris, A., (2006). Teacher led school improvement: Teacher leadership in the UK. *Teaching and Teacher Education, 22*(8), 961–972.

Nieto, S. (2007). The color of innovative and sustainable leadership: Learning from teacher leaders. *The Journal of Education Change, 8*(4), 299–309.

Nieto, S., & Bode, P., (2012). *Affirming diversity: The sociopolitical context of multicultural education*. Boston, MA: Pearson.

Oakes, J., Welner, K., Yonezawa, S., & Allen, R. L. (2005). Norms and politics of equity-minded change: Researching the 'zone of mediation.' In M. Fullan (Ed.), *Fundamental change: International handbook of educational change* (pp. 282–305). Dordrecht, The Netherlands: Springer.

Onore, C., Goeke, J., Taylor, M., & Klein, E. J. (2009, Summer). Teacher leadership: Amplifying teachers' voices. *Academic Education Quarterly, 13*(2), 78–83.

Opfer, V. D., & Pedder, D. (2011). Conceptualization of teacher professional learning. *Review of Educational Research, 8*(3), 376–407.

Payne, C. (2008). *So much reform, so little change: The persistence of failure in urban schools*. Cambridge, MA: Harvard Education Press.

Reason, P. W., & Bradbury, H. (2008). *The Sage handbook of action research: Participatory inquiry and practice* (2nd ed.). London, UK: Sage Publications, Ltd.

Silva, D. Y., Gimbert, B., & Nolan, J. (2000). Sliding the doors: Locking and unlocking possibilities for teacher leadership. *Teachers College Record, 102*(4), 779–804.

Stigler, J. W., & Hiebert, J. (1999). *The teaching gap: Best ideas from the world's teachers for improving education in the classroom*. New York, NY: The Free Press.

Stone, R., & Cuper, P. (2006). *Best practices for teacher leadership*. Thousand Oaks, CA: Corwin Press.

Taylor, M., & Otinsky, G. (2007). Becoming whole language teachers and social justice agents: Pre service teachers inquire with sixth graders. *International Journal of Progressive Education, 3*(2), 59–71.

Taylor, M., Goeke, J., Klein, E. J., Onore, C., & Geist, K. (2011). Changing leadership: Teachers lead the way for schools that learn. *Teaching and Teacher Education 27*(5), 920–929.

Taylor, M., Klein, E. J., & Abrams, L. (2014). Tensions of re-imagining our roles as teacher educators in a third space: Revisiting a co/autoethnography through a faculty lens. *Studying Teacher Education, 10*(1), 3–19.

Theoharis, G. (2007). Social justice educational leaders and resistance: Toward a theory of social justice leadership. *Educational Administration Quarterly, 43*(2), 221–258.

Villegas, A. M., & Lucas, T. (2001). *Educating culturally responsive teachers: A coherent approach*. Albany, NY: State University of New York Press.

York-Barr, J., & Duke, K. (2004). What do we know about teacher leadership? Findings from two decades of scholarship. *Review of Educational Research, 74*(3), 255–316.

293

2

Monica Taylor
Department of Secondary and Special Education
Montclair State University
Montclair, New Jersey

Anna Karina Monteiro
East Side High School
Newark, New Jersey

Cristina Morales
East Side High School
Newark, New Jersey

Michael De Antonio
East Side High School
Newark, New Jersey

Mario Santos
East Side High School
Newark, New Jersey

EMILY J. KLEIN AND MONICA TAYLOR

12. EPILOGUE

Ripple Effects and Reinvention in the Third Space

SCALING DOWN

It's a beautiful spring day in 2014 when I walk back into East Side High School. I have been on family medical leave for months caring for a sick family member and although I have kept up with the residents I know that it's a far cry from seeing what is actually happening in the classroom. I know from the most recent evaluation report that overall, the residency continues to be successful. With a 90% retention rate, far higher than most teaching retention rates (Ingersoll & Strong, 2011; Papay, 2007), our residents also report high efficacy scores on *Teachers' Sense of Efficacy Scale* as documented in the program's evaluation done by Kyse, Arnold-Berkovits, Bentley, Oshman, and Lyman (2014). I know from dinners and Facebook and emails and texts that these months have been turbulent and also exuberant. I wonder what I will find.

Walking into East Side High School's science wing I am bombarded with kids experiencing hands on science—in one of our mentor classrooms they are looking at a puddle outside the window through a prism; in Dave's classroom students are testing water for pollutants from local companies, and in Antonio's classroom they are creating hypotheses about how to speed up the process of dissolving an Alka Seltzer. Even walking by Suzanne's classroom a student taps me on the arm to say with genuine excitement—"we just turned aluminum into copper—it was SO COOL." Every classroom seems to be on the same philosophical and pedagogical page. (Emily, May 22nd, 2014)

Within a week of Emily's visit, Dale Russakoff's (2014) extensive investigative piece for the New Yorker about the history of Newark school reform came out. In it she describes the complex layers of top down reform instigated by Corey Booker, Chris Christie, Chris Cerf, and Cami Anderson, and the many levels of resistance and entrenched bureaucracy they faced. At the end of the piece, despite millions of dollars from Mark Zuckerberg, scores of new principals, teachers, and schools, the reader is left with the impression "Everybody's getting paid, but Raheem still can't read." Spreading school reform across a district as large and complex as Newark is hard. Cami Anderson, Newark's current superintendent, compares it to "sixteenth

dimensional chess." Part of this is because the reform story as conceived by Booker and the administration is one that ignores the area of reform that involves changing the practice of teaching and learning that happens in practice, or what Elmore (1996) and McDonald (1996) refer to as *scaling down* "the process whereby a spreading reform challenges habitual practice in the new contexts and habitual practice yields to new ways of working" (McDonald, Buchanan, & Sterling, 2004, p. 82). Scaling down involves not only a "spread" of ideas, but "penetration," meaning that *knowledge and skills* are disseminated across a network, and also deeply absorbed by teachers on the ground. The story told about Newark reform has been one of scale, but not of scaling down. The vision is large, but not deep, and the philosophy for teaching and learning has not been conveyed in any way to teachers as something that they own.

And yet there is a missing piece to the story.

What the second cohort of residents has managed is scaling down, is changing the way science, and to some degree math, is taught at East Side High School. In a relatively short amount of time, and with a relatively small influx of resources (as compared, say, to the massive amounts of money infused by Mark Zuckerberg), there has been a focused effort to revise the curriculum, align the assessments, and provide consistent and coherent experiences for the students there. For two years in a row, for a few thousand dollars, the residents have worked together over the summer to revise the curriculum and assessments of another content area (this year environmental science), and have worked to share and align significant project based learning experiences too. Dave tells us their goal is to align all of their curricula with the Common Core and Next Generation Science Standards: "People say the standards aren't coming to Newark but they're wrong. We want to be ahead of the curve." The day Emily visited, Dave was willing to try a complex project that involved students testing water from around Newark's rivers because Alex was working on it as well and they provided each other feedback about challenges that arose during implementation. Coming from the same paradigm eases their work together and supports them in taking risks.

They are also expanding their sphere of influence to impact teachers and students in the larger district beyond East Side High School. Over the summer our resident graduates and mentors led several science professional development and curricular initiatives. For instance, Alex and Antonio led a district wide professional development workshop for environmental science teachers to help them think about transitioning from the New Jersey Curriculum Science Standards to the Next Generation Science Standards. Additionally Karina and Rosie designed a biology curriculum that was aligned with these new standards as well. This fall they are piloting the curriculum and Karina has facilitated multiple important biology professional development workshops for the district. Despite turbulence, turnover, and challenges in the district, this cohort in particular has managed to begin to operate as district science teacher leaders.

EPILOGUE

RESILIENCY

Why has this cohort been so resilient? They all remain in teaching, and with two exceptions, all in Newark,[1] and all seem to be emerging teacher leaders in their departments or schools. This past summer, Antonio and Alex were the two science teachers leading the "bridge" program at East Side for 9th graders, a program that helps transition 8th graders to 9th grade as well as develop their skills for high school. They created a curriculum for the summer that involves "data collection, graphing, air pollution, and social justice." Dave was similarly involved in summer curriculum development and looking to revise the physics curriculum as he has taken over teaching the majority of the physics courses for the school. Resiliency and "grit" in teacher recruitment and retention have been gaining credibility as possible criteria for making sense of who stays in teaching. The work of Robertson-Kraft and Duckworth (2014) suggests that "gritty teachers" in urban districts, as "defined by perseverance and passion for long term goals" (p. 2), outperform other teachers and are more likely to stay in their classrooms. Although our residents were not evaluated using Robertson-Kraft and Duckworth's grit measurement, and although the authors are careful to distinguish their measure of grit from our measures of perseverance and resilience described in the admissions chapter, we wondered from the biographical descriptors in their admissions data if many of our residents from this cohort did not, in fact, have "gritty" characters. For example, teachers were awarded higher "grit" scores who were multi-year members of teams and often went on to leadership positions on those teams. Work experience and other organizational leadership also contributed to higher grit scores. As we examined the applications of our cohorts, we noticed many of them would have received high grit scores. For example, Marc spent years involved in his chess team and Antonio worked as a camp counselor and a series of other job experiences. Suzanne spent all her high school and college years on the basketball team, becoming the team captain her senior year of high school. She spent four years in choir and band and was a member of the national honor society ("I was MS. High School" she once told us). She worked the same job each summer during high school and college, worked for four years as a housecleaner and dogwalker, and was a resident assistant in college. According to Robertson-Kraft and Duckworth (2014), she earns high points for grit. Other residents had corollary kinds of life experience that might not have shown up on such a measure, but we believed counted; for example Janae had essentially raised her younger sister, an act of deep commitment and responsibility that we believe mimicked the same characteristics of someone engaged in a long term committed out-of-school job.

But the success of this cohort can be attributed to more than just their personal characteristics (and the success of the program). Even Robertson-Kraft and Duckworth (2014) note that it is not clear the mechanism that allows gritty teachers to be successful, suggesting perhaps "gritty teachers are better able to maintain confidence in their ability and a sense of purpose, perhaps through support seeking

297

or other adaptive coping skills" (p. 22). It is the latter that we believe the NMUTR fostered in this community specifically. In at least the cases at Arts and East Side High Schools, the professional environment that fostered collaboration and supported improved teaching has been significant (Kraft & Papay, 2014). In both those cases, the schools were relatively untouched by the chaos of Newark reform and included strong cohorts of mentors who themselves were modeling the qualities and behaviors of emerging socially just teacher leadership. Kraft and Papay's research (2014), affirms that "if teachers in more supportive environments improve more and feel more successful because of this improvement, this 'sense of success' can increase the likelihood they remain at their schools .... As effective teachers remain in schools, opportunities for meaningful peer collaboration and a positive organizational culture become even more possible" (p. 495). This positive cycle was clearly in play in the science department at East Side High School, and was part of the success of the residency model there.

TEACHING IN AN IMPERFECT DISTRICT IN UNUSUAL TIMES

But even with these successes, there are cracks in this learning community. No matter how much we as a third space community of educators collaboratively thought through, planned, or organized the residency, we could never have predicted or prepared our residents for the kinds of challenges that they would face in NPS. Newark is an imperfect school district with frequent administrative change, a continual stream of newly imposed initiatives, and a top down model of leadership. After begging to get a job at East Side High School after her first school, Barringer High School, closed (as part of Cami Anderson's reforms), Suzanne left; she had difficulties with the disciplinary team, she did not feel as supported last year by the administration as she had hoped, and her schedule was challenging—three preps and multiple classrooms; privately other residents tell me they see both sides. One day when Emily visited her classroom, she witnessed firsthand the nature of a particularly challenging class. She told Emily of the struggles with them, of how midway through the year she was managing and how she would gather them in a circle and teach them chemistry that way, but that each week administrators would send another student with special needs to her, doubling the class size and adding every challenging student in her room, with new ones still coming in as late as May. Suzanne admits she did not take our advice not to "make waves" as a new teacher. We feel badly our advice came across that way; we want her to be the strong advocate for kids that we know she is and we also want her to feel supported. There are other examples of change too. Bryan, Marc's mentor, moved to New Hampshire, crossing the border to teach in Massachusetts; he cannot afford to raise a family in New Jersey. Rob from cohort one left teaching to pursue his passion as a musician. When Emily suggests a particular resident from cohort three fill his place, she hears he too is leaving Newark and potentially leaving teaching for good. After he completed the residency, he chose a position in a school with no other residents or mentors for

support and the experience has been challenging; rumor has it he would rather pay back what he owes. Dave tells Emily that while he is not planning to leave Newark all the residents see what teachers make in other urban districts, and while they feel protected at East Side High School, they are deeply concerned about what they see in the elementary cohort—residents unable to get positions, colleagues losing jobs, and schools being gutted. A few days after Emily's first day back there we received an email that the fourth cohort would not be placed in Newark at all; they were to seek jobs outside Newark. Many of cohort four residents hustled and found jobs in Orange. Later that decision was reversed, but the anxiety that it created leaves a bitter taste in the mouths of many.

DISTRICT LEVEL SUPPORT

One of the lessons that emerged for us as we made sense of the NMUTR years was that without significant high-level district support, the most well conceived residency cannot be successful. Even now, viewing the success of the program at East Side High School, we know that much of the collective work done by residents, mentors, faculty, and administrators can quickly be undone by the larger district level upheavals that seem likely with a new Newark mayor openly hostile to Cami Anderson. During the residency we experienced the leadership of three very different superintendents, one with a radically different vision for Newark school reform, and we realized in that latter case that we did not do enough work to build a relationship and a vision for how the residency could meet the needs of the district. Cami Anderson has been charged with implementing a strong charter school agenda from Christie and Booker, and has turned to Teach for America as a means for fulfilling that agenda (Russakoff, 2014). This is not necessarily antithetical to a strong residency model—in fact, in a number of cities urban residencies co-exist well with Teach for America. However, our vision for school change and school development through a socially just lens may not have been so easily aligned and so easily self-explanatory that we could allow it to speak for itself. In hindsight we needed to do a more effective job at advocating for both our vision and our program, but at the very least, our program. As we reflected we wondered if we had relied too heavily on the relationship that our own university administrators had cultivated with the district leaders rather than developing our own relationships. As faculty working in the schools on a day to day basis, building strong third space partnerships with Newark students, teachers, administrators, and staff, our perspective on the work was more immediate and urgent. More deliberately including the district leaders in our third space negotiation may have opened up communication and more readily facilitated shared visioning and democratic decision-making. We know we have made strides in this area with NPS through the residency but had we made enough progress to weather the significant change in district leadership and the more corporate models of school reform to convince district officials to equally invest in the preparation of teachers as socially just change agents?

BUILDING THE PLANE WHILE FLYING IT

What kept us from such advocacy? It is an oft-told story of educational change—we were building the plane (and in some cases shaping the tools) while flying it. Although we had many relationships with Newark schools, because of leadership changes and staffing issues in the secondary schools, we ended up with our primary partnership in a relatively new school (in terms of partnership)—East Side High School, and were simultaneously building relationships with teachers as we were developing curriculum, creating an admissions program, and working on school leadership. The nature of third space work is that you build the plane—and navigate it—while flying it; it is part of what makes it emergent and not emergency. However, we underestimated how much even a year of building teacher leadership and mentoring capacity would have helped us in advancing the program. Much of the co-construction of curriculum and mentoring work in which we really wanted to engage with the mentors did not begin until cohort two because during the first year we were busy trying to build collegial relationships with the mentors. The first stages of trust and collegiality simply could not be passed over.

MOVING FORWARD SCALABILITY

As the four years of the grant wind down, as this book is completed, there has been endless analysis and reflection about the impact of the program, both on Newark, but also on MSU and on its teacher education. As we write this, we are preparing to pilot the initial phase of a master's program that will incorporate some of the lessons learned from the residency. Neither of us is naïve enough to think that we can easily transport the work from one site to another, but we reject the notion that the residency was merely a nice boutique program with nothing to offer our traditional preservice teacher education programs. Each of our sections will be placed in a single school offering opportunities for rounds and other field based learning opportunities provided during the residency. Monica will bring her students to East Side High School and continue to build on the partnership established there. Emily forges a new partnership at Clifton High School. It is our hope that we can begin to think about the scalability of the residency.

THE HYBRID ROLE OF FACULTY

We believe faculty must continue to engage in this kind of partnership work—intensive, on site, third space partnership work. But as we have written about previously (Klein, Taylor, Onore, Strom, & Abrams, 2013), such work often comes up against certain institutional barriers and constraints: faculty load, and semester start and stop times that do not align well with the secondary school's calendar. We also found that over the course of three years, there was a personal toll that this work took; the unrelenting nature of working in schools, of running in a program that ran

12 months a year without break, of beginning a new cohort before a previous one was finished. We often felt the pull from the university to be more involved in university committees and responsibilities when we were already overloaded with work in NPS. Institutional barriers were not single but multiple and sometimes it felt as if we were fighting on a variety of fronts, making our work ever more complex. It would behoove teacher educator institutions to expand their structures to better support faculty doing such work. As Zeichner and Pena-Sandoval (2015) suggest, "We are on a course to dismantle and replace the college and university system of teacher education in the United States that continues to prepare most of the nation's teachers" (p. 15). More and more, "reformers" of teacher education are building and supporting teacher education structures outside of the university system. Like Zeichner and Pena-Sandoval, we align ourselves with "transformers"—those who "see the need for substantive transformation in the current system of teacher education but do not support 'blowing up' the current system and replacing it with deregulated market economy" (p. 2). But we urge institutions of higher education to take seriously the threat to teacher education and to think flexibly and creatively about how to best support the innovative work of faculty in the field. Without finding ways to bring serious innovation to the traditional teacher education programs we risk such programs becoming dinosaurs—and sooner rather than later.

THE INVENTIVENESS OF THE THIRD SPACE

Despite the personal toll and professional weight of running the NMUTR, we end this book with a feeling of optimism. This residency program was only possible because of the "deep well of generosity" (Burnett, 2014) and the openness to creativity of faculty, mentors, administrators, community organizers, and residents. The third space structure invited participants to take risks, think imaginatively, and invent practices for urban preservice teacher education. Although these collaborative dialogues could be difficult at times to navigate they resulted in a collective richness that was much greater than its parts. There is no perfect model of teacher education—we know that there is always more work to be done and new practices to develop—but our collective experience of the residency has reminded us of the wonderful possibilities of radically imagining teacher education and the power and importance of educators shifting identities and crossing boundaries. As Maxine Greene (2010) once wrote, "There can be no final solution; but there is time—always time—to reject somnolence, to choose to begin" (p. 1).

NOTE

1 Marc is currently teaching physics in Florence High School, which is considered a high needs district. He left his first school in Newark because his principal did not renew his contract and although Marc was willing to continue to teach in Newark, he was not offered a job in time, and in August 2014

took a position outside in Florence. Barb had a physical injury during her first year teaching at a middle school in Newark. She is currently a special education high school biology resource teacher in Voorhees, New Jersey.

REFERENCES

Burnett, T.B. (20 July 2014). T Bone Burnett: How I set lyrics for Bob Dylan's new Basement Tapes to music. *The Guardian.* Retrieved from http://www.theguardian.com/music/shortcuts/2014/jul/20/lyrics-bob-dylan-new-basement-tapes-t-bone-burnett

Elmore, R. (1996). Getting to scale with good educational practice. *Harvard Educational Review, 66*(1), 1–26.

Greene, M. (2010). Prologue to art, social imagination and action. *Journal of educational controversy 5*(1), 1–2.

Ingersoll, R. M., & Strong, M. (2011). The impact of induction and mentoring for beginning teachers: A critical review of the research. *Review of Educational Research, 81*(2), 201–233.

Klein, E. J., Taylor, M., Onore, C., Strom, K., & Abrams, L. (2013). Finding a third space in teacher education: Creating an urban teacher residency. *Teaching Education, 24*(1), 27–57.

Kraft, M. A., & Papay, J. P. (2014). Do supportive professional environments promote teacher development? Explaining heterogeneity in returns to teaching experience. *Educational Evaluation and Policy Analysis, 36*(4), 476–500.

Kyse, E. N., Arnold-Berkovits, I., Bentley, S., Oshman, M., & Lyman, C. (2014). *Newark-Montclair urban teaching residency (NMUTR): Year 4 (2012–2013) Evaluation Report.* Montclair, NJ: Center for Research and Evaluation on Education and Human Services.

McDonald, J. P. (1996). *Redesigning school: Lessons for the twenty first century.* San Francisco, CA: Jossey Bass.

McDonald, J. P., Buchanan, J., & Sterling, R. (2004). The national writing project: Scaling up and scaling down. In T. K. Glennan, S. J. Bodilly, J. R. Galegher & K. A. Kerr (Eds.), *Expanding the reach of education reforms,* (pp. 81–105). Washington (DC), WA: Rand.

Papay, J. P. (2007). *Aspen institute datasheet: The teaching workforce.* Washington (DC), WA: The Aspen Institute.

Robertson-Kraft, C., & Duckworth, A. L. (2014). True-Grit: Trait Level perseverance and passion for long-term goals predicts effectiveness and retention among novice teachers. *Teachers College Record, 116,* 1–27.

Russakoff, D. (2014, May 19). Schooled. *The New Yorker.* Retrieved from http://www.newyorker.com/reporting/2014/05/19/140519fa_factu sakoff?currentPage=all

Zeichner, K., & Pena-Sandoval C. (2015). Venture philanthropy and teacher education policy in the U.S.: The role of the new schools venture fund. *Teachers College Record, 117*(6), 1–24. Retrieved from http://www.tcrecord.org (ID Number: 17539)

Emily J. Klein
Department of Secondary and Special Education
Montclair State University
Montclair, New Jersey

Monica Taylor
Department of Secondary and Special Education
Montclair State University
Montclair, New Jersey

AFTERWORD

On April 7, 2015, Monica and Emily got notice that NPS Superintendent Cami Anderson was designating East Side High School as a "turnaround" school for the 2015–2016 academic year, one of 8 schools "turned around." The Newark Teachers Union (NTU) contract (2012) reads, "NPS will consult with the NTU on the number of schools it designates as Turnaround. NPS will designate a maximum of ten (10) schools as Turnaround Schools each year for the duration of this contract" (p. 9). Within the contract, it is explained that schools become turnaround based on "a variety of data points including but not limited to the following: enrollment patterns over time, proficiency over time, and growth over time" (p. 9). East Side was deemed a "turnaround" school despite the school's rising HSPA scores under Mario's leadership, among other significant examples of evidence of improvement. "Turnaround" may look different for different schools, but as part of the process teachers are asked to sign an "EWA" or an Election to Work Agreement.

The template for the EWA is provided in the 2012 NTU contract. Some of the conditions of the agreement include: 1) extending the school day to a total of 7.5 hours per day; 2) teachers will attend school planning and curriculum development sessions for 2 weeks (10 school days) every summer; 3) there will be up to four staff retreats throughout the school year; 4) all teachers may have to advise a group of students for an extra-curricular student activity (up until now teachers have compensated for advising extra-curricular activities); and 5) every teacher, including the professional staff, will act as an advisor to a group of no more than 25 students. These additional responsibilities come with a stipend of a total of $3000.00, which works out to approximately $10 an hour. Finally, the EWA states that teachers should be prepared to be flexible since there may be year-to-year or even intra-year changes in terms of their responsibilities, faculty meetings, their courses and schedules or professional development. Any specific conditions are subject to change.

East Side teachers, many of them resident graduates and mentors who contributed to this book, have rallied to protest what they see as a misguided understanding of their school as needing "turnaround." A school pep rally was organized on a Saturday to educate parents and the community about the designation. This pep rally encouraged the teachers and students of Weequahic High School to organize their own Saturday protest. East Side students and teachers joined them in an act of solidarity. Alex and a 3rd year cohort member spoke at the Newark Advisory Board meeting. East Side students, in collaboration with the Newark Student Union, have staged several walkouts and sit ins. On May 1st, 1000 students walked out of East Side and headed to the Court House and later 2 Cedar Street, the district office. On May 13th, East Side High School students and teachers marched to 2 Cedar Street to let their voices be heard. There they met fellow teachers and students from the other

AFTERWORD

designated turnaround schools. Mayor Ras Baraka gave a moving speech about the need to take back the leadership and management of schools in Newark.

On May 15th, the deadline for signing the EWA, only five teachers, out of 130, signed the EWA. Teachers were told that if they did not sign the EWA they may not be allowed to stay at East Side or they will be moved either to the "oops" list, from which they could be assigned to any school, or if they are untenured, they could be let go.

On June 18, Cami Anderson met with some of our resident graduates at East Side High School. She explained that East Side would no longer be considered a full "turnaround" school and that teachers would not have to sign the EWA. Unless notified, they would all be able to return there to teach for the following year. There will however be an extended day for the incoming freshmen.

On June 22, Cami Anderson announced her resignation. Chris Cerf, former New Jersey state education commissioner, will replace her for the next three years. His past record as a proponent of charter schools and his role as the CEO of Amplify, an educational consulting firm, leaves us skeptical but only time will tell.

REFERENCE

NPS-NTU 2012 Memorandum of Agreement. (2012, October 18). Memorandum of agreement between the Newark State operated school district and Newark teachers union (pp. 1–35). Retrieved from http://www.ntuaft.com/Info_Center/NTU_Archive/NPS_NTU_MOA_FINAL_101512_dated_101812.pdf